Managing Global Legal Systems

This unique text develops a framework for understanding the corporate strategy–public policy interface as it relates to human capital management and treats legal systems as factors that must be actively managed in the pursuit of international competitive advantage.

Comparative law material is integrated with up-to-the-minute research to explain the structural characteristics of legal systems around the world, document the variance in labor and employment regulation they have produced, and to assess the opportunities nongovernmental actors have to influence the state's underlying relationship with national IR/HRM systems through political action. In the process, readers are provided with the most comprehensive discussion to date of the roles that transnational, regional, and national institutions play in the evolution of domestic and international labor standards.

Key concepts are illustrated with high-profile news events from diverse country settings, offering additional cross-cultural insights into the challenging regulatory environment that multinational enterprises face when managing an international work force. Taking an applied approach to the subject of labor-market regulation on six continents, *Managing Global Legal Systems* is a valuable reference for students and practitioners alike in the fields of HRM, business management and law.

Gary W. Florkowski is a faculty member at the Katz Graduate School of Business, University of Pittsburgh, USA.

Routledge Global Human Resource Management Series

Edited by Randall S. Schuler, Susan E. Jackson, Paul Sparrow and Michael Poole

Routledge Global Human Resource Management is an important new series that examines human resources in its global context. The series is organized into three strands: Content and issues in global human resource management (HRM); Specific HR functions in a global context; and comparative HRM. Authored by some of the world's leading authorities on HRM, each book in the series aims to give readers comprehensive, in-depth and accessible texts that combine essential theory and best practice. Topics covered include cross-border alliances, global leadership, global legal systems, HRM in Asia, Africa and the Americas, industrial relations, and global staffing.

Managing Human Resources in Cross-border Alliances
Randall S. Schuler, Susan E. Jackson and Yadong Luo

Managing Human Resources in Africa
Edited by Ken N. Kamoche, Yaw A. Debrah, Frank M. Horwitz and Gerry Nkombo Muuka

Globalizing Human Resource Management
Paul Sparrow, Chris Brewster and Hilary Harris

Managing Human Resources in Asia-Pacific
Edited by Pawan S. Budhwar

International Human Resource Management (second edition)
Policy and practice for the global enterprise
Dennis R. Briscoe and Randall S. Schuler

Managing Human Resources in Latin America
An agenda for international leaders
Edited by Marta M. Elvira and Anabella Davila

Global Staffing
Edited by Hugh Scullion and David G. Collings

Managing Human Resources in Europe
A thematic approach
Edited by Henrik Holt Larsen and Wolfgang Mayrhofer

Managing Human Resources in the Middle East
Edited by Pawan S. Budhwar and Kamel Mellahi

Managing Global Legal Systems
International employment regulation and competitive advantage
Gary W. Florkowski

Global Industrial Relations
Edited by Michael J. Morley, Patrick Gunnigle and David G. Collings

Managing Global Legal Systems

International employment regulation and competitive advantage

Gary W. Florkowski

Routledge
Taylor & Francis Group

LONDON AND NEW YORK

First published 2006
by Routledge
2 Park Square, Milton Park, Abingdon, Oxon OX14 4RN

Simultaneously published in the USA and Canada
by Routledge
270 Madison Ave, New York, NY 10016

Routledge is an imprint of the Taylor & Francis Group, an informa business

© 2006 Gary W. Florkowski

Typeset in Times New Roman by
Keystroke, Jacaranda Lodge, Wolverhampton
Printed and bound in Great Britain by
TJ International Ltd, Padstow, Cornwall

British Library Cataloguing in Publication Data
A catalogue record for this book is available from the British Library

Library of Congress Cataloging in Publication Data
Florkowski, Gary W.
Managing global legal systems : international employment regulation and
competitive advantage / Gary W. Florkowski.
p. cm.
Includes bibliographical references and index.
1. Labor laws and legislation–Political aspects. 2. Labor policy. 3. Industrial
relations–Political aspects. 4. Competition, International. I. Title.
K1705.F57 2006
344.01–dc22
2005030134

ISBN10: 0–415–36944–4 (hbk)
ISBN10: 0–415–36945–2 (pbk)
ISBN10: 0–203–50291–4 (ebk)

ISBN13: 978–0–415–36944–2 (hbk)
ISBN13: 978–0–415–36945–9 (pbk)
ISBN13: 978–0–203–50291–4 (ebk)

To my wife, Tina, who gave unbounded encouragement, understanding, love and sacrifice in support of this project

Contents

Illustrations

Tables

Boxes

Legal Systems in Action

Foreword

Global Human Resource Management is a series of books edited and authored by some of the best and most well-known researchers in the field of human resource management. This series is aimed at offering students and practitioners accessible, coordinated, and comprehensive books in global HRM. To be used individually or together, these books cover the main bases of comparative and international HRM. Taking an expert look at an increasingly important and complex area of global business, this groundbreaking new series answers a real need for serious textbooks on global HRM.

Several books in the series are devoted to human resource management policies and practices in multinational enterprises. For example, some books focus on specific areas of global HRM policies and practices, such as global leadership development, global staffing, and global labor relations. Other books address special topics that arise in multinational enterprises across the globe, such as managing HR in cross-border alliances, developing strategies and structures, and managing legal systems for multinational enterprises. In addition to books on various HRM topics in multinational enterprises, several other books in the series adopt a comparative, and within-region, approach to understanding global human resource management. These books on comparative human resource management can adopt two major approaches. One approach is to describe the HRM policies and practices found at the local level in selected countries in several regions of the world. This approach utilizes a common framework that makes it easier for the reader to systematically understand the rationale for the existence of various human resource management activities in different countries and easier to compare these activities across countries within a region. The second approach is to describe the HRM issues and topics that are most relevant to the companies in the countries of the region.

Managing Global Legal Systems is intended to describe global legal systems and the relevant institutions and their laws, regulations, and guidelines that multinational enterprises face as they operate around the world. Gary Florkowski does a superb job in identifying and thoroughly describing the complexity and extensiveness of the various legal systems and relevant institutions that MNEs need to be aware of and comply with. The topics covered include global and regional institutions and the evolution of employment regulation, industrial relations in a global perspective, and a final chapter on managing global legal systems for competitive advantage. He does this in seven chapters containing a wide variety of highly informative tables and figures. Each chapter also has numerous boxed features that further highlight the application of the topics being discussed. This book is an extremely well written and highly valuable book for any global human resource scholar or global human resource professional.

This Routledge series, Global Human Resource Management, is intended to serve the growing market of global scholars and professionals who are seeking a deeper and broader understanding of the role and importance of human resource management in companies as they operate throughout the world. With this in mind, all books in the series provide a thorough review of existing research and numerous examples of companies around the world. Mini-company stories and examples are found throughout the chapters. In addition, many of the books in the series include at least one detailed case description that serves as a convenient practical illustration of topics discussed in the book.

Because a significant number of scholars and professionals throughout the world are involved in researching and practicing the topics examined in this series of books, the authorship of the books and the experiences of companies cited in the books reflect a vast global representation. The authors in the series bring with them exceptional knowledge of the HRM topics they address, and in many cases the authors have been the pioneers for their topics. So we feel fortunate to have the involvement of such a distinguished group of academics in this series.

The publisher and editor also have played a major role in making this series possible. Routledge has provided its global production, marketing, and reputation to make the series feasible and affordable to academics and practitioners throughout the world. In addition, Routledge has provided its own highly qualified professionals to make the series a reality. In particular we want to indicate our deep appreciation for the work of our series editor, Francesca Heslop. She has been very supportive of the series right from the beginning and has been invaluable in providing the needed support and encouragement to us and to the many authors in the series. She, along with her staff, including Emma Joyes, Victoria Lincoln, Jacqueline Curthoys, and Lindsie Court, has helped make the process of completing this series an enjoyable one. For everything they have done, we thank them all.

Randall S. Schuler, Rutgers University and GSBA Zurich
Paul Sparrow, Manchester University
Susan E. Jackson, Rutgers University and GSBA Zurich
Michael Poole, Cardiff University

Abbreviations

AFL-CIO	American Federation of Labor – Congress of Industrial Organizations
AFTA	ASEAN Free Trade Area
AIE	advanced industrialized economy
ASEAN	Association of Southeast Asian Nations
ATCA	Alien Tort Claims Act (United States)
BIAC	Business and Industry Advisory Committee (OECD)
CAN	Community of Andean Nations
CARICOM	Caribbean Community and Common Market
CFA	Committee on Freedom of Association (ILO)
CNA	competent national authority
COE	Committee of Experts (ILO)
COMESA	Common Market for Eastern and Southern Africa
EEO	equal employment opportunity
EIRO	European Industrial Relations Observatory
EM	emerging market
EPL	employment-practice lawsuit, employment-practices liability
EPZ	export processing zone
EU	European Union
FDI	foreign direct investment
FFCC	Fact-Finding and Conciliation Commission on Freedom of Association (ILO)
FTA	free trade area
GATT	General Agreement on Tariffs and Trade
GB	Governing Body (ILO)
GSP	Generalized System of Preferences
HCN	host-country national
HR	human resource
HRM	human resource management
ICFTU	International Confederation of Free Trade Unions
IHRM	international human resource management
ILC	International Labor Conference (ILO)
ILO	International Labor Organization
ILS	International Labor Standard
IMF	International Monetary Fund
IOE	International Organization of Employers
IR	industrial relations

IT	information technology
MERCOSUR	Southern Common Market
MFN	most favored nation
MNE	multinational enterprise
NAFTA	North American Free Trade Area
NCP	National Contact Point (OECD)
NGO	nongovernmental organization
OECD	Organization for Economic Cooperation and Development
OSH	occupational safety and health
PCN	parent-country national
RIF	reduction(s) in force
SADC	Southern African Development Community
SAFTA	South Asia Free Trade Area
TCN	third-country national
TUAC	Trade Union Advisory Committee (OECD)
UN	United Nations
WTO	World Trade Organization

Global legal systems and the employment relationship

1

Government interfaces with IR/HRM systems

General considerations

The terms and conditions of employment often emerge as coveted spheres of influence for government and business entities alike. As Brewster (1993: 771) noted, there is no consistent body of evidence supporting a conclusion that *societal*-level gains automatically redound from human resource management (HRM) initiatives enhancing organizational competitiveness. Top management's quest to increase market share, profitability, or shareholder wealth rarely is constrained by an unwavering commitment to minimize potential hardships that may befall employees or communities housing the firm's operations. While potentially beneficial to the "bottom line," decisions to exploit contingent staffing arrangements, variable compensation, offshore sourcing, and information technology innovations can create serious income and employment risk for the work force in advanced industrialized economies (AIEs). Emerging markets run the risk of accepting foreign direct investment (FDI) that utilizes aging or obsolete technologies, thereby impeding the transfer and assimilation of cutting-edge job skills to accelerate industrialization and sustain long-term employment growth. Governments in both types of economies arguably have vested interests in resisting cross-border transfers and indigenous development of HRM practices that are culturally incompatible with existing labor-market institutions. Accordingly, politicians and public administrators should exhibit a universal tendency to monitor and, at times, intervene in employment decisions perceived to threaten critical social policies or macroeconomic performance.

Yet, little agreement is evident in the business or economics literature regarding the state's actual role in HRM and industrial relations (IR) systems.[1] Nor is there consensus about the underlying dynamics of employment regulation or the ultimate function that it serves. For example, Dunlop (1993) tags government as one of three core actors shaping the substantive and procedural elements of employment relationships in national IR systems. Several forms of state action are identified that can influence a given system's overarching "web of rules," including (1) the promulgation of legislation and regulations, (2) the enforcement of legally permissible provisions that have been voluntarily adopted by management and workers or their respective agents, and (3) the utilization of sovereign authority to require review and approval of tentative contracts or unilateral actions by nongovernmental actors before they can be implemented. None of these initiatives occurs in a political vacuum—a reality that this framework shuns by treating the locus and distribution of power in society as an exogenous variable. Political action is acknowledged to exist, but no explanation is offered in terms of the relative power of government *vis-à-vis* the other actors over time within or across countries. Begin's (1992) treatment of the political system during the evolution of national HRM systems displays similar drawbacks.

A more enigmatic account of the sociopolitical context of industrial relations appears in Cooke (2003: 3–4). The text suggests that unions and multinational enterprises (MNEs) seek to influence political systems at home and abroad to increase the likelihood of achieving their respective goals; however, the framework itself only depicts organized labor attempting to do so. Why this environmental dimension should be fixed for companies alone is not clear. Even if this glaring inconsistency is an unintended artifact, one is left wondering about such issues as the relative importance of private versus political action in different IR systems, the portfolio of employment-related political behaviors that firms and organized labor engage in across markets, and the relative efficacy of those strategies.

In contrast, Boivin (1989: 101) places lobbying and other political-activity mechanisms on an equal footing with collective bargaining at the heart of IR systems. Still, no predictive insights are offered regarding the form, intensity, and relative sophistication of political behaviors that management and unions deploy in different legal systems. Boivin also fails to account for political actions instituted by numerous entities which exist outside of a particular country context, such as independent nongovernmental organizations (NGOs), trading-partner nations, and transnational bodies like regional trade blocs or the Organization for Economic Cooperation and Development. The same oversight is observed in the models discussed earlier as well.

Others have rejected these "pluralist" characterizations of government's nexus with industrial relations (i.e., as a neutral or competing actor in policy-making processes fraught with political maneuvering by major interest groups). Alternative paradigms have been developed rooted in "unitary" or Marxist theories of the state (e.g., Giles 1989; Adams 1992), as well as microeconomic theory of the firm (Dow 1997). These IR systems generally operate very differently from the one described above.[2] Unitary-based models implicitly endow government with the ability to detect and distill the prevailing values and preferences of society, which provide guidance for rational policy making. The state also is presumed to have sufficient power to unilaterally institute such policies to defend the public interest. Common justifications for such action might be an asserted need to heal conflict between industrial parties, ensure that fair employment practices prevail in the workplace, restore functionality to markets, or preserve social order.

Through the lens of Marxist thought, government institutions historically exist as manifestations of capitalist domination that are exploitive to the working class. Therefore, industrial relations policies and structures are branded as inevitably favoring capitalists until the state restructures economic, political, and social relations in society to the contrary. One might argue that little is gained by adding this perspective to our discussion in light of unmistakable signs that viable Marxist states are a dying political reality. Yet, clarifying its tenets may help to explain the agendas of some nongovernmental actors and opposing political factions relegated to minority positions in certain nations.

At the other ideological extreme reside the "new" institutional economists, who rely on microeconomic theory to hawk the general superiority of private governance structures in labor markets. Pursuant to this mindset, government intervention becomes justifiable only when there is evidence that inefficient governance structures have materialized due to market failure. Serious information asymmetries, unequal market power, and high exit costs are among the factors that may precipitate dysfunctional market outcomes that otherwise would be avoided (Dow 1997). The underlying assumptions of individual actor rationality and competitive market forces give rise to a minimalist view of regulation, though. These core beliefs are in stark contrast with those held by old-school institutionalists like John R. Commons and Selig Perlman, who contended that employers had enduring, disproportionate market power that had to be perpetually offset by government regulation in key areas like collective bargaining and labor standards (Kaufman 1997).

Thus, widely divergent views exist regarding the objectives for, and centrality of, state action in HRM/IR. A major challenge one encounters when trying to manage legal systems is discerning which of these regulatory orientations government officials follow now and will embrace in the future. This dynamic view of employment regulation is consistent with the position taken by Poole (1986: 102–104) that agents of the state make strategic choices about the level of control to exert over economic markets, IR institutions, and individual establishments. Cultural and structural constraints (i.e., ethico-political philosophies, politico-economic structures, political systems) may preclude radical shifts in regulatory philosophy in the short run, but they do not necessarily guarantee that the regulatory superstructure will remain static indefinitely. These issues will be dealt with more systematically in Chapters 3 and 4.

Deciphering the appropriate outlet for behaviors directed at the state and other nongovernmental actors is a related challenge. Societies vary in the extent to which structured, hierarchical linkages have evolved to orchestrate dealings among the system's participants. This fact calls for informed, well reasoned choices when attempting to exert influence on employment relationships. One must assess how strongly these connections interlock management, trade unions, and government, and in what areas, as a prelude to any planned course of action. The following structural arrangements will be highlighted to elaborate on this point: state corporatism, pluralism, concertation without labor, and societal corporatism (Dekker 1989; Poole 1986). While definitional nuances pepper the literature, corporatism usually refers to settings where government *voluntarily* shares power with centralized bodies representing employers and labor to *jointly* engineer solutions that promote desired macroeconomic or other policy outcomes. These tripartite relationships arguably ask all of the actors to surrender some of their traditional areas of control to consensus-based decision making in exchange for industrial peace and other advancements in social welfare.

Based on this definition, the term "state corporatism" is a misnomer. Places with this configuration (e.g., China, the former Soviet Union, Spain during the Franco era) lack union movements and a private sector with sufficient power and influence to be independent of government. Centralized labor federations and employer associations may exist, but their interactions with the state are largely ritualistic endorsements of the latter's agenda. Since these peak organizations have been captured by the state, their willingness and ability to meaningfully influence policy making are highly suspect, especially if the changes sought would call for major compromises by the ruling political party. In this kind of environment, there seems to be little practical value attached to individual employers (particularly MNEs) subordinating their own political-action strategies to these centralized bodies for IR or other matters.

A similar conclusion is reached where pluralism reigns (e.g., the United States, Canada, New Zealand) for different reasons. The independence of nongovernmental actors is not in question; however, their peak organizations have not been vested with the authority to bind affiliates to IR agreements. They also traverse a landscape where well entrenched competing political parties rotate into and out of office on a frequent basis, economic planning is not revered as a mainstream responsibility of the state, and there is no tradition of power sharing for critical social issues. For example, a series of high-profile presidential labor–management committees have been convened in the United States since 1945 to advise on far-reaching macroeconomic issues. These initiatives had a minor impact on subsequent policy at best, and did not foster an enduring infrastructure for corporatist-like interactions (Moye 1980). Decentralized political-action mechanisms are much more potent channels of influence in these nations. Consequently, employers may be well served by supplementing individual political undertakings with active participation in employer associations to shape the latter's lobbying priorities. Influence synergies may result from this tiered approach to wielding political pressure on public officials.

Concertation without labor materializes as a possibility when there is a societal affinity for state-led economic planning, and indigenous labor is relatively weak (e.g., Singapore, Japan, France). Although it may not openly court big business as a planning partner, the state generally is more amenable to structured, high-level input from peak management organizations than from their union counterparts. Asymmetric access may be an outgrowth of labor's inability to formulate a coherent socioeconomic platform because of internal discord, or outright relegation to an outsider's role by government leaders. Even so, employers do not always get what they want in the regulatory arena. France's legislated 35 hour work week is a good illustration. Employer associations nevertheless have the capacity to be more potent liaisons with the state than was the case under pluralism. This development argues against passive membership because of the sizable risk that government bureaucrats might take an association-endorsed position on market reforms that would neutralize one's factor advantages in HRM. Greater balance needs to be engineered between individual and collective political action in this scenario.

How much of a firm's labor-market fate should be entrusted to peak employer organizations is a key issue in countries that have opted for societal corporatism. In its weaker incarnations (e.g., Italy, the United Kingdom, Ireland, Belgium, Germany), the state provides recurrent opportunities for management and union federations to consult on limited socioeconomic issues and participate in their implementation. Government still formulates its policy responses unilaterally, albeit with more diversified input than was the case in the previous three configurations. The addition of a consolidated voice for labor in the policy-making equation makes it even more important to leverage the individual and group-based vehicles for political action available to firms. The relative emphasis needs to tilt more to the latter, though, as the IR system becomes more centralized (i.e., regional, industry, and national negotiations displace plant-level bargaining as the primary means of generating collective agreements). Peak IR organizations not only negotiate these accords on behalf of their respective affiliates, but also are more likely to draw attention from government as necessary economic stakeholders to interact with on a frequent basis.

MNEs based in countries that do not practice corporatism may be slow to make this adjustment. Ford-Werke's IR experiences in Germany illustrate this point (Copp 1977: 47). The subsidiary's longstanding practice of negotiating company-specific agreements with its works councils—an outlier stance among large employers—eventually was reassessed in the early 1960s. An extensive internal review of Ford's bargaining relationships in Germany made it apparent to local and corporate IR staff that this approach was not adequately serving the firm's interests. As a result, the company elected to join regional and industry employer associations and adhere to their settlements. Much ado might be made about the deference headquarters displayed from the outset in allowing host IR personnel to ultimately decide how the business unit would structure its dealings with employee representatives. On the other hand, one can criticize the parent firm for being complacent in originally allowing local industrial relations to be practiced in a format that was more palatable in terms of home-country norms but dysfunctional in the context of the host IR system. From the beginning, corporate IR staff should have balanced any perceived benefits from exercising more direct, short-term control over the itinerary of collective bargaining against the long-term opportunity costs of isolating the subsidiary from the economic and political clout of employer associations in that country.

Strong societal corporatism is much less common (e.g., Austria, Sweden, Norway, the Netherlands). Capstone IR groups at last become integral players in the creation and deployment of core economic and social policies. Concentrating political-influence tactics on intraorganizational bargaining in these organizations should yield greater dividends than operating as an isolated, external constituent in larger governmental processes. We will return to the topic of political behavior and its ramifications for industrial relations in Chapter 6.

Finally, it is critical to recognize that the very process by which law is crafted differs markedly across countries. National legal systems can be classified into distinct groups based on the principles and institutions that shepherd its formulation, institutionalization, and modification. Parliamentary bodies are the dominant wellspring of law in some societies, with the judiciary occupying a very circumscribed support role. In others, judges can be independent engines of law who rival legislators in their ability to fashion new legal entitlements and dramatically alter existing ones. Still others may have an executive branch that hoards sovereign authority, permitting legislatures and judicial agents to do little more than carry out the dictates of central-government leaders. These institutional contingencies must be reflected in the choice and prioritization of political behaviors that will be utilized to advance one's position within a given IR/HRM system.

Organizational resources should be selectively distributed across government branches to maximize the probability of (1) detecting significant impending changes in employment regulation, and (2) directing timely, efficacious political action at the appropriate decision makers. Should employers lobby legislators, administrators, or both sets of officials? Should companies intervene in lawsuits in which they are not the direct parties in dispute to lobby judges with *amicus curiae* (i.e., "friend of the court") briefs? The correct answers to such questions will vary from nation to nation. A more in-depth comparative analysis of legal-system attributes will follow later in this chapter.

Reality check

Theoretical considerations aside, how much influence does government actually exert over employment relationships? Is there evidence of substantial international variation in the intensity of the state's intrusion into employment decision making? In the aspects of work where it will try to intervene? How should the legal system's presence in HRM/IR systems be gauged—by the presence of official enactments and enforcement structures or the assessments of nongovernmental actors? What is the appropriate frame of reference to use when evaluating prevailing levels of employment regulation—general labor-market indicators or corporate performance and projected competitiveness? These issues will be encountered throughout the book with special attention devoted to the ways that they have been addressed in previous research.

For now, Figure 1.1 supplies an entry point into this area of government relations. While the underlying data reflect the perceptions of corporate respondents, one can begin to grasp the complex boundary spanning that firms must engage in to make informed market entry and exit decisions. Three major dimensions are examined: employment-related intervention by the state, wage-related intervention, and the extent to which labor regulation impedes present and future performance. Nations are clustered into three groups on these dimensions: low (less than 30 percent agreement with the item description), moderate (31–60 percent agreement), and high (more than 60 percent agreement). Potential geographic and economic idiosyncrasies are well represented. The 30 countries depicted span six continents and the continuum of industrial development.

Interesting patterns appear when one pairs ratings for the first two items. Emerging markets account for every instance (15 overall) where government seems to be unobtrusive in employment and wage decisions. A minimalist stance on regulation cannot be taken for granted in such economies, though. While the nations in Central/Eastern Europe, Asia, and the Middle East/Africa seem to reflect this orientation, Latin American countries do not. There was at least moderate agreement that frequent intervention was common in both areas in Argentina, Peru, Venezuela, and Mexico. In Chile, feelings that the state regularly injected itself into these aspects of HRM were even more widespread. Some variation also was evident in the distribution of AIEs. Most advanced economies elicited only moderate levels of agreement that state intervention was normal in such decisions. Portugal, Sweden, and Canada distinguished themselves as places with the most pervasive views of recurrent state involvement in employment and wage determinations.

Perhaps more intriguing is the highly attenuated relationship between state intervention in these areas and perceived performance. The fact that firms in Russia, China, and Singapore did not think labor regulations were seriously curtailing operations or growth is not unexpected, given their assessments that the state generally stays out of key HRM decisions. While companies in India and South Africa also characterized state

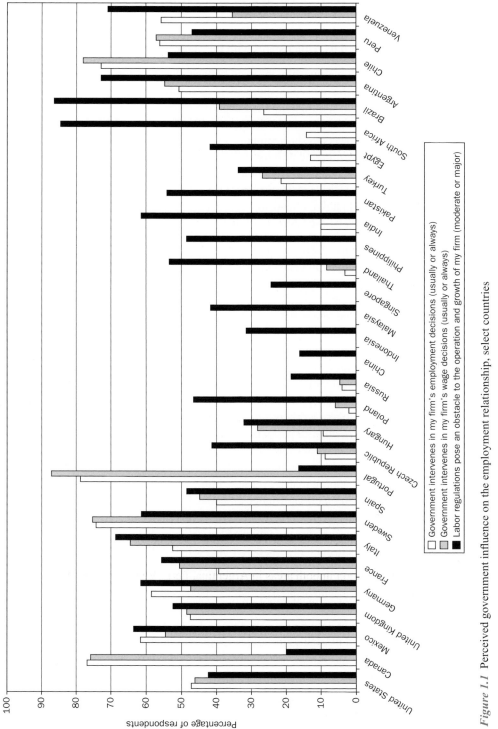

Figure 1.1 Perceived government influence on the employment relationship, select countries

Source: Based on data from World Bank Group (2001). Several countries profiled in this book did not participate in that investigation, including Australia, Ireland, Japan, New Zealand, South Korea, and Taiwan.

intervention as uncommon, they indicted labor regulation as a major threat to present and future success. The converse can be seen among AIEs. Portuguese and Canadian respondents, who were the most likely to portray government interference as high, generally did not identify labor regulations as a performance inhibitor. Sweden, on the other hand, enhanced its outlier status with this item.

Why isn't a more direct relationship observed between these factors? It may be that firms in some countries have become more adept over time at coping with regulatory constraints in employment, mitigating their negative effect on company outcomes. If true, then one could encounter variable judgments like those described above. Another potential explanation speaks to shortcomings in the research design that generated the underlying data. The wording of all three dimensions leaves much to be desired. For example, it is unclear whether the employment and wage scales implicitly incorporate labor-law mandates or exclude them outright. One could see a noticeable discrepancy between scores on the first two dimensions and those on the third if the latter is alone in capturing industrial relations obligations and procedural requirements.

What are the implications of the state and companies being at loggerheads over the issue of control in employment decision making? Profit-seeking firms have a defensible interest in containing legal encumbrances on their employment relationships, notwithstanding a growing international debate over the boundaries of corporate social accountability.[3] HRM-based competitive advantage ultimately rests on the ability to foster superior organizational capabilities in the areas of talent management, performance management, knowledge management, and stakeholder management. Talent management traditionally encompasses activities like external recruitment and selection, employee retention, and career development. More recently, its content domain has expanded to include the exit process and workforce survivors in downsizing situations, the location and integration of contingent workers, and the synergistic utilization of employee competencies residing in alliance partners. Performance management has at its epicenter the creation and maintenance of strategically appropriate evaluation systems, remuneration policies, and training practices. Knowledge management seeks to facilitate aggressive boundary spanning to discover new information streams impacting the firm's competitiveness, to codify tacit knowledge embedded in the work force to create an institutional memory and reduce barriers to information exchange, and to promote efficient, widespread internal dissemination of critical knowledge. The overall quality of these major activity clusters, in turn, determines whether the firm can achieve effective stakeholder management. Here, the focus is on steering the expectations and behaviors of external organizations and groups purporting to have a vested interest in HRM decision making (i.e., government, labor unions, customers, and investors).[4]

National employment regulation may play a pivotal role in determining the fate of these undertakings. Countries remain sharply divided in the legal restrictions placed on workforce internationalization, reductions in force, and alternative forms of employment. Politicians, unions, and NGOs in many advanced economies actively oppose company efforts to capitalize on offshore sourcing opportunities, alien work visas, and contingent employment relationships. For example, six state legislatures in the United States were deliberating the passage of Bills at the time of this writing making companies that employ workers overseas ineligible for state-government contracts (Executive Briefing 2003).

Talent management initiatives are not the only work practices that might be impaired by political-system activity. Incentive compensation strategies may falter because of isomorphic legal pressures. Global stock plans can be undermined or outlawed in a particular economy due to local securities regulations or taxation schemes. Global HR information systems can be disrupted by national variations in privacy laws, which inhibit cross-border flows of employee data. Internal development and knowledge-management programs could be compromised as a result.

International plant-location studies corroborate the influence that national employment-law profiles have on MNE entry and exit decisions. Ulgado (1996) investigated the relative importance that foreign companies attach to location attributes when making inward investment decisions in the United States. Overall, host labor law ranked seventeenth among 58 potential site-characteristics. Japanese MNEs assigned a slightly higher priority to this attribute, German and other European MNEs a slightly lower one. Outward investment by U.S. multinationals also has been examined to assess its sensitivity to workplace regulation (Cooke 1997; Cooke and Noble 1998). Pre-existing layoff restrictions were negatively associated with FDI in both studies, especially when prior government authorization or broad consultation is required before large-scale reductions in force can be instituted. UK firms similarly have been deterred from closing plants and investing in potential greenfield sites within Europe because of local employment legislation (Marginson *et al*. 1995). This inverse relationship appears to hold for FDI decisions in all developed economies (Cooke 2001). Stronger employment laws do not automatically drive away foreign investors, though. To illustrate, mandated works councils and the adoption of International Labor Organization (ILO) conventions have been linked to higher levels of inward investment (Cooke and Noble 1998; Kucera 2002).

Domestic firms also may exodus from their home countries because of HRM-related laws. Anecdotal support for this possibility abounds. For example, Valeo warned that it would move its operations to Great Britain if the French government followed through with its pledge to lower the work week to 35 hours without permitting a reduction in pay (Iskandar 1997). While that statement proved to be an idle threat, numerous French firms did relocate plants to England in the late 1990s due in large part to lower employment costs (Adams and Jack 1997; Groom 1997). For these companies, added transportation costs did not outweigh saving 75 percent or more on payroll taxes by operating in the United Kingdom. Brussels-based Virgin Express airlines announced plans to apply for an Irish air operator's certificate as a prelude to relocating its headquarters to Ireland and issuing Irish employment contracts to its work force (Ford 1998). Belgian social security costs equaled 37 percent of salaries at the time, compared to 9 percent in Ireland. Substantial cost savings were anticipated even though most of the carrier's services would continue to originate in Brussels. Belgium's national carrier, Sabena, likewise expressed an interest in relocating its pilots to Luxembourg or in shifting their employment contracts to Switzerland to reduce its employment-related tax liability (Skapinker 1998). Similar forces were behind much of the leakage of German operations into Eastern Europe during the decade (e.g., Gumbel 1993).

Employees are becoming increasingly militant in trying to secure their legal rights and entitlements as well. The United States often is labeled a litigious society, no less so in the workplace than in any other facet of social relations. This characterization is not without merit, given the explosive growth of employment-practice lawsuits (EPLs) in recent years. Discrimination claims alone grew by 2,200 percent from 1974 to 1999 (HR Briefing 1999). Moreover, the costs of noncompliance can be staggering, as Coca-Cola and Texaco discovered in two class-action lawsuits brought by disgruntled minority and female employees during the late 1990s. Out-of-court settlements were entered into with the plaintiffs in both instances totaling $192.5 million and $176 million, respectively. Legal fees for the plaintiffs' attorneys topped $20 million in the Coca-Cola case, and were incorporated in the defendant's payout figure. Although such outcomes are the exception, the price tag for mounting a defense can be formidable. One source reported that employers pay an estimated $60,000–$300,000 defending against a single employment-practices claim in court (Lenckus 1998).

It would be naïve to assume that such legal entanglements are a uniquely American phenomenon. Other nations are experiencing dramatic upswings in these lawsuits as well. Canada and Australia have become "hot spots" for employment litigation, giving rise to sophisticated markets for EPL insurance products along with the United States (Howard 1998). Europe appears to be headed in the same direction. For instance, nearly 165,000 legal actions were filed against British employers in 2000, a 32 percent jump from the previous year (Aldred 2000). Settlement costs also seem to be marching upward in the United Kingdom—by as much as 20 percent in discrimination cases. The number of lawsuits filed annually by Japanese employees may pale in comparison, but it continues to grow (Daily Yomiuri 1999; Japan Economic Newswire 1995).[5] Thus, while litigation volume and award size do not approach U.S. levels in these AIEs, the trends are unmistakably similar. Legal Systems in Action 1.1 suggests that analogous patterns are surfacing in emerging markets.

Given this backdrop, one assumes that managing legal systems would be a high-priority service area for HR's internal customers. Surprisingly, the research record is mixed. Some findings are consistent with this expectation (Tsui and Milkovich 1987); others are not (IBM/Towers Perrin 1992: 85–8; Mitsuhashi et al. 2000; Wright et al. 2001).

The IBM/Towers Perrin study is particularly helpful in sorting out perceived linkages between regulation, HRM, and firm performance in a cross-cultural context. Executives, academics, and consultants from 12 nations projected the impact that numerous environmental and organizational attributes would have on HR departments by the year 2000. Less than 20 percent of the overall sample ranked increased regulation as the first or second most influential factor. Slightly more HR executives did so than did other groups. North Americans were more likely to attach high salience to it than were individuals based elsewhere. Views that employment regulation would be a critical determinant of competitiveness were even harder to locate. Less than 5 percent of the sample considered legal compliance to be one of the top two goals for HR in order to achieve business success. This assessment transcended region, stage of industrial development, and type of respondent.

Rather than presenting a paradox, these findings underscore the need for corporate planners and researchers to think broadly when trying to assess the opportunities and constraints that legal systems present to competitiveness. The last set of investigations relied on very narrow wording to operationalize firm–government relations, thereby undersampling its content domain. At best, respondents were asked to evaluate the potential contributions of one of its facets—compliance management activities. This

Employment litigation and arbitration are on the rise in China

Until the mid-1990s, most Chinese employees were ill equipped to access the country's court system to defend their workplace rights. Many labor laws were kept secret by the government, fostering uncertainty about the entitlements and protections workers should be receiving. Those who somehow knew their rights were not much better off because they generally could not afford the services of licensed lawyers, whose fee usually equaled several months' wages. Not surprisingly, Chinese businesses experienced very little compliance pressure from below or above in this environment.

Things started to change dramatically when the government aggressively pursued admission to the World Trade Organization. The media were given more leeway to report employer abuses, and employees were encouraged to redress workplace grievances in the legal system. A series of labor-law reforms also took effect, making it less burdensome for individuals to do so. Employees were authorized to represent themselves in legal proceedings. Legal-aid offices (2,400) were established throughout the country to provide free advice on compliance questions. A new class of *de facto* attorneys also emerged from the ranks of the labor force. These lay practitioners provide counsel and representation services to co-workers—often free of charge—at quality levels that compete with, if not surpass, what is delivered by licensed lawyers.

With more avenues of recourse available, labor-related arbitration claims and lawsuits have skyrocketed. According to the Chinese Ministry of Labor, 184,000 claims were filed in 2002—nearly twice the number processed just four years earlier.

Source: Adapted from Wonacott (2003)

deterministic treatment of law is at odds with reality in many instances. Opportunities frequently exist to proactively influence the contents of regulation and its enforcement through lobbying and other forms of political action. There also are nonregulatory relationships that can be pursued with the state to create a more supportive environment for effective HRM. Mercedes-Benz's decision to build M-class sports utility vehicles in Tuscaloosa, Alabama, illustrates this point. While competing incentive packages and adequate supplies of skilled workers were available in nearly 150 potential locations, Alabama officials further distinguished themselves by pledging funds for on-site training facilities and submitting a plan to promote the successful adjustment of German expatriates and the families (Camp 1994; Wolffe 1998). Legal Systems in Action 1.2 highlights that even more creative arrangements may be engineered with government to realize the opportunities for HR-based competitive advantage that otherwise exist. Failure to incorporate these activities in a "managing legal systems" construct could lead one to seriously undervalue its importance to HR outcomes and firm performance.

What needs to be done in light of these observations? It is clear that previous models have inadequately addressed how *individual* employers can orchestrate their composite legal environment for competitive advantage. The call for the international HRM field to embrace a more strategic approach to government relations is consistent with the general contention that political behavior should be managed as though it was another factor of production for the firm (e.g., Boddewyn and Brewer 1994). To accomplish this, one must identify a more robust framework for managing employment rights and liabilities across countries. Greater precision is required in the delineation of relevant stakeholders in HRM decisions. A more dynamic view of law also is necessary—one that not only catalogs existing obligations and entitlements, but also prospects for opportunities to reshape them in the future. The next section expands on these points.

Superior plant performance in Mexico: government relations as a key HRM activity

Enactment of the North American Free Trade Act (NAFTA) was one of the most contentious political issues of the early 1990s in America. One of the more memorable comments against its passage was the warning there would be a "giant sucking sound" generated by the exodus of U.S. manufacturing jobs to lower-paid Mexican workers. While economists continue to debate the net effects of NAFTA's passage, specific states and industries did experience major reductions in factory work. For example, most of the 20,000 textile jobs that Alabama lost from 1995 to 1998 went to Mexico. Available data suggesting that U.S. compensation costs were five to ten times higher than those in Mexico undoubtedly influenced relocation decisions in this industry and others. However, firms that transferred operations often were unable to reap significant savings in operating costs due to unforeseen productivity problems and supply-chain inefficiencies. Outdated equipment, ineffective local managers, poorly educated employees, and transportation bottlenecks were obstacles commonly encountered by foreign companies.

Some firms avoided these pitfalls and experienced productivity levels that were above average, if not world-class, for their industry. For example, Ford Motor Company's Hermosillo facility ranked among the top one-third of auto plants in terms of productivity. Ford accomplished this feat by instituting several progressive measures, including overseas training for hundreds of host workers, employee busing, and political lobbying for the construction of additional dwellings to overcome housing shortages in the region.

Thomson, a French electronics company, achieved even better performance from its factory in Juarez. This plant quickly became the parent firm's most efficient production unit, turning out television sets at 80 percent of the cost of the best plant in France, and 50 percent of a sister facility in Beijing. Again, government relations and aggressive training policies were crucial elements of the startup strategy. Thomson's management deployed a comprehensive lobbying strategy that focused on (1) rezoning the land around the plant for residential construction and a school, (2) improving local bus services, (3) expediting the processing of employee mortgage applications for state-subsidized housing in the surrounding community, and (4) securing day passes for workers to shop across the border in nearby El Paso, Texas.

Both success stories indicate that cross-border relocations and greenfield operations may call for more than the cultural adaptation of home-country work practices. The ability to harness political-action mechanisms may be an indispensable component of effective workforce management, especially in emerging markets.

Sources: Adapted from Davis (1993) and Millman (1998)

Framework for managing legal systems

As shown in Figure 1.2, three factors will determine the breadth and complexity of effort that must be marshaled to manage legal systems effectively. First, the firm must precisely identify current and potential stakeholders that are subject to, or impact the creation and implementation of, legal instruments and processes bearing on HRM. Individuals can meet this criterion through their participation in employment relationships or their dealings with workers of the firm or its alliance partners. Labor unions qualify as stakeholders to the extent they attempt to supply formal or informal representation services to the existing work force (e.g., negotiating collective agreements, pressing the state for stronger IR/HRM regulation). Various entities within the labor movement may go on the offensive to defend or expand workplace rights, including national unions, domestic union federations, and international labor confederations.

Government must be included in the mix of external stakeholders for obvious reasons. Like unions, it can be stratified into multiple layers that may choose to act independently in setting or enforcing employment-related standards. Accordingly, firms must understand the jurisdictional limits that exist for local, national, and supranational (e.g., EU, OECD, WTO) legal institutions to ascertain their relevance in particular situations. There also is a need to distinguish among different kinds of government interactions (Florkowski and Nath 1993). *Ministerial* interactions are typified by compliance reporting and by requests for mandated approval of pending HRM actions or policies. Consultations to improve one's compliance posture under existing regulation (e.g., submission of voluntary affirmative actions plans for review and input prior to implementation) also would be considered ministerial in nature. *Adversarial* interactions encompass situations where companies must defend their activities during formal proceedings. Government may drive such encounters, as would be the case in congressional investigations and litigation initiated by agents of the state (e.g., federal

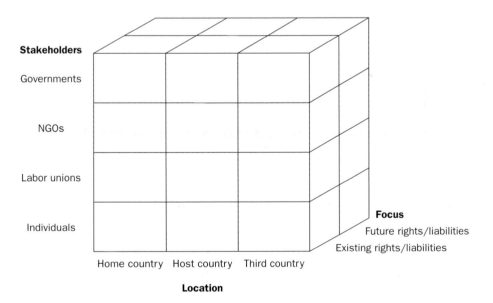

Figure 1.2 Framework for managing legal systems

lawsuits brought by the U.S. Equal Employment Opportunity Commission after conciliation negotiations with defendant employers fail to produce a consent decree). Alternatively, government may play a more indirect role serving as adjudicator in legal actions brought by employees, unions, or other system actors. *Participative* interactions, in turn, are proactive efforts to influence the scope of future rights and entitlements in the larger legal system. Illustrations would include lobbying, providing formal input to public officials during the formulation of regulations (e.g., notice-and-comment hearing in the United States), and submitting *amicus curiae* briefs in cases where the firm is not a direct party in the dispute. Intraorganizational bargaining in peak employer associations would qualify as well to the extent the objective is to influence policy development in corporatist societies.

Nongovernmental organizations loom as another self-proclaimed stakeholder albeit in a more limited range of circumstances. While a universal definition of NGOs is lacking, it is widely acknowledged that thousands of these nonprofit, private groups are in existence worldwide. Their willingness and ability to intervene in legal systems is common knowledge. Some function exclusively within a specific nation, others are truly global in scope. Of those that seek to become involved in employment regulation and its enforcement, relatively few seek to advance the interests of companies. Thus, firms must be aware of their *modus operandi* and be prepared to respond in whatever forum and venue NGOs choose to leverage.

The spatial context of these multifaceted encounters and their underlying purposes are additional factors to consider. Some companies confine their operations to a single nation, while others orchestrate a value chain that stretches across countries or regions. Domestic firms can concentrate on the substantive and procedural intricacies of one legal superstructure. Multinational employers not only face the prospect of having to simultaneously interact with different kinds of legal systems, but also must overcome the challenge of having to correctly ascertain which legal systems govern their dealings with particular stakeholders at any moment in time. Balance also must be sought between actions that optimize the firm's present legal standing and those that will improve its position *vis-à-vis* other system actors in the future. The former thrust places a premium on tracking, executing, and protecting all employment-related obligations that have been perfected, the latter on identifying and influencing the most potent sources of regulatory change.

These points are expanded upon below.

Dealings with individual stakeholders

The following litigation scenarios typify how employees and companies can become embroiled in legal proceedings over employment-related issues:

● A British MNE was sued in its home country by representatives of 20 Zulu employees who had died from mercury exposure that was linked to the firm's subsidiary in South Africa. Local authorities had determined that the poisonings resulted from poor working conditions and safety practices at the host production facility—problems that had plagued these operations before they were transferred from England to South Africa. Unfortunately, the survivors had no recourse under

South African law because workers generally do not have the right to sue their employers. Refusing to dismiss the suit, the English Court of Appeal rejected the company's claim that the United Kingdom was not an appropriate jurisdiction to litigate the dispute (i.e., *forum non conveniens*). The parties subsequently settled out of court for the equivalent of US$2.1 million (Rice 1997; Aldred 1998).

- An American energy firm was dragged into its home-country court system for alleged human-rights abuses that were perpetrated by its host-country alliance partner. The company had entered into an agreement with local government officials to provide manpower and security for an offshore natural-gas-field project. With the help of human rights activists, Myanmar villagers sued in the United States, asserting that they had worked as forced labor in the joint venture rather than risk imprisonment or death at the hands of the military—a situation that the American organization was well aware of and profited from. In 2002, the Los Angeles Superior Court ruled that a trial could proceed to determine whether it was vicariously liable for the behavior of its alliance partner's actions in their common business (Malkani 1999; Waldman 2002).

- Forty Japanese companies were named defendants in a U.S. lawsuit filed on behalf of Chinese nationals (some having become American citizens) who worked as slave laborers during World War II. No viable recourse was deemed to exist in China because the government had abandoned diplomatic efforts to secure official reparations for wartime damages. Japan's legal system was available but hostile to these actions. Several prior cases based on similar war crimes had been rejected by Japanese courts. Japan's largest construction firm became the first defendant to settle with these litigants shortly after the U.S. suit began, establishing a $4.5 million fund to be administered by the Chinese Red Cross (Forney 2000; Bannon 2000; Tett 2000).

- An American computer firm was sued by U.S. nationals in state court for allegedly discriminating during a 2,500 person reduction in force. Plaintiffs claimed that the firm not only shielded East Indian employees from termination, but also continued to hire more than 2,000 Indian H-1B visa holders, many of whom were performing work formerly done by laid-off Americans. Legal proceedings continue (Morrison 2003; Moad 2003).

- A U.S. air carrier was sued in the United Kingdom by four flight attendants who sought maternity benefits guaranteed by UK law. Although all of the plaintiffs were based in London, only one was a British citizen. Moreover, they spent most of their working time outside of the United Kingdom and originally were hired and trained in the United States. A host employment tribunal ruled that these employees could pursue a cause of action for British maternity employment rights (Aldred 2001).

Dealings with union stakeholders

The following events are representative of the legal jousting that can go on between unions and employers over workplace issues:

- Australian employers encountered a stern warning from the Australian Council of Trade Unions (ACTU) on the heels of new legislation allowing financial institutions to offer retirement savings accounts (RSAs) as an alternative savings vehicle for superannuation monies that are mandated for all employees. In an alleged effort to thwart "sweetheart" deals between companies and banks (e.g., benefits conveyed to the firm in exchange for employees being directed to open RSAs), the federation announced that its law firm would take legal actions on behalf of workers against employers who pressured or misled individuals into channeling their superannuation entitlements into RSAs (Davis 1997).

- A South Korean multinational was accused of breaching the OECD Guidelines by illegally suppressing union activity in its Guatemalan operations. The ITGLWF, an international federation of garment-industry unions, followed procedures set out in the Guidelines and raised the case with the Korean National Contact Point (NCP). NCP administrators were requested to set up a meeting between ITGLWF officials and the MNE's president to redress the situation (ITGLWF 2002a).

- Argentine labor federations reacted angrily to, and ultimately overturned, a set of labor-law reforms that created more labor flexibility for employers, decentralized collective bargaining, and provided for the renegotiation of collective agreement (many of which been in effect for decades). The legislation was part of a series of economic reforms demanded by the IMF as a condition for a multibillion dollar bailout package. Union leaders mobilized thousands of rank-and-file members in demonstrations outside of the Congress while voting on the Bill took place. Having failed to derail the Bill's passage, federation leaders continued to aggressively negotiate with government officials and called for a series of general strikes to disrupt an already wounded economy. Approximately 18 months later, the labor movement had precipitated the downfall of the existing administration and witnessed its successor submit a new Bill to repeal the reforms (Torres 2000; Warn 2000; Saa 2001).

- A U.S. technology union received approval from its membership to formally lobby Congress for legislation designed to curtail the growing practice of outsourcing IT jobs overseas. The union's objective was to pressure legislators to tighten visa requirements for foreign IT workers and create meaningful incentives for U.S. firms to keep IT jobs in America (Economist Intelligence Unit 2003).

- The ICFTU, a global confederation of national labor federations, developed and submitted proposals to the European Union to provide input for pending trade negotiations with several dozen developing nations. These recommendations sought to influence how EU negotiators attempted to structure the content and style of future trade relations with African, Caribbean, and Pacific countries that were partners in the Lomé Convention that was set to expire in 2000 (ICFTU 1999).

Dealings with government stakeholders

The following situations highlight the wide-ranging interactions that may occur between government and firms as they jockey to influence and control employment decisions:

- UK employers watched from the sidelines as British employees successfully challenged legal restrictions on older workers' ability to file unfair dismissal claims and receive statutory redundancy pay. Both policies were ruled to be discriminatory[6] by a low-level employment tribunal. Contending that the tribunal had been influenced by erroneous statistical evidence, the government formally appealed the decision to a higher-level judicial body. Left unchanged, the ruling would expand workplace rights for hundreds of thousands of persons over the age of 65 (Tait 2003).

- Exercising an option specified in Canadian federal legislation, British Columbia passed its own privacy law to regulate the collection, use, and disclosure of personal data within the province. Over 170 organizations had consulted with local government officials regarding the introduction and composition of this Bill. Provinces that failed to enact their own laws by 2004 were covered by PIPEDA, the federal privacy law, by default (Canadian HR Reporter 2003).

- A large Italian manufacturer applied for and received government approval to carry out a large-scale reduction in force (RIF) in its domestic operations. Thousands of employees were slated for temporary and permanent layoffs in an effort to save upwards of US$1 billion in a multifaceted turnaround strategy. Securing the classification of being in "crisis status" was a prerequisite to tapping an industry-funded but state-administered program that pays those experiencing short-term layoffs as much as 60 percent of their former wages, provided they are rehired within one year. Pursuant to the deal struck between these two system actors, the company shortened the period for which its Sicilian plant would be closed and agreed to have workers at other plants only suffer reduced hours through job sharing rather than being laid off outright. In exchange, the state issued the appropriate designation and acquiesced to nearly six times as many terminations as had been sought initially. It marked the second time within a decade that the firm qualified for this subsidy (Galloni and Di Leo 2002; Galloni and Boudette 2002; Kapner and Barber 2002).

- The Federation of Korean Industries (FKI), a powerful lobbying group, squared off against President Roh Moo-hyun's government over labor-law reform and the future direction of industrial relations in that country. Favoring U.S.-style changes, the federation advocated tougher civil and criminal penalties against the instigators of illegal strikes and the right to withhold pay from those who participate in such activities. Greater labor participation, desired by the state, was strongly disavowed. Fifty-nine core member firms signed the FKI statement articulating these positions (BBC Monitoring International Reports 2003).

- Peak employer associations in the United Kingdom and Italy delivered formal letters to the prime ministers of their respective nations demanding that they block all future labor-market regulations from the European Commission. For British employers, the overriding concern was the growing ossification of the European Union's least regulated labor market. Their Italian counterparts were trying to contend with the fact that Italy already stood as one of the most heavily regulated markets in the region (Champion 2002).

- The leading HRM professional association and industrial group in the United States filed *amicus curiae* briefs with the Supreme Court in a sexual harassment case that had been successfully appealed. The core issue being litigated was the standard that should be utilized to guide the imposition of punitive damages. Both organizations sought to share their expertise and insights with the justices, asserting that punitive damages would not be an appropriate remedy where firms had proactively implemented anti-discrimination measures. While there is no evidence confirming that this input materially impacted judicial thinking, the court's ruling did reflect this stance (Bisom-Rapp 2001).

Dealings with NGO stakeholders

Illustrations of legal-system skirmishes between nongovernmental organizations and employers would include:

- A U.S.-based MNE settled a protracted legal battle with worker-rights activists over public statements defending its oversight of Asian suppliers and their HRM policies. While denying any wrongdoing, the firm agreed to pay $1.5 million to the Fair Labor Association to help fund a wide variety of initiatives including monitoring conditions in foreign factories, advancing the development of global reporting standards, and educating workers. The company also agreed to honor existing commitments to conduct after-hours training in all its overseas locations. The settlement was reached after the U.S. Supreme Court declined to review earlier state-court decisions. Interestingly, six major MNEs had filed *amicus curiae* briefs in support of the defendant's review request (Kang 2003).
- The National Employment Law Project (NELP) filed a "friend of the court" brief with the U.S. Supreme Court on behalf of illegal immigrant workers in an effort overturn a law denying them organizing rights. An unfavorable ruling prompted Mexico to request an advisory opinion from the Inter-American Court of Justice, a supranational judicial body attached to the Organization of American States. At the behest of the Mexican government, NELP attorneys filed a second *amicus curiae* brief—joined by dozens of U.S.-based NGOs—arguing that the contested provisions violated fundamental international norms of nondiscrimination and freedom of association (National Employment Law Project 2002a, b, 2003).
- A third NGO, the Lawyers' Committee for Human Rights, tried to impact trade negotiations by testifying in a public hearing conducted by the Office of the U.S. Trade Representative. The group levied accusations of rampant labor-rights abuses in all of the countries seeking to negotiate a Central American free-trade area with the United States. Federal officials were urged to conduct a country-by-country assessment of labor rights prior to finalizing a trade deal for that region (Lawyers' Committee for Human Rights 2002).

The intricacies of these relationships will be examined in the last three chapters of the book.

It would be useful at this juncture to profile the diversity of legal systems in place around the world. The location dimension in Figure 1.2 deals with much more than geographic proximity and the number of countries where legal issues may arise. One must be mindful of critical distinctions in the underlying principles of law along with the ways it is fashioned. Region and industrialization stage are relevant but not determinative factors in explaining the substantive and procedural variance across nations. Separated by a small body of water, the United Kingdom and France share little in their respective approaches to jurisprudence. Nigeria has more in common with Malaysia and Indonesia in this regard than it does with the Congo Republic or Egypt. We explore these differences in next section.

Alternative legal systems

Table 1.1 organizes the global community of nations into eight regions and three overarching legal systems: common law, civil law, and mixed. Table 1.2 profiles the regulatory scope, sources of law, and judicial process associated with each system.

Looking across the rows in Table 1.1, it is obvious that system heterogeneity varies from area to area. This fact dispels any notion that familiarity with one legal system automatically equips firms to handle those in neighboring countries. Proceeding down its columns, one can identify sets of nations that display similar patterns in the creation and application of law. Countries sharing the same classification do not necessarily have common policy objectives. Nor is it guaranteed that the substantive content of regulation will overlap.

Common law systems

Having their genesis in the legal history of England, common law systems empower courts to utilize statutory law or legal principles that judges have evolved (i.e., common law and equity) to make determinations in a particular lawsuit. Such rulings can have dramatic consequences extending far beyond the immediate dispute if they create legal precedent.[7] To establish precedent, judicial opinions must contain at least one *ratio decidendi* (i.e., a new or modified legal principle derived from the judge's decision on the material facts at hand). Legal professionals are saddled with the challenge of extracting this component from surrounding case-specific language that is referred to as *obiter dicta*. Once set, precedent generally is binding on lower-level courts unless subsequent cases can be distinguished based on their facts, or an even higher-level court modifies or overturns it. Statutes, in turn, typically codify common law principles spanning a body of case law, or introduce regulation to issues that have received little attention from the courts.

The international proliferation of this legal family is closely tied to the British Empire's expansion over several centuries. It remains fundamentally intact in colonial settings that lacked a politically organized local population at the time of settlement (e.g., the United States, non-French territories in Canada, Australia, and New Zealand). In essence, the home-country legal system was extended to British colonists as their birthright, and there was no indigenous counterpart with which it needed to interface. This does not mean that these countries failed to develop their own legal identities post-independence. Noticeable variation exists in the way that law is structured, the methods and procedures that underlie legal practice, and the inclination to treat English judicial decisions as precedent. Australia has retained the closest connection with English law, the United States has differentiated itself the most, and Canada falls somewhere between the two (Zweigert and Kötz 1987: 226–245; David and Brierley 1978: 377–391).

In other instances, the British took control of regions that had pre-existing legal systems of Western or other origin. English law (and judicial administration) was "received" in these settings as a matter of colonial policy, coexisting with the indigenous legal superstructure. This practice led to the emergence of the following types of mixed legal systems: common–civil (e.g., Quebec (Canada), South Africa), common–customary

Table 1.1 Typology of national legal systems

Region	Common law	Civil law	Mixed					
			Common–civil law	Common–customary law	Civil–customary law	Common–Islamic law	Civil–Islamic law	Other
North America	United States, Canada *except Quebec*	Mexico	Quebec (Canada)	–	–	–	–	–
Western Europe	UK *except Scotland,* Northern Ireland, Ireland	Germany, France, Italy, Sweden, Austria, Belgium, Netherlands, Denmark, Norway, Finland, Spain, Portugal, Greece, Switzerland, Iceland	Scotland (UK)	–	–	–	–	–
Central and Eastern Europe	–	Czech Republic, Poland, Hungary, Slovakia, Estonia, Latvia, Lithuania, Belarus, Ukraine, Romania, Bulgaria, Slovenia, Russia	–	–	–	–	–	–

Asia and Oceania	Australia, New Zealand	Vietnam, Kazakhstan, Tajikistan, Turkmenistan, Uzbekistan	Thailand, Philippines	Myanmar, Papua New Guinea	China, Taiwan, South Korea, Japan	Pakistan, Bangladesh, Singapore	–	India,[a] Malaysia,[b] Indonesia[b]
Middle East and Africa	–	Turkey	South Africa	Tanzania, Uganda, Zambia	Congo, Niger	Oman, UAE, Qatar, Sudan	Egypt, Kuwait, Lebanon, Iraq	Nigeria,[b] Kenya,[c] Saudi Arabia,[d] Iran,[d] Israel[e]
Central America and Caribbean	Belize, Bahamas, Bermuda, Jamaica	Cuba, Costa Rica, Dominican Republic, El Salvador, Guatemala, Panama, Honduras, Nicaragua	–	–	–	–	–	–
South America	–	Brazil, Argentina, Chile, Peru, Venezuela, Colombia, Ecuador, Bolivia, Paraguay, Uruguay	–	–	–	–	–	–

Source: University of Ottawa Faculty of Law website (http://www.droitcivil.uottawa.ca/world-legal-systems/eng-tableau.html)

Notes

a Common/Hindu/Islamic law.
b Common/customary/Islamic law.
c Civil/customary/Islamic law.
d Civil/common/Islamic law.
e Civil/common/Jewish law.

Table 1.2 Select characteristics of major legal systems

Characteristic		Common law	Civil law	Customary law	Religious law (special case of customary law)		
					Islamic	Hindu	Jewish
Regulatory scope	Issues to which the law applies	*General* • May not apply to some areas of private law in mixed systems	*General* • May not apply to some areas of private law in mixed systems	*Private law only* • Family law and succession law • Land law (Africa)	*Private law only* • Family law and succession law	*Private law only* • Family law and succession law	*Private law only* • Family law and succession law
	Persons to whom the law applies	*General population* • Choice-of-law rules may lead the court to apply principles from other legal systems	*General population* • Choice-of-law rules may lead the court to apply principles from other legal systems	*Native population* • Option may exist to select common/civil law to govern one's legal relationships	*Muslim population*	*Hindu population*	*Jewish population*
Potential sources of law	Legislation	*Major influence* • Statutes frequently address gaps in common law • 'Codes' typically represent compilations of discrete statutes that may not encompass all of the law on a given subject	*Major influence* • Codes are integrated, comprehensive bodies of private law in basic areas (e.g., civil, penal) • Special 'codes' regulate areas not covered by the basic codes (e.g., labor and employment law)	*Major influence* • May exist in written or oral form (Africa) • Chieftains may have the authority to declare the content of customary law for publication as legislative instruments (e.g., Ghana)	*Limited influence* • Certain aspects are formally codified in some countries (e.g., Egypt)	*Limited influence* • Certain aspects are codified in some countries (e.g., India)	*Limited influence* • Takkanot

Judicial process	Common law	Civil law	Customary law	Islamic law	Hindu law	Jewish law
Court decisions	*Major influence* • Superior courts create binding precedent for lower-level courts • Highest court not bound by own precedent	*Limited influence* • May be cited as persuasive authority on recognition of custom or statutory interpretation	*Limited influence* • Statutes may empower local courts to declare the content of customary law (e.g., Nigeria)	—	—	—
Court organization	*Unified system* • Ordinary courts preside over private and public law cases without recognizing a distinction • May have parallel ordinary-court systems (i.e., federal and state) • 'Legislative' courts may exist, but their decisions normally are subject to review by ordinary courts	*Bifurcated system* • Ordinary courts preside over private law cases; administrative courts handle public law cases • Different judicial structures are utilized to resolve conflicts that arise when both systems assert jurisdiction over the same dispute	*Unified system* • Ordinary courts apply customary law where it pertains and common or civil law elsewhere	*Unified system* • Ordinary courts apply Islamic law where it pertains (Iran is an exception) and common or civil law elsewhere	*Unified system* • Ordinary courts apply Hindu law where it pertains and common or civil law elsewhere	*Bifurcated system* • Ordinary courts preside over public and private law cases; religious courts handle disputes involving Jewish law

Sources: Abdal-Haqq (2002), David (1984), Essien (1994), Goldstein (1996), Radford (2000), Zweigert and Kötz (1987)

(e.g., Myanmar, Zambia), and common–Islamic (e.g., Pakistan, Singapore). Reception did not necessarily end when independence and statehood were achieved. For example, an independent Zambia continued to adopted newly enacted UK legislation for a time pursuant to the 1965 British Acts Extension Act (Kalula 2004: 15). Singapore did not end the practice until 1993, when legislation prohibited further reception and specified the statutes and common law that would carry over into the future (de Cruz 1999: 122). Colonies and protectorates like India, Malaysia, Indonesia, and Nigeria actually added a third legal system with the onset of British rule. While Israel also combines elements from three legal systems, the infusion of civil law happened after the modern state's founding.

Choice-of-law rules guide the identification and application of relevant legal principles in mixed systems. To illustrate, Nigerian courts preside over legal disputes in the following manner:

- Customary law is applied to transactions between Nigerians unless (1) the parties have expressly or implicitly decided that English law will govern, or (2) the essence of the transaction deals with a subject unknown to customary law. A complementary set of decision rules may be invoked if completing systems of customary law are involved in the dispute.
- English law is applied to transactions between Nigerians and non-Nigerians unless it will substantially injure one of the parties. If so, then customary law becomes the default option.
- English law is applied to transactions between non-Nigerians (Essien 1994: 178).

Civil law systems

Civil law systems have an altogether different character. To begin with, there is a fundamental bifurcation of law into two domains, public law and private law, each having its own hierarchy of courts. Public law typically encompasses such areas as constitutional law, public international law, the structure and function of public services, and tax law. Private law defines the rights and duties of private persons and corporations, spanning family law, inheritance law, contract law, tort law, commercial law, employment law, private international law (e.g., conflict of laws in disputes where the state is not a party), etc. More mercurial in nature, penal law is considered an aspect of public law in some nations (e.g., Germany) and private law in others (e.g., France). Ordinary courts have the authority to preside over private law matters; administrative courts over those involving public law. A "conflict of competence" arises when both systems assert jurisdiction over the same case. Nations have developed varied mechanisms for coping with this problem, including review by a special tribunal (e.g., France) or constitutional court (e.g., Austria), deferral to the judgment of the highest ordinary court (e.g., Italy, Belgium), and respect for the judgment of the first court to rule on the issue (e.g., Germany) (Szladits 1975: 2–48 and –49).

Legislation is the paramount source of law, though. While judges have the power to determine whether existing statutes govern a particular dispute, they have no authority to create new law. Two kinds of legislation coexist in these systems. Codes integrate the full set of legal principles governing particular areas. For example, much of private law is codified in a single civil code. Matters not addressed in the basic codes still may be controlled in piecemeal fashion by separate legislation. These auxiliary statutes, sometimes labeled "special codes," are closer in spirit to the laws enacted in common law nations. Commercial transactions are regulated in this manner, as are IR/HRM systems with the exception of Italy, whose civil code has an employment subdivision.

Modern-era civil law systems first surfaced in Continental Europe during the late eighteenth century. France was the starting point, where newly formulated legal codes sought to institutionalize sociopolitical changes ushered in by the French Revolution. Napoleon's military campaigns were instrumental in spreading the civil code's influence over much of Western Europe. Belgium, the Netherlands, and numerous regions in latter-day Germany, Poland, Latvia, and Italy received the French code in the aftermath of conquest. It proved resilient enough to survive the end of Napoleon's regime and subsequent backlashes of nationalism, albeit in modified form. Spain eventually agreed upon a civil code in the late 1800s derived largely from French sources. Germany carried these reforms the furthest, creating a very distinctive code in 1896 that was highly technical in nature and more strongly rooted in Roman legal principles than its French-based antecedent. The German code later spread through much of Central and Eastern Europe,[8] Italy, and Portugal.

Scandinavian nations belong to this legal family, but were not directly impacted by the French or German codification movements. The civil law systems in Sweden, Norway, Denmark, and Finland are based on statutory law and have bifurcated court systems, but uniformly lack comprehensive, integrated codes (Berkowitz *et al.* 2003; Ortwein 2003). Instead, their codes more closely resemble legislative compilations found in the United States.

Latin America's wholesale conversion to the civil law system was a matter of choice as well as history. Its colonial relationship with Spain and Portugal clearly exposed the population to Roman law principles and institutions. However, fledgling nations in the region turned to other European countries, and sometimes one another, to develop their own civil codes (Murillo 2001; Zweigert and Kötz 1987: 117–118). France's civil code was thought to embody the values and ideals spurring the movement for independence in the western hemisphere. Some national codes amounted to little more than translations of their French counterpart (e.g., Bolivia), while others built upon its core elements to generate codes with a very local flavor (e.g., Chile, Argentina, and Venezuela). Brazil's civil code, which did not appear until 1916, drew upon its predecessors on both sides of the Atlantic.

Of course, most countries systematically overhauled their codes in the mid to late twentieth century to preserve their relevance and vitality.

France's colonial empire spawned mixed legal systems as well. The Middle East and Africa house numerous examples of civil–customary, civil–Islamic, and other more exotic permutations. Egypt provides an excellent illustration of the intermingling of civil law and Islamic law over time. When the arrival of Islam displaced Roman law during the first millennium, Sharia courts were empowered to hear civil, criminal, and family matters within their territories—a situation that would remain largely unchanged for the next 1,100 years. During the 1870s, Egypt allowed treaty-based "mixed tribunals" to acquire jurisdiction over civil and commercial suits where at least one of the parties was a foreigner (Zweigert and Kötz 1987: 113). These tribunals were administered primarily by Europeans, who applied French-oriented legislation. A parallel system of native courts was created shortly thereafter based on these principles, limiting religious courts to cases involving family law and inherence law. The post-World War II period brought a national civil code of French influence, the disbanding of mixed tribunals, and the reassignment of jurisdiction over conflicts governed by Islamic law to ordinary courts. In an interesting twist, Egypt's civil code directs the judiciary to fill any gaps in the law according to Islamic law principles (David and Brierley 1978: 431).

The cross-pollination of civil and customary legal systems in Asia manifested in one of two ways. Civil and commercial codes were imposed on some nations (e.g., Vietnam, the Philippines) during their colonial occupation by European powers. In contrast, voluntary reception occurred in Japan and China as a calculated strategy to eliminate treaty-sanctioned "consular courts" which had jurisdiction over foreign nationals within their borders (Zweigert and Kötz 1987: 367–368; Epstein 1998). Japanese and Chinese drafters were strongly influenced by the German code when developing their own civil legislation. Left undisturbed in all of these instances were matters of family law and inheritance law, which stayed in the domain of customary law.

Macro-level linkages like those described in Table 1.2 can make some systems easier to understand and step into than others. Micro-level linkages (i.e., commonalities in the substantive and procedural aspects of employment regulation) would be even more useful. The latter are unmistakable at times. To illustrate, many French-speaking African countries drew heavily from France's Labor Code for Overseas Territories when enacting their own national labor codes (Schregle 1985). A decidedly British influence is evident in India's employment regulation after more than a half-century of political independence (e.g., Mankidy 1995; Ratnam 1995). In other instances, nations in the same legal family have markedly different institutional structures for regulating labor-market activity. For example, mandated state arbitration mechanisms have a major impact on wage determination in Australia and New Zealand, while the United States and United Kingdom generally treat arbitration and wage determination as matters that are voluntarily negotiated by management and labor. MNEs should experience less difficulty adjusting to legal systems that exhibit strong macro- and micro-linkages with those they have dealt with in the past.

These materials also begin to suggest ways that multinational firms can leverage a presence in multiple locations to improve their legal position. To illustrate, the choice-of-law clause is a pivotal element of international employment agreements because it specifies which nation's law affords the substantive and procedural backdrop for work assignments. While host-country nationals undoubtedly will be governed by local law, this is not necessarily true for expatriates. MNEs generally have considerable latitude to negotiate which laws will be applied to parent-country nationals and third-country nationals during their stints overseas. Consequently, firms need to assess the strengths and weaknesses of structuring their contracts to tap host- or third-country employment regulation. We will return to this topic in Chapter 7.

Comparing abstract principles of law tells only part of the story in distinguishing legal systems. Figures 1.3 and 1.4 critique the relative performance of the state as gatekeeper to legal entitlements and liabilities.[9] The first item in Figure 1.3 focuses on public-sector service delivery. Most countries scored poorly here. There were only three nations (all Asian emerging markets) where more than 30 percent of respondents agreed that government provided services in an efficient manner. A similar outcome was obtained for regulatory predictability. The Czech Republic, Poland, Singapore, and India were the only locations where there was at least moderate agreement that business regulation was more predictable now than in the recent past. Belief that the legal system would protect vested rights in business disputes was more widely shared. While the composition of individual nations changed, developing economies again led in the ratings. Interesting regional variations surfaced as well. Indonesia and Thailand received a much weaker vote of confidence on this issue than did other Asian economies. Europe's AIEs differed considerably on this dimension. Sweden, France, and Spain outperformed the United Kingdom, Germany, Italy, and Portugal by sizable margins. With the exception of Chile, Latin America reflected high levels of cynicism that government was inclined to defend corporate rights.

Regulatory transparency and voice speak more pointedly to legal-system performance. At a minimum, companies should be able to access the details of existing regulations and rely on previous interpretations of them by the state to clarify the scope of their compliance obligations. Advance notice of pending regulatory changes, as well as opportunities to provide input during their formulations, would further ensure that government was functioning effectively and fairly. Figure 1.4 displays comparative data on these issues. Information on applicable regulations was deemed available in most countries, although Singapore and South Africa were the only places where most respondents concurred. Europe again was split with Germany, Italy, and Sweden lagging behind other EU members. Two-thirds of the nations exhibited low agreement (i.e., 30 percent or less) that the interpretation of regulations was consistent and predictable. Canada and France were the only AIEs to score moderately well. Even fewer countries won approval for their notification tendencies. The United States and United Kingdom fared best among developed economies, but were surpassed by Singapore, China, and South Africa. No nation received accolades for its treatment of the input business supplies when important changes in law or policy are afoot.

Successfully integrating these puzzle pieces in pursuit of competitive advantage is a daunting task. Its systematic undertaking is the focus of the rest of this book.

Overview of chapters

2 Global institutions and the evolution of employment regulation

This chapter examines the impact that transnational entities like the ILO, WTO, and OECD can have on employment regulation at the country level. Special attention will be devoted to the diversity of approaches that are utilized to facilitate legal change, as well as the opportunities firms have to influence their scope and intensity.

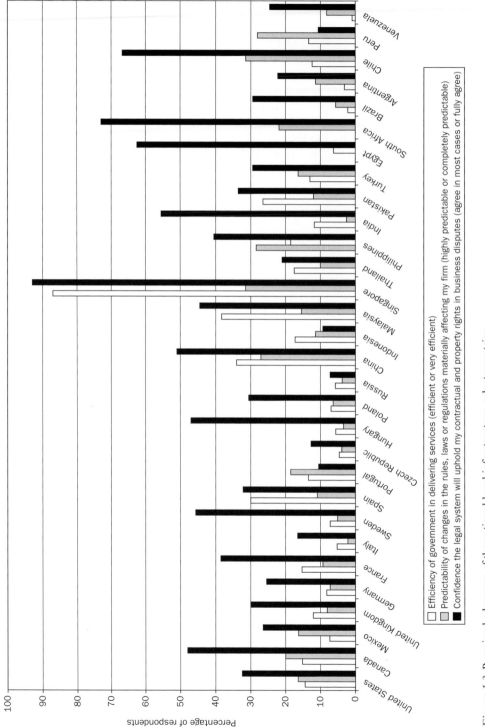

Figure 1.3 Perceived adequacy of the national legal infrastructure, select countries

Source: Based on data from World Bank Group (2001).

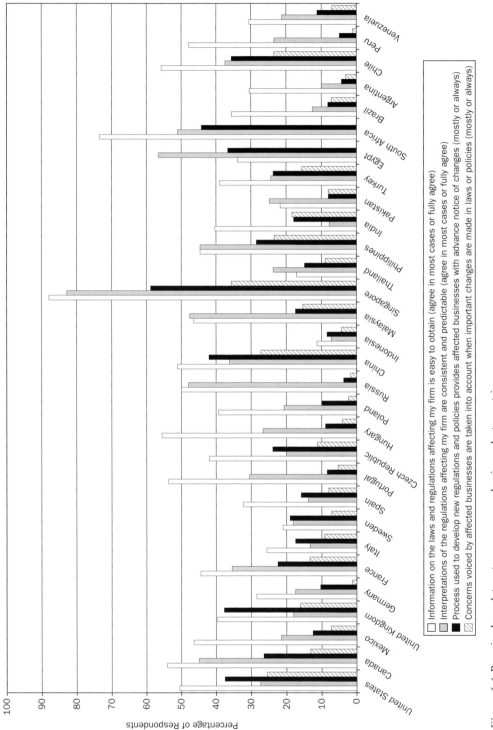

Figure 1.4 Perceived regulatory transparency and voice, select countries

Source: Based on data from World Bank Group (2001).

3 Regional institutions and the evolution of employment regulation

Chapter 3 profiles the effects that trade blocs can have on the labor and employment laws of member states. Fundamental differences in the underlying goals and control mechanisms of these supranational bodies are highlighted to clarify the prospects for greater harmonization of employment regulation in various regions. Historical and current developments within the European Union, NAFTA, and MERCOSUR are featured prominently in the discussion.

4 National institutions and the evolution of employment regulation

The executive, legislative, and judicial branches of government play distinct, but complementary, roles in the creation and enforcement of workplace rights in any given state. This chapter analyzes how each actor operates within the context of its overarching legal system to influence the regulatory framework governing employment relationships. Emphasis is placed on understanding how their actions enable "foreign" legal principles and international commitments to find their way into domestic labor and employment law.

5 The state and IR in global perspective

Chapter 5 provides a comparative overview of the level and form of government involvement in the establishment and internal affairs of unions, the formation of collective labor agreements, and resolution of industrial disputes. Recommendations for the development and administration of labor-relations strategies follow.

6 Managing domestic and transnational political behavior

This chapter highlights the opportunities and constraints associated with HRM/IR political action on an international scale. After exploring the general dynamics of MNE–government relations, we look specifically at the use of lobbying and other tactics to proactively influence employment regulation within and across legal systems. Whenever possible, the patterns evident in developed economies are compared with those observed in emerging markets.

7 Managing global legal systems for competitive advantage

The final chapter encourages more systematic efforts to manage legal systems. Drawing on earlier chapters, an integrated framework is presented summarizing the domestic and cross-border forces that drive employment regulation. The ensuing discussion highlights its implications for the HRM profession and academics who have a serious interest in advancing our understanding of the environmental challenges associated with international HRM.

Conclusion

The mosaic of global legal systems is difficult to comprehend, let alone master. Nations vary considerably in their propensity to regulate the terms and conditions of employment. The ways that management, labor, and government interact with each other are not standardized. Even the processes that give rise to law can be fundamentally different. Yet, domestic and multinational firms must cope with workplace regulation to have any chance of realizing their strategic business goals. As reflected in EPL trends worldwide, corporate adherence to existing mandates is being scrutinized more closely and challenged more often than ever before. There also are clear signs that unions and NGOs are aggressively expanding their political involvement to influence the course of future regulation.

It is a primary contention of this book that the legal environment cannot be treated as an exogenous variable in strategic HRM decision making. Firms need to become proactive in furthering their position across the legal systems impacting present and future operations. MNEs, in particular, have a need to evolve a core capability in public affairs management at least with respect to work-related matters. By analogy, some firms in the pharmaceutical industry have derived competitive advantage from developing superior competencies in handling the regulatory process for drug approvals.

The first step in this process is acquiring a more thorough understanding of the transnational and domestic sources of employment regulation. This topic is examined at length in the next chapter.

Global institutions and the evolution of employment regulation

While law makers tend to view regulation as a manifestation of national sovereignty, there is no guarantee the world at large will acquiesce in its outcomes. Nowhere is this more evident than in the context of labor markets, where countries often are at odds over acceptable employment practices. Conflicts are most likely to occur when there is regulatory competition over labor standards that are economically or socially redistributive in nature (e.g., jointly funded social insurance programs, union protections, mandatory information sharing and consultation with workers), as more demanding jurisdictions worry about negative investment effects (Charny 2000). Hoping to avert the flight or withholding of capital, disadvantaged nations could offer affected firms direct subsidies to counteract the higher standards' distributive impact. Even if one assumes government officials have the expertise to design and administer effective transfer payment schemes, the additional taxes needed to fund them are politically daunting. Alternatively, standards could be pared down, with the accompanying risk that domestic working conditions might deteriorate as a byproduct of saving jobs. A final option might be to push for international labor standards that bring local workplace rules into closer alignment. This response is fraught with challenges as well, since standards must be developed and diffused in a manner that not only wins acceptance from competing political entities, but also avoids high transaction costs.

One source discusses the spread of international standards in the context of four regulatory models (Block *et al.* 2001). The legislative model has two distinguishing features: a permanent supranational decision-making mechanism, and laws that at least partially harmonize labor standards. European Union work directives and ILO conventions are cited as representative outcomes. Neither attribute is present in the multilateral enforcement model, where countries do little more than add parallel conflict resolution structures to their IR/HRM systems. To illustrate, the NAFTA labor side agreement obligates Canada, Mexico, and the United States to utilize the same expedited procedures when processing complaints that their respective laws are not being adequately enforced. This collaboration arguably reduces the likelihood that local regulation will be selectively enforced to worsen the labor-rights disparities that already exist among bloc members. The trade-sanctions model is even more circumscribed in scope, finding expression in unilateral and bilateral initiatives that link trade preferences to the level of conformity with international labor standards (e.g., U.S. Trade Act, U.S.–Cambodian Textile Agreement). The final model, voluntary standards, is exemplified by the Global Sullivan Principles and corporate codes, as well as social labeling programs like Social Accountability International's SA8000 certification.

While their attempt to devise a regulatory typology is applauded, much work needs to be done to refine its component parts. To begin with, it is questionable whether voluntary standards should be treated as a regulatory modality at all, especially when the state plays no formal role in their formulation—as would be the case for codes compiled by individual companies and most NGOs. Even if one limits this category to codes developed with tripartite input (e.g., UN Global Compact), one cannot overlook the deliberate avoidance of formal enforcement mechanisms to ensure adherence. The legal significance of privately codified standards remains suspect even if one argues that they contribute to the autonomous body of transnational commercial rules known as *lex mercatoria*.[1] Extrapolating from Horn (1980: 62), it is premature to treat them as elements of customary law, not only because courts have yet to recognize them as such, but also because consensus principles are still lacking across sources. Since their potential hold on corporate behavior has nothing to do with the way that legal systems function, voluntary standards will not be delved into further, with one exception—the OECD Guidelines for Multinational Enterprises—for reasons that will become apparent. Interested readers are referred to the foundation book in this series by Dennis Briscoe and Randall Schuler (2004), as well as Sethi (2003), O'Rourke (2003), and Diller (1999) for more detailed discussions of the voluntary-standards phenomenon.

It also should be noted the other three models are not mutually exclusive in their underlying dynamics. While EU directives satisfy the litmus test for multi-jurisdictional lawmaking, ILO conventions do not. Unlike the European Parliament, the ILO International Labor Conference has no power to legislate on behalf of member states. Adopted conventions do not take on the force of law unless individual governments subsequently ratify them and enact tailored implementing legislation. Consequently, they are more creatures of national legislative processes than supranational ones. If this distinction is ignored, then one is hard pressed to explain why the laws used to illustrate the trade-sanctions model are not classified under the legislative model as well. ILO core labor standards figure prominently in GSP eligibility determinations under all of the statutes that Block *et al.* refer to. The same holds true for the multilateral enforcement model, since each NAFTA member has assimilated ratified ILO conventions into local law to some degree. At best, one can say that these models highlight differences in the driving force behind regulation (i.e., supranational in the first one, national in the second and third).

Finally, their regulatory typology excludes several legal devices that can foster the application or enforcement of indigenous law in foreign settings. *Extraterritoriality clauses* extend the reach of home-country legislation by awarding parent-country nationals who work overseas the same general protections as are conveyed to domestic employees. The United States and European Union have laws that incorporate this feature, a practice we will revisit in Chapter 4. Certain litigation principles can "internationalize" locally defined rights as well. *Choice-of-law rules* operate as legal algorithms, shepherding judicial decisions about the appropriate laws to apply when cases unite parties or events that span multiple jurisdictions. The fact that a lawsuit is brought in country X does not necessarily guarantee that its laws will define the underlying rights being adjudicated. At the other end of the litigation spectrum, national courts may be asked to enforce judgments that were rendered somewhere else to give them practical effect (e.g., holding parent MNEs accountable for labor and employment law violations that their host alliance partners are unwilling or unable to redress). Those pressing for the *recognition of foreign judgments* must be able to demonstrate that the ruling comports with the enforcing legal system's own public policies and expectations of procedural due process. All three devices have the potential to compress labor-standard variability on a limited scale.

This book takes a different path, organizing discussion around the institutional sources that evolve country-level employment regulation. As shown in Figure 2.1, global entities, regional bodies, bilateral relationships, and national institutions can be the impetus for change. The rest of this chapter examines how the landscape of labor and employment law can be altered by interactions that governments and private actors have with the ILO, WTO, and OECD. These exchanges take place in an environment that is strongly rooted in public international law with a reach that transcends region, economic development stage, and political ideology regarding the state's role in IR/HRM.

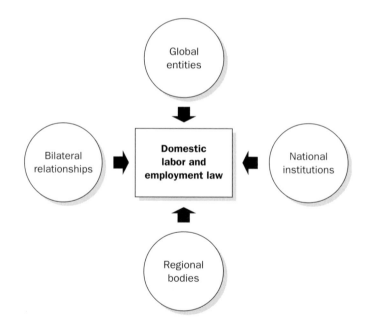

Figure 2.1 Evolutionary forces in labor and employment law

International Labor Organization (ILO)

For more than 80 years, the ILO has tried to advance the cause of minimum labor standards worldwide. This UN-affiliated agency has evolved an elaborate infrastructure to formulate international standards, monitor compliance efforts, and enforce the commitments of member states. The precise obligations that a given labor standard imposes is dependent on the form it has taken. *Conventions* are treaty-like agreements that must be brought before law makers for a formal ratification decision. As will be seen, however, ratification alone may not be sufficient to actually improve the lot of labor-market participants or IR actors. In contrast, *recommendations* contain technical or general guidelines that are designed to increase the likelihood that ILO-favored principles can be translated into domestic policy, legislation, and practice. At the time of this writing, 185 conventions and 194 recommendations had been adopted, covering a wide array of IR/HRM activities. Eight conventions articulate norms that are viewed as fundamental rights for all workers and therefore considered high-priority items in terms of proliferation. Box 2.1 summarizes their key provisions, while Table 2.1 documents national and regional ratification patterns.

Box 2.1 ILO core labor standards

Freedom of Association and Collective Bargaining

Rights of Association (Convention 87)

Requires that individuals and firms have unrestricted rights to form and join IR organizations, and that these organizations have the right to operate freely without government interference. Major provisions include:

- Employees and employers have the right to organize and to affiliate with organizations of their own choosing.
- Employee and employer organizations have the right to create and join domestic and international (con)federations.
- The state shall not condition the establishment, functioning, and ongoing legal existence of IR organizations on requirements that abridge the rights of association identified above.
- Employees, employers, and IR organizations must respect local laws that do not abridge rights specified in this convention.

Rights of Organization and Collective Bargaining (Convention 98)

Requires that individuals be free of anti-union discrimination, IR organizations be safeguarded against acts of interference by their counterparts, and voluntary collective bargaining be promoted and encouraged. Major provisions include:

- Employees must be protected against hiring and retention policies that preclude persons from acquiring or retaining union membership.
- Employees must be protected against prejudicial work treatment or discharge because of union membership or involvement.
- Employee organizations must be protected against control or domination by employers or their organizations.
- The state must establish appropriate mechanisms, where necessary, to ensure that the rights specified above are respected.
- The state must institute appropriate measures, where necessary, to facilitate the full development and utilization of collective bargaining to establish the terms and conditions of employment.

continued

Freedom from Discrimination in Employment and Occupation

Equal Remuneration (Convention 100)

Requires that the principle of equal remuneration for work of equal value be applied to all workers. Major provisions include:

- Gender must not be a factor in the determination of employment-related economic rewards.
- All elements of the compensation package adhere to this principle (i.e., direct *and* deferred compensation, cash *and* payments in kind).
- The state must cooperate with employers' and workers' organizations for the purpose of giving effect to the convention.
- The state must advance this principle by appropriate legal mechanisms (i.e., laws, regulations, wage-determination vehicles) to the extent it is not redressed by collective agreements.

Discrimination in Employment and Occupation (Convention 111)

Requires the formulation of a national policy designed to eliminate work-related discrimination[1] and promote equality of opportunity and treatment. Major provisions include:

- The state must repeal any statutory provisions and modify any administrative policies or practices that are inconsistent with this policy.
- The state must enact legislation and promote educational programs which favor its acceptance and implementation in cooperation with employers' and workers' organizations.
- All stages of labor-market participation must be covered (i.e., access to vocational training, access to employment and specific occupations, terms and conditions of employment).

Elimination of Forced and Compulsory Labor

Forced Labor (Convention 29)

Requires the suppression of forced or compulsory labor[2] in all of its forms. Major provisions include:

- The state must make the illegal use of forced labor a penal offense with "really adequate" penalties.
- The state must take adequate measures to ensure that this law is strictly enforced.

Abolition of Forced Labor (Convention 105)

Requires the prohibition of all forms of forced or coerced labor (e.g., debt bondage, serfdom and other relationships that deprive workers of a genuine opportunity to terminate their employment). In particular, the state must refrain from using and otherwise suppress the practice of forced labor as a means of (1) political coercion, indoctrination or punishment regarding political or ideological views, (2) mobilizing workers for economic development, (3) disciplining or punishing employees for work- or IR-related activities, and (4) advancing racial, social, national or religious discrimination.

Abolition of Child Labor

Minimum Age (Convention 138)

Requires the formulation and implementation of a national policy designed to effectively abolish child labor and progressively increase the minimum age for employment to levels consistent with the fullest development of young persons. More specifically, the state is directed to set the minimum age for employment at:

- no less than 13 years[3] for light work;
- the time for completing compulsory schooling or 15 years,[4] whichever occurs later, for non-hazardous work;
- no less than 18 years for hazardous work, with national laws or regulations defining the types of work that fall within this category after consultation with employers' and workers' organizations.

Worst Forms of Child Labor (Convention 182)

Requires the immediate development and implementation of effective measures to eliminate the worst forms of child labor[5] involving persons under age 18. The state also is encouraged to:

- provide support for the removal and rehabilitation of child victims;
- ensure access to free basic education or vocational training for all those removed from these settings;
- identify children at special risk; and
- take into account the special situation of girls.

Notes

1 Involving race, color, gender, religion, national extraction or social origin, political opinion and any other motive identified by a particular government.
2 Does not include military service, normal civic obligations, and work obligations exacted as a consequence of emergencies or legal convictions (provided the person is under the supervision and control of a public authority and is not hired or placed at the disposal of private individuals, companies, or associations).
3 Can be lowered by one year where the national economy and educational facilities are insufficiently developed, and there has been consultation with employers' and workers' organizations.
4 Can be lowered by one year where the national economy and educational facilities are insufficiently developed, and there has been consultation with employers' and workers' organizations.
5 Defined as slavery and practices similar to slavery (i.e., sale and trafficking of children, debt bondage, serfdom, forced labor), compulsory recruitment of children for use in armed conflict, involvement of children in prostitution and the generation of pornography, use of children in the production and trafficking of drugs, and other work likely to harm the health, safety or morals of children.

Source: Adapted from ILO website, http://www.ilo.org/public/english/standards/norm/whatare.htm

Table 2.1 Ratification dates of ILO core labor standards, select countries

Region	Country	Freedom of association and collective bargaining		Freedom from discrimination in employment and occupation		Elimination of forced and compulsory labor		Abolition of child labor	
		Convention 87 (1948)	Convention 98 (1949)	Convention 100 (1958)	Convention 111 (1951)	Convention 29 (1930)	Convention 105 (1957)	Convention 138 (1973)	Convention 182 (1999)
North America	United States	–	–	–	1991	–	–	–	1999
	Canada	1972	–	1972	1964	–	1959	–	2000
	Mexico	1950	–	1952	1961	1934	1959	–	2000
Europe	United Kingdom	1949	1950	1971	1999	1931	1957	2000	2000
	Ireland	1955	1955	1974	1999	1931	1958	1978	1999
	Germany	1957	1956	1956	1961	1956	1959	1976	2002
	France	1951	1951	1953	1981	1937	1969	1990	2001
	Italy	1958	1958	1956	1963	1934	1968	1981	2000
	Sweden	1949	1950	1962	1962	1931	1958	1990	2001
	Spain	1977	1977	1967	1967	1932	1967	1977	2001
	Portugal	1977	1964	1967	1959	1956	1959	1998	2000
	Czech Republic	1993	1993	1993	1993	1993	1996	–	2001
	Hungary	1957	1957	1956	1961	1956	1994	1998	2000
	Poland	1957	1957	1954	1961	1958	1958	1978	2002
	Russia	1956	1956	1956	1961	1956	1998	1979	2003

Asia and	Japan	1965	1953	1967	–	1932	–	2000	2001
Oceania	Australia	1973	1973	1974	1973	1932	1960	–	–
	New Zealand	–	2003	1983	1983	1938	1968	–	2001
	South Korea	–	–	1997	1998	–	–	1999	2001
	China	–	–	1990	–	–	–	1999	2002
	Indonesia	1998	1957	1958	1999	1950	1999	1999	2000
	Malaysia	–	1961	1997	–	1957	1958[a]	1997	2000
	Singapore	–	1965	2002	–	1965	1965[b]	–	2001
	Thailand	–	–	1999	–	1969	1969	–	2001
	Philippines	1953	1953	1953	1960	–	1960	1998	2000
	India	–	–	1958	1960	1954	2000	–	–
	Pakistan	1951	1952	2001	1961	1957	1960	–	2001
Middle East	Turkey	1993	1952	1967	1967	1998	1961	1998	2001
and Africa	Israel	1957	1957	1965	1959	1955	1958	1979	–
	Egypt	1957	1954	1960	1960	1955	1958	1999	2002
	South Africa	1996	1996	2000	1997	1997	1997	2000	2000
South	Brazil	–	1952	1957	1965	1957	1965	2001	2000
America	Argentina	1960	1956	1956	1968	1950	1960	1996	2001
	Chile	1999	1999	1971	1971	1933	1999	1999	2000
	Peru	1960	1964	1960	1970	1960	1960	2002	2002
	Venezuela	1982	1968	1982	1971	1944	1964	1987	–

Source: ILO website

Notes:

a Convention denounced in 1990.
b Convention denounced in 1979.

How are these standards created? What role do employers and workers play in the process? Both groups are well represented in the organization's administrative machinery. At a grassroots level, local IR actors normally choose some of the delegates that their country will send to the annual International Labor Conference (ILC). Table 2.2 presents an abridged list of employer and labor organizations that have contributed members to ILC delegations in recent years. Conference attendees, in turn, play a major part in the development and ongoing oversight of ILO standards during ILC plenary sessions. Employer and worker delegates also elect individuals from their ranks to serve as regular or deputy members of the Governing Body[2] (GB), the ILO's most powerful executive committee. This group sets the agenda of future ILC sessions, elects the Director General, and appoints committees that play integral roles in the life cycle of ILO standards.

Employers and unions can influence ILO thinking and outcomes through other channels as well. International NGOs offer one potential means for doing so. Nongovernmental entities that secure general or regional consultative status have standing arrangements to participate in ILO meetings. Many of these qualifying organizations have strong ties to organized labor (e.g., ICFTU, World Confederation of Labor, International Confederation of Arab Trade Unions, Caribbean Congress of Labor, Brotherhood of Asian Trade Unionists, ETUC) or to the business community (e.g., International Organization of Employers (IOE), Pan-African Employers' Confederation, Association of Latin American Industrialists, ASEAN Confederation of Employers). Such access can be exploited to influence GB members and ILC delegates. To illustrate, the IOE (2000, 2001) shared major position papers with the Governing Body recommending specific actions that the ILO should take with respect to international labor standards and global economic integration. Peak IR associations also can be leveraged at the country level. Member states often consult with these groups to formalize their position on the wording and ultimate adoption of newly proposed standards. The timing and form of these interactions will be discussed more fully in the next section. Finally, individual firms and unions can directly submit complaints to the ILO alleging that their government has failed to comply with one or more of its ratified conventions, triggering investigative and reporting activities that might not have happened otherwise.

The International Labor Standard (ILS) life-cycle depicted in Figure 2.2 is described more fully below. This level of detail is warranted not only because it further details the opportunities private IR actors have to influence ILO processes, but also because ILO standards ultimately define the substantive expectations member nations of the WTO and OECD inherit in terms of labor-market regulation. Thus, decisions about the resources to invest in ILS-related activities have far-reaching ramifications.

ILS development and adoption

It usually takes several years to forge new ILO standards; a fact that should not be surprising given the multitude of sovereignties and private entities that are involved. Potential standards begin their journey as official discussion topics on the agenda of an annual ILC meeting. The Governing Body may decide this action is warranted based on information it has received from internal sources (e.g., individual GB members, reports from ILO-sponsored regional or technical meetings) or external ones (e.g., materials furnished by NGOs). Several activities will be carried out behind the scenes by GB staff to pave the way for a "first discussion" at the conference. A summary report is prepared initially, detailing the pertinent laws and practices of each member state. Such information guides the development of a questionnaire that seeks to clarify the operation of these regulatory schemes and uncover national idiosyncrasies that might make the envisioned ILS impractical to apply. Responses to this mandatory survey are integrated into a final report delineating the major issues that arise if the ILO seeks to intervene in this area of employment. The report is circulated among member states at least four months ahead of the ILC session where the potential standard will undergo its first formal review, enabling countries to clarify their information needs and refine their official positions on the matter.

Once the ILC convenes, a tripartite committee of appointed delegates will deliberate on the appropriate way to handle prospective standards listed on the agenda. Substantial bargaining may occur at this time as employer and worker representatives on the committee seek to build consensus within their own ranks, and then to get their counterparts to endorse the outcome desired. The committee's official conclusions are incorporated in a formal report that is submitted to the full ILC for a vote. The report usually indicates what form the proposed instrument should take—convention only, recommendation only, or convention with supporting recommendation. A simple majority vote to adopt the committee's work product allows the proposed standard to be placed on the following year's agenda (i.e., a "second discussion").

Provisional wording for the fledgling standard is hammered out and sent to member states within two months of the session's close. Affiliated governments then have three months to submit amendments or other suggestions to the ILO, often involving peak union and employer organizations in the process. These responses are incorporated in a final ILO report that is put back in the hands of member states several months ahead of the next ILC session where the second discussion is slated to occur. At the conference, a newly appointed tripartite committee relies on the same document to finalize the standard's wording, then passes it on to the full ILC for approval. Formal adoption proceeds on a clause-by-clause basis with two-thirds or more of the delegates needing to vote in favor each time for ultimate passage. Convention instruments that fall short of this threshold but still register majority support can be referred back to the tripartite committee for redrafting as a recommendation. However, the newly crafted recommendation still must garner two-thirds of the ballots cast in another round of voting before it can become operative.

ILS implementation

Despite its formality, the process described so far lacks the authority to vest anyone with legally enforceable rights, even in nations that voted in favor of ILS adoption. Conventions, like other treaty instruments, must be formally incorporated into the local legal system of each member state subsequent to their passage. Countries differ considerably not only in the way that they internalize treaty obligations, but also in the relative importance attached to them. Leary (1982: 36–37) identified three distinct approaches that sovereignties use to diffuse treaty provisions into domestic law: automatic, quasi-automatic, and legislative incorporation. Automatic incorporation tends

Table 2.2 Peak IR associations serving on national ILC delegations, select countries

Region	Country	Employer associations	Labor associations
North America	United States	United States Council for International Business	American Federation of Labor–Congress of Industrial Organizations (AFL-CIO)
	Canada	Canadian Employers' Council	Canadian Labor Congress (CLC)
	Mexico	Confederación de Cámaras Industriales de los Estados Unidos Mexicanos (CONCAMIN)	Confederación de Trabajadores Mexicanos (CTM)
Europe	United Kingdom	Confederation of British Industry (CBI)	Trades Union Congress (TUC)
	Ireland	Irish Business and Employers' Confederation (IBEC)	Irish Congress of Trade Unions (ICTU)
	Germany	Confederation of German Employers' Associations (BDA)	German Confederation of Trade Unions (DGB)
	France	Mouvement des Entreprises de France (MEDEF)	Confédération Française Démocratique du Travail (CFDT)
	Italy	Confindustria	Confédération Générale Italienne du Travail (CGIL)
	Sweden	Confederation of Swedish Enterprise	Swedish Trade Union Confederation
	Spain	Confederación Española de Organizaciones Empresariales (CEOE)	Confédération Syndicale des Commissions Ouvrières (CCOO), Confédération Générale des Travailleurs (UGT)
	Portugal	Confederação da Indústria Portuguesa	Union Générale des Travailleurs (UGT-P)
	Czech Republic	Union of Industry and Transport	Czech-Moravian Confederation of Trade Unions
	Hungary	National Association of Entrepreneurs and Employers	Democratic League of Independent Trade Unions
	Poland	Confederation of Polish Employers	Independent Self-governing Trade Union (Solidarność)
	Russia	Coordinating Council of Employers' Union of Russia (KSORR)	Federation of Independent Trade Unions of Russia (FNPR)
Asia and Oceania	Japan	Japan Business Federation (JBF)	Japanese Trade Union Confederation (JTUC-RENGO)
	Australia	Australian Chamber of Commerce and Industry (ACCI)	Australian Council of Trade Unions (ACTU)
	New Zealand	Business New Zealand	New Zealand Council of Trade Unions (NZCTU)
	South Korea	Korea Employers' Federation (KEF)	Korean Confederation of Trade Unions (KCTU)
	China	China Enterprise Confederation	All-China Federation of Trade Unions (ACFTU)

Region	Country	Employers' Association	Trade Union
	Indonesia	Employers' Association of Indonesia	Confederation of Indonesian Workers Union (KSPSI)
	Malaysia	Malaysian Employers' Federation	Malaysian Trades Union Congress
	Singapore	Singapore National Employers' Federation	Singapore National Trades Union Congress
	Thailand	Employers' Confederation of Thailand	Thai Trade Union Congress
	Philippines	Employers' Confederation of the Philippines	Trade Union Congress of the Philippines (TUCP)
	India	Council of Indian Employers	Bhartiya Mazdoor Sangh (BMS)
	Pakistan	Employers' Federation of Pakistan	All Pakistan Federation of Trade Unions
Middle East and Africa	Turkey	Turkish Confederation of Employers Associations (TISK)	Confederation of Turkish Trade Unions (TURK-IS)
	Israel	Manufacturers' Association of Israel	Histadrut
	Egypt	Egyptian Federation of Industries	Federation of Egyptian Trade Unions
	South Africa	Business Unity of South Africa (BUSA)	South African Transit and Allied Workers' Union (SATAWU)
South America	Brazil	Confederação Nacional do Transporte (CNT)	Central Unica de Trabalhadores (CUT)
	Argentina	Unión Industrial Argentina (UIA)	Confederación General del Trabajo (CGT)
	Chile	Confederación de la Producción y del Comercio	Central Unitaria de Trabajadores (CUT)
	Peru	Confederación Nacional de Instituciones Empresariales Privadas	Confederación General de Trabajadores del Perú (CGT-P)
	Venezuela	Federación de Cámaras y Asociaciones de Comercio y Producción de Venezuela (FEDECAMARAS)	Confederación de Sindicatos Autónomos de Venezuela (CODESA)

Source: International Labor Organization website (http://www.ilo.org/public/english/standards/relm/ilc/ilc92/index.htm)

Note: Organizations designated as advisors or substitute delegates are not included. These entities nevertheless play a vital role in countries where management or labor has not coalesced into a single association, often representing rival groups that might otherwise challenge the actions of national delegates.

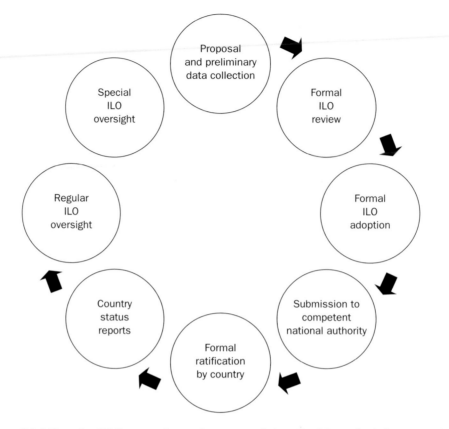

Figure 2.2 Life cycle of ILO conventions and recommendations. Revisions of existing conventions and recommendations tend to follow the same procedural stages

to be the least administratively cumbersome, and therefore quickest, route. Here, the act of ratification itself, usually involving only the state's executive branch, is sufficient to make the treaty part of local law. This approach is evident in numerous countries, including the United States, France, the Netherlands, Belgium, Switzerland, Mexico (along with most of Latin America), and Japan.[3] However, critical legal issues still may arise regarding the treaty's legal status. For example, some provisions may be classified as non-self-executing, meaning that they lack sufficient detail to be applied directly by judges and administrators.[4] As such, they remain outside of the law until implementing legislation is enacted to overcome the problem. Similarly, a treaty may be silent about the penalties for violating its principles, again calling for supplemental government action before meaningful recourse is available to claimants. Quasi-automatic incorporation also provides for the internalization of treaties at the time of ratification, but preconditions the executive branch's authority to ratify them on consent from the legislative branch. The latter often signifies its support *post hoc* by issuing an implementing order or an order of execution that gives legal authority to the treaty's language. Absent such endorsements, ratification is not deemed to have occurred. Germany and Italy embrace this practice.

The third mode, legislative incorporation, treats ratification as a foreign-policy initiative that is beyond the purview of domestic law. While the failure to adhere to a ratified treaty *ex post* may be challenged by other countries and supranational political bodies, those exchanges play out in international forums (e.g., International Court of Justice) and are governed by public international law—at least until there is a subsequent act of transformation by the signatory nation (Jackson 1992). To become part of the fabric of local law, a treaty's contents must be legislatively enacted by the appropriate parliamentary body. Statutory language tends to closely resemble, but not necessarily mirror, the original treaty language when this happens, as legislators seek to customize its dictates to the indigenous environment. Great Britain, Canada, Australia, India, South Africa and the Scandinavian countries typify this approach.

Once treaty provisions find their way into the local legal system, it becomes critical to know what hierarchical status they enjoy as a source of law. This issue is most salient when indigenous legislation, administrative regulations, or judicial precedents (where relevant) are inconsistent with treaty mandates. A variety of decision rules are used to resolve these conflicts where automatic or quasi-automatic incorporation reigns. Some countries award signed treaties primacy over all sources of law except the national constitution. To illustrate, Venezuela's highest court has ruled that ratified ILO conventions supersede all conflicting statutory language in the domestic labor laws (ILO 1995). Hanami (1981: 778) contends that several judicial decisions in Japan have implied the same approach would be taken there. At the other extreme are states where statutory provisions tend to prevail, even when they are enacted *after* the treaty in question has been ratified (Leary 1982: 40). A middle ground exists in nations like the United States, where deference is given to the requirement that was put into effect later in time. The solution is much more straightforward in legislative-incorporation states, where one simply assesses the treatment of statutes *vis-à-vis* other sources of law to determine how to proceed.[5]

Given this divergence in national practice, the ILO constitution obligates member states to bring adopted conventions and recommendations to the attention of competent national authorities (CNAs) (i.e., those with legislative authority) within 12–18 months of their passage. This duty entails more than supplying legislators with a copy of the instrument's provisions. Governments also are expected to recommend an official course of action that should be taken—ratification/acceptance, deferral until such time as an adequately informed decision can be made, or rejection.[6] They also must submit a follow-up report to the ILO detailing the steps that have taken in this regard and the legislative body's response. An obligation exists to provide copies of that document to the country's most representative workers' and employers' organizations as well.

Member states that succeed in getting a particular convention ratified still must have that action officially recognized by the international community. This is accomplished by dispatching a duly signed *instrument of ratification* to the ILO Director General, who then certifies it. Ratified conventions normally become effective 12 months after the ILO certification date,[7] ushering in new responsibilities for government officials. For example, there are initial obligations to (1) repeal inconsistent laws and regulations, and (2) enact new ones redressing pre-existing gaps in domestic law that would otherwise limit the convention's application. Afterward, there is a mandate to facilitate ILO oversight of the measures taken to advance its provisions. The process associated with these periodic reviews will be discussed at length in the next section.

In principle, the state has no residual obligation to champion adopted conventions if they are not ratified by the CNA the first time around. A critical exception exists for the 110 countries that have ratified ILO Convention No. 144. In these nations, tripartite consultation procedures must be used on a regular basis to re-examine conventions (recommendations) that could not be given effect earlier, and to contemplate actions that might promote their eventual ratification (acceptance).

ILS monitoring mechanisms

Ratification is expected to be more than an empty, ceremonial gesture of socially desirable behavior. Accordingly, compliance monitoring is a well structured process. Much of the input is derived from cyclical, self-reported data from member states, although the ILO has the ability to accelerate data collection and to diversify the set of materials used to assess a given nation's compliance posture. The reporting cycle[8] is set in motion each February by a letter requesting government administrators to identify measures that have been taken to give effect to particular conventions. These Article 22 reports are due back at the ILO by the beginning of September, where they will be reviewed sequentially by two administrative entities: the Committee of Experts (COE) and the Conference Committee.[9] State efforts to adhere to the envisioned timetable have been lacking in recent years. Less than one-third of the reports submitted in 2001 and 2002 conformed to the deadline, the vast majority instead arriving up to three months later during the time when the Committee of Experts was convened to evaluate their contents (ILO 2003a).

While government reports are vital to the assessment process, they are not the only items considered. Representative organizations of employers and workers also receive letters inviting them to contribute data and commentary bearing on the application of said conventions in their home countries. Several hundred of these *observations* are submitted to the ILO each year, either as direct filings or as appendices to the government reports discussed above. As might be expected, labor groups tend to be more proactive in this regard. In 2002, employers' organizations accounted for approximately one-fifth of the observations that were recorded (ILO 2003a).

Compliance levels in each member state are evaluated on a convention-by-convention basis during the annual COE meeting. Those satisfying all requirements earn a brief respite until the next reporting cycle begins in the new calendar year. Countries that have failed to meet their obligations, or provide sufficient data to make an assessment, are pressed for additional information. While most nations formally respond to these *direct requests* when asked, there are exceptions. To illustrate, 29 nations chose not to reply to most or all of the comments that were directed to them in 2002 (ILO 2003b: 24/44). Major compliance departures or the persistent refusal to cooperate can lead to the issuance of COE *observations*, which are incorporated in a report that is forwarded to the ILC for further deliberations.

Documentation of these interactions is forwarded to the tripartite Conference Committee, which will examine the exchanges during broader discussions at the next ILC annual meeting. This gathering affords governments one last forum to defend their record or explain ongoing difficulties in achieving compliance. In 2002, 67 countries availed themselves of this opportunity to appear before the committee, providing information to members and participating in discussions of their cases (ILO 2003b: 24/50). The

Conference Committee ultimately submits its own report to the larger ILC for discussion at several plenary sessions. If adopted, the report becomes part of the annual meeting's official record. Governments also receive copies of the report with points tailored to reflect current compliance needs or future disclosure instructions.

Complementary reporting responsibilities also attach for unratified conventions and recommendations. The Governing Body identifies a small cluster of ILS instruments each year that will be the focal points of a general survey. Member states that have not fully internalized their dictates are expected to submit Article 19 reports detailing the provisions that have been or are set to be enacted, as well as difficulties preventing or delaying more extensive ratification. At a minimum, countries must provide copies of what is turned in to representative employers' and workers' organizations. Submissions are processed in the same manner as described for ratified conventions (i.e., COE review with or without comment followed by deliberations and potential adoption by the Conference Committee).

ILS enforcement and evaluation

While recurring obligations to report on ILO standards can be viewed as an enforcement tool, it is a modest one at best. More direct means exist to challenge errors of omission in ILS implementation, particularly with respect to ratified conventions. Some of these mechanisms are available to unaffiliated IR organizations around the world; others are reserved for the ILO community. All are complaint driven and have trappings of formal adjudication. The three primary enforcement modes are summarized below.

Any national or international organization of employers or workers can invoke an Article 24 proceeding against ILO member states alleging that ratified conventions are not being fully applied. Such *representations* are filed with the Governing Body, which not only determines their receivability (i.e., conformity with substantive and procedural requirements), but also creates an *ad hoc* committee to examine those that can be pursued. The committee is composed of an equal number of members from the GB's business, labor, and government factions. Additional fact finding likely will occur based on supplemental documentation or oral presentations from the parties. The committee's subsequent conclusions and recommendations are fed back to the Governing Body, setting the stage for a final discussion of the matter.

The desired result in this context is that the country under fire privately agrees to rectify shortcomings brought to its attention. A 1990s case involving Venezuela showcases how this may unfold. There, a local employers' federation and the IOE filed a representation questioning the recently enacted Organic Labor Act's compatibility with two ratified ILO conventions. They argued that far more restrictive controls were imposed on the formation and internal administration of employers' organizations than on other kinds of associations, and that government officials were wrongly authorized to mandate labor negotiations whenever they had direct or indirect knowledge of problems considered to be collective in nature. The allegation was formally evaluated,[10] culminating in a report advancing preliminary conclusions and a request for additional information from the parties. Although nearly 18 months elapsed before the Venezuelan government submitted its reply, the intent to cooperate was unmistakable when it communicated that

(1) a troublesome provision would be voided and a second amended consistent with the committee's 1993 report, (2) discussions were being initiated with both social partners to better understand their positions as a basis for proposing revisions to seven additional provisions, and (3) regulations would be developed in consultation with the social partners to further the remainder of the Act (ILO 1995). The committee's final report recommended that the promised changes be effectuated, two other challenged provisions be amended, and the case be brought to the attention of the COE for legislative monitoring. When such cooperation is not forthcoming, the Governing Body may decide to bring attention to the problem by publishing a compilation of the materials it has amassed, or by launching an independent adjudicatory process that will be discussed next.

A second means of redressing convention-linked irregularities would be to lodge an Article 26 *complaint* as provided in the ILO constitution. However, the only parties authorized to do so are member states that have ratified the same convention, ILC delegates, and the Governing Body itself. Some illustrations include:

- the government of France filing a complaint against Panama for failing to observe ratified Convention Nos. 53, 23, and 68 (1978);
- the workers' delegate of India filing a complaint against India concerning the inadequate observance of ratified Convention No. 1 (1934);
- the employers' delegate of Sweden filing a complaint against Sweden for its failure to observe ratified Convention Nos. 87, 98 and 147 (1991);
- a group of delegates filing a complaint against Poland for its nonobservance of ratified Conventions No. 87 and 98 (1982).

It should be noted that the window of opportunity for delegates to file is during the actual ILC meeting each year. Complaints deemed to have merit may be delegated to the Commission of Inquiry, an independent, *ad hoc* group appointed by the Governing Body. The commission formulates procedures for its investigation on a case-by-case basis, issuing a report with recommendations back to the Governing Body for official notice. Nations objecting to the outcome have the option of bringing the matter before the International Court of Justice for a final, binding decision. Otherwise, there is an expectation that the recommended actions will be pursued in good faith with monitoring as needed by the Committee of Experts.

Yet another process may be invoked when there are specific allegations that IR practices, laws, or draft legislation are hostile to freedom of association or collective bargaining. Actions that improperly circumscribe these fundamental labor rights fall within the purview of the Committee on Freedom of Association (CFA), a tripartite, nine-person group of GB members that meets three times a year.[11] Relying on documentary evidence, and possibly hearings, the committee reports its findings and recommendations back to the Governing Body for consideration. For example, the committee examined 28 of the 114 cases pending before it in November 2003, reaching definitive conclusions in 23 instances and interim ones in five others (ILO 2003c). Further measures will not be taken by the GB unless the record establishes that such rights were, in fact, encumbered.

Unlike Article 24 and 26 proceedings, the nation being challenged does not have to be a signatory to the applicable conventions (i.e., Nos. 87 and 98). To illustrate, the CFA investigated a complaint that New Zealand's Employment Contracts Act violated both of these core labor standards even though government officials had never ratified them (Wilson 2000). The committee eventually issued two reports determining that certain provisions were inconsistent with these conventions. A series of recommendations emphasized the desirability of undertaking statutory revision to remove problematic language and to provide explicit penalties for offenders. A similar scenario played out in Zambia, where the state was urged to remove provisions of the Industrial Relations Act that improperly restricted the rights of labor organizations affiliated with the Zambian Congress of Trade Unions (Panford 1994: 62).

Where problems do exist, the process for redressing them will move in one of two directions. If the pertinent convention has been ratified, government officials typically will be asked to take specific measures to remedy the situation. Oversight tends to become the COE's responsibility, particularly when the changes sought raise legislative issues. The Venezuelan case described above played out in this fashion. A different path will be followed if the relevant convention has not been ratified. Here, the CFA may recommend that the Governing Body seek consent to refer the dispute to the Fact-Finding and Conciliation Commission on Freedom of Association (FFCC).[12] The FFCC operates in a manner similar to the Commission of Inquiry, generating a report that articulates conclusions and recommendations based on information it has assembled from the parties and through its own independent efforts. Attempts are then made to mediate a mutually agreeable settlement between the parties. If that fails, the matter reverts back to the Governing Body, which will be updated on the situation periodically in progress reports supplied by the CFA.

Despite being highly formalized and multifaceted, this enforcement scheme depends heavily on goodwill from the community of nations to be effective. Lacking the power to authorize trade sanctions or other forms of remedial or punitive action, the ILO has to rely on pressure from other member states to rein in persistent violators after they have been outed. Even then, there is no guarantee that the regime in question actually will return to the fold.

A perfect illustration is the meandering, and frequently obstructed, ILO effort to eliminate forced labor in Myanmar (e.g., ILO 1998a, 2000a, 2003b, d). This compliance saga begins in 1991, when the Committee of Experts received an ICFTU report documenting systemic use of forced labor in violation of Convention No. 29. COE attempts to secure a reply and the mandatory Article 22 report were unsuccessful, prompting the ICFTU to file an Article 24 representation in 1993. A duly appointed *ad hoc* committee found support for the allegations and recommended several legislative changes in a report that was adopted by the Governing Body in 1994. Government officials disputed the validity of the charges during the 1995 ILC session and refused to implement any of the suggested reforms. These stonewalling tactics prompted workers' delegates to lodge an Article 26 complaint when the ILC next met, one year later. Myanmar's leaders submitted observations on the complaint in 1997, essentially denying that any problems existed. Unable to reconcile government claims with the evidentiary record, a Commission of Inquiry was formed to assess the situation. The state remained defiant throughout its dealings with the commission, abstaining from the hearing, refusing to provide the names of witnesses who could be called to testify, and denying requests for a country visit on the grounds that it would be an improper interference in the nation's internal affairs. The investigation proceeded anyway, producing a factual record that corroborated earlier findings and recommendations for major reform. Myanmar still had not implemented any of those recommendations two years after the commission's report was issued. Accordingly, the ILC adopt a resolution in 2000 encouraging individual member states to review their relations with Myanmar and take appropriate measures to refrain from supporting forced labor in any way.[13] Since then, several ILO/UN delegations have visited Myanmar and an ILO liaison officer has been appointed to facilitate local compliance efforts. The Governing Body characterized these interactions as a "last chance call," expressing concerns that progress was falling far short of expectations (ILO 2003d). While this case is an outlier, it does expose the shortcomings of the present system.

One way of confirming the efficacy of ILO standards would be to verify that they have precipitated enduring positive changes in the legal systems of member states. Such imprinting is suggested by the following anecdotes:

● Sweeping labor-law reforms in Eastern Europe during the early 1990s drew heavily from ILO conventions (especially Nos. 87 and 111).
● South Africa's new labor code was significantly influenced by FFCC recommendations and meetings between the parliament's drafting committee on labor legislation and ILO staff.
● Australian legislation regulating the minimum size of employers' and workers' organizations was modified in 1995 in response to ILO pressure.
● The European Code of Social Security and Social Charter, as well as MERCOSUR's social pact, were drafted to be consistent with principles espoused in multiple ILO standards (de la Cruz *et al.* 1996: 31–33).

Similarly, the Russian government invited ILO commentary on the draft version of its new labor code, incorporating several COE recommendations in the final legislation that became effective in 2002 (Lyutov 2003). While some suggestions were ignored, the state modified notice requirements in strike situations, established a ceiling on the proportion of wages payable in nonwage form, reaffirmed a preference for workers in firm-insolvency situations with respect to wage claims, and expanded the number of groups specifically protected against discrimination.

Are these events isolated incidents or a sampling of recurrent change? Surprisingly little research has been conducted on this subject. While numerous studies have assessed the effects that national labor standards have on trade performance and the ability to attract inward investment (e.g., Aggarwal 1995; Cooke and Noble 1998; Flanagan 2003; Hasnat 2002; Kucera 2002; Mah 1997; OECD 1996; Rodrik 1996; Van Beers 1998), they do not speak to the issue at hand for several reasons. First, ILO convention ratification was not uniformly factored into the operationalization of labor standards in these investigations. Second, those that did factor it in failed to look beyond the ratification event to ascertain the extent to which conventions actually became infused into local law. Recall that convention provisions must be truly self-executing or properly transformed into law in nations with automatic or quasi-automatic incorporation policies. Similarly, legislative-incorporation states must enact statutes to implement the entire convention, or none of its provisions will create indigenous rights and entitlements. This shortcoming may partially explain previous findings that ratified conventions had little, if any, positive effect on indigenous labor market conditions (Flanagan 2003: 26–35; Galenson 1981: 216–232).[14] Third, even if one were to assume that all conventions were fully enacted soon after ratification, it is impossible to determine how much local legal systems *changed* because pre–post measures of labor and employment laws and their administration were not gathered, let alone compared. In a similar vein, it seems reasonable to assume that the greater the local system's deficiency at the time of ratification, the longer it will take government to devise and implement the regulatory rules and processes needed to effectuate conventions. Yet, none of the cross-sectional analyses control for the magnitude of the initial compliance gap or the length of time ratified conventions have been in place.

A more direct way of assessing the impact of ILO standards would be to document how often they (1) engendered supplemental or revised legislation to achieve initial compliance, and (2) inspired new statutes thereafter as reflected in statutory language and legislative histories. From 1964 to 2003, there were 2,342 instances where the COE expressed satisfaction with government efforts to implement measures that were recommended to bring domestic law and practice into conformity with ratified conventions[15] (ILO 2003b: 24/46). While impressive on the face of it, this figure may seriously underestimate the changes that have occurred because it recognizes only actions taken in response to direct requests or observations from the committee (i.e., where deficiencies were thought to exist). Legislative revisions put into effect pre-ratification, a customary practice in Japan, as noted earlier, would not be commented on by the committee and therefore not counted. It also ignores instances where laws enacted during the post-ratification period contain provisions influenced by convention norms. Again, there would be nothing to trigger further committee involvement. Content analyses of Article 22 reports may help to quantify both kinds of events. In short, future studies need to address these methodological concerns.

Table 2.3 summarizes the ways private IR actors can influence the development and application of ILO conventions and recommendations during each life-cycle stage.

A final caveat is warranted. Unratified conventions still may find their way into domestic law in special circumstances, albeit on a limited scale. The creative use of statutes provides one means of facilitating their entry, although the outcome is by no means certain. A U.S. case exemplifying this tactic pits a Colombian union and the survivors of its murdered leaders against an American-based MNE.[16] Their complaint is rooted in the Alien Tort Claims Act (ATCA), which empowers foreign nationals to bring civil lawsuits against U.S. defendants who engage in actions that violate international law. In a groundbreaking argument, plaintiffs asserted that the freedom to associate and organize, as embodied in ILO conventions, is a norm of international law that gives rise to actionable torts if abridged even though the corresponding ILO instruments had not been ratified by the U.S. government. The company tried without success to have the case dismissed as a matter of law (i.e., summary judgment), paving the way for it to go to trial. Recall from the previous chapter that an eventual decision on the merits would be treated as precedent in common law systems. In contrast, a German firm was unsuccessful in leveraging that country's Unfair Competition Law to prevent a local competitor from utilizing asbestos suppliers from a nation that had not ratified the pertinent ILO convention on occupational cancer. Noting that the foreign state was not even an ILO member at the time, the court felt that the convention had not yet been ratified by enough countries to reflect internationally recognized ethical rules of production (Charnovitz 1987: 576).

Table 2.3 Influencing the development and application of ILO conventions and recommendations[a]

Phase	Direct opportunities to exert influence	Indirect opportunities to exert influence
Initial proposal	• *Employer members of the ILO Governing Body* can (1) unilaterally introduce reports or documents identifying the need for new labor standards, or (2) advocate a consensus position for business in deliberations on placing a potential ILS on the next ILC agenda • *Employer-oriented NGOs* can (1) send materials to the ILO suggesting the need for new labor standards, or (2) participate in ILO regional and technical meetings to consult on the need for new labor standards	• Member states are expected[b] to consult with the *most representative employer organization* when developing responses to the (1) ILO law-and-practice questionnaire, and (2) follow-up report identifying principal issues to be discussed at the upcoming ILC session
Formal ILO review (*first discussion*)	• *Employer members of the tripartite committee appointed by the Governing Body* can advocate a consensus position for business in deliberations on the merits and provisions of a potential ILS • *Employer-oriented NGOs* having standing arrangements or an invitation to attend the ILC session can consult on the merits and provisions of a potential convention or recommendation • *ILC employer delegates* cast ballots in the plenary-session vote that determines whether a proposed ILS is placed on the next ILC agenda	—
Formal ILO adoption (*second discussion*)	• *Employer members of the tripartite committee appointed by the Governing Body* can advocate a consensus position for business regarding the final wording of a new ILS • *Employer-oriented NGOs* having standing arrangements or an invitation to attend the ILC session can consult on the desirability of adopting the proposed convention or recommendation • *ILC employer delegates* cast ballots in the plenary-session vote that determines whether the proposed ILS will be adopted	• Member states are expected[b] to consult with the *most representative employer organization* when developing suggestions or amendments to the ILO's proposed wording of a new convention or recommendation
Submission to competent national authorities	—	• Member states that ratified Convention No. 144 are required to consult with the *most representative employer organization* when deciding what action they will recommend should be taken on the adopted ILS

Formal ratification by country	—	• *Employer organizations* can mobilize available forms of political action to influence the national legislative body's ratification decision • Member states that ratified Convention No. 144 are required to set up a consultation process with *employer organizations* to periodically reexamine unratified ILSs and consider further measures to promote their ratification
Country status reports	• *Employer organizations* can submit "observations" to the ILO at any time regarding their government's application of ratified conventions • *Employer organizations* can submit "observations" to the ILO discussing the status of unratified ILS • *Employer members of the tripartite ILS application committee* can advocate a consensus position for business regarding the conclusions to incorporate in its general report to the ILC	• *Employer organizations* can submit "observations" regarding the application of ratified conventions to member states for inclusion in their periodic reports to the ILO Committee of Experts
Regular oversight procedures	• *Employer members of the ILO Governing Body* can advocate a consensus position for business in deliberations about what noncomplying nations must do to more fully apply ratified conventions	—
Special oversight procedures	• *ILC employer delegates* can file complaints against member states that are not securing effective application of ratified conventions • *Employer organizations* can submit "representations" to the ILO claiming member states have failed to apply ratified conventions • *Employer members of the ILO Governing Body* can advocate a consensus position for business in deliberations on the appropriate response to valid representations (e.g., the Governing Body itself bringing a complaint)	—

Notes:

a The same opportunities exist for workers' representatives and organizations during each phase.

b Consultation is mandatory for nations that have ratified Convention No. 144, *Tripartite Consultation Regarding International Labor Standards and Other ILO Activities*. Overall, 110 member states have done so. Six of the 36 countries profiled in this book have not (i.e., Canada, Russia, Singapore, Thailand, Israel, and Peru).

Bilateral trade negotiations also have been used in this manner. U.S. agreements with Cambodia and Jordan highlight how public international law can give life to ILO standards in settings where they otherwise would not be present. The 1999 Cambodian textile pact contained an innovative incentive-based provision that more than doubled the authorized base-level increases in imports each year if a U.S. government panel could verify substantial compliance with indigenous labor laws and ILO core labor standards. Only one of the eight conventions in Box 2.1 had been ratified by Cambodia at the time the agreement became operative.[17] U.S. negotiators went even further in 2001, securing an economy-wide arrangement with Jordan that listed ILO labor standards among the criteria that had to be honored to avoid formal trade sanctions. Again, Jordan's obligations went beyond the subset of core standards that it had ratified at the time the agreement took effect. We will return to the impact bilateral treaties can have on national employment regulation in Chapter 4.

Discussion now turns to two other supra-regional forums where nations and IR stakeholders may lock horns over international labor standards.

World Trade Organization (WTO)

Since 1947, the General Agreement on Tariffs and Trade (GATT) and its progeny have guided trade liberalization in the global economy.[18] Four principles underlie this trade regime: nondiscrimination, reciprocity, transparency, and impartial dispute settlement. Nondiscrimination is achieved when signatory countries honor their most-favored-nation (MFN) and national-treatment commitments. The former requires that trade concessions awarded to one member state be extended to all others; the latter that imported items be treated the same post-entry as their locally produced counterparts. Reciprocity is secured when the trade benefits one receives from fellow members are extended back in kind. Acting in concert, the MFN and reciprocity obligations become powerful means of dismantling barriers on a global scale. Transparency, in turn, is attained when there is greater clarity about national practices that distort trade. While tariffs are readily recognizable impediments, nontariff barriers[19] may be of even greater concern because they often foster hidden transaction costs. "Tariffication" (i.e., converting noneconomic trade barriers into specific tariff levies) and recurrent trade-policy disclosures can be utilized to attack this problem. Finally, there is an expectation that trade disputes will be brought to the community of member nations if they cannot be resolved bilaterally. An elaborate system of mediation services, expert-panel decisions, appeals, and community-wide reviews has been instituted in hopes of precluding unilateral punitive trade sanctions.

The diverse activities associated with this framework are overseen by the World Trade Organization. Given its centrality to ongoing trade negotiations and dispute resolution, the WTO is a natural forum to debate the role labor standards should play in trade arrangements. AIEs tend to support some kind of linkage to preclude nations from acquiring a superior trade position by way of labor exploitation. Emerging markets often respond with allegations that any explicit connection would be veiled protectionism to defuse a legitimate factor advantage. The issue has been formally raised in several WTO proceedings, faring no better than earlier attempts to join the two under GATT.[20] The difficulties encountered highlight how governments can be at loggerheads on employment regulation and the political maneuvering that they, and private IR actors, engage in to advance their policy objectives.

The first WTO Ministerial Conference in Singapore is a prime example, eliciting the same categorical refusal to redress labor concerns in the trade arena that had aborted previous GATT initiatives. A U.S. and Norwegian proposal to incorporate international labor standards in multilateral trade agreements (i.e., a "social clause") acted as a lightning rod, drawing strong opposition from developing countries and key AIEs like the United Kingdom and Australia (Turnell 2002: 5). After much wrangling, a superficial compromise was incorporated in the ministerial declaration that framed what had been accomplished at the meeting. Pertinent text identified the ILO as the competent body to set and deal with labor standards, affirmed the intention of WTO members to observe international labor standards, rejected the use of labor standards for protectionist purposes, and expressed a commitment to have the WTO secretariat continue collaborating with its ILO counterpart (WTO website).

The declaration did little, if anything, to spur real progress on the underlying issues despite its positive tone. The fact the ILO has demonstrated a longstanding aversion to acting decisively on the issues of ILS enforcement and trade questions the logic of deferring these matters to that organization. Upon closer examination, one discovers that:

- A provision in the original ILO constitution empowering the Commission of Inquiry to recommend appropriate economic sanctions against governments defaulting on their convention-related obligations was deleted in 1946 without ever being used (Charnovitz 1987: 576).
- The ILC similarly rejected a "social labeling" proposal in 1997 that would have committed the ILO to regular monitoring and inspections of member states with an eye toward certifying those that respected core labor standards (Turnell 2002).
- An ILO working group assessing the social dimensions of liberalized trade had been unable to examine potential links between labor standards and trade since its inception in 1994 because of stern opposition from emerging-market members. The ILO Governing Body was forced to reconstitute the group in 2000 in an effort to jumpstart progress (Mah 1998: 297; Singh 2000).
- The ILO Director General publicly stated a year *before* the Singapore Declaration that it was the role of the WTO, not the ILO, to rectify distortions in international competition arising from national differences in the levels of social protection afforded to workers (Mah 1998: 294).

Additional concerns should be noted. The declaration was generous in labeling the state of affairs between the two secretariats as "an existing collaboration." Others have characterized their nexus as largely nonexistent (Leary 1997; Turnell 2002). While document exchanges and informal cooperation have been evident from time to time, meetings between the Director Generals are rare. Moreover, while the WTO has been accorded full observer status in the ILO, the relationship is not reciprocal. The ILO has not been designated as an observer of the General Council, precluding attendance at ministerial conferences and other major meetings unless it is invited to attend, and then only on the WTO's terms. To illustrate, after failing to receive an invitation to the Singapore Ministerial Conference, the ILO Director General was invited to observe the one in Seattle *without* the right to speak directly to attendees.[21]

Undeterred, several developed countries reintroduced labor standards as a topic of discussion at the Seattle Ministerial Conference. The United States, Canada, and the European Union each submitted proposals for that session, albeit with very different aspirations (Turnell 2002; WTO website). Expressing opposition to the Singapore Declaration, the United States fielded an ambitious proposal advocating the creation of a Working Group on Trade and Labor to be supervised by the WTO General Council, as well as a formal expression of receptiveness to the ILO requesting full observer status. Securing a thorough study of trade's impact on the (1) level and composition of national employment, (2) scope and structure of social protections, and (3) implementation of core labor standards, among other things, was a key objective. Although the Canadian proposal also envisioned a WTO working group, labor rights were subsumed in a wider range of social and environmental issues to be examined in the context of trade. The EU initiative was even more modest, seeking a joint WTO/ILO Standing Working Forum on trade, globalization, and labor to promote substantive dialogue among interested parties. One of its provisions expressly excluded any issues related to trade sanctions from that conversation. Regrettably, the Seattle meetings ended in turmoil before any of these proposals was formally considered.

The issue resurfaced two years later during the Doha Ministerial Conference, where the European Union once more called for a strengthened declaration regarding WTO–ILO cooperation. Although numerous countries indicated willingness to support the proposal (i.e., Canada, New Zealand, South Africa, as well as many Latin American and Caribbean states), no formal action was taken to effectuate it (ICFTU 2001a). South Asian nations again led the charge against more explicit WTO language linking trade and labor.

There is no shortage of recommendations from external sources as to how the WTO–ILO relationship could be improved. At the extreme is the highly formalized, jointly administered enforcement scheme put forth by Ehrenberg (1996). This complaint-driven procedure would become available if there was documentary evidence that the production of internationally traded goods in an ILO or WTO country was tainted by gross and persistent violations of labor rights. Standing to bring these actions would be extended to governments (directly) and private IR actors (indirectly) of nations affiliated with either organization. Appointees from each body would staff the series of committees engaged in a three-stage dispute resolution process: complaint admissibility; merit determination; and remediation of confirmed violations. While time limits on the activities within and across stages are not fully demarcated, the experience is projected to take approximately two to three years from start to finish. Alternatively, the ICFTU (2000: 3; 2001b) has called for ILO participation in a permanent WTO group or forum that would analyze the relationship between trade and core labor standards and recommend procedures, instruments, and incentives to promote their observance. As such, it is reminiscent of the U.S. proposal to the Seattle Ministerial. Zaheer's (2003) proposed innovation may be the least controversial, recasting the ILO as a designated labor expert available for consultation within the confines of the existing WTO dispute settlement process. We are not likely to see any of these modifications in the foreseeable future, given the WTO's track record in this area.

The unwillingness or inability to structurally involve the ILO in a meaningful way does not mean the WTO turns a deaf ear to nongovernmental organizations in general. To the contrary, a formalized system of NGO contact has been evolving since 1996 providing recurrent opportunities to interact with WTO personnel. To qualify for the most coveted form of involvement, conference attendance, NGOs must document that they are engaged in matters within the penumbra of the WTO and register in a timely manner. Nearly 1,000 NGOs satisfied these criteria for the most recent Ministerial Conference in Cancún, many of them private IR actors.[22] Those making the trip can receive real-time progress briefings, participate in WTO-sponsored workshops, conduct press conferences and parallel seminars in close physical proximity to the meeting, and try to informally interact with council and committee members working on new or revised trade agreements.

NGOs can attempt to influence ministerial thinking in other ways. The WTO has a habit of scheduling public symposia shortly before these gatherings, inviting broad-based participation from external stakeholder groups. To illustrate, the June 2003 symposium, "Challenges Ahead on the Road to Cancún," featured working sessions on key issues under negotiation. Global Unions[23] was permitted to organize one of the sessions, bringing in union leaders from national and international labor federations to lead panel discussions and presentations on sustainable trade in the context of social development and decent work (WTO website). NGOs also can post trade-related position papers on a dedicated WTO webpage—an option labor and employer groups have exercised on occasion. For example, an IOE (1999) statement posted one month before the Seattle Ministerial urged governments to refrain from extending WTO jurisdiction to labor matters out of respect for the ILO's mandate. Finally, NGOs can publicize their own internal reports just prior to scheduled WTO events, as demonstrated by the ICFTU's calculated release of a study criticizing WTO outcomes just days before the Cancún meetings were set to begin. The report chastised the "Doha Development Round" for failing to benefit emerging markets as envisioned, as well as being oblivious to the pressure they face to undercut labor standards in the quest to remain competitive in exporting (ICFTU 2003a).

What are the chances of mounting a successful WTO challenge to objectionable labor practices in the absence of a social clause? Aside from prison labor, the parade of multilateral trade agreements over the last 60 years has not explicitly targeted work policies for regulation. Alben (2001) nevertheless contends that certain GATT provisions were viewed as protective of labor standards early on, at least with respect to wages. One finds little comfort in the formal language of the GATT accords and their WTO successors, though, when working toward that end—even less when the definition of fair labor standards goes beyond earnings to include issues like child labor, discrimination, and unionization. In spite of this, the following have attracted attention as possible bases for redressing disputes rooted in labor standards: anti-dumping agreement (Article VI), subsidies agreement (Article XVI), safeguards agreement (Article XIX), "opt-out" clause (Article XII), "general exception" clause (Article XX), and "nullification or impairment" clause (Article XXIII). Each is assessed briefly below.

The first three trade rules clarify when and how governments can protect indigenous industries from damaging trade practices or patterns. Each responds to a different kind of problem: product "dumping" in an overseas market, government subsidization of exports, and a dramatic upswing in import penetration.[24] Dumping occurs when export prices are set below what is charged for like items in the ordinary course of business in the exporter's home market or a third country.[25] If this occurs, the importing nation may be allowed to impose anti-dumping duties on such goods to neutralize the economic threat they pose. Alternatively, foreign governments may directly or indirectly subsidize the operations of local producers, conveying an improper pricing advantage. Some subsidies are prohibited outright under WTO/GATT (e.g., linking taxation to export performance, granting export credits at rates below those that could be obtained in international capital markets), while others are "actionable" if certain evidentiary standards can be met (e.g., direct forgiveness of debt, financial contributions to cover sustained operating losses). In such instances, importing countries may be justified in levying countervailing duties on the products destined for their markets. Finally, a major surge in imports itself can lead to protective action, even when nothing improper has been done in the underlying value chain. Here, the objective is to temporarily fend off the influx of foreign goods so that the domestic industry can regroup and increase its competitiveness.

Discussion remains polarized as to the relevance that labor practices have in these matters (e.g., Diller and Levy 1997; Trebilcock and Howse 1999). On balance, the prognosis is not encouraging. While the production of items under sub-par working conditions can be described as "social dumping" (Brown 2000), the analogy is imperfect at best. The dumping construct embraced by the WTO/GATT framework is based on the premise that foreign producers are deviating substantially from their *own* pricing policies in other markets to gain an unfair trade advantage. Producers in emerging markets may enjoy labor-cost advantages that fuel exports, but the goods sold abroad are made under the same conditions as those they sell in the local market. The fact that competitors in advanced economies may feel pressured to relax their own labor standards to compete is a legitimate public-policy concern (i.e., organized labor's emotional "race to the bottom" argument for employment practices), but those decisions are made by *other* firms—again falling outside the content domain of dumping. Similar definitional problems arise when trying to classify inferior labor standards as improper government subsidies. The pertinent WTO agreement defines subsidies as financial contributions that indigenous companies receive from governmental units. Enacting less rigorous employment laws is not a financial contribution *per se*, nor does it bear any resemblance to the subsidy modalities articulated in the text. The same would appear to hold true for failures to collect civil or criminal fines for employment-law breaches if noncompliance is detected.

Leveraging safeguard measures to apply economic pressure to nations with objectionable IR/HRM is even more problematic. To begin with, aggrieved industries face the heightened evidentiary standard of serious injury. Those able to meet its requirements face other obstacles. Safeguards were legitimized to offer domestic companies a temporary, metered reprieve from imports *in general*, not to prosecute individual states that produce goods destined for international commerce in a controversial manner. For this reason, the tools available (e.g., tariff alterations, quotas) operate with blunt force rather than surgical precision. To illustrate, exporting nations collectively experience fallout from restrictive import quotas, not just the trading partner at the heart of the labor standards dispute.[26] Adding insult to injury, states that are negatively impacted by safeguards have the right to seek compensation to offset their trade losses, making it difficult to see where the incentive is for regulatory reform.

The remaining trade principles bring different challenges to the table. The "opt-out" clause essentially authorizes existing WTO nations to deny new members rights that they otherwise would be entitled to upon accession. This course of action will not be sanctioned unless it is communicated to the Ministerial Council while the target's accession is under consideration. Can labor-standard disparities give rise to such behavior? The flurry of diplomatic activity associated with Japan's entry into GATT provides a dramatic example that it can. Protracted negotiations during the early 1950s failed to alleviate concerns held by many Western economies that lower-cost Japanese goods—supported by inadequate wages and labor standards—would overrun their markets. In the end, these reservations prompted Great Britain and 13 other nations to deny tariff and other benefits to Japan at the time that it joined (Alben 2001). While the coalition later relented, precedent was established for advancing a labor-rights agenda in this manner. The obvious drawback to this tactic is that it cannot be mobilized against existing members.

The "general exceptions" clause allows members to institute trade restrictions that deviate from WTO/GATT requirements if, among other things, they are necessary to protect public morals or human life and health. Normally, the focus is on preserving the well-being of the government's own civilian population. There is a more radical view that this language might authorize states to protect persons in other jurisdictions as well. If this liberal interpretation is valid, the argument can be made that it is permissible to use trade sanctions to pressure local officials to deliver their people from exploitative IR/HRM systems. Despite the intuitive appeal of casting weak labor standards as systematic assaults on the human condition, few work practices seem critical enough to threaten morals, life, or health on a broad scale. Proponents have tried to make this case for extreme forms of child labor (e.g., Diller and Levy 1997; Mitro 2002). The WTO has not formally embraced this proactive stance, though, in any of its adopted decisions.

At first glance, the "nullification and impairment" clause appears to be a powerful weapon against policies that threaten trade performance. According to its terms, governments that believe they are losing out on GATT-related benefits because of another member's actions may initiate bilateral negotiations to arrive at a satisfactory adjustment. The offending policies do not have to violate a specific provision of the GATT agreements; just impede or invalidate their intended benefits or objectives. Thus, it is possible to challenge "nonviolations" as well as breaches of formal clauses. If settlement efforts fail to resolve the matter, formal WTO review can be requested in an effort to ratchet up the level of diplomatic pressure or receive authorization to initiate retaliatory trade actions. While the United States has long maintained that inadequate labor standards are actionable nonviolations (Charnovitz 1987: 574–575), a test case has yet to be brought before the organization's Dispute Settlement Body (DSB). More important, there is no indication that the U.S. view on this subject has much backing within the WTO community.

This does not mean that WTO proceedings never revolve around labor and employment law issues. A transatlantic dispute over the banning of asbestos-containing imports illustrates this point (WTO 2000). The ban came about as a result of occupational safety and health legislation that was added to the French Labor Code after the 1994 GATT agreement went into effect. Canada, a major exporter of asbestos and asbestos-based products, claimed that the restriction met the requirements for an actionable nonviolation. Among other things, Canadian officials asserted that (1) such products had been subject to tariff concessions for decades, (2) the prohibition on imports created a monopoly for substitute fibers in the French marketplace, and (3) the ban was not a reasonably foreseeable action at the time tariff concessions were being negotiated.[27] The European Communities countered that (1) the World Health Organization had been classifying the targeted materials as a dangerous carcinogenic product since the mid-1970s, (2) ILO Convention 162 calls for national legislation that provides for the replacement of asbestos-linked products by less harmful alternatives, and (3) an EU directive recommends a similar course of action. In the end, the DSB-appointed panel ruled that Canada had not established the existence of a benefit nullification or impairment within the meaning of GATT Article XXIII 1(b). It should be underscored that the rigor of the safety legislation *vis-à-vis* international norms was not at issue, just its deleterious economic impact on trade.

Given these developments, considerable inertia must be overcome before the WTO becomes a noteworthy engine of change in employment regulation.

Organization for Economic Cooperation and Development (OECD)

Having its genesis in post-World War II reconstruction efforts in Europe, the OECD has expanded and diversified its membership over the last few decades to encompass 30 countries on five continents. One of the organization's longstanding goals has been the promotion of foreign investment that simultaneously benefits firms and the societies harboring their operations. Toward that end, a set of formal instruments was adopted in 1976 committing member states to (1) treat foreign-controlled companies no less favorably than local businesses (i.e., national treatment principle), (2) collaborate with one another to minimize the imposition of conflicting requirements on MNEs, (3) improve cooperation on measures affecting international direct investment (e.g., formal FDI incentives), and (4) promote adherence to a recommended code of conduct for MNEs. The last agreement, known as the *OECD Guidelines for Multinational Enterprises*, is of particular interest here because it advocates numerous policies that have a bearing on employment and labor relations. Box 2.2 displays the principles that multinationals are encouraged to follow in their global operations.

The guidelines received a much needed facelift in 2000, when major revisions were implemented. Two changes stand out. First, substituting the term "applicable" for "host" in Chapter IV's opening sentence dramatically altered the frame of reference that firms are expected to use when sizing up employees' rights. Although local law remains highly salient, transnational sources cannot be overlooked even though they may not have been ratified by the state or benefited from implementing legislation. A dispute between the American subsidiary of a French MNE and a U.S. union supports this point. The union filed a complaint under the guidelines requesting host-government assistance in protecting the association rights of subsidiary employees (Clean Clothes Campaign 2002). Many of the alleged abuses by management were potential violations of U.S. labor law; others were not but could be interpreted as being inconsistent with the ILO Declaration on Fundamental Principles and Rights at Work, and ultimately, therefore,

Box 2.2 Revised OECD guidelines for multinational enterprises

Chapter IV Employment and Industrial Relations

Within the framework of applicable law and prevailing IR/HRM practices, MNEs should:

- Respect employees' right to be represented by trade unions and other bona fide entities, engaging in constructive negotiations with such representatives in pursuit of agreements on employment conditions.
- Provide employees and their representatives with sufficient information to convey an accurate, fair view of firm performance, and to conduct meaningful negotiations on conditions of employment. Employee representatives also should be provided facilities, when needed, to assist in the development of effective collective agreements.
- Enable authorized employee representatives to engage in collective bargaining negotiations and to consult on matters of mutual concern with management representatives authorized to make decisions on these matters. Consultation and cooperation on matters of mutual concern should be promoted as well.
- Refrain from using threats to relocate operations or transfers of foreign employees to hinder local organizing efforts or to unfairly influence local collective-bargaining negotiations.
- Avoid discrimination against employees with respect to employment or occupation on the basis of race, color, gender, religion, political opinion, national extraction or social origin, *unless* doing so furthers established government policies to promote greater EEO or can be justified as job related.
- Contribute to the elimination of all forms of forced or coerced labor and the effective abolition of child labor.
- Take adequate steps to ensure occupational safety and health.
- Observe employment and IR standards no less favorable than those adhered to by comparable employers in the host country.
- Employ local personnel and provide training to improve skill levels *to the greatest extent practicable*. This strategy should be executed in cooperation with employee representatives and, where appropriate, relevant government authorities.
- Provide reasonable notice of operational changes that would have a major effect on employees' livelihood (e.g., plant closures) to employee representatives and, where appropriate, relevant government authorities, cooperating with them so as to mitigate the adverse effects *to the maximum extent practicable*.

Chapter II General Policies

Taking into account established national policies and the views of other stakeholders, MNEs should:

- refrain from seeking or accepting exemptions not contemplated in the statutory or regulatory framework related to labor;
- abstain from any improper involvement in local political activities;

continued

> ● encourage, *where practicable*, suppliers, sub-contractors and other business partners to apply principles of corporate conduct compatible with the Guidelines.
>
> Source: Adapted from OECD (2000d)

an attack on rights promoted by the guidelines. While the case's disposition did not hinge on this creative argument, it was not rejected as an appropriate justification for invoking OECD proceedings. The other noteworthy revision expanded MNE responsibilities in the area of supply chain management, calling for good-faith efforts to persuade foreign suppliers to operate in a manner consistent with the guidelines regardless of where they are located.

The voluntary nature of the guidelines indicates that the OECD, like the WTO, has chosen to leave the systematic development and proliferation of international labor standards in the hands of the ILO (OECD 2000). That being said, the guidelines effectively complement ILO instruments by translating their public-policy expectations into recommendations for corporate practice. There is an obvious parallel, for instance, between the first six bullets in Box 2.2 and major ILO conventions, recommendations, and declarations. More important, signatory governments take on the independent responsibility of working with multinationals that operate or are based within their borders to facilitate compliance. This duty, and the administrative infrastructure that has been created to execute it, make it necessary to treat this code differently than other initiatives rooted in voluntary standards.

National contact points (NCPs) shoulder most of the work load that adhering countries incur under the guidelines. Each unit is responsible for promoting more widespread acceptance of its principles, mediating disputes over MNE compliance, and tracking country experiences for the OECD as a whole. Little commonality is evident in their governance features, as shown in Table 2.4. While most NCPs are run by a single government agency, a relatively high number of states (15) delegate oversight to an interdepartmental committee. The coordination challenges of the latter approach are obvious. Even greater variation exists with respect to their positioning within the executive branch. While the agency responsible for commerce/economic affairs runs or chairs NCP activities in nearly two-thirds of the countries (e.g., the United Kingdom, Hungary, South Korea), others vest this authority in the ministry of foreign affairs (e.g., the United States, Canada, Sweden, Japan), finance/treasury (e.g., Brazil, Turkey), or labor (e.g., Denmark). NCPs also differ markedly in their dealings with external stakeholders. Sixteen do not have systematic contact with business, organized labor, or NGOs (e.g., Mexico, Ireland, Poland, Israel). Five others periodically disseminate information and solicit input during informal meetings (e.g., Australia, Spain, the Czech Republic). The remaining contact points provide for direct participation in decision making. Advisory groups support NCP activities in countries like Germany, New Zealand, and Chile. The most extensive form of involvement, tripartite membership, is confined to the Baltic States and Continental Europe. Mindful of the potential inequities that may be created by these organizational differences, the OECD tries to promote "functional equivalence" among NCPs by insisting that four operational criteria are met: visibility, accessibility, transparency, and accountability (OECD 2000). Whether or not this has been achieved will be discussed shortly.

How does one mount a guidelines-based challenge to MNE behaviors or policies? Complainants begin the process by requesting that a *specific instance* be reviewed by one or more contact points. Sixty-four instances had been filed by the summer of 2003, most alleging nonobservance of Chapter IV principles (OECD 2003:17). Requests often are put forward in detailed letters, although some NCPs have created an official form that must be utilized (e.g., Australia). Regardless of the format, the document must specify such critical information as:

- the party's identity and interest in the matter;
- the materiality of the issues raised and ability to substantiate them;
- the relevance of applicable law and procedures;
- the treatment that has been accorded similar issues in domestic and international proceedings;
- how the guidelines' purposes and effectiveness would be advanced by considering these issues (OECD 2000: 60).

Independent fact finding is unlikely to occur at this stage, making it imperative that review requests are paired with high-quality documentation. There is no appeal from an NCP decision not to accept a case. Contact points remain divided on whether the possibility of legal recourse under local law bars them from becoming involved.

Which stakeholder groups have requested a review? Organized labor has been the most prolific source, being responsible for more than 30 instances[28] (OECD 2003: 94). The anti-union charges that have been leveled against subsidiaries and suppliers are not confined to a particular region or market type. NGOs also have presented themselves as interested parties, launching or supporting five employment-related instances (OECD Watch 2003). Some of these cases witnessed parallel filings in multiple NCPs. Governments occasionally have sought the assistance of NCP staff as well—to clarify the meaning of certain provisions of the guidelines, for example. This was France's initial response to a decision by Hoover Europe to transfer 700 jobs to Scotland without informing the local work force in a timely manner. The French NCP was asked to clarify the meaning of three phrases: "the entities of multinational enterprises located in various countries are subject to the laws of these countries," "provide reasonable notice in case of changes in operations," and "about the transfer of employees in order to influence unfairly negotiations with the representatives of employees" (OECD 2002a).

NCPs will flesh out the record for accepted review requests as needed to set the stage for relevant support services (e.g., mediation). This may entail consultations with other NCPs, or the solicitation of advice from outside experts, IR organizations, and NGOs. Guidance also may be sought from a higher-level OECD body, the Committee on International Investment and Multinational Enterprises (CIME). Composed of all member and observer nations, the CIME is responsible for issuing clarifications on the guidelines. To illustrate, the Belgian and French NCPs jointly requested the CIME to explain two passages as they processed an instance involving Renault's controversial decision to permanently close its Vilvorde plant in 1997. After an 18 month interlude, the committee provided feedback on the text in question (OECD 2002a). It should be noted that the committee's input is couched in terms of general principles, not rulings *per se* that apply

Table 2.4 OECD national contact points

Region	Country	Designated government unit	IR actors' role in NCP
North America	United States	Department of State—Office of Investment Affairs (*sole administrator*)	Tripartite advisory group
	Canada	Department of Foreign Affairs and International Trade (*interdepartmental coordinator*)	–
	Mexico	Ministry of Economy (*sole administrator*)	–
Europe	Austria	Ministry of Economic Affairs and Labor—Export and Investment Policy Division (*sole administrator*)	Tripartite advisory group
	Belgium	Ministry of Economic Affairs (*interdepartmental coordinator*)	Tripartite membership
	Denmark	Ministry of Employment (*interdepartmental coordinator*)	Tripartite membership
	Finland	Ministry of Trade and Industry—Advisory Committee on International Investment and MNEs (*interdepartmental coordinator*)	Tripartite membership
	France	Ministry of Economy and Finance—Treasury Department (*interdepartmental coordinator*)	Tripartite membership
	Germany	Ministry of Economics and Labor (*sole administrator*)	Tripartite advisory group
	Greece	Ministry of Economy—Directorate for International Organizations and Policies (*sole administrator*)	Tripartite advisory group
	Iceland	Ministry of Industry and Commerce (*interdepartmental coordinator*)	–
	Ireland	Department of Enterprise, Trade and Employment—Enterprise Policy Unit (*sole administrator*)	–
	Italy	Ministry of Production Activities (*sole administrator*)	–
	Luxembourg	Ministry of Economics (*interdepartmental coordinator*)	Tripartite membership
	Netherlands	Ministry of Economic Affairs—Investment Policy and International Organizations Division (*interdepartmental coordinator*)	Periodic consultations
	Norway	Ministry of Foreign Affairs—Department for Trade Policy, Environment and Resources (*interdepartmental coordinator*)	Tripartite membership
	Portugal	Portuguese Investment Promotion Agency—Foreign Investment Department (*sole administrator*)	–
	Spain	Ministry of Economy—General Secretary for International Trade (*sole administrator*)	Periodic consultations
	Sweden	Ministry of Foreign Affairs—Department for International Trade Policy (*interdepartmental coordinator*)	Tripartite membership
	Switzerland	State Secretariat for Economic Affairs—International Investment and Multinational Enterprises Unit (*sole administrator*)	Tripartite advisory group

Region	Country		Consultation
	United Kingdom	Department of Trade and Industry—International Investment and Competition Policy Unit (*sole administrator*)	Periodic consultations
	Czech Republic	Ministry of Finance—International Organizations Department (*sole administrator*)	Periodic consultations
	Hungary	Ministry of Economic Affairs and Transport—Department of Economic Development Programs (*interdepartmental coordinator*)	–
	Poland	Polish Agency for Foreign Investment (*sole administrator*)	–
	Estonia	Ministry of Economic Affairs and Communication—Foreign Trade Policy Division (*interdepartmental coordinator*)	Tripartite advisory group
	Lithuania	Ministry of Economics—Company Law Division (*sole administrator*)	Tripartite advisory group
	Slovak Republic	Ministry of Economics (*sole administrator*)	–
	Slovenia	Ministry of Economy—Foreign Economic Relations Division (*sole administrator*)	–
Asia and Oceania	Japan	Ministry of Foreign Affairs—Second Division of International Organizations (*interdepartmental coordinator*)	–
	Australia	Ministry of Treasury—Foreign Investment Policy Division (*sole administrator*)	Periodic consultations
	New Zealand	Ministry of Economic Development (*sole administrator*)	Tripartite advisory group
	South Korea	Ministry of Commerce, Industry and Energy—Executive Committee on FDI (*interdepartmental coordinator*)	–
Middle East and Africa	Turkey	Undersecretariat of Treasury—General Directorate of Foreign Investment (*sole administrator*)	–
	Israel	Ministry of Trade, Industry and Labor (*sole administrator*)	–
South America	Brazil	Ministry of Finance—Deputy Secretary for International Affairs (*sole administrator*)	–
	Argentina	Ministry of Foreign Affairs, International Trade and Worship—DINEI (*sole administrator*)	–
	Chile	Ministry of Foreign Affairs—Directorate of International Economic Relations (*interdepartmental coordinator*)	Tripartite advisory group

Source: OECD (2003)

to individual firms. Accordingly, they are not adjudicatory of specific rights or obligations.

NCP efforts to 'offer good offices' to help resolve disputes can lead to two outcomes fundamentally. The envisioned accomplishment is a mutually agreeable settlement that is exemplified by an agreement the Dutch NCP brokered between the India Committee of the Netherlands and Adidas. At issue was the firm's use of foreign suppliers that produced footballs under conditions which were inconsistent with the dictates of the guidelines. Note that the NGO was complaining about work practices in a nonadhering nation. The agreement called for more communication and transparency in dealings between the parties, and reserved a future role for the NCP in the event the situation deteriorated (OECD 2002b). Short of an agreement, the NCP can issue a report with recommendations to strengthen observance of the guidelines. The least desirable result is that there are irreconcilable differences which preclude any kind of amicable resolution. If that happens, the voluntary OECD process has run its course.

There is another reason why the OECD is profiled in our discussion of global institutions. Emerging markets that desire to become members must be willing to open themselves up to a formal review process—an encounter that can have significant fallout for employment regulation. The triggering event is an invitation from the OECD Council to discuss accession prospects. Assuming the contacted government is receptive, specialist committees will be formed to compare local policies and regulations with the organization's core principles and legal instruments.[29] Legal reforms will be recommended if significant disparities are identified. The council relies on this input to structure the conditions, if any, that will be linked to an invitation to join. The fact that no country reaching this stage has ever been denied admission speaks to the growing practice of not approaching states until they have a history of involvement as nonmembers.[30] Accession becomes a reality once the candidate nation's legislative body ratifies the membership agreement that has been duly signed by the executive branch.

The potential impact that this process can have on labor and employment law is demonstrated by events surrounding South Korea's entry in the mid-1990s. Early in the examination period, the Directorate of Employment, Labor and Social Affairs (ELSA) determined that several aspects of indigenous law were inconsistent with OECD obligations. Government officials were presented with three recommendations to overcome this problem: make a best-faith effort to align labor laws with ILO standards; minimize arrests and imprisonment of union members; and lessen the hostility in labor relations (Jeong 2000). After pledging to rectify the situation, South Korea received an invitation to join, with the stipulation that a special monitoring procedure would remain in effect until its labor legislation was brought into line with international standards. The first post-accession evaluation was completed in April 2000, uncovering several instances where legislation had been enacted or repealed with an eye toward compliance.[31] Both advisory committees took advantage of the opportunity they were given to comment on the draft report. The BIAC submitted a document prepared by the Korean Employers' Federation conveying managements' perspective on what had been accomplished and what still needed to be done (BIAC 2000). A core element of its feedback was the request to end the special monitoring procedure in light of the gains that had been made. The TUAC predictably had a different take on this situation. Claiming substantial disparities *vis-à-vis* internationally accepted standards, organized

Organized labor wages a global fight against two South Korean subsidiaries in Guatemala

In 2002, the International Textile, Garment and Leather Workers' Federation (ITGLWF) notified several transnational bodies that the rights of Guatemalan workers were being systematically violated by two South Korean subsidiaries. Over the next two years, this case would be formally reviewed by the ILO, three OECD national contact points, and at least two Guatemalan ministries. At the heart of the dispute was a series of incidents that had taken place *after* local unions perfected their representational status under Guatemalan law. The alleged misconduct included:

- formal efforts to get workers to switch their affiliation to "solidarista" associations that received employer funding and allowed managers to be members;
- attempts to pressure workers to sign documents expressing opposition to the union;
- threats of plant closures if the unions were not rejected;
- attempts to get union leaders to relinquish their posts through financial inducements, comments about potential blacklisting, and physical violence;
- the failure to discipline individuals who had committed acts of violence against union representatives;
- a suspicious two-day lockout during which wages were withheld; and
- demands for membership lists under the guise of contesting that unions had the level of support mandated by the labor code.

Labor Ministry officials tried to redress the problems early on, with limited success. After being warned that their export licenses were at risk, both employers signed an agreement pledging to respect freedom-of-association rights, reinstate dismissed employees without any loss of seniority, adhere to international standards and local legislation, and publicly state that their plants would not be closed because of union activity. Any sense of victory within labor's ranks would be short-lived, as it became increasingly obvious in the months that followed that management had no intention of fulfilling these obligations. Sporadic tripartite meetings continued anyway at the behest of public officials, but little real progress was evident by the end of January 2002.

Dissatisfied with the ongoing stalemate, the ITGLWF intervened on behalf of the host unions and took the case international. Its first line of attack was to send a letter to the WTO Director General urging that the Guatemalan government be held accountable for these violations. The timing of the communication was no accident, occurring just days before Guatemala was scheduled to undergo its first country-review by the WTO Trade Policy Review Body (TPRV). The letter went on to argue that an intended goal of the trade policy review mechanism was to encourage governments to fulfill their WTO commitments, including the obligation to respect core labor standards as stated in the Singapore and Qatar Ministerial Declarations. Available records do not indicate that the issue received any attention in the review process, though (WTO 2002). The closest the TPRB apparently came was comments by the Korean representative which pointed out the contribution Korean investments had made to Guatemala's export performance. He also is on record expressing the hope that Guatemala would "continue to offer favorable incentives to foreign investors, and to improve its business environment."

continued

Undeterred, the federation filed a parallel complaint with the ILO Committee on Freedom of Association (CFA) in February 2002. Thirteen months passed before the CFA issued a case report. The report did little to alter the situation, though, given the committee's determination that additional fact-finding was necessary. Guatemalan officials were instructed to submit a complete observation on all facets of their investigation into the allegations, expanding on matters that had not been adequately explained in two earlier replies.

While those proceedings remained in a holding pattern, the ITGLWF broadened its counteroffensive. Several national contact points became involved as the federation successfully argued that the underlying pattern of misconduct was a "specific instance" that called for OECD assistance. Korea's NCP was the main body targeted in hopes of securing a commitment from the parent firm to rein in the offending host units. In addition to soliciting advice from the TUAC, NCP staff coordinated and chaired meetings with representatives from several Korean ministries and senior management. This dialogue ultimately resulted in headquarters agreeing to punish the individuals who were at fault and to distribute easily comprehended summaries of Guatemalan labor law to local employees. The U.S. and Dutch NCPs had agreed to look into the dispute as well, but neither played a significant role in its final outcome.

Meanwhile, the situation in Guatemala continued to evolve. The Minister of Finance issued a press release in June 2003, warning that sanctions would be imposed on all companies that failed to comply with their obligations under the labor code. On the heels of that announcement, both subsidiaries were told their export licenses would be revoked unless a collective bargaining agreement was quickly negotiated. An agreement on working conditions was signed less than four weeks later, officially bringing the conflict to an end. In addition to providing for wage increases, day care facilities, and improved access to medical care, the contract was accompanied by a side agreement which stipulated that the company would provide a positive environment for the union. These developments were summarized in the observation that Guatemala submitted to the CFA in late August 2003. The follow-up case report issued several months later acknowledged "with interest" that a collective agreement had materialized, but voiced deep concern about the seriousness of the allegations regarding acts of violence against trade unionists.

Sources: ITGLWF (2001, 2002b), ILO (2003e, f), OECD (2002d: 20–1), United States Council for International Business (2002: 4); US/LEAP (2003); WTO (2002)

labor not only wanted monitoring continued, but also urged that its scope be expanded. In the end, the committee decided that special monitoring no longer was warranted for labor-law reform, but would remain in effect for another 18–24 months for labor-market and social security policies (Jeong 2000).

Having provided a bird's-eye view of process in these global organizations, the chapter closes with materials that hopefully bring it to life. Legal Systems in Action 2.1 illustrates the opportunities and pitfalls of using ILO, WTO and OECD procedures to redress employment-related disputes. Their relative efficacy obviously varies from case to case, but the institutional behaviors depicted therein are representative of what one encounters in practice.

Conclusion

International organizations that have sufficient membership diversity and administrative capacity to influence the dynamics of regulation on a global scale are few and far between. The International Labor Organization, World Trade Organization, and Organization for Economic Cooperation and Development are three entities that potentially fit the bill. Each has an extensive decision-making infrastructure and base of nation states that could be highly influential in bringing about unifying principles for workplace public policy. To date, the political will and consistency of purpose to aggressively orchestrate widespread standardization have been not been evident. The ILO has been most active in this regard, which is not surprising given that its mission is most closely aligned with labor-market reform. The path it has traveled to advance labor and employment law in national legal systems places emphasis on the development and promotion of minimum international labor standards. Highly structured tripartite processes enable labor organizations, employer associations, governments, and NGOs to devise new conventions and recommendations, as well as to update those that have become antiquated. Multitiered oversight and complaint procedures are designed to keep the international community abreast of indigenous efforts to satisfy the tenets contained therein.

Yet, for all of the formality and broad-based participation, ILO efficacy ultimately rests in the hands of local government officials. Standards that are adopted by the ILC still have to be ratified by national legislatures before they take effect. If the language of the instrument is not self-executing under local law, implementing legislation will be required to make the provisions operative in that jurisdiction. Oversight and enforcement of ratified standards rely heavily on self-reported data and analyses. Lacking the power to award damages or issue injunctive relief, ILO bodies are dependent on government cooperation to resolve disputes through negotiations. As the Myanmar case demonstrates, such behavior is not always forthcoming. In light of these constraints, it is remarkable that there have been more than 2,000 instances where states voluntarily altered their laws or sought drafting assistance to advance principles embodied in conventions and recommendations.

While there appears to be ample historical justification for bringing labor issues into the realm of multilateral trade negotiations, previous attempts to do so have been opposed by many emerging markets and developed economies. Thus, the World Trade Organization has purposely shied away from exerting any direct influence on the course of employment standards, content to have the ILO deal with such matters. Beginning with the Ministerial Conference in Singapore, member states repeatedly have gone on record supporting the labor standards of their sister organization—just as long as they are not part of a social clause that could impact trade rights and privileges. The WTO is likely to remain an inconsequential force in the evolution of labor and employment law until that stance changes, given the very limited circumstances when the general-exceptions and opt-out clauses might come into play.

The Organization for Economic Cooperation and Development occupies a middle ground of sorts. It is clear member states have little interest in saddling local law makers with yet another amalgam of legislative expectations. That being said, it would be erroneous to describe their stance on labor standards as *laissez-faire*. OECD activities nurture the global convergence of some aspects of labor and employment law in two subtle ways. First, the guidelines for multinational enterprises synchronize corporate norms for IR/HRM practices with the overarching policy goals that ILO core standards seek to foster in national legal systems. The most recent iteration further challenges this influential cohort of employers to promote socially responsible behavior throughout their global supply chains. To increase the likelihood that MNEs will heed that calling, member states operate a network of national contact points that fields stakeholder complaints about MNE misconduct, provides dispute resolution services, and facilitates improvements in the quality of government oversight. While this administrative system is still in its infancy, all signs point to its continued viability and positive impact.

Second, OECD accession can have a standardizing influence on legal systems in its own right. Candidates for membership must show that their regulatory practices are, or imminently will be, consistent with OECD values and legal instruments as a condition of entry. The committee-driven process that assesses whether such alignment exists will judge the substantive and procedural adequacy of indigenous law based on prevailing international labor standards. This process, in turn, can evoke changes in labor and employment law, as occurred in South Korea's case.

We now turn our attention to the impact that trade blocs and other regional organizations have on country-level employment regulation.

Regional institutions and the evolution of employment regulation

3

The political, economic, and cultural diversity that global organizations must contend with during the course of decision making understandably limits their impact on labor and employment law. Large and enduring differences on these dimensions suggest that it will be the exception rather the rule when there is agreement on the objectives, form, and enforcement priority of labor-market regulation. Where consensus is achieved on threshold norms and principles (e.g., ILO conventions and recommendations), implementation can be uneven because individual countries risk little if they fail to conform. Devoid of real police powers, entities like the ILO and OECD are limited to moral suasion, offers of technical assistance, and threats of expulsion when dealing with recalcitrant governments. These points raise an intriguing question: are geopolitical arrangements at the regional level, most notably trade blocs, better situated to evolve employment regulation?[1] While it would be naïve to assume that geographically proximate nations are homogeneous with respect to factor endowments, political systems, and social policies, there should be a meaningful reduction in the divergent interests that must be accommodated, if for no other reasons than the number of state actors involved is much smaller. Stiffer penalties also may be available, depending on what the architects are striving to accomplish.

Regional networks can take many forms and serve very different ends. Some have a purely military focus, orchestrating broad collaboration as a means of enriching national defense capabilities (e.g., North Atlantic Treaty Organization). Others are more humanitarian in nature, seeking to promote social progress and cultural development through peaceful, cooperative interactions (e.g., Association of Southeast Asian Nations). The ones of particular interest to our analysis have economic growth as their dominant goal, especially in the context of the global economy. Regional trade agreements (RTAs) exemplify this group.

The proliferation and expansion of RTAs has been nothing short of remarkable in recent years. As many as 300 agreements may be in force by the end of 2005, more than twice the number in place a decade earlier.[2] Various mechanisms can be utilized to foster economic integration. The most conservative approach, creating a *free trade area* (FTA), selectively phases out the tariff and nontariff barriers that member states previously imposed on each other. No concerted effort is made to coordinate the entry barriers that each party applies to nonmembers, though. If the latter does occur (e.g., common external tariff), the FTA is transformed into a *customs union*. Making further provision for the free movement of capital, labor, goods, and services within the bloc spawns a *common market*. Affiliated nations tend to cooperate closely on monetary, fiscal, and employment policies, but do not surrender their sovereignty over them. An *economic union* comes into being when member states finally adopt common monetary and fiscal policies, as well as a common currency. The three regional organizations choosing this path—the European Union, CARICOM, and COMESA—are at varying points in their journey.

Such variability in purpose must be taken into account when predicting bloc efforts to harmonize work-related statutes, edicts, and court rulings. It is unlikely that major investments in monitoring and enforcement infrastructure will be observed when economic integration is not in the offing. The same can be said for jointly developed legal instruments. At most, member states are expected to exchange best-practice information on labor administration and loosely coordinate labor-market policies when they face common pressures from external trading partners or the international community. FTA participants have a greater need to know the regulatory workings of their peers and have some kind of process outlet to challenge specific HR mandates (e.g., indigenous employment quotas) or the selective enforcement of workplace laws that operate as nontariff barriers. More resources should be allocated to bloc activities as a result, earmarked primarily for knowledge management (e.g., funding comparative law studies, conducting public conferences and workshops) and compliance reviews. Regional employment standards should remain low-priority items because the free movement of workers is not an existing or nascent objective of the network and there is little else from a public-policy standpoint the parties are intent on synchronizing.

Things should be markedly different where member states are obligated to facilitate intrabloc labor flows. Regional instruments and institutions are expected to play more prominent roles as governments try to efficiently execute this charge. In common markets, regional law making should not go beyond measures that support cross-border migrations (e.g., relaxed visa requirements, social security participation, and portability) and core labor standards (e.g., occupational safety and health). Further regulation at this level exceeds what the parties agreed to do: enable the free movement of workers—a far cry from standardizing employment rights across countries. Ongoing, broad-based harmonization of HR/IR law is likely to be the province of economic unions—increasingly so as they mature. The shared vision of society arguing for common taxation, spending, monetary, and infrastructure policies should carry over and impact socio-labor policies in the same manner. Both integration approaches call for well-resourced, permanent administrative units that are attached to the larger governance mechanism overseeing regional affairs.

Table 3.1 puts a face on this discussion by highlighting the linkages between regional blocs and national legal systems in different parts of the world. All three integration strategies are represented in this mix of locations, as are the various stages of economic development. Most of the alliances are a product of the 1990s, although some can trace their roots back several decades. An array of administrative structures is leveraged in the pursuit of labor and employment objectives—some amounting to little more than add-on departments or staff within domestic labor ministries, while others have the trappings of independent supranational bodies with executive and legislative responsibilities. The tangible outcomes of their operations range from research reports on workplace trends and needs to comprehensive directives that must be incorporated into local law. The history, institutional features, and impact of each bloc are examined in more detail below.

European Union

By far the most sophisticated and prolific bloc when it comes to labor-market regulation, the European Union has been perfecting its craft for several decades. A long line of agreements has transformed the region into a community that leads all others in economic and social integration. The 1957 Treaty of Rome, which created the European Economic Community, generally provides the constitutional basis for all EU law. Six nations were the initial signatories—France, Germany, Italy, Belgium, the Netherlands, and Luxembourg. Since then, the group has expanded to 25 countries, with the most recent influx coming from Central and Eastern Europe as a result of the 2004 Treaty of Accession. Along the way, additional measures were ratified, coalescing member states into an economic union that proactively manages its social dimension. Some of the more notable instruments include the Single European Act (1986), Maastricht Treaty (1992), Treaty of Amsterdam (1999), and Treaty of Nice (2000). All have played key roles in evolving the institutional processes that shape Community law and orchestrate its activities.

Community law, which enjoys supremacy over conflicting domestic law, manifests itself in different types of instruments. *Directives* require member states to implement community policies into domestic law, but leave it to national legislative bodies to determine the exact form the regulatory adjustments will take. This allows states to honor community obligations without turning a blind eye toward national HR-system characteristics. Most aspects of industrial relations are so steeped in local culture and tradition that the European Union refrains from trying to regulate them. This principle is embodied in the Maastricht social protocol, which prohibits directives on union organizing, collective bargaining, or strike-related activity. *Regulations*, a second form of EU law, must be received into domestic law in their exact form even if there is no legislation on the topic. *Decisions* and *recommendations*, the remaining two variants, have more limited relevance. The former are case-specific, factual determinations that primarily impact the rights of the immediate disputants, while the latter are nonbinding opinions that member states are free to adopt or bypass. While directives occupy our attention for the rest of this section, the other instruments are not completely irrelevant. Däubler (1996: 160–162) discusses several examples where nondirectives contributed to Community labor law.

New directives follow a well defined course. The process typically begins with a directive proposal that has been prepared by the European Commission after preliminary consultations with the social partners (e.g., tripartite Economic and Social Committee) regarding the need for an initiative in this area of employment and its content. Next, the proposal will be forwarded to the European Parliament for review and comment. The parliament can endorse the proposal in its existing form or propose amendments that the commission is free to accept or ignore. Once the proposed instrument's wording is finalized, it will be submitted to the Council of Ministers, which is composed of top government officials from each member state. The proposal's fate will be determined by a Council vote, which is subjected to a different standard for passage depending on the

Table 3.1 Labor-rights initiatives of regional blocs

Region		Labor and employment objective(s)	Dedicated infrastructure for labor-rights issues	Labor-rights initiatives
Americas and the Caribbean	North American Free Trade Area (NAFTA)	• Ensure domestic laws are effectively enforced	• Commission for Labor Cooperation • National Administrative Offices	• List of principles (11) that domestic law should advance (in treaty)
	Dominican Republic–Central American Free Trade Area (DR-CAFTA)	• Ensure domestic laws are consistent with international labor standards • Ensure domestic laws are effectively enforced	• Labor Affairs Council • Labor Cooperation and Capacity Building Mechanism	• List of internationally recognized rights (5) that domestic law should advance (in treaty)
	Caribbean Community (CARICOM)	• Promote and coordinate policies for full employment and improved work standards • Establish an integrated labor market with free movement of labor	• Council for Human and Social Development • Regional Business and Labor Advisory Committee • National Committees (charter implementation)	• Charter of Civil Society (Article XIX) • Declaration of Labor and IR Principles • CARICOM Agreements (2) • Model legislation (7)
	Community of Andean Nations (CAN)	• Coordinate policies for employment promotion, training, safety and health, social security and migration	• The Conference • Specialized Labor Committees • Advisory Council of Labor Ministers • Andean Advisory Business and Labor Councils	• Andean Social Charter • Andean Charter for the Protection and Promotion of Human Rights • Andean Instruments (3)
	Southern Common Market (MERCOSUR)	• Coordinate policies for employment promotion, safety and health, and other areas linked to economic integration	• Working Group 10 (Labor, Employment and Social Security) • Economic and Social Consultative Forum • Socio-Labor Commission	• Socio-Labor Declaration • MERCOSUR Agreements (2)

Region	Organization	Objectives	Institutions	Instruments
Europe	European Union (EU)	• Promote high employment, fair pay, better working conditions, and equal opportunity • Establish an integrated labor market with free movement of labor	• Directorate General for Employment and Social Affairs, European Commission • Economic and Social Committee	• Charter of Fundamental Social Rights for Workers • Social Protocol and Agreement • EU work-related directives (21[a])
Asia	ASEAN Free Trade Area (AFTA)	• Promote capacity building to develop productive and competitive work forces • Share experience and best practice in developing social protection systems	—	• ASEAN Occupational Safety and Health Network (OSHNET)
	South Asia Free Trade Area (SAFTA)	• Promote skills development across the region	—	—
Africa	South African Development Community (SADC)	• Promote employment creation and the efficient utilization of human resources • Ensure minimum labor standards and social protection	• Directorate of Social and Human Development and Special Programs, SADC Secretariat • SADC National Committees	• Charter on Fundamental Social Rights • Codes of conduct (3) • Protocol facilitating the movement of persons (draft)
	Common Market for Eastern and Southern Africa (COMESA)	• Establish an integrated labor market with free movement of labor • Cooperate closely with respect to labor laws	—	• Protocol on relaxation of visa requirements (PTA carryover) • Protocol on free movement of persons, labor and services (draft)

Sources: American Center for International Labor Solidarity/AFL–CIO (2003), ASEAN website (www.aseansec.org), CARICOM website (www.caricom.org), COMESA website (www.comesa.int), European Union website (www.europa.int), ILO website, Staff (2003a), Mark and Oxman (2002), Olivier *et al.* (2002), Rohter (2002), SADC website (www.sadc.int).

Note:
a Does not include sector-specific directives.

matter being regulated. Unanimity is required for directives involving social security, worker participation, the employment of TCNs, and job creation. A lesser threshold, qualified majority support, applies when the focus is on occupational safety and health (OSH), working conditions, information and consultation, gender equality, and persons excluded from labor-market participation. In many instances, proposals that have been supported by the Council will be passed by the European Parliament as well, enabling them to be issued as joint Acts (i.e., codetermination of EU legislation). More insights into the EU legislative process can be found in Barnard (2000: 85–110).

Box 3.1 lists the nearly two dozen employment directives that have been issued to date. One thing that went unmentioned in the preceding paragraph is the bargaining that goes on behind the scenes to get member states to throw their support behind a draft directive. For example, the proposed temporary workers directive was the subject of extensive bargaining between the Directorate General for Employment and Social Affairs and two member states in 2002. The United Kingdom, which has more temporary workers than other EU members, and Ireland were not prepared to support the proposed instrument unless changes were made. Several concessions were offered at one point, including a longer transition lag period before it would become operative and simplified monitoring procedures for compliance (Parker 2002a). The United Kingdom wanted more, particularly an extension of the qualifying service period. Proposal COD 2002/0072 does not seem to reflect these exchanges, perhaps explained by the fact that the measure would require only qualified majority support for passage by the Council down the road.

Box 3.1 Major work directives of the European Union

Information and consultation of workers

Collective Redundancies (98/59/EC) specifies the information and consultation rights that employees have in collective redundancy settings
- Consolidates directives 75/129/EEC and 92/56/EEC

European Works Council (94/45/EC and 97/74/EC) creates an obligation to form EWCs or comparable bodies to inform and consult with employees in Community-scale firms and units

European Company Statute (2001/86/EC) supplements the European company statute with regard to the involvement of employees

European Co-operative Society (2003/72/EC) supplements the statute for a European co-operative society with regard to the involvement of employees

Information and Consultation of Employees (2002/14/EC) establishes a general framework for information and consulting workers in the European Community

Transfer of Undertakings (*Acquired Rights*) (2001/23/EC) articulates the rights employees have when a firm or business unit is transferred to a new employer
- Consolidates directives 77/187/EEC and 98/50/EC

Working conditions

Employer Insolvency (2002/74/EC) protects employees' rights to unpaid wages and other claims
- Amends Directive 80/987/EEC

Fixed Term Work (1999/70/EC) gives effect to the framework agreement on fixed-term contracts negotiated by the ETUC, UNICE and CEEP

Health and Safety in Fixed Term and Temporary Employment (91/383/EEC) requires equal application of health and safety practices regardless of the nature of the employment relationship

Information on Individual Employment Contracts (91/533/EEC) creates the obligation to inform employees of the conditions associated with their contract of employment

Part-Time Work (97/81/EC and 98/23/EC) gives effect to the framework agreement on part-time work negotiated by the ETUC, UNICE and CEEP

Posting of Workers (96/71/EC) requires that legal standards on working conditions and pay in a member state be applied equally to domestic workers and expatriates during the course of their assignment there

Working Time (93/104/EC and 2000/34/EC) specifies minimum requirements with respect to scheduling

Protection of Young People (94/33/EC) prohibits child labor

Equal opportunity

Equal Treatment in Employment and Occupation (2000/78/EC) updates the requirement to treat men and women equally regarding access to employment, vocational training, promotions and working conditions
  - Amends directive 76/207/EEC

Burden of Proof in Sex Discrimination Cases (97/80/EC) sets standards for this legal issue

Racial Equality (2000/43/EC) requires equal treatment in employment and access to occupations regardless of racial or ethnic origin

Employment Framework Directive (2000/78/EC) establishes a framework for equal treatment employment and access to occupations regardless of religion, disability, age or sexual orientation

Other

Parental Leave (96/34/EC) gives legal effect to the framework agreement negotiated by the ETUC, UNICE and CEEP

Personal Data Protection (95/46/EC) limits the processing and cross-border transfer of personal information

Activities and Supervision of Institutions for Occupational Retirement Provision Pension (2003/41/EC) establishes a framework for the operation and supervision of occupational pension plans

Working Conditions for Temporary Workers (COD 2002/0072) is an amended proposal that has been forwarded to the European Parliament and the Council for possible adoption

Source: Directorate General for Employment and Social Affairs, European Commission (http://europa.eu.int/comm/employment_social/labour_law/directives_en.htm#4.%20%20%20INFORMATION%20AND%20CONSULTATION%20OF%20EMPLOYEES)

Leaving directive implementation in the hands of member states does have its risks. A significant time lag is inevitable from the point in time that the EU hierarchy adopts a directive to its bloc-wide appearance in local law (i.e., transposition). Legal Systems in Action 3.1 illustrates how the process works and highlights the challenges. Even if transposition occurs with minimal delay, there is the prospect that individual members will mistakenly or intentionally fall short of what needed to be done in the reforms that were made. This development would necessitate follow-up action by EU officials, including bringing the matter before the European Court of Justice. Given transposition's centrality to the enactment of EU policy, there has been surprisingly little research on the dynamics of the process. Three recent works hopefully signal a change in the situation (see Falkner *et al.* 2004; Linos 2004; Tallberg and Jönsson 2001). Further studies are needed to clarify the relative importance of national preferences and national administrative capacity in the compliance posture of member states.

Conforming to the European Works Council Directive: a tale of three nations

On September 22, 1994, the European Council adopted Directive 94/45/EC, obligating member states to recognize and enforce the right to establish European Works Councils or comparable arrangements in multinationals meeting certain size and location criteria (see Box 3.1). Minimal procedural constraints would be imposed on parties that voluntarily created these structures during the directive's two-year transposition period. These "Article 13" committees could be negotiated and renewed using local IR-system processes, so long as they encompassed all workers covered by the directive and facilitated meaningful information sharing and consultation. The situation would be handled differently if action had not been taken before the transposition deadline expired. From that point forward, EWCs had to be negotiated in a manner that was consistent with procedures outlined in the directive. If those negotiations failed to secure an agreement, default committees would be established with powers and rules that were listed therein.

This was not the first time that there had been a concerted effort to harmonize aspects of worker participation within the European Union. A series of proposals had spoken to the issue in various ways over the previous two decades (e.g., draft "Fifth" Company Directive, draft Vredeling Directive, draft European Company Statute Directive), only to be tabled. What had changed? The single most important development undoubtedly was the 1992 Treaty on European Union (i.e., Maastricht Treaty) and the accompanying Social Policy Protocol, which marked a new legislative philosophy. Functional equivalence became an acceptable path toward harmonization at the expense of rigid insistence on uniform practice. The EWC Directive was the first legally binding instrument to arise from this revised strategy, drawing its essence from the European Social Charter.

However, the post-adoption situation was not problem-free. To begin with, the United Kingdom was exempt from the directive's requirement, having negotiated the right to opt out of Maastricht's social component and, before that, the Charter itself. The Conservative-led government's primary reason for doing so was unwillingness to reverse more than 10 years of domestic reforms promoting profitability-oriented decision making and supply-side policies. This did not mean that the directive was totally inoperative within its borders.

Firms based in other European countries generally extended EWC participation to their UK subsidiaries, and some UK-based companies chose to enter into voluntary arrangements sanctioned by Article 13. While the state did nothing to disrupt either phenomenon, its refusal to enforce the directive certainly limited proliferation.

That policy stance was reversed when the Labour Party came into power following the spring 1997 elections. Within days of taking office, the new government announced that it would agree to be bound by this and other social directives. The change of heart was not surprising, for ideological and pragmatic reasons. The newly elected Labour government was more amenable to the norms and policies associated with Community social initiatives. A significant political complication also loomed at year's end, when the United Kingdom was scheduled to take its turn leading the European Union's Social Affairs Council. Earlier opt-out decisions would bar it from even attending meetings where key social policy issues were discussed, let alone chairing the sessions. The loss of political prestige and potential forfeiture of an opportunity to directly influence future policy clearly had to be averted.

Other member states were happy to oblige. Several harbored feelings that British employers had enjoyed an unfair competitive advantage by being beyond the directive's reach. This loophole was closed by the Amsterdam Treaty and its social policy agreement, which were universally endorsed. Six months later, the European Council adopted Directive 97/74/EC, which extended the EWC Directive to the United Kingdom and Northern Ireland, and set a two-year time limit on bringing their regulations and administrative procedures into compliance.

Delay in getting all of the Community's members on board for adoption only tells part of the story. There also was the challenge of transposing the directive's requirements into each country's law, since EU instruments are not self-executing. A special working group of national experts was charged with recommending draft legislation toward that end—the first time the European Union had utilized this practice. The end product was a set of clarifications and suggestions that was passed on to the government officials responsible for industrial relations. The transposition experiences of three states are briefly summarized next to highlight the dynamic, highly variable nature of the process.

Germany was the seventh nation to align its labor laws with the EWC Directive, missing the original implementation deadline by one month. The process was smooth and orderly, buttressed by extensive negotiations with the peak IR actors. When all was said and done, the transposing legislation ended up being little more than a replication of the directive's text with minor exceptions. Were these developments surprising? The notion of works councils certainly was compatible with the German industrial relations system, having been legislated at the national level for decades. In fact, local law extended WC rights to employees in much smaller firms than those covered by the directive, and conveyed more entitlements—in particular, the right of codetermination. However, the country's major business federations (i.e., BDA and BDI) had steadfastly opposed EU-wide initiatives for worker consultation throughout the 1980s and early 1990s. Among the concerns voiced were (1) adding yet another level of participation apparatus, especially if that obligated German multinationals to deal with foreign worker representatives with communist affiliations, and (2) emboldening national unions to push for expanded codetermination rights. Working behind the scenes, federal officials managed to soften employers'

continued

opposition and temper organized labor's demands so that the directive's language could find its way into domestic law largely undisturbed.

Luxembourg, in contrast, was the last member state to enact transposing legislation, and then only after formal action was taken against it to secure compliance. Lacking any information on Luxembourg's implementation plans nearly four months after the September 1996 deadline had passed, the European Commission invoked infringement procedures under Article 226 of the EC Treaty. The process begins with a formal request for an observation explaining the situation. This was done in mid-January 1997, prompting a reply one month later which confirmed that draft legislation was under discussion and projected that a final version would be laid before the Parliament shortly. The imminent submission of a draft Bill was reaffirmed in a second letter to the Commission dated May 2, 1997. Eleven months passed, though, without further word, leading Commissioners to send a "reasoned opinion" inviting the government to satisfy its obligation (i.e., stage two). A two-month time limit was attached, after which the case could be referred to the European Court of Justice as specified in the treaty. Luxembourg's subsequent failure to respond triggered the next logical step when the matter was brought before the European Court.

Hoping to diffuse the controversy, the government pointed to draft legislation that had been adopted in January 1999 and was now awaiting approval from the professional chambers and State Council. Unpersuaded, the Court ruled that Luxembourg had not taken all necessary steps to insure compliance, as it was bound to do. That finally became a reality in 2000 when the requisite legislation for transposition took effect. While the state's foot-dragging has been attributed to apathy, given the small number of firms affected and highly evolved level of indigenous participation, corroborative evidence is elusive.

Slow to make a policy commitment to EWCs, the United Kingdom moved swiftly to fulfill its obligations under the Amsterdam Treaty and Council Directive 97/74/EC. Transposition efforts were spearheaded by the Department of Trade and Industry (DTI), which retained a consulting firm to identify the full range of costs and benefits associated with the directive as part of a regulatory impact assessment. Armed with these data, the government issued draft regulations and a consultation document for its social partners in the summer of 1999. Extensive negotiations produced a final iteration that was laid before Parliament five months later. The only question remaining was whether an annulment by negative resolution would occur over the next 40 days, derailing this initiative. While a timely motion to debate the matter was filed by the Conservative opposition in the House of Commons, the Standing Committee on Delegated Legislation ultimately voted 9:3 in favor of the regulations, paving the way for them to become operative. Compliance had been achieved less than two months after the deadline set in the 1997 directive.

Sources: Callaghan (2003), Carley and Hall (2000), EIRO (1998b, 1999a, b, 2001a, 2003a), Müller and Hoffmann (2001), Weber *et al.* (2000)

We now move to what might be considered the opposite end of the continuum in terms of regional influences on labor rights.

North American Free Trade Area

The very limited labor-rights paradigm found in North America might be altogether nonexistent had the 1992 U.S. presidential election turned out differently. FTA negotiations between the United States, Canada, and Mexico were at a critical juncture in 1991 just as the American President's fast-track negotiating authority was coming to an end. Needing to have it renewed to finalize an agreement, President Bush tried to reassure congressional members that the state of labor law and labor administration south of the border would not unfairly prejudice American workers—even though the draft instrument for NAFTA said nothing about labor standards. To make his case, the President cited a 1991 memorandum of understanding (MOU) between the US Department of Labor and Mexico's Secretariat of Labor and Social Welfare that already had facilitated a string of cooperative initiatives strengthening the latter's inspection and reporting capabilities (U.S. General Accounting Office 1993: 120–121). The memorandum was being supervised by the US–Mexico Bilateral Commission, an intergovernmental body that officially dated back to the early years of the Reagan administration. Fast-track authority was extended by the Senate, allowing NAFTA negotiations to continue without changing the underlying approach to labor issues.

Parallel efforts to advance labor cooperation continued over the next 18 months. For example, Canada and Mexico entered into a similar memorandum of understanding in April 1992. The U.S. and Mexico signed a second memorandum that fall, expanding the scope of their joint activities (U.S. General Accounting Office 1993: 121–122). Both governments agreed to work to develop common approaches to improve workplace safety and to seek opportunities for greater uniformity in safety regulations. The centerpiece of the agreement was a commitment to establish the Consultative Commission on Labor Matters as a permanent forum for bilateral labor issues. Impending changes in the political landscape would prevent it from becoming a reality, although many of its elements arguably would resurface in another form two years later.

The December 1992 signing of NAFTA validated several years of effort to negotiate a mutually acceptable trade liberalization initiative for the continent. However, President Bush's recent election defeat presented a major complication—he no longer was positioned to submit the agreement to Congress for ratification when it reconvened. That task would fall to President-elect Bill Clinton, who not only was on record being critical of its current structure, but also would be urged by fellow Democrats to make labor rights a more visible, prominent part of the arrangement. Wanting to garner broader domestic support for NAFTA, the new administration made it clear that ratification would not be pursued unless the NAFTA instrument was accompanied by subsidiary labor and environmental agreements. Trilateral discussions between March and September 1993 satisfied this stipulation, paving the way for the entire NAFTA framework to take effect on January 1, 1994.

Key sections of the North American Agreement on Labor Cooperation (NAALC or labor side agreement) can be found in Box 3.2. The labor principles listed in Annex 1 encompass issues that are commonly associated with internationally recognized labor rights, but there is no requirement that the parties ratify or follow specific international instruments. It would be incorrect to view them as a preliminary step in the evolution of binding regional standards, given the disclaimer on that point. Instead, the main focus is on the consistent enforcement of domestic law, the substance of which is deemed best left in the hands of national political systems. Idiosyncrasies in those systems bring more than qualitatively different labor and employment laws. For instance, the NAALC applies only in certain parts of Canada, for constitutional reasons. Since labor law is primarily under provincial jurisdiction, the federal government has no authority to commit individual provinces to follow its terms in settings that they control. They nevertheless can choose to participate by way of an intergovernmental agreement, an option that four provinces have exercised (i.e., Alberta, Manitoba, Quebec, and Prince Edward Island). The procedures described below are available only in these provinces and in establishments coming within the scope of federation jurisdiction (see Chapter 5).

Box 3.2 North American Agreement on Labor Cooperation (NAALC): select provisions

Article 1 Objectives

The objectives of this Agreement are to:

1 improve working conditions and living standards in each Party's territory;
2 promote, to the maximum extent possible, the labor principles set out in Annex 1;
3 encourage cooperation to promote innovation and rising levels of productivity and quality;
4 encourage publication and exchange of information, data development and coordination, and joint studies to enhance mutually beneficial understanding of the laws and institutions governing labor in each Party's territory;
5 pursue cooperative labor-related activities on the basis of mutual benefit;
6 promote compliance with, and effective enforcement by each Party of, its labor law; and
7 foster transparency in the administration of labor law.

Article 2 Levels of Protection

Affirming full respect for each Party's constitution, and recognizing the right of each Party to establish its own domestic labor standards, and to adopt or modify accordingly its labor laws and regulations, each Party shall ensure that its labor laws and regulations provide for high labor standards, consistent with high quality and productivity workplaces, and shall continue to strive to improve those standards in that light.

. . .

Article 4 Private Action

1. Each Party shall ensure that persons with a legally recognized interest under its law in a particular matter have appropriate access to administrative, quasi-judicial, judicial or labor tribunals for the enforcement of the Party's labor law.

2. Each Party shall ensure that such persons may have recourse to, as appropriate, procedures by which rights arising under:

1 its labor law, including in respect of occupational safety and health, employment standards, industrial relations and migrant workers, and
2 collective agreements, can be enforced.

. . .

Article 43 Private Rights

No Party may provide for a right of action under its domestic law against any other Party on the ground that another Party has acted in a manner inconsistent with this Agreement.

. . .

Annex 1 Labor Principles

The following are guiding principles that the Parties are committed to promote, subject to each Party's domestic law, but do not establish common minimum standards for their domestic law. They indicate broad areas of concern where the Parties have developed, each in its own way, laws, regulations, procedures and practices that protect the rights and interests of their respective workforces.

1 *Freedom of association and protection of the right to organize.* The right of workers exercised freely and without impediment to establish and join organizations of their own choosing to further and defend their interest.
2 *The right to bargain collectively.* The protection of the right of organized workers to freely engage in collective bargaining on matters concerning the terms and conditions of employment.
3 *The right to strike.* The protection of the right of workers to strike in order to defend their collective interests.
4 *Prohibition of forced labor.* The prohibition and suppression of all forms of forced or compulsory labor, except for types of compulsory work generally considered acceptable by the Parties, such as compulsory military service, certain civic obligations, prison labor not for private purposes and work exacted in cases of emergency.
5 *Labor protections for children and young persons.* The establishment of restrictions on the employment of children and young persons that may vary taking into consideration relevant factors likely to jeopardize the full physical, mental and moral development of young persons, including schooling and safety requirements.
6 *Minimum employment standards.* The establishment of minimum employment standards, such as minimum wages and overtime pay, for wage earners, including those not covered by collective agreements.
7 *Elimination of employment discrimination.* Elimination of employment discrimination on such grounds as race, religion, age, sex or other grounds, subject to certain reasonable exceptions, such as, where applicable, *bona fide* occupational requirements or qualifications and established practices or rules

continued

governing retirement ages, and special measures of protection or assistance for particular groups designed to take into account the effects of discrimination.

8 *Equal pay for women and men*. Equal wages for women and men by applying the principle of equal pay for equal work in the same establishment.

9 *Prevention of occupational injuries and illnesses*. Prescribing and implementing standards to minimize the causes of occupational injuries and illnesses.

10 *Compensation in cases of occupational injuries and illnesses*. The establishment of a system providing benefits and compensation to workers or their dependents in cases of occupational injuries, accidents or fatalities arising out of, linked with or occurring in the course of employment.

11 *Protection of migrant workers*. Providing migrant workers in a Party's territory with the same legal protection as the Party's nationals in respect of working conditions.

. . .

Source: United States Department of Labor website (www.dol.gov/ILAB/regs/naalc/naalc.htm)

Administratively, the labor side agreement operates in a decentralized fashion, functioning more as a confederation of units than as a single, well oiled machine. The coordinating mechanism is referred to as the Commission for Labor Cooperation, which consists of a Ministerial Council (MC) and dedicated secretariat. The council is composed of the top labor officials in each country, who meet annually to set priorities for cooperative action, approve planned activities for the Labor Cooperation Program (e.g., trinational conferences and workshops), and assess the NAALC's ongoing effectiveness. They also may gather in special sessions if there is a need for consultations to resolve complaints. The secretariat is staffed by a cross-national team of labor lawyers, labor economists, and other professionals who are knowledgeable about the respective HR/IR systems. This group provides operational support to the council and conducts periodic reports on labor law and administrative procedures, trends and strategies related to implementation and enforcement, and national labor market conditions.

The National Administrative Offices (NAOs) are the actual "workhorses" of the NAALC. Structurally, they are nothing more than dedicated subunits in each country's labor ministry. Each NAO executes the framework's day-to-day activities by coordinating the execution of cooperative ventures, serving as the contact point for intergovernmental exchanges, and handling all dealings with external stakeholders. Each has the authority to determine what standards and procedures will govern the acceptance and processing of complaints (i.e., submissions). To illustrate, the Mexican NAO tends to hold private sessions that are considered to be informational in nature, while its U.S. and Canadian counterparts conduct public hearings. While any person or legally recognized organization can file a submission, one of the oddities of the agreement is that it is not done in the country where the alleged misconduct occurs. Instead, one must go to an NAO in one of the other two countries to set a review in motion. Individual NAOs also decide whether there will be national advisory committees and who will comprise their membership.

A sequence of stages is laid out to try to resolve situations where the NAALC's objectives are being thwarted. Accepted submissions will be examined by NAO staff with additional fact finding and consultations as needed. If the matter is not amicably resolved within a set timeframe, an MC ministerial consultation can be requested. These two stages are available for all submissions. Whether additional avenues of recourse are available depends on the labor principle from Annex 1 that is involved. Conflicts rooted in the first three principles from Box 3.2 have nowhere else to go. Submissions based on any of the remaining principles have at least one more stage they can pass through provided it can be shown there is a link to trade. If ministerial consultations fail to settle the issue, an Evaluation Committee of Experts (ECE) can be formed upon request. This MC-appointed body will conduct an independent analysis of the pattern of practice in enforcing the laws in question and issue a report with recommendations. Each party has the right to submit written responses to its findings, conclusions, or recommendations. One last vehicle, an arbitration panel, can be invoked for three specific labor principles: child labor, minimum wage, and the prevention of workplace injuries. Fines ultimately would be available for continuing violations of this narrow cluster of labor principles, with the amount capped at 0.007 percent of the total trade in goods between the disputing countries during the most recent year. Unpaid fines could be converted into trade sanctions against Mexico or the United States, but not against Canada, because it agreed to make the panel's decision enforceable in its courts.

How has this conflict resolution system performed? Legal Systems in Action 3.2 chronicles the events associated with one submission for consideration. The general sentiment is perhaps best summed up in the following statement:

> The practical experience of the complaints procedure under NAALC has demonstrated the extremely narrow scope and ineffectiveness of this legislation. . . . The procedural system for resolving disputes . . . has demonstrated its inability to remedy violations of even the most fundamental labor rights, such as freedom of association. The process itself is effort- and time-consuming and the outcome morale-crippling for workers and their organizations.
>
> (Tsogas 2001: 163)

More than 12 years out, a total of 30 submissions have been filed. Most have been directed to the U.S. NAO and have targeted behaviors in Mexico. None has proceeded beyond the point of ministerial consultations. Although numerous suggestions have been offered to improve the process (e.g., Human Rights Watch 2001), significant reform is unlikely in the foreseeable future.

It should be noted that the Clinton administration's first proposal for a side agreement called for a trilateral commission on labor standards that would have been empowered to broadly impose trade sanctions on nonconforming members. Mexico and Canada opposed this feature, mindful of what they believed to be a U.S. propensity to use trade complaints and sanctions as political weapons to coercively grow market share (Mazey 2001). Dombois *et al.* (2003) put another kind of political spin on the NAALC's design "flaws." They argue that the governments essentially agreed to establish an ambiguous, "toothless" labor-rights process in pursuit of different ends. The United States wanted a public monitoring device that would show it was sensitive to social standards without

The NAALC and workers' rights in Mexico: winning the battle only to lose the war?

At first glance, U.S. NAO Submissions No. 9702 and 9702-Part II (Han Young de Mexico) seem like uninspired choices to illustrate the inner workings of NAFTA's labor side-agreement. The underlying dispute was confined to a single assembly plant in Tijuana, Baja California, that supplied tractor-trailer chassis and platforms to a larger manufacturing facility owned by Hyundai Precision America. Peak employment at the facility never exceeded 150 workers. Work practices and government relations—at least at the local level—were not materially different from what has been reported for countless *maquiladora*. So why highlight this case, especially since other NAALC filings have involved more employees, contained more pervasive or egregious allegations of wrongdoing, and produced more convoluted cross-border dealings between member states? In a nutshell, the Han Young submission aptly portrays the strengths *and* core shortcomings of labor-rights oversight in the North American context. From virtually every perspective, the binational process worked as envisioned when the dispute resolution framework was adopted. Yet, it is hard to see how justice was served in the end, given the way things turned out.

While the substantive harmonization of labor laws was never a serious prospect in NAFTA's creation, the NAALC reflected a consensus that existing regulations should be consistently enforced in transparent administrative proceedings. Any aggrieved person or organization with a legally recognized interest was to be afforded meaningful extralegal recourse to have the situation redressed. In October 1997, NGOs from both sides of the border submitted a complaint to the U.S. NAO alleging that rampant IR and workplace safety violations at Han Young's factory were being enabled by Mexican officials. Claims of governmental nonfeasance and malfeasance proliferated over the next few months as additional parties (e.g., United Steelworkers' Union, United Auto Workers, and Canadian Auto Workers) filed addendums to the original document.

Most of their ire was directed at the local conciliation and arbitration board (CAB) for repeatedly sabotaging attempts by employees to be represented by a union of their own choosing. To illustrate, the local board was accused of turning a blind eye to representation-election irregularities on October 6, 1997, that allowed ineligible persons favoring management to cast ballots. When that didn't stop a popular independent union from winning, the election was nullified for reasons that were inconsistent with earlier rulings in the case and Mexican law in general.[1] A negotiated settlement between management and disgruntled workers would have recognized the independent union and reinstated workers who were fired during the organizing drive, but CAB members refused to sign off on it. Federal officials finally intervened, brokering a deal to administer a second election before year's end. The independent union emerged victorious once more and was certified as the workforce representative in January 1998. However, management was not required to honor its bargaining obligation later that spring when the existing "ghost union" collective agreement was set to expire. It also appeared to be acting with impunity in discharging and replacing members of the union's newly constituted rank and file. Assorted charges were levied against Mexico's labor department as well for lax enforcement of health-and-safety violations that had been documented in several inspections.

Consistent with its fact-finding charge, the NAO did not restrict the review to materials that had been supplied by the parties. Interviews, a public hearing, and correspondence with the

Mexican NAO provided additional information. The two-part report was published in April and August of 1998, respectively, conveying serious concerns that the local board had not consistently and impartially enforced laws pertaining to (1) representation rights, and (2) the protection of workers exercising their right to organize and bargain. More equivocal statements were made about health-and-safety compliance, which was attributed to incomplete documentation of the process for conducting inspections and determining financial penalties.

Ministerial consultations were recommended in both areas, a course of action the U.S. Secretary of Labor agreed to pursue. Two months later, the Mexican Secretary of Labor and Social Welfare confirmed that his government was amenable to such talks. Subsequent discussions culminated in a ministerial agreement signed on May 18, 2000. Pursuant to the accord, Mexico agreed to hold a public seminar in Tijuana to inform workers on their organizing and representation rights, conduct a trilateral seminar on the regulatory scheme governing its labor boards, rededicate itself to ensuring that collective bargaining contracts were registered in conformity with the law, and participate in an intergovernmental meeting on health-and-safety issues raised in the case.

NAALC proponents could draw much encouragement from these developments. The U.S. NAO had responded expeditiously in building a comprehensive record and rendering both sets of findings. Its counterpart, in turn, provided needed expertise regarding the intricacies of Mexican industrial relations law and practice in a timely manner. The two nations also were able to identify sufficient common ground in the end to execute a ministerial agreement. Moreover, the agreed-upon terms emphasized education, administrative reform and joint activities—behaviors that were at the heart of what the side agreement was meant to foster.

Still, the process was not problem-free. Mexico's displeasure with the initial NAO report was unmistakable as it publicly criticized the Department of Labor for inappropriately taking sides and trying to rewrite the parties' NAFTA obligations. And while the Mexican labor secretary seemed to get past that sentiment rather quickly in agreeing to ministerial consultations, nearly two years would elapse before the two countries could hammer out mutually acceptable terms for signing. Although the labor-organizing seminar was conducted shortly thereafter as promised, it wound up being controversial in its own right. Attendees looked on as two dozen persons who had supported the formation of an independent union at Han Young were physically attacked and beaten by members of government-affiliated unions in the audience. Rather than evoking a strong and indignant response from Mexican and U.S. officials on the scene, the meeting was allowed to continue as though nothing of real consequence had occurred. Finally, it is questionable whether the stipulated intergovernmental meeting on safety and health infractions ever took place. Formal documentation of its occurrence does not appear in the public record, and the parties who filed the submission never received notice that it had been scheduled or held.

Perhaps the unkindest cut of all was that nothing in the agreement was designed to make whole the workers who had been victimized. No form of restitution was imposed directly or indirectly on company representatives for their illegal actions. This becomes even more incredible when one learns that management capped off its spree of misconduct by closing down the plant in December 1998.[2] Relegated to self-help, workers looked for new

continued

opportunities to keep their struggle in the public eye. In May 1999, they tried to occupy the firm's new operating facility to halt production but were unsuccessful. They also were behind a citywide *consulta* (i.e., referendum) that called for a general strike in support of a higher minimum wage and compliance with profit-sharing laws. However, their plight soon began to fade from the headlines without any tangible gains being secured.

Washington bureaucrats apparently lost interest or decided to formally distance themselves from the situation by the time the ministerial agreement was announced. Not long afterward, a DOL publication matter-of-factly stated that no respondents from the firm could be found to pay striking workers' demands. Management's reported ability to avoid detection by the legal system is curious, given that redundant employees had no problem locating and trying to occupy the new plant in 1999. In all likelihood, the troubled case wore out its political welcome as it became increasingly clear Mexico's federal government was unwilling to impose its will on local authorities.

Rather than emerging as a shining example of enlightened binational cooperation, the Han Young submission underscores the difficulty of engineering meaningful regional checks on employment regulation when the underlying framework gives primacy to national sovereignty and bars private causes of action against member states that do not comply with their treaty obligations.

Notes

1 The first justification offered was that the independent union could not be vested with representation rights for auto workers because its existing registration was confined to the federal metalworking sector. This contention not only misapplied pertinent law, but also conflicted with the board's own pre-election ruling that STIMAHCS did not lack the appropriate certification to represent Han Young workers in Baja California. The second argument in support of this action had more legal merit (i.e., that representation rights could not be conveyed in an election unless the number of votes received by the winning party equaled a majority of the workers eligible to participate). Neither union involved in the election could meet that standard. Yet, the board had no problem awarding representation rights to CROC, the government-affiliated "ghost union"—even though it received fewer votes than STIMAHCS.
2 The firm had brazenly announced its intention to close down the factory in March—around the time it received notification that the independent union had acquired representation rights and one month *before* the first NAO report was released. More and more independent-union supporters lost their jobs in the weeks that followed. An ill-fated strike in May sought to perfect the right to sell off plant equipment in lieu of severance pay once it became clear the shutdown was inevitable. By September, the firm was gearing up to reopen under a different name in another section of Tijuana.

Sources: Brown (2004), Bureau of International Labor Affairs, USDOL (2002a: 13–14), ICFTU (2000), U.S. National Administrative Office (1998a, b, 2005), Williams (2000)

having to materially alter its policy position on the internalization of international labor-rights instruments. Not having insisted that labor standards be part of the NAFTA agreement in the first place, Mexico and Canada wanted maximum flexibility to direct attention away from conflict resolution toward intergovernmental cooperation.

The European Union and NAFTA seem to receive the lion's share of attention whenever talk turns to regional influences on labor standards. Having discussed both blocs at length, we now look elsewhere to ascertain how representative these models are for the world at large. Our search for answers begins in Latin America, heads eastward to Africa, and concludes in Asia.

Other blocs

Latin America

Dominican Republic–Central American Free Trade Area (DR-CAFTA)

Desirous of extending NAFTA's trade principles southward, the United States has kept an ear to the ground for receptive partners elsewhere in the hemisphere. The five countries initially courted—Costa Rica, El Salvador, Guatemala, Honduras, and Nicaragua—had their own history of dealings on the trade front. For forty years, they had been struggling to orchestrate a viable Central American Common Market (see Bulmer-Thomas 1998). Active negotiations on an FTA began in January 2003 and were concluded within twelve months. The Dominican Republic elected to join the group the following year after a very brief negotiating period. By August 2004, all seven nations had signed off on the agreement. If the arrangement actually does come to pass, most tariffs would be eliminated immediately, with the rest being phased out over a 10 year span.

Unlike NAFTA, the labor-rights provisions in CAFTA have been incorporated in the main document (chapter 16). A Labor Affairs Council (LAC) would be created to oversee implementation and review progress under the chapter. Rather than being an independent regional body *per se*, the LAC is structured as an *ad hoc* forum of cabinet-level representatives. Administrative subunits (i.e., contact points) operating within the existing labor ministries would provide operational support for all internal and external activities. Parallels to the NAALC national administrative offices are obvious. However, CAFTA's "labor cooperation and capacity building mechanism" (Mechanism) adds a unique twist. Contact points would be empowered to mobilize and deploy interagency teams with the requisite expertise to assist interested governments to bolster their ability to comply with the agreement's labor requirements. The Mechanism's charge includes (1) disseminating information on labor laws and best practices in labor administration, (2) establishing priorities for cooperation and capacity building, (3) developing relevant programs, and (4) seeking support, as appropriate, from international organizations. Each nation also has the option of utilizing tripartite advisory committees as it sees fit.

No sovereignty would be surrendered over the content of domestic labor-market regulation. Signatory governments instead promise to respect internationally recognized labor rights and enforce their own laws in a consistent and effective manner. A specific process has been designed to handle complaints that chapter obligations are being abridged. The first two stages would involve cooperative consultations with the contact points and LAC. Once these options run their course, the complaining state could bring the issue before another entity created by the agreement, the Free Trade Commission. If the commission failed to settle the matter within specified time limits, an arbitration panel could be requested. The panel would issue preliminary and finals reports with recommendations based on the information that had been submitted for review. A key point for us is that any nongovernmental entity (e.g., company, union, NGO) would have the right to attend panel hearings and contribute oral or written submissions for consideration so long as it first served written notice on the disputing governments (Article 20.11).

A panel determination of non-conformity would trigger a 45 day window for the disputing governments to negotiate mutually acceptable compensation. What happens if they are unable to come to terms? The prevailing party could request that the panel be reconvened to impose an annual monetary assessment on the offending member, which is capped at $15 million per year. Such fines would be paid to a fund administered by the commission for discretionary allocation to initiatives that would improve the situation in the violating country. The only recourse the prevailing party would have if the fine went unpaid would be to withdraw tariff benefits for an equivalent amount. Here, CAFTA clearly departs from its North American predecessor.

Where does the CAFTA agreement stand at the moment? While the legislatures of El Salvador, Honduras, and Guatemala have ratified the instrument, Nicaragua and Costa Rica are unlikely to do so in the near term, given their current political climate (Business Coalition for U.S.–Central American Trade 2005; Nicaragua Solidarity Campaign 2005; Staff 2005). The agreement also faces an uphill battle in the U.S. Congress as organized labor and pro-labor NGOs voice continuing opposition to its passage (e.g., AFL-CIO 2005; Human Rights Watch 2004, 2005; Labor Advisory Committee for Trade Negotiations and Trade Policy 2004). The fast-track authority conveyed to the executive branch to negotiate the deal does not preclude Congress from rejecting the finalized terms. In May 2005, Central American leaders received assurances from President Bush that he would personally intervene to facilitate congressional approval of the pact (Reuters 2005). Regardless of how this situation breaks, the approach to labor rights is different enough from NAFTA to be independently profiled.

Caribbean Community (CARICOM)

Nations in this part of the hemisphere have been somewhat enigmatic when it comes to collective regulation. As we will see, there are an impressive number and variety of instruments that have the capacity to homogenize labor-market institutions and employment terms. That being said, it is difficult to predict what the future holds, because CARICOM's key organs have very circumscribed powers. There is no supranational parliament or commission like the ones we will see below in CAN and MERCOSUR. CARICOM members nevertheless have chosen repeatedly to back harmonization initiatives, differentiating themselves from their neighbors to the north and west. The question is, how long will this decentralized approach continue to yield such outcomes?

One of the older economic blocs, CARICOM brings together 20 national governments[3] seeking to better represent their development and foreign-policy interests on the world stage. Over time, the underlying economic linkages have run the gamut of integration forms discussed in this chapter. After establishing an FTA in the late 1960s, member states had no intention of standing pat. They quickly resolved to transition further into a common market and secured that outcome with the 1973 Treaty of Chaguaramas. By the mid-1980s, local political leaders had become convinced that deeper integration was necessary to make the region's small markets more attractive for inward investment. This realization paved the way for the 1992 decision to formally endorse the creation of a CARICOM Single Market and Economy (CSME). Although nine years would pass before all of the requisite treaty amendments were finalized, the CSME took flight in 2001 with a four-year timetable to become fully operational. In 2005, trade ministers received word that all member states were on track to satisfy their obligations by year's end as required.[4]

CARICOM's strategic and operational needs are serviced by a diverse set of administrative units. The conference of Heads of Government determines bloc policy. That task, challenging in its own right, is especially difficult here because unanimity is required for decisions to take effect. Strategic planning, external relations, and the coordination of economic integration are handled by a council of ministers. Both entities are supported by a cluster of lower-level "themed" councils (e.g., trade and economic development, finance and planning). The one most germane to our discussion is the Council for Human and Social Development (COHSOD), which is responsible for promoting cross-country intersectoral cooperation in such areas as education, health, culture, sport, crime, and work.[5] A directorate in the CARICOM secretariat supplies technical support for COHSOD activities. In 2001, a regional business and labor advisory committee was added to the mix (Mark and Oxman 2002: 71). Attempts to learn more about its structure, activities, and place in the general hierarchy did not pan out.

The Caribbean Community has gone to considerable lengths to codify the principles, and in some instances legislative provisions, that member states should receive into local law. Adopted in the mid-1990s, the Charter of Civil Society could lay claim to being the desired ethical grounding for labor-market regulation in the region. Two of its articles have a direct bearing on HR/IR systems. Article XIX lists numerous rights that employees have concerning industrial relations, OSH, social security, employment security, and basic working conditions; resonating on the whole with internationally recognized labor standards. In contrast, Article XXII speaks to the state's obligation to facilitate genuine consultation in the development and implementation of national economic and social programs. Formal reporting and complaint systems are part of the charter (Article XXV), underscoring the seriousness of the initiative. Signatory governments agree to constitute a tripartite national committee to monitor implementation and receive allegations of wrongdoing. A three-year reporting cycle is specified, with each report conveying the nation's compliance posture and factors that are impeding further progress. It is expected that the social partners will actively participate in the preparation of these documents. The first wave of reports was presented to CARICOM's executive secretary in 2000 (American Center for International Labor Solidarity/AFL-CIO 2003: 143).

Perhaps more intriguing is the prospect that *individual* citizens and organizations can file complaints against the state or *a social partner* for charter noncompliance. In the interests of procedural due process, accused parties will be notified about the filing and given an opportunity to comment on the allegation(s). National committees have the option of including their view of the matter in reports that will be forwarded to the bloc's executive secretary. The intended consequences of bad acts are a mystery, though, as the charter is silent about sanctions. This may go a long way in explaining why no complaints had been lodged by mid-2003, six years after the charter was adopted (American Center for International Labor Solidarity/AFL-CIO 2003: 143).

Other CARICOM instruments build on this effort. The 1995 Declaration of Labor and Industrial Relations Principles fleshes out the charter's implications for national employment policies and tripartite relations. With ILO technical assistance, model Acts have been drafted to promote equal opportunity (four), the formation and recognition of IR organizations (one), OSH (one) and employment security (one). While Belize and Guyana are the only members to have implemented any of these measures outright, several others have been mindful of their contents when formulating local Bills (Mark and Oxman 2002: 26). The only instances of coordinated legislation so far apply to immigration and social security entitlements. Separate agreements have been entered into at the community level to facilitate the free movement of skilled persons (i.e., university graduates) and other approved categories (e.g., media workers, musicians). Twelve member states have done what is necessary legislatively and administratively to give effect to the first agreement; 10 for the second one. Individuals making the move for work purposes have to obtain a "certificate of recognition of CARICOM skills qualification" from a designated home- or host-country ministry. An ancillary agreement on social security has been signed, ratified and enacted by 13 nations, guaranteeing CARICOM nationals access to local benefits during their stint as a migrant worker and credit for years worked abroad in the computation of home-country benefit levels.

The decision to assimilate the group that spearheaded these innovations into a much larger unit with a predominantly nonwork social agenda does raise concerns about the future. Will the community's labor ministers be able to command sufficient attention and resources from COHSOD to promote more widespread acceptance and internalization of existing labor-rights instruments? Where do additional innovations in labor-market regulation rank in COHSOD's plans, given competing commitments to advance education, public safety, and other facets of society? It is too early to tell whether CARICOM's impact on local labor and employment law has already peaked or is just beginning to show.

Community of Andean Nations (CAN)

The objectives and structure of Latin America's second oldest bloc have their roots in three watershed events. First constituted under a different name (i.e., Andean Pact), the group has its genesis in the 1969 Cartagena Agreement. While there were high hopes at the time of signing that economic development and social integration would be stimulated, little changed for member states deep into the 1980s. The disappointing results prompted a reassessment of their relationship with an eye toward change. The 1989 Galápagos summit accomplished just that when a strategic repositioning plan was approved by the attending heads of state. In essence, a decision was made to favor regional trade liberalization over tariff protection and import-substitution policies. Over the next decade, an FTA and customs union would materialize, and a framework would be successfully negotiated with MERCOSUR to eventually merge into a South American Community of Nations (CSN) modeled after the European Union.[6] The 1999 Act of Cartagena represents a third turning point, laying out plans for an Andean common market by the end of 2005.

The Community's governance structure has expanded and been refined to keep pace with its increasingly ambitious agenda. Strategic direction comes from a presidential council, which relies on a council of foreign ministers and commission for trade and investment to manage all stages of the policy cycle in their respective spheres of influence. The latter two bodies can issue "decisions" that amount to regional legislation which automatically becomes part of the domestic law of member states. While nothing further has to be done to have decisions received into local law, there still may be a need to transpose their dictates into national legislation or decrees similar to the EU (i.e., decision language is not necessarily self-executing). This explains why decisions sometimes include specific deadlines for government action. Draft proposals and decisions normally originate with the Andean parliament and general secretariat, which pass them on for consideration and formal adoption.

The secretariat also processes and can self-initiate complaints that individual countries are not complying with community instruments. Follow-up may entail a pre-litigation investigation, a written observation requesting the offending government to provide a response, and a justified opinion based on the data finally assembled. If the problem is not rectified, the case will be forwarded to the Andean Court of Justice for a ruling that can lead to the suspension or restriction of bloc-related benefits if noncompliance is found. Individuals and organizations whose rights have been negatively impacted by the behavior in question have legal standing to file complaints with the secretariat and to appeal secretariat determinations to the court of justice.

CAN has done more than any other bloc outside of Europe to shepherd social integration. In 2000, an advisory council of labor ministers was established to furnish strategic guidance on five priority aspects of the impending common market: employment promotion, labor education and training, social security, labor migration, and security and health at work. The group has met several times, reporting directly to the council of foreign ministers. To increase the probability that the resources and processes available to labor officials will be optimized, a protocol was adopted that same year revising the Simón Rodriguez Convention—an organizing framework for social dialogue and planning that had been moribund for the most part since its enactment in the 1970s. Three administrative bodies are planned to deliver focused, tripartite attention to the community's social and labor issues. The conference, comprising labor ministers and the representatives of labor and business advisory committees in each country, would meet annually at minimum to evaluate the outcomes of convention-related activities, authorize new programs and budget requests, and propose modifications that might improve future performance. Special committees (tripartite) and a technical secretariat are slated to provide operational support as directed. The protocol will come into effect once all member states deposit an instrument of ratification with the community's general secretariat (Article 13). So far, only Peru has done so (Cortés *et al.* 2003: 15).

Andean advisory committees for labor and business began meeting in 1998 to channel the concerns and priorities of their constituencies to bloc leaders. A reinvigorated Simón

Rodriguez Convention obviously contains the prospect of multilevel regular interactions with labor officials, but their opportunities do not stop there. In fact, they are *required* not only to attend meetings of the council of ministers, Andean commission, and working groups connected with the Andean integration process, but also to offer opinions on relevant issues to the community's two primary organs and general secretariat (Andean Commission Decision 464). Organized labor has fulfilled these expectations without any prodding. That has not been true for its business counterpart, at least on the social dimension. Its patterned failure to attend sessions of the labor ministers' advisory council prompted the group to request assistance from the general secretariat in securing more participation (Cortés *et al.* 2003: 12).

More tangible progress is discernible in the generation of labor-rights instruments. Two social charters offer a window into the labor-market principles that member states are trying to foster. Article 15 of the Andean social charter makes it clear that ILO core conventions are a beginning rather than end point in the state's obligation to employees. A nonexhaustive list of 24 rights is articulated, including freedom of movement, vocational training, employment, and meaningful consultation. The charter was adopted by the Andean parliament in 1999. A complementary measure, the Andean charter for the promotion and protection of human rights, was approved by the Andean presidential council three years later. Neither has the force of law in its present form (i.e., declaration).

Since 2003, the council of foreign ministers has approved three work-related CAN agreements that must be received into local law (Decisions 545, 583, 584). These instruments establish common policies on (1) the right of insured individuals to receive social security benefits while working outside of their home country, (2) the right of migrant workers to move freely through community space, and (3) basic OHS standards. At the time of this writing, the advisory council of labor ministers was preparing draft regulations for these instruments with technical assistance from the ILO and International Organization for Migration. New agreements on labor administration and the elimination of child labor purportedly are in the works as well (Staff 2003a).

The Andean community has the mechanisms in place to rival the European Union in imprinting regional values on domestic labor-market regulation. How willing local officials and the business community are to go down that route remains to be seen.

Southern Common Market (MERCOSUR)

MERCOSUR officially came into being in 1991 when the Presidents of Brazil, Argentina, Paraguay, and Uruguay signed the Treaty of Asunción.[7] Unfortunately, little forethought had been given to the socio-labor issues that would arise in the transition to a common market. The only pertinent language in the treaty merely intimated that economic development could not be pursued at the expense of social justice. That omission began to be redressed a few months later when "subgroup 11" was formed by the Common Market Group (CMG)—the bloc's executive organ—to assess integration's likely effects on labor relations, employment, and social security. The subgroup quickly divided itself into a network of subcommittees concentrating on the following topics: individual labor relations, collective labor relations, employment and migration for employment, vocational training, OSH, social security, specific sectors, and international principles and conventions. One of its first contributions was a recommendation to the CMG that all member states ratify 33 delineated ILO conventions (Perez del Castillo 1993: 646). This arrangement was short-lived, however, supplanted by a new working group when the 1994 Protocol of Ouro Preto finalized MERCOSUR's institutional infrastructure.

Bringing together the region's labor ministers, Working Group 10 has tripartite features and reports direct to the CMG, like its predecessor. Its bailiwick includes ILO compliance reviews for the region, comparative law studies, and proposals for new labor instruments. Work formerly handled by the highly fragmented subcommittee system has been consolidated and reassigned to three new committees: employment relations; employment, migration, and training; and OHS, labor inspection, and social security. Labor and management representatives on each committee have the right to participate in all deliberations and vote on recommendations and conclusions to forward to the larger working group; however, they have no voice in what gets passed on to the CMG.

The Ouro Preto protocol also established the Economic and Social Consultation Forum (ESCF), a purely advisory body comprising labor, management and NGO designees. This body interacts directly with the CMG, seemingly ensuring the social partners have high-level access to bloc decision making. But appearances can be misleading. In general, the ESCF has been resource starved and unable to get any of its recommendations adopted (American Center for International Labor Solidarity/ AFL-CIO 2003: 132). Part of the reason for this may be the diversion of attention to a more focused tripartite entity, the Socio-labor Commission. The commission is a creature of the Socio-labor Declaration, which was jointly issued by the bloc's heads of state in 1998. In addition to reviewing annual compliance reports that member states must submit, commissioners have the authority to unilaterally conduct investigations and propose modifications to the declaration's provisions. An ever-present hurdle that must be overcome is the requirement that consensus be achieved before any actions are taken. No updates of its experiences or performance have been reported in English-speaking sources.

The declaration itself champions the standard fare of labor standards endorsed in multilateral social charters. One of its distinctive characteristics is the inclusion of a "management rights" section (Article 7), which releases employers from doing anything more than following national law and practice in running their enterprises to demonstrate compliance. Another is the explicit bar on trade or financial sanctions for nonadherence (Article 25). Thus, the declaration's practical significance will be determined by the actual legal reforms that individual governments choose to make and enforce within their own borders.[8]

Other instruments are trying to formally synchronize how affiliates manage certain aspects of employment. A social security agreement was adopted in 1997 by MERCOSUR's highest-level authority, the Common Market Council. Similar to what we saw in CARICOM, the accord seeks to guarantee migrant workers access to local benefits as well as credit for time spent in covered foreign work once they return home. Six years later, the document still had not been ratified by the respective national parliaments (American Center for International Labor Solidarity/AFL-CIO 2003: 130). An agreement on the free movement of persons also was signed in 2002 with a considerable fanfare from attending ministers. Ordinarily seen as an essential component of common markets, the free-movement accord has drawn criticism from outsiders. For example, Albarracin (2005) asserts that the agreement was ill timed, given the longstanding inability of member states to effectively administer their underlying FTA and customs union. The decision to liberalize immigration policies is portrayed as a public relations device to divert attention away from the lack of progress on trade issues that have higher transaction costs. Even if this is not true, the fate of the social security agreement does not bode well for this initiative.

Before we leave this part of the world, a few comments are warranted about ongoing efforts to erect the Free Trade Area of the Americas (FTAA)—a development that would dramatically alter the economic landscape of the western hemisphere. Approved in principle at a historic 1994 summit in Miami, the new bloc would stretch from northern Alaska to the southern tip of Chile, linking the economies of 34 nations. Active trade negotiations officially began four years later with considerable institutional support from the Organization of American States,[9] the Inter-American Bank, and the United Nations. Eleven major negotiating groups were assembled to facilitate integration: market access; agriculture, rules of origin; customs procedures; investment; standards and technical barriers to trade; subsidies, anti-dumping and countervailing duties; government procurement; intellectual property rights; services; competition policy; and dispute settlement. Surprisingly, nothing was done to insure the accompanying socio-labor challenges would receive focused attention, a point that was not lost on several external stakeholders. It is unclear from public records whether the omission was a deliberate snub—as the union movement has contended (e.g., American Center for International Labor Solidarity/AFL-CIO 2003: 146)—or a miscalculation of the topic's significance.

Trade unions and pro-labor NGOs mobilized quickly, hoping to move employment-related issues into the mainstream of negotiations. Lacking opportunities to provide direct input, they conducted "people's summits" in Santiago and Quebec as high-level FTAA meetings were about to begin (American Center for International Labor Solidarity/AFL-CIO 2003: 147). Thousands of labor representatives and social activists gathered to develop and publicize socially responsible policy options. The resultant declaration and action plan called for major changes, including (1) a labor equivalent to the "business forum" already afforded ready access to trade negotiators, (2) explicit language in the final agreement requiring adherence to ILO core labor standards, and (3) adoption of a broader FTAA social charter. These demands were presented to the governments chairing the respective FTAA proceedings, Chile and Canada.

While a hemispheric social charter and reconfigured negotiating structures would not be on the cards,[10] the coalition of labor interests did succeed in modifying the *status quo*. Trade ministers started to interact more regularly with the Inter-American Conference of Ministers of Labor afterward. Noting with interest an IACML study on globalization's labor-market effects, the ministers requested a copy of the findings in their 2002 Quinto declaration. Labor ministers from Canada, Mexico, and Brazil delivered the report and commented further on IACML activities one year later at the Miami meeting. More important still was a fundamental shift in thinking about the treatment of labor topics in the FTAA agreement. The first two drafts lack any affirmations or obligations linked to labor rights, a situation that changed in November 2003 when the third version was released. Chapter VII of the latest iteration would obligate signatory nations to ensure that domestic employment regulation is consistent with internationally recognized labor standards. No provision is made for supranational law making, and the processes and penalties for noncompliance mirror the language of the DR-CAFTA agreement.

Wanting more, labor supporters continue to push for reforms. In May 2004, a special FTAA committee for societal participation received critical feedback from the organizers of a labor-law roundtable. The contributed statement urged negotiators to demonstrate a more aggressive commitment to ILO requirements and recommended several changes. The list of proposals included establishing a negotiating group on labor issues, opening up dispute-settlement procedures to individuals and organizations, and substantially fortifying the terms for Chapter VII (Jiménez and Morales 2004). No institutional follow-up has been observed to date.

The FTAA's future remains uncertain beyond the fact that it will not take effect at the end of 2005 as envisioned. Little has been accomplished since the Miami Trade Ministerial, as the parties struggle to find common ground in such key areas as market access, competition policy, and trade remedies. Tangible progress is further compromised by a self-imposed requirement that FTAA provisions be adopted as a unified package rather than on an issue-by-issue basis. How labor and employment law will be managed in a hemispheric free trade area—should it come to pass—will be revealed with the passage of time.

Africa

Southern African Development Community (SADC)

Having demonstrated the capacity to cooperate on social issues and development projects in key sectors for more than a decade, 10 southern African nations[11] opted to integrate their economies on a more systematic basis in the early 1990s. Their decision was formalized in a 1992 treaty marking the beginning of the SACD. Growth and self-reliance objectives certainly were behind the move as member states tried to overcome the economic doldrums besetting much of the continent. Not long afterward, a trade protocol was adopted that set an eight-year timetable for the establishment of a free trade area. But there also was an intersection of sociopolitical interests at the time of signing, evident in the treaty's avowed commitment to evolving common political values, systems, and institutions.

The bloc's administrative structure was overhauled in 2001 to better support the FTA and other causes. Overall responsibility for the formulation and effective implementation of SADC policies is vested with three organs: a summit of the heads of state and government, a council of ministers, and an integrated committee of ministers. The SADC secretariat, in turn, carries out all of the operational activities associated with program planning and management; most notably, bringing policy harmonization proposals to the attention of the council and assessing how well regional policies are being implemented. Work-related programs and policies are the charge of one of its subunits, the Directorate of Social and Human Development and Special Programs (SHDSP). Finally, there are the SADC national committees, another governance innovation. These tripartite advisory bodies are expected to help shape regional strategies and assist in their execution. On the surface at least, it appears that the social dimension of integration will receive ample attention as the planning process moves forward.

The SADC has championed several labor-rights initiatives in recent years consistent with this view. Adopted in 2003, the Charter of Fundamental Rights details the overarching labor-market principles that SADC countries have agreed to follow. Legal and social policy harmonization is a central objective, especially for social security entitlement, health and safety standards, labor mobility, and basic working conditions (Articles 2 and 11). Information and consultation rights at the enterprise level are featured prominently as well (Article 13). Signatory governments also are pressed to make the ratification and incorporation of core ILO standards high-priority items, and to establish regional mechanisms to assist member states comply with ILO reporting systems (Articles 4–7 and 12). To lend more credibility to the project, public officials are directed to report annually on the extent to which the charter's dictates are being advanced. Article 16 further specifies that reports must be prepared with input from the most representative organizations for management and labor, and that SADC institutions have an obligation to prevent non-implementation in any affiliated country. However, it is difficult to imagine how the latter obligation will be satisfied without an obvious enforcement mechanism.

Other protective measures have been devised. For example, codes of conduct on child labor, the employment of persons with HIV/AIDS, and the handling of workplace chemicals have been prepared and disseminated to supply interested governments with drafting principles for domestic legislation. A draft protocol on the cross-border movement of persons within the SADC was hammered out in 1998, ending protracted negotiations on the subject.[12] The designated time frame for harmonizing immigration practices varies from three to five years, depending on the migration activity in question (i.e., visitation, residence, establishment). Some states have formally agreed to its terms; others continue to canvass key stakeholders. To illustrate, South Africa's Immigration Advisory Board conducted a public consultation in October 2003 to explore the document's public safety and labor implications. The protocol will take effect once two-thirds of the member states deposit an instrument of ratification or accession with the SADC executive secretary.

This bloc has the necessary structures in place to go beyond mere coordination of labor-market policies. Yet, the collective will to aggressively pursue area-wide regulation has not been very strong so far, with no signs there will be a deviation from this pattern in the decade ahead.

Common Market for Eastern and Southern Africa (COMESA)

Selective trade liberalization can be observed in other parts of Africa. Since 1981, a large band of nations extending from Egypt to Swaziland[13] has been forging closer economic ties to bolster competitiveness. In 1994, their preferential tariff arrangement became the cornerstone of a more comprehensive framework, COMESA, which would be phased in over several decades. Over the next 10 years, agreements were secured on an FTA and customs union (at least for raw materials and capital goods). Half of the countries have met the qualifying criteria for FTA membership, and there is continuing hope that the remainder will choose to undertake the necessary reforms to gain entry. That and much more has to occur, though, if the ultimate goal of a functioning economic union is to be achieved by the year 2025.

COMESA's bureaucratic engine looks very similar to what has been installed elsewhere. There is an authority of heads of state and government, council of ministers, and secretariat to fashion regional policies, set program priorities, assist member states with treaty implementation, and evaluate the performance of bloc activities. A consultative committee facilitates interactions with external stakeholders. What does differentiate COMESA is the low-level position that the unit handling employment-related issues occupies. It is not a main component of the secretariat, as was true for the SADC. Nor is it an independent network of high-level ministers like the IACLM in the Organization of American States. The Labor, Human Resources, and Social Affairs committee is one of 12 "technical committees" mapping implementation plans for COMESA programs and monitoring their operations. The recommendations it can make are tactical, not strategic, in nature.

Is there likely to be much activity on the labor-rights front when the social dimension of integration lacks a champion in policy-making circles? The 1994 treaty is very explicit about the reforms that need to be engineered. Article 143 calls for close cooperation on labor laws and the adoption of a social charter, while Article 164 obligates member states to agree on a protocol for the free movement of labor. Nothing has been reported to suggest that real progress has been made on the first two items. The situation does not appear to be much better for the third when one considers a report from the June 2004 meeting of the council of ministers.[14] Few countries had completed national consultations on a draft version of the protocol even though it had been open for signature since the fifth COMESA authority summit in 2000. The council further noted that it had not yet determined how the programs associated with Article 9 (movement of labor) would be implemented. On a positive note, a new timetable was laid out for protocol implementation, with 2008 identified as the target date for agreement on the movement of skilled labor. Some degree of skepticism is unavoidable given the added revelation that the protocol on relaxed visa requirements, which predates the COMESA treaty, still was not being implemented at all or only partially by most member states. To invoke a popular phrase, this bloc certainly has talked the talk in terms of putting a regional stamp on employment regulation. Whether it can walk the walk with the meager institutional apparatus that exists in this area is in serious doubt.

We would be remiss in leaving the continent without briefly taking stock of what has been happening in western Africa, where there is a heavy concentration of francophone countries. Dating back more than a quarter-century, the Economic Community of West African States[15] (ECOWAS) was relatively lax about integration until 1993, when the founding treaty was revised. A new economic agenda prompted the community to revamp its administrative structure along the lines of neighboring blocs. Ambitious goals were set for a customs, and then economic, union to become fully operational 10 and 15 years out, respectively. Translating the vision into practice has been tougher than anticipated, leading to a postponement of the former until 2007 at the earliest.

The new direction in trade relations also brought greater sensitivity to the social dimension of integration. Roberts (2005) presents an interesting, and very much needed, review of the bloc's link to labor-market regulation before and after the early 1990s.

In a nutshell, no systematic effort was made to monitor or influence labor and employment laws in the region prior to 1993. The original ECOWAS treaty made no mention of work-related issues, and bloc officials did nothing independently to promote the idea that labor ministers should interact on anything other than an *ad hoc* basis. This *laissez-faire* attitude was formally abandoned in the revised treaty. First, an explicit commitment was made to harmonize labor laws and social security legislation (Article 61). Second, a human resource commission was identified as one of eight new technical committees that would monitor and facilitate the treaty's application within their specific area of competence (Article 22). The commission met for the first time in March 2004 and resolved to take a proactive, results-oriented stance on regional activities. Several months later, the council of ministers adopted a commission recommendation to institute the draft social security convention[16] that had been tabled for 10 years. Beginning in 2005, there also will be an annual forum of labor ministers to facilitate more information sharing and collaboration on labor-market matters.

Asia

ASEAN Free Trade Area (AFTA)

Conceived during a time of major political unrest, the Association of Southeast Asian Nations (ASEAN) tended to focus more on regional security than on economic development during the first two-plus decades of its existence. That appeared to change in 1992 when member states decided to form a free trade area.[17] While earlier attempts at economic cooperation had languished (e.g., ASEAN industrial projects, ASEAN industrial complementation), the ASEAN Free Trade Agreement received strong governmental backing—to the point where full implementation of the common effective preferential tariff was moved up five years to 2003 for the first set of signatory nations. Oversight responsibilities are discharged by an AFTA Bureau housed in the ASEAN secretariat and the AFTA Council of Ministers, a higher-level body that reports directly to the ASEAN heads of government.

Given the steadfast opposition that Malaysia and its neighbors have expressed to social clauses in trade arrangements (e.g., Singapore and Seattle WTO Ministerials, ILO International Labor Conferences), it is no surprise that the AFTA agreement is silent about labor rights and their enforcement. Labor ministers do meet annually under ASEAN's larger bureaucratic superstructure, but that forum has not embraced the harmonization of employment regulation as an explicit or implicit goal. Instead, the gatherings serve as an information clearinghouse on HR/IR practices and vehicle to orchestrate technical studies and collaborative development projects.

Two recent ASEAN initiatives nevertheless may signal growing interest in limited standardization. In 2000, a memorandum of understanding was executed, establishing the ASEAN Occupational Safety and Health Network (ASEAN-OSHNET), a regional body responsible for strengthening and coordinating national policies on workplace safety and health. The organization is headed by a coordinating board that reports direct to the ASEAN Subcommittee on Labor Affairs. One of the priority areas identified in its first action plan was the formulation of ASEAN guidelines for OSH management systems and the classification, labeling, and packaging of hazardous chemicals. Another project is striving to create a framework for mutual skills recognition to facilitate labor mobility within the region. Australia has channeled some funding to this endeavor through the ASEAN–Australian Development Cooperation Program, and the European Union has volunteered to share expertise on integrated social protection for workers through the ASEAN–EU Project on Regional Integration Support.[18] Whether this foreshadows uniform relaxed visa requirements is anyone's guess. The ASEAN Economic Community, which was endorsed at the 2003 ASEAN summit (Bali Concord II), speaks glowingly about the free flow of goods, services, and capital but makes no mention of the free movement of workers.

The Bali Concord II envisions an ASEAN Socio-Cultural Community (ASCC) as well. The ensuing action plan underscores the need to effectively manage the social impact of economic integration, but does not offer any principles to guide labor-market reforms. This has not stopped the academic community from debating the prospects for an ASEAN social charter. Serrano et al. (2004: 82–86) go so far as to develop a charter prototype espousing values and interactions reminiscent of those inhabiting the North and Central American free trade areas. Countries would strive to adhere to internationally recognized labor standards without abdicating any control over domestic law. Noncompliance would be channeled through a multitiered process involving NAOs, the ASEAN Labor Ministers' Meeting, and finally an Evaluation Committee of Experts. No stance is taken on whether charter participation would be voluntary or mandatory, with financial sanctions for violations. The likelihood that this or any other supranational labor-rights body will gain favor with local politicians in the near term is remote.

South Asia Free Trade Area (SAFTA)

The South Asian Association for Regional Cooperation (SAARC) officially got its start at a summit in Dhaka, Bangladesh, in 1985. Uniting nations that spanned the Indian subcontinent and the Maldives, SAARC's institutionalized collaboration on economic, social, cultural, and technical matters was intended to foster greater regional self-reliance. Member states demonstrated the ability to work together on noneconomic issues (e.g., "designated year" initiatives focusing on drug abuse, female children, and the environment) early on; however, economic integration proved to be a tougher nut to crack. Eight years would elapse before the group successfully negotiated its first preferential trade deal, and 11 more until a free trade area was inked. The latter is set to be phased in over a 10 year period beginning on January 1, 2006.

SAFTA's institutional arrangements vest primary decision-making authority in a ministerial council. The council, in turn, is supported by a committee of experts and regional secretariat. Most interesting from our perspective is the failure to create an autonomous labor-rights entity or make one of the three bodies responsible for this issue. The terms "labor," "employment," and "work" are not mentioned *anywhere* in the SAFTA agreement or press releases that summarize COE negotiations on outstanding trade issues. One might argue that this was not necessary because SAARC already has a dedicated HR unit in place, the Human Resources Development Center (HRDC). Closer scrutiny of the HRDC's mandate and activities dispels that notion. HRDC programs to date are confined largely to cataloging governmental resources devoted to education, poverty reduction, etc., as well as limited public-sector training. Legal reform or harmonization is unmistakably beyond its purview.

Labor-oriented legal instruments also are missing from the SAFTA framework. Interestingly, an SAARC social charter was discussed and approved at the same ministerial summit that produced the free trade agreement. Does the charter obviate the need for more focused policy statements about workplace practices? For all of its laudatory language, the document makes no references to work relationships or labor markets. All of the responsibilities are couched in general terms, encouraging member states to elevate the social status of women, advance the well-being of children, improve the capacity to fight drug trafficking, and promote population stabilization among other things. One can extrapolate from such objectives to employment decision making, but the connection is indirect at best.

There has been no shortage of ideas from external stakeholders on how these shortcomings might be redressed. In 1996, a diverse group of labor activists and social reformers from India, Pakistan, Sri Lanka, Bangladesh, and Nepal participated in the "Kathmandu Consultation" on labor rights in multilateral trade agreements. Consensus was reached on the principles and components of a draft charter on South Asian labor rights, a development that was personally communicated to the SAARC Secretary General (South Asia Citizens Web 2005a). While the Secretary General expressed vague support and interest in the initiative, there is no indication of a formal response from the council or other SAARC organ. Undeterred, consultation organizers formed a preparatory committee to flesh out its provisions. The final product was incorporated in a far-reaching resolution that called for (1) regional harmonization of labor laws with specific international conventions and declarations, (2) a tripartite SAARC-level labor rights commission to monitor progress, (3) institutional mechanisms for SAARC work permits, and (4) national policies guaranteeing the right to work and need-based minimum wages (South Asia Citizens Web 2005b).

A regional coalition of labor organizations reiterated the need for governmental action on the charter's substantive and procedural elements in the months leading up to the SAFTA agreement (Mishra 2003). Two days before the signing, a people's summit in Islamabad issued a declaration pressing member states to take immediate steps to eliminate child labor, ensure strict compliance with core ILO conventions, adopt the aforementioned labor-rights charter, and guarantee free mobility for workers within the SAARC bloc (SAP International 2004). The ministers in attendance and their respective governments were not persuaded. Nothing that has materialized since then gives one reason to believe the *status quo* will be meaningfully altered any time soon.

Conclusion

Looking back on the chapter, one sees wide variation in the goals, institutions, and processes that guide member-state relations in regional trade blocs. The classification scheme depicted in Figure 3.1 may convey a better sense of the core similarities and differences that exist. According to the framework, a bloc's capacity to act as a change agent in national legal systems will be determined by two factors: the amount of authority the regional institution has over member-state policy making, and the level of substantive integration that affiliates are seeking to achieve. The two Asian blocs appear in the lower left-hand corner of the diagram because they presently lack the institutional infrastructure to generate or enforce regional instruments and are strong proponents of national sovereignty over labor-market regulation. NAFTA and DR-CAFTA rate slightly higher on both dimensions, but still are on the low end of each scale. While the underlying agreements recognize the parties' right to control their own labor and employment laws, they target adherence to specific principles rooted in internationally recognized labor standards. There also is a formalized process to resolve complaints and the potential for financial penalties for non-conformity. The lack of permanent legislative and judicial organs at the regional level keeps them from appearing further to the right on the *x* axis.

Four other blocs have set goals to coordinate multiple aspects of community IR/HR systems: SADC, COMESA, MERCOSUR, and CAN. Meaningful levels of sovereignty have not been delegated to the African entities, evident in the absence of regional law-making powers and lack of enforcement mechanisms to deter charter and protocol nonobservance. Their South American peers have more going for them in this regard, with well developed regional oversight of labor rights during the course of integration. In addition, the Andean community has two bodies (i.e., council of foreign ministers, Andean commission) whose decisions are tantamount to regional legislation that must be received into local law.

The remaining two blocs, CARICOM and the European Union, have aspirations for labor-market regulation that goes beyond mere coordination. Substantial integration is envisioned in both instances, although they differ radically on the authority dimension.

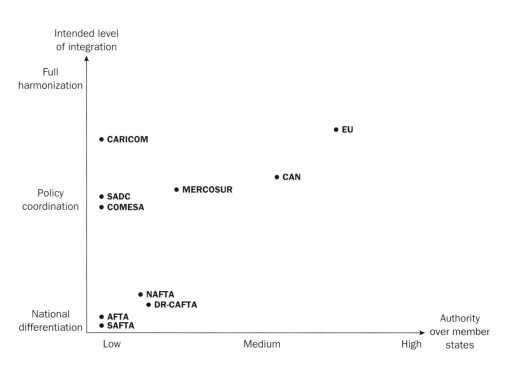

Figure 3.1 Capacity of regional blocs to act as change agents in labor and employment law

Across blocs, there has been a concentration of effort on "soft law" (i.e., non-binding instruments such as charters, social declarations, codes of conduct, model Acts) for the most part. Acknowledging the value of shared principles, the recalibration of local law to meet their specifications is spotty at best outside of the European Union. Accordingly, the next chapter concentrates on the heart and soul of employment regulation: national governments.

National institutions and the evolution of employment regulation

4

The phrase "stick to your knitting" (i.e., concentrate your activities and resources on what you already do well) has become a popular business-strategy mantra. Its public-sector ramifications are somewhat muddied by the diversity of governance forms that nations have implemented to direct their affairs. What individual and joint responsibilities do the various branches of government have in common law and civil law systems to make effective governance a reality? How do they interact with other sovereignties and international organizations to advance the interests of the societies they represent? How do these patterns impact labor-market regulation? The rest of this chapter will attempt to answer these questions.

Figure 4.1 orients all of the interactions within and across governmental units toward two fundamental activities: law creation and law enforcement. As discussed in Chapter 1, enforceable rights, entitlements, and obligations in a given society can flow from various sources, including legislation, court decisions, administrative rule making, custom, and religious texts. Whether a given source has relevance in terms of law creation, and how much influence it has, will be a function of the particular legal system in place (i.e., common, civil, mixed). Enforcement, the necessary complement to creation, encompasses the formal and informal processes leveraged by government officials to give practical effect to established laws. Adjudication is but one manifestation of this phenomenon. While there is some specialization of labor within government for these core activities, a systems approach is better suited to understanding and managing the public-sector dynamics. Concentrating on the left or right side of the diagram allows one to examine these interrelationships in a purely domestic context. Considering the entire set of paths shows how components of the domestic political system participate in bilateral and multilateral exchanges with other sovereignties.

Heads of state, ministries and agencies

Previous chapters are replete with examples of the executive branch advancing local interests in supranational bodies. For example, members of the tripartite delegations sent to ILO conferences are directly or tacitly appointed by this unit. All of the reporting obligations inherent in ILO membership reside here as well. We see high-ranking administrators interacting regularly in such regional forums as MERCOSUR's working

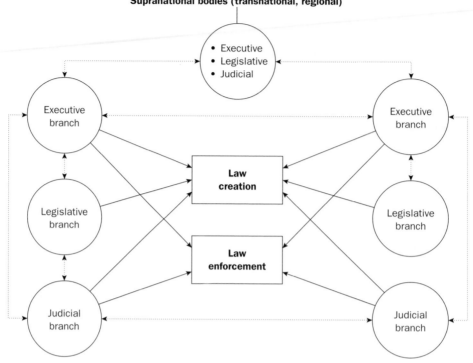

Figure 4.1 Institutional interfaces in labor and employment law

group of labor ministers. Heads of state and foreign ministers legislate in the European Union and CAN by approving directives and issuing decisions. Should the need arise, it will be this branch of government that represents the nation in judicial proceedings like those before the European Court of Justice or Inter-American Court of Human Rights.

The executive branch also interfaces with its foreign peers in diverse ways. Bilateral and multilateral agreements are negotiated by their respective staffers and signed by the heads of state. This area of government is the conduit through which intergovernmental communications and assistance will pass typically in the servicing of treaty obligations (e.g., OECD national contact points). Technical cooperation may occur as well. DR-CAFTA will give rise to a capacity-building mechanism for labor administration if it is ratified by all of the parties. The experience would not be entirely new for the United States. For years, the U.S. Department of Labor has been working to professionalize the enforcement and reporting abilities of emerging markets (EMs) through bilateral deals. An example of this is the 2003 agreement with China's Ministry of Labor and Social Security to cooperate on labor law implementation, labor law education, and labor legal aid (Xinhua News Agency 2003).[1]

Sometimes the cooperation is more strategic in nature. In 2004, the British Prime Minister and German Chancellor joined forces to influence a contentious employment matter that was being reviewed by the European Commission. The UK's opt-out exception for the EU work-time directive was about to expire, and government officials were very interested in securing an extension. Germany's decision to support the request made it unlikely that opposing interests would be able to convince the Commission to deny the proposal (Parker 2002b). It was the second time in just a few months that the two nations had worked together in this fashion. Shortly beforehand, Germany had assisted Great Britain in thwarting a Commission initiative to regulate temporary workers.[2] The *quid pro quo* was a UK-supported measure diluting the takeover directive that would have made it easier to acquire German-based firms.

At times, the executive branch even may take on the role of enforcer, pressuring counterparts overseas to adopt or maintain policies that benefit home-country stakeholders. Legal Systems in Action 4.l encapsulates how emerging markets can find themselves on the horns of a dilemma when it comes to FDI, and what one country did to extricate itself.

Labor rights in Bangladesh's export processing zones: can't live with them, can't live without them?

Bangladesh's Export Processing Zones Authority (BEPZA) cited "production-oriented" labor laws and a general bar on union activity in its promotional materials for inward investment as recently as July 2004. At first glance, these statements appear to be inaccurate or misleading. Core ILO conventions protecting union rights had been ratified back in the 1970s, and numerous laws were in place governing employment within its borders. However, EPZs had been selectively exempted from measures like the Industrial Relations Ordinance, Employment of Labor (standing orders) Act, and Factories Act in the 1980s, the government exercising discretionary powers that had been conveyed in § 11A of the enabling legislation. In their place was a sketchy set of "instructions" on employment standards developed by the BEPZA and administered by an industrial relations department in each zone. Neither the Labor Ministry nor organized labor had representatives on any of the Authority's main bodies. Meaningful inspection and enforcement procedures to foster compliance with the instructions also seemed to be missing. Investors evidently liked what they saw. Foreign direct investment from Japan and South Korea alone rose to US$600 million, dwarfing capital inflows from other sources.

The reaction of labor NGOs and the U.S. government differed markedly. Having been an instigator of trade-law reform linking tariff concessions to the observance of international labor standards, the AFL-CIO submitted a petition to the U.S. Trade Representative (USTR), seeking to revoke Bangladesh's newly minted GSP privileges. The ensuing review and intergovernmental negotiations culminated in an agreement which expressly conditioned the preservation of GSP entitlements on reinstituting two of the suspended laws by 1997 and the third by 2000. When the first deadline came and passed without full compliance, the USTR received another request from the American labor federation to revoke GSP eligibility. Bangladesh officials had not only failed to withdraw the exemptions for the EPZ at the heart of the dispute, but also extended them to a second zone established in the interim (and possibly still others that were in the planning stages). Formal discussions to resolve the matter began in June 1999 and continued into the following summer in hopes of engineering a compromise.

Outraged by these developments, local and regional investors mounted a counteroffensive to preserve the original labor-law restrictions. Although the United States was Bangladesh's

continued

Legal Systems in Action 4.1

largest export market, most of the goods shipped there were produced *outside* of the EPZs. That fact, combined with the modest level of U.S. investment in these zones, made the stakes much higher for them in this situation. During a special conference held in December 1999, the U.S. ambassador was informed that investors would consider a repeal of the exemptions to be a breach of contract by the host government because assurances of a peaceful labor climate had been instrumental in securing their investment. Adamant on this point, they followed up with a strong letter of protest to Bangladesh's foreign secretary threatening to cease operations and withdraw if trade unions were allowed to operate in the zones. The Japanese ambassador also met independently with the BEPZA chairman and explicitly stated that his country did not want trade unions in those areas at that time. The pressure became so intense that Bangladesh made an announcement in June 2000 that trade unions would not be allowed in its EPZs. Instead, the government endorsed a proposal to create neutral labor relations tribunals for each zone as well as workers' welfare panels (WWPs) composed of representatives from the BEPZA, larger government, and individual employees—changes that were not opposed by Japan, South Korea, or Hong Kong.

Hoping to diffuse a potential backlash from the United States, the BEPZA retained a lobbyist to sell this concept stateside. In an attempt to bolster their government's bargaining position, the Bangladesh Garment Manufacturers' and Exporters' Association offered to have the work force in each of its locations vote on the introduction of WWPs. The Authority's services would be enlisted to assist workers to select representatives in places where a majority of voters favored their establishment. A three to five year moratorium on this issue would be imposed wherever employee support fell short. The Prime Minister's official visit to Washington, DC, provided another opportunity to make a case for the initiative later that fall.

Unmoved, the United States continued its push for compliance with the original agreement, spurred by yet another petition from the labor movement. An updated country-practice review was completed in late October, prompting the USTR to recommend that the President alter the country's GSP status. Negotiations continued behind the scenes for several months, resulting in a three-year extension one day before GSP eligibility was set to end. For its part, Bangladesh officially announced that freedom of association would be permitted in EPZs and published a timeline specifying how full-fledged organizing and bargaining rights would be phased in by January 1, 2004. Workers' committees were recognized to be an interim step in this transition.

Not willing to surrender without a fight, investors pushed back. Dire predictions were released forecasting precipitous declines in sales, and public statements lamented how nearly a billion dollars of FDI might be in jeopardy due to the "premature introduction" of trade unions in EPZs. A group of investors even filed suit and convinced a Bangladesh court to stay implementation of the memorandum of understanding with the United States. Recognizing the need to extricate itself from a seemingly no-win situation, the government brought all of the interested parties together in December 2003 for a meeting. In attendance were several high-ranking local officials, the U.S., Japanese, and South Korean ambassadors, the World Bank's country director, and a representative from the AFL-CIO Solidarity Center. While the United States agreed to extend the deadline for compliance beyond January 1 to accommodate yet another round of negotiations, the multilateral group failed to make much headway. In response, the United States specified that May 12 would be the deadline for action if GSP participation was still desired.

On May 11, Bangladesh announced that a new trade union Bill would be finalized for EPZs in a matter of days and implemented within the next 12 months. The Bill, which emulated key provisions of US labor law, was passed by Parliament two months later, authorizing workers' committees in the zones until October 31, 2006, and trade unions thereafter. The USTR terminated its ongoing review in light of these developments.

Sources: Clay (2001), Independent (2000a, b, c, d), Kahn (2003), Siddiqui (2001), Union Network International (2004), United States Trade Representative (2005: 239), Xinhua News Agency (2000a, b, 2004)

On the domestic front, there are numerous ways that senior administration officials can initiate contact with legislative bodies. Recall from Chapter 2 that adopted ILO conventions must be submitted to the competent national authority (i.e., legislature or parliament) of member states within 18 months, along with a recommended course of action on ratification. It is the executive branch that carries out this responsibility. Similar dynamics can be seen in the trade arena. The fast-track authority that President George W. Bush wielded to negotiate DR-CAFTA was linked to notification and consultation requirements. Under the Trade Promotion Act of 2002, Congress must receive at least 90 days' notice of impending trade negotiations and be approached after their conclusion for mandatory consultation. Only then can the President move forward to sign an agreement. Turning the tables somewhat, the U.S. constitution vests the President with veto power over all Bills (which can be overridden only by a supramajority vote in Congress). This is not universally true, though. In France's parliamentary system, for example, the President lacks this power but can request that objectionable legislation be reconsidered—having the authority to dissolve Parliament and call for new elections. Finally, there are the recurring informal efforts to get supportive members of the legislature to collaborate on new legislation that advances the administration's policy objectives.

Links with the judiciary are more infrequent. The executive branch may have a hand in staffing key components of the national court system. To illustrate, the U.S. President nominates individuals for federal judgeships who in turn must secure Senate approval to ascend to the Bench. In many countries, the highest court can be approached by other parts of the government for advisory opinions on pending domestic legislation or general policy matters. Germany, Canada, and Hungary are a sampling of nations that specifically allow for this activity. The practice is far from universal, though. Australia and the United States are counterexamples where a conscious decision has been made to avoid such behaviors. U.S. aversion to abstract judicial review (i.e., lacking a party that has experienced or will experience a specific injury from the matter) dates back to the early 1790s, when the first chief justice declined President Washington's request for advice on international law and the position the country should take in the ongoing war between France and Great Britain. While some would argue that the court did not mean to foreclose this *ad infinitum* (e.g., Jay 1997), the principle has stuck. Modern justifications for it include the need to promote the finality of judicial decisions, respect for separation of powers in government, and the benefits of deciding cases and controversies only where adversaries have the incentive to fully develop plausible ways of resolving the dispute.

There are two avenues by which persons affiliated with this branch create new law. Heads of state invariably will have the authority to issue legal instruments that are binding on the public sector and perhaps even society at large. One sees the latter in Greece's Presidential Decree on Fixed-Term Contracts (81/2003), which implemented an EU directive on the subject. While that decree automatically took effect once it was published in an official government source, additional requirements may be imposed. Many countries (e.g., India) make such decrees contingent on parliamentary approval, for instance. American presidents have used executive orders to establish standards and processes for collective bargaining and EEO for decades, with more than 100 directed at private-sector firms since the early 1940s (LeRoy 1996). However, their reach is limited to vendors that transact business with federal departments and agencies, being derived from broad powers the President has been given over federal procurement.

New law also can emanate from administrative rule making by departments, commissions, and other branch subunits. Often referred to as delegated legislation in common law systems, the legislative branch passes a "primary" statute that (1) articulates broad principles of public policy that are being codified, and (2) empowers an existing or new regulatory agency to fashion supplemental regulations that will flesh out more specific expectations and requirements for HRM/IR practices. The United States makes a distinction between two kinds of activities in this vein, with corresponding variation in the procedural demands that agency decision makers are saddled with. *Informal rule making* produces standards and policies that will be applied generally to all persons and entities within the scope of the overarching statute. Under the Administrative Procedures Act, federal agencies are obligated to provide notice whenever they are contemplating new rules and afford interested parties timely, structured opportunities to supply feedback and recommendations. The final rule(s) must be published with a concise general statement of the basis and purpose as well. "Circulars" could be considered a UK variant on informal rule making. These documents are shared with other units of government, detailing administrative procedures, stating regulatory policies, and interpreting new legislation. *Formal rule making*, in contrast, is enforcement oriented. Here, administrative law judges adjudicate the rights of individual parties under a given statutory scheme, rendering decisions that may be reviewed by the courts.

These legal concepts also can be found in civil law systems. For example, France recognizes the executive branch's right to unilaterally implement normative Acts (*pouvoir réglementaire*), as well as the delegated power to execute Acts that are constitutionally vested with the legislature (*pouvoir réglementaire subordonné*). Further distinctions are made between circulars that interpret existing law (*circulaires interprétatives*) and those that create law (*circulaires réglementaires*).

Treaty negotiations offer the executive branch a potent means of reshaping labor and employment law for the set of participating countries involved. International social security agreements are a common example of this, coordinating how social security rights and entitlements will be handled for posted workers. See Table 4.1. These agreements can greatly simplify benefits planning and administration for work performed in the affected locations. Coping with parallel bureaucratic infrastructures and double taxation are facts of life for IHRM staff supporting expatriates in nonsignatory countries. Friendship, Commerce, and Navigation (FCN) treaties can have relevance for MNE staffing policies. On one hand, equality of treatment is generally pledged between the indigenous individuals and the resident expatriated nationals of the other signatory country. Juxtaposed in many FCN accords is the right of foreign MNEs to choose persons for sensitive positions in their host branch offices without regard to domestic employment laws (e.g., equal employment opportunity). Finally, there are bilateral trade agreements that are linked to labor rights reform. The United States has been the most active in this regard, conditioning trade benefits under the agreement on the promotion of, and adherence to, internationally recognized labor rights (e.g., agreements with Cambodia, Vietnam, Jordan, Chile, Singapore). As discussed in earlier chapters, ratification and enabling legislation may be needed to give full effect to the negotiated instruments.

Law enforcement activities of the executive branch manifest in several ways. As mentioned earlier, agency personnel may be the initial decision makers in a dispute over the extent of compliance with particular regulations. Many countries have labor inspectorates to monitor compliance with diverse labor and employment laws. There also is the prospect that a dedicated justice ministry will engage in prosecutorial actions to secure adherence to the statutory requirements of legal codes. In all likelihood, litigation will be preceded by negotiations to settle the conflict. To illustrate, the U.S. Equal Employment Opportunity Commission will enter into conciliation negotiations first upon making a determination that infractions have occurred—the ultimate goal being a signed, enforceable consent decree. Only when this effort fails will the agency decide whether to file a lawsuit to stop the practice and secure appropriate remedies. Participative interactions that dispense advice on ways to voluntarily achieve compliance are another form of enforcement action.

Legal Systems in Action 4.2 highlights some of the added complexities that arise when nations try to prosecute illegal work behaviors that occur in MNEs. As this high-profile case demonstrates, having the unilateral will to pursue enforcement is not sufficient to bring about justice. Cooperation from other sovereignties may be required that is not necessarily forthcoming.

While developed economies certainly are not above reproach when it comes to enforcing labor and employment laws, pervasive enforcement lapses seem endemic to emerging markets. For example, the Chinese government allegedly waives restrictions on work hours for extended periods so that firms can consistently meet orders from Western suppliers (Blecher 2004: 482). Vietnamese authorities reportedly relaxed enforcement efforts on a broad scale to pacify MNEs in the textile and apparel sector (Manyin *et al.* 2001: 10). Willful neglect or intentional nonfeasance is the root cause in both instances.

Inadequate institutional capacity is the problem in other settings. The ILO has documented repeatedly that the labor inspectorates of most SADC countries are resource starved and staffed with personnel who often lack appropriate training (Kalula 2004: 9–10). These findings echo what has been reported for many Asian nations. Less than 200 inspectors are responsible for monitoring the compliance of 80,000 enterprises in the Philippines (Serrano *et al.* 2004: 69). The same source reports that each labor inspector in Thailand is responsible for more than 1,000 establishments on average. Many Central American governments have struggled to find the financial and human resources needed to conduct competent inspections, provide effective conciliation and mediation services, and properly administer labor courts (Working Group of the Vice Ministers Responsible for Trade and Labor 2005: 21, 37, 45, 55, 61–62).

Table 4.1 International social security agreements,[a] select countries

Region	Country	In effect				Signed but not in effect	Ongoing negotiation
		Europe	Asia and Oceania	Middle East and Africa	Americas		
North America	United States	Austria, Belgium, Finland, France, Germany, Greece, Ireland, Italy, Luxembourg, Netherlands, Norway, Portugal, Spain, Sweden, Switzerland, UK	Australia, South Korea	–	Canada, Chile, Quebec	Japan, Mexico	Argentina, Brazil, Croatia, Denmark, India, Israel, New Zealand
	Canada	Belgium, Croatia, Cyprus, Czech Republic, Denmark, Finland, France, Germany, Greece, Hungary, Iceland, Ireland, Italy, Luxembourg, Netherlands, Norway, Portugal, Slovakia, Slovenia, Spain, Sweden, Switzerland, UK	Australia, South Korea, New Zealand, Philippines	Israel[b]	Chile, Jamaica, Mexico, US	Morocco, Turkey	Estonia, Latvia, Lithuania
	Mexico	Spain	–	–	Canada	US	Netherlands, Uruguay
Europe	United Kingdom	All EU members, Bosnia and Herzegovina, Croatia, Iceland, Macedonia, Norway, Serbia and Montenegro, Switzerland	Japan, New Zealand, Norway, Philippines, South Korea	Israel, Mauritius, Turkey	Bermuda, Canada, Jamaica, US	–	–
	Ireland	All EU members, Iceland, Norway, Switzerland	Australia, New Zealand	Turkey	Canada, Québec, US	–	South Korea
	Germany	All EU members, Bosnia and Herzegovina, Bulgaria, Croatia, Iceland, Macedonia, Norway, Serbia and Montenegro, Switzerland	Australia, China,[b] Japan, South Korea	Israel, Morocco, Tunisia, Turkey	Canada, Chile, Quebec, US	–	Romania, Russia, Ukraine, Uruguay

France	All EU members, Bosnia and Herzegovina, Croatia, Iceland, Macedonia, Norway, Romania, Serbia and Montenegro, Switzerland	Philippines	Algeria, Cameroon, Israel, Morocco, Niger, Tunisia, Turkey	Canada, Chile, Quebec, US	South Korea	Argentina, Brazil, Japan
Italy	All EU members, Bosnia and Herzegovina, Croatia, Iceland, Macedonia, Norway, Switzerland	Australia	Libya, Tunisia, Turkey	Argentina, Brazil, Canada, Quebec, US, Uruguay, Venezuela	Chile, New Zealand, Philippines, South Korea	–
Sweden	All EU members, Albania, Croatia, Iceland, Norway, Serbia and Montenegro, Switzerland	Australia	Algeria,[b] Israel, Morocco, Turkey	Canada, Chile, Quebec, US	–	New Zealand, Philippines
Spain	All EU members, Bulgaria, Iceland, Norway, Russia, Switzerland, Ukraine	Australia, Philippines	Morocco, Tunisia, Turkey	Argentina, Brazil, Canada, Chile, Ecuador, Mexico, Paraguay, Peru, US, Uruguay, Venezuela	Dominican Republic	Israel, Romania
Portugal	All EU members, Iceland, Norway, Switzerland	Australia	Morocco, Mozambique, Turkey	Argentina, Brazil, Canada, Chile, Quebec, US, Uruguay, Venezuela	Ukraine	Angola, Bulgaria, East Timor
Czech Republic	All EU members, Bosnia and Herzegovina, Bulgaria, Croatia, Iceland, Macedonia, Norway, Romania, Russia, Serbia and Montenegro, Switzerland, Ukraine	–	Israel	Canada, Chile, Quebec	Turkey	South Korea
Hungary	All EU members, Belarus, Bosnia and Herzegovina, Bulgaria, Croatia, Iceland, Macedonia, Moldova, Norway, Romania, Russia, Serbia and Montenegro, Switzerland, Ukraine	Azerbaijan, Kazakhstan, Kyrgyzstan, Tajikistan, Turkmenistan, Uzbekistan	–	Canada	Quebec	Israel, Turkey, Uruguay

continued

Table 4.1 continued

Region		In effect				Signed but not in effect	Ongoing negotiation
		Europe	Asia and Oceania	Middle East and Africa	Americas		
Europe continued	Poland	All EU members, Albania, Belarus, Bosnia and Herzegovina, Bulgaria, Croatia, Iceland, Macedonia, Norway, Russia,[b] Serbia and Montenegro	China[b]	–	Tunisia	Switzerland	Ukraine
	Russia	Bulgaria, Czech Republic, Hungary, Lithuania, Moldova, Romania, Poland,[b] Slovakia, Spain, Ukraine	Georgia, Mongolia	–	–	Azerbaijan, Estonia, Kyrgyzstan	Germany, Latvia, Turkey
Asia and Oceania	Japan	Germany, UK	–	–	–	South Korea, US	Belgium, France
	Australia	Austria, Croatia, Cyprus, Denmark, Finland,[b] Germany, Ireland, Italy, Netherlands, Portugal, Slovenia, Spain, Sweden[b]	New Zealand	–	Canada, Chile, US	Belgium	Finland, Greece, Norway, Switzerland, Turkey, Uruguay
	New Zealand	Denmark, Greece, Ireland, Netherlands, UK	Australia	–	Canada	Italy	Cyprus, Sweden, US, Uruguay
	South Korea	Germany, Netherlands, UK	China	–	Canada, US	Belgium, France, Italy, Japan	Czech Republic, Denmark, Ireland, Switzerland
	China	Germany,[c] Poland[b]	South Korea	–	–	–	–
	Philippines	Austria, France, Spain, Switzerland, UK	–	–	Canada, Quebec	Belgium, Italy, Netherlands	Sweden

Region	Country					
Middle East and Africa	Turkey	Albania, Austria, Belgium, Cyprus, Denmark, Estonia, France, Germany, Greece, Ireland, Italy, Latvia, Lithuania, Luxembourg, Macedonia, Netherlands, Norway, Portugal, Romania, Spain, Sweden, Switzerland, UK	Libya	—	Azerbaijan, Bosnia and Herzegovina, Canada, Croatia, Czech Republic, Georgia, Quebec	Australia, Bulgaria, Hungary, Russia, Ukraine
	Israel	Austria, Belgium, Czech Republic, Denmark, Finland, France, Germany, Netherlands, Sweden, Switzerland, UK	—	Canada,[b] Uruguay	—	Chile, Hungary, Norway, Spain, US
South America	Brazil	Greece, Italy, Luxembourg, Portugal, Spain	—	Argentina, Chile, Uruguay	Angola, Paraguay	France, Netherlands, Ukraine, US
	Argentina	Greece, Italy, Portugal, Spain	—	Brazil, Chile, Uruguay	Netherlands, Paraguay, Peru	France, Slovenia, Switzerland, Ukraine, US
	Chile	Belgium, Czech Republic, Denmark, France, Germany, Luxembourg, Netherlands, Norway, Portugal, Spain, Sweden, Switzerland	Australia	Argentina, Brazil, Canada, Quebec, US, Uruguay	Colombia, Italy, Finland, Venezuela	Israel
	Peru	Romania, Spain	—	—	—	—
	Venezuela	Greece, Italy, Portugal, Spain	—	Uruguay	Chile	Bolivia, Colombia, Ecuador, Peru

Source: Mercer Human Resource Consulting (2004)

Notes:

a Malaysia, Singapore, Thailand, Taiwan, Pakistan, Egypt, and South Africa are not listed because they have no agreements pending or under negotiation. India does not appear either, although it should be noted that a bilateral agreement is being discussed with the United States.

b Medical benefits only.

c Only applies to employees sent abroad for a limited time period.

General Motors and Volkswagen litigate an executive defection on two continents

The executive juggernaut that was José Ignacio López de Arriortua appeared destined for greatness in GM's global empire during the early 1990s. Starting out as a low-level purchasing agent in Spain, Mr. López rose swiftly through the ranks to become vice-president of European supply within a decade. He was the head of global purchasing by 1993, with plans in place to elevate him to the company's second most powerful position, President of North American Operations. A press conference set up to announce the promotion did not turn out as planned, though. In a surprise appearance, GM's CEO made the startling revelation that Mr. López had quit unexpectedly to become Volkswagen's chief of purchasing and production. In the days that followed, it came to light that secret negotiations had been going on for months trying to finalize a deal that would cause the wunderkind to jump ship. Shock was replaced by anger when GM discovered that Mr. López had taken more than a handful of key associates along with him. Up to 20 boxes of confidential corporate documents were nowhere to be found.

GM's legal team sprang into action. Civil lawsuits were filed in Germany and the United States in quick succession asserting that trade secrets had been misappropriated, to the company's detriment. Two core allegations were raised—that Volkswagen's "new" purchasing strategy, as well as its plans for an innovative manufacturing facility, were based on confidential information stolen from GM. By initiating a parallel suit in the United States, the firm sought to preserve access to remedies that might be denied or unavailable in the German legal system. For example, there was no foreign counterpart to the American cause of action rooted in the Racketeer Influenced and Corrupt Organizations (RICO) Act, which held out the prospect of triple damages.

Lawyers representing VW countered with a motion to dismiss the U.S. lawsuit, arguing that the cases were virtually identical and that the present location of important evidence and witnesses made Germany the more appropriate forum. A federal judge disagreed, ruling that much of the alleged wrongdoing had occurred in Michigan, where the individual defendants had lived for a time, and that local law legitimately afforded the plaintiff different remedies and legal opportunities. The fight was on.

Developments on the public relations front only added fuel to the fire. GM repeatedly accused senior Volkswagen executives of assisting the conspiracy to commit industrial espionage. The German auto maker scoffed at such claims and leveled accusations that its rival was fabricating evidence. A story also was circulated alleging that GM was conspiring to attack Germany as an industrial location.

After four years of acrimonious exchanges, the two firms decided to settle the matter out of court in January 1997. Pursuant to the agreement, Volkswagen would pay GM $100 million in damages, purchase more than $1 billion in parts from GM suppliers over a designated interval, release several of the alleged co-conspirators, and refrain from using the services of Mr. López in an employment or consulting capacity until 2000. Memos also were exchanged between the respective boards conveying regrets for inflammatory rhetoric. Capital markets on both sides of the Atlantic reacted positively to the announcement.

Mr. López's legal troubles were not necessarily over, as ongoing criminal proceedings remained untouched by the deal. Less than a month earlier, German prosecutors had charged him with embezzlement and corporate spying following a three-year investigation. The indictment did not prove to have much staying power. All of the criminal charges were dropped in 1998 after López complied with an order to pay DM 400,000 to an unnamed charity. Undeterred, the U.S. Justice Department continued its pursuit of the Spanish national. In October 1999, a federal grand jury returned a six-count indictment against him. Charges in hand, American officials submitted a formal request to Spain for López's extradition. The Spanish high court eventually turned down the extradition request, holding that the underlying charges did not amount to serious offenses in that country.

Mr. López is not expected to be seen in the United States anytime soon.

Sources: El Mundo (2001), Facts on File World News Digest (1996), Kerwin (1996), Marcus (1996), Münchau and Althaus (1997), Schmid (1998), Smith (1997), U.S. Justice Department (2000)

What is being done to redress these shortcomings? Technical assistance and capacity-building initiatives are becoming increasingly common interventions. To illustrate, the United States Trade and Development Agency approved a $500,000 grant in 2000 to study the feasibility of automating Vietnam's social security agency (Manyin *et al.* 2001: 9). These funds were add-ons to the $3 million in technical assistance that had been pledged in a memorandum of understanding between the two countries' labor ministries. In like fashion, El Salvador completed a reorganization assessment of its labor ministry with ILO assistance. A series of recommendations was generated advocating significant organizational restructuring, the rationalization of services, and reformulation of the existing personnel system (Working Group of the Vice Ministers Responsible for Trade and Labor 2005: 37). Related self-help measures include:

- combating uneven enforcement by centralizing authority over labor inspections and labor mediation—Indonesia;
- substantially increasing the labor ministry's budget for compliance management—Costa Rica;
- transitioning labor inspectors from being political appointees to career civil service positions—Guatemala;
- instituting comprehensive training programs for labor inspectors under the auspices of the judiciary—Dominican Republic (Sijabat 2004a; Working Group of the Vice Ministers Responsible for Trade and Labor 2005: xi–xiii).

As customers and investors become more focused on corporate social responsibility, there is a growing need to develop a framework that systematically compares national capabilities and tendencies in labor and employment law enforcement. Verité (2003) presents an interesting starting point to work from. Commissioned to evaluate country-level compliance on international labor standards, this NGO rated 27 emerging markets in a report that was issued to the California Public Employees Retirement System (CalPERS) to guide investment decisions. "Institutional capacity," one of five dimensions utilized to determine the overall rankings, had a weight of 15 percent. This construct, in turn, was composed of two subscales: government capacity (80 percent) and NGO freedom (20 percent). Government capacity was defined by such things as the breadth of administrative coverage of enforcement departments, adequacy of personnel and budgets, frequency and adequacy of inspections and penalties levied for infractions, and extent of departmental corruption. Diverse qualitative and quantitative data were combined to derive ratings. More research is needed to expand and refine this kind of approach.

Discussion now turns to the legislative branch and how it contributes to the dynamics of national legal systems.

Legislatures and parliaments

Controlling the ultimate fate of nominees to the bench and key ministry positions is only one way that this branch influences the behaviors and performance of its executive counterpart. Legislative oversight of policy implementation and administration plays an even more critical role in effective government by advancing the cause of effective checks and balances. There are numerous justifications for legislators to assume this role, including (1) ensuring administrative compliance with legislative intent, (2) preventing executive encroachment on legislative authority and prerogatives, (3) detecting and preventing poor administration or illegal conduct, (4) improving the efficacy, economy, and effectiveness of governmental operations, and (5) gathering information to formulate new legislative proposals or revise existing statutes (Kaiser 2001). How frequently this activity is engaged in, and what form it takes, vary across countries.[3] Many possible forms have been implemented, such as committee and plenary-session hearings (e.g., appropriations), evaluative studies, interpellations, ombudsmen, and special prosecutors.

Pelizzo and Stapenhurst (2004) utilize World Bank data to investigate the extent to which the form of constitutional government, national income, and democracy levels for a sample of 82 countries impacts the construct "oversight potential." Oversight tools were classified along two dimensions. The first deals with the timing of the activity. Some are implemented before the executive branch enacts a policy or engages in a specific activity (instruments of control *ex ante*); others are performed after either has occurred (instruments of control *ex post*). A second dimension captures whether the activities are conducted by the legislature itself or an external source. Several important findings were reported. To begin with, oversight was universally practiced, with multiple forms in place in most instances. Legislative bodies in parliamentary systems of government tended to have more oversight tools at their disposal than did their counterparts in presidential or semi-presidential (i.e., president and prime minister have considerable influence and involvement in the day-to-day operations of government) systems. Preference patterns for oversight mechanisms also varied with national *per capita* income and prevailing levels of democracy.

Unfortunately, there is a paucity of research on the oversight mechanisms that different countries utilize in the area of labor market regulation. Jensen's (2004) study of the oversight practices used for labor inspectorates in EU member states is an exception. "Police patrol" mechanisms (e.g., mandatory activity reports, performance-based pay, inspections of local offices) were more likely to be deployed in countries that had low levels of ideological division within the government. While effective in ferreting out bureaucratic misconduct in the abstract, this approach is best suited for settings where strong opposing factions are not present to engage in obstructionist behaviors. Reinforcement for this notion was found in the fact that police patrol oversight was highest in Spain, Greece, and Sweden, while being nonexistent in Denmark, Finland, and the Netherlands. Judicial oversight mechanisms were more likely to be observed in countries that have strong, enduring ideological divisions in the ruling polity. These techniques operate as a dual-edged sword, though. They clearly allow legislators to distance themselves from the social and political costs of oversight—transferring a good deal of it to the judiciary—but open themselves up to judicial actors expanding their own oversight powers somewhat unchecked. This phenomenon is illustrated by the extensive oversight role that Italian, German, and Finnish courts have embraced.

Legislative bodies also pass statutory instruments to directly modify policies formulated by the other two branches. After congressional allies twice failed to secure labor law amendments that would have outlawed the permanent replacement of strikers, President Clinton decided to take matters into his own hands. In March 1995, executive order No. 12954 was issued, barring firms from engaging in this practice if they were working on federal contracts that exceeded $100,000. Republicans were outraged, claiming the chief executive was usurping power over labor law that the constitution had reserved exclusively for Congress. Moreover, they cited a report which projected that the measure could cost the US economy from $520 million to $2 billion each year (Ponessa 1995). In response, Bills were drafted and circulated in the House of Representatives and Senate to legislatively override it. Although neither was passed into law, the actions of their sponsors demonstrate how statutes can be crafted to neutralize objectionable policy positions.

A successful example of this practice comes from the discrimination area. Here, Congress was intent on overturning a curious ruling of the US Supreme Court regarding the selective exclusion of pregnancy-related costs from employees' health insurance coverage. Female employees asserted that this benefits policy was a prohibited form of sex discrimination, particularly since medical expenditures incurred treating the male reproductive system were reimbursed under the plan. The Supreme Court disagreed that the policy violated the underlying EEO statute. In its view, gender had nothing to do with the situation at all. This was an instance of differential treatment between two groups: pregnant persons and nonpregnant persons. Since women were represented in both categories, this situation was beyond the bounds of what law makers had intended to guard against. Congress disagreed and passed the Pregnancy Disability Act shortly thereafter, amending the statutory language to explicitly ban the denial of equal opportunity in the workplace for reasons related to pregnancy.

Much of the labor and employment law handiwork of legislative bodies is featured in Chapter 5 and Appendix B, where domestic markets are the focus of regulation. Accordingly, we will limit discussion here to legislative initiatives that have international repercussions.

The WTO/GATT framework contains an "enabling clause" that allows developed economies to provide more favorable tariff treatment to developing nations to spur growth. Many AIEs have done so though a legislative vehicle described as the Generalized System of Preferences (GSP). While Japan, Canada, and Australia have not linked GSP benefits to labor rights, the United States and European Union have. The mechanisms that are used to advance labor rights are different, though, as detailed in Box 4.1. The American approach is punitive in nature, while the European Union has adopted more of an incentive-oriented approach.[4] The GSP–labor rights linkage in the United States came about as a result of a 1984 amendment that required countries to meet a new labor standard to retain eligibility. Full compliance with internationally recognized labor standards is not a minimum threshold to qualify. However, it must be shown that meaningful steps are being taken to pursue them. The statute allows all interested parties to petition the U.S. Trade Representative to initiate public reviews of whether nations with GSP status are complying with this mandate. A formal determination by the USTR that they are not could lead to suspension or termination of these trade benefits. Compa and Vogt (2001) summarize the U.S. experience with this and similar legislative schemes—a glimpse of which we saw in Legal Systems in Action 4.1.

Box 4.1 Linking labor policies to GSP eligibility: U.S. and EU approaches

United States

Trade Act of 1974, as amended (Title V)

SEC. 502 Designation of Beneficiary Countries

. . .

(b) Countries Ineligible for Designation.—

. . .

(2) Other bases for ineligibility.—The President shall not designate any country a beneficiary developing country under this title if any of the following applies:

. . .

(G) Such country has not taken or is not taking steps to afford internationally recognized worker rights to workers in the country (including any designated zone in that country). Subparagraph . . . (G) shall not prevent the designation of any country as a beneficiary developing country under this title if the President determines that such designation will be in the national economic interest of the United States and reports such determination to the Congress with the reasons therefore.

(c) Factors Affecting Country Designation.—In determining whether to designate any country as a beneficiary developing country under this title, the President shall take into account—

. . .

(7) whether or not such country has taken or is taking steps to afford to workers in that country (including any designated zone in that country) internationally recognized worker rights.

. . .

SEC. 504 Review and Report to Congress

The President shall submit an annual report to the Congress on the status of internationally recognized worker rights within each beneficiary developing country.

. . .

SEC. 507 Definitions

For purposes of this title:

   . . .

   (4) Internationally recognized worker rights.—The term "internationally recognized worker rights" includes—

   (A) the right of association;
   (B) the right to organize and bargain collectively;
   (C) a prohibition on the use of forced or compulsory labor;
   (D) a minimum age for the employment of children; and
   (E) acceptable conditions of work with respect to minimum wages, hours of work, and occupational safety and health.

. . .

European Union

Council Regulation (EC) No. 2501/2001 of 10 December 2001 applying a scheme of generalized tariff preferences for the period 1 January 2002 to 31 December 2004

. . .

Title III Special Incentive Arrangements

Section 1 Special incentive arrangements for the protection of labor rights

ARTICLE *14*

1 The tariff preferences referred to in Article 8(1) shall apply to products originating in a country which according to Annex I benefits from the special incentive arrangements for the protection of labor rights, or which has subsequently been granted those arrangements by a decision taken in accordance with Article 19, for the sector concerned, . . .

2 The special incentive arrangements for the protection of labor rights may be granted to a country the national legislation of which incorporates the substance of the standards laid down in ILO Conventions No. 29 and No. 105 on forced labor, No. 87 and 98 on the freedom of association and the right to collective bargaining, No. 100 and No. 111 on non-discrimination in respect of employment and occupation, and No. 138 and No. 182 on child labor and which effectively applies the legislation.

continued

ARTICLE 15

1 The special incentive arrangements for the protection of labor rights shall be granted provided that:

   – they are requested by a country or territory listed in Annex I,
   – examination of the request shows that the requesting country fulfills the condition laid down in Article 14(2),
   – the requesting country has given an undertaking to monitor the application of the special incentive arrangements and to provide the necessary administrative cooperation,
   – the requesting country has given the agreement referred to in Article 17.

2 The requesting country shall submit its request to the Commission in writing and shall provide comprehensive information concerning:

   – the national legislation referred to in Article 14(2), the measures taken to implement it and to monitor its application,
   – any sectors in which that legislation is not applied.

3 The full official text of the legislation referred to in Article 14(2) and the implementing measures shall be attached to the request.
4 Where the legislation referred to in Article 14(2) is not applied in certain sectors, a country may request the special incentive arrangement only for those sectors in which it is applied.
   . . .

ARTICLE 17

During the examination of the request, the Commission shall determine, in agreement with the requesting country,

(a) the authorities of that country that will be in charge of the administrative cooperation,

. . .

Sources: United States Trade Representative (1999), Official Journal of the European Communities (2001)

"Domestic" labor and employment legislation also can have international dimensions when the laws have extraterritorial application (i.e., extend the full set of rights and entitlements to PCNs while they are working abroad). Most U.S. EEO laws explicitly provide for this contingency: amendments that were made to comply with holdings by the courts that such an extension of coverage would not be read into statutes by the judiciary. The geographic reach of Japanese labor and employment law is less settled, although some legal scholars have suggested that extraterritoriality applies only to international business travelers whose ordinary place of work is Japan (Yamakawa 1996). Pertinent sections of the civil code and Labor Standards Law lack provisions that would signal there was legislative intent for more widespread application. Turning to the European Union, there are some directives that have extraterritorial application to non-EU countries (e.g., data privacy). In this instance, practices occurring outside the region will be treated as though they were performed within the European Union when compliance determinations are made involving European-based business units. Crutchfield George *et al.* (2001) discuss the ramifications that the directive's "safe harbor" principles have for U.S.-based multinational firms.

Whether legislative bodies will exempt export processing zones (EPZs) from regular labor-market legislation has international overtones as well. The quest for FDI has led many emerging markets to characterize their EPZs as having "flexible labor laws" (e.g., Pakistan, Iran). The root question is whether they are willing to engage in "labor derogation" to secure it. Legal Systems in Action 4.1 discussed the stance that Bangladesh has taken on this issue. Table 4.2 summarizes the extent to which there is selective application and enforcement of national labor laws in key targets of inward investment around the world. With a few exceptions, official regulations extend into these areas. This provides little comfort if, in fact, there is a general lack of enforcement. Most of the responsibility for that problem resides with the executive branch, not the legislature.

The last major component of national government that we encounter is the court system.

Judiciary

There are wide-ranging views on the appropriate role of judges in constitutional forms of government. Some would assert that members of the judiciary have an independent responsibility to ensure the legal system evolves with, and is responsive to, the times we live in. When there are gaps in law or policy that are not being properly redressed by the executive and legislative branches, the courts should step in to rectify the problem. This behavior is easier to perpetrate in nations where the legal superstructure is based in whole, or in part, on common law systems. Such judicial activism is much less likely to be successful in jurisdictions that are governed by some form of civil law system, for reasons we have discussed before. Others would argue that such conduct is indefensible for those serving on the bench. Instead of deciding new policy directions, judges are expected to ensure there is consistent, impartial administration of existing law. Their focus is to be on strengthening the rule of law by strictly construing such legal instruments as the constitution, statutes, regulations, etc. When interpretation is required, they are to discern the original intent of the legislators or administrators who devised the legal rule involved in the dispute, not substitute personal values or expectations of what the law should be to society and the individuals who comprise it. It is beyond the scope of this book to establish which perspective is the correct one for a given country, let alone the community of nations. We instead will briefly assess the decision-making dynamics of courts, especially where there are interfaces with other branches or foreign governments.

Figure 4.2 provides an initial window on to this discussion. Court systems appear to have a long way to go to be considered user-friendly and effective in resolving business

Table 4.2 Export processing zones and domestic labor law, select countries

Region	Country	Export processing zones[a]	Main sources of inward investment	National labor and employment laws applied to EPZs without modification?	Applicable labor laws are enforced with regularity
Americas and the Caribbean	Mexico	n.a. 1,081,553	US, Canada, France, South Korea, Taiwan, Germany, Hong Kong (China)	Yes	No
	Costa Rica	12 34,000[b]	US, South Korea, Mexico, Dominican Republic, Germany, Taiwan, Singapore, Hong Kong (China), Guatemala, Italy	Yes	No
	El Salvador	17 70,000	US, South Korea, Mexico, Dominican Republic, Germany, Taiwan, Singapore, Hong Kong (China), Guatemala, Italy	No (union organizing and strikes prohibited)	No
	Guatemala	20 69,200	n.a.	Yes	No
	Honduras	28 106,457	US, South Korea, Mexico, Dominican Republic, Germany, Taiwan, Singapore, Hong Kong (China), Guatemala, Italy	Yes	No
	Nicaragua	n.a. 40,000	Taiwan, US, South Korea, Nicaragua, Italy, Hong Kong (China), Honduras, Belize, Mexico	Yes	No
	Dominican Republic	53 181,130	US, South Korea	Yes	No
Asia	Bangladesh	6 138,341	China, US, UK, India, Japan, Belgium, Pakistan, South Korea	No (union organizing and strikes prohibited)	No
	China	15 30,000,000[b]	US, Germany, France, Switzerland, Netherlands, Canada	Yes	n.a.
	India	7 95,000	n.a.	No (longer notice period for strikes)	No

Malaysia	14 200,000	Japan, US, UK, Germany, Switzerland, Taiwan, South Korea, Italy, Netherlands, Finland	Yes	n.a.
Pakistan	22 410,540	US, UK, UAE, Germany, France, Hong Kong (China), Italy, Japan, Saudi Arabia, Canada, Netherlands, South Korea	No (union organizing and strikes prohibited)	n.a.
Philippines	34 820,000[b]	US, Japan, UK, Malaysia, Singapore	Yes	No
Sri Lanka	12 111,033	South Korea, Japan, Hong Kong (China), Singapore, UK	Yes	No
Vietnam	10 107,000	Japan, Taiwan, Hong Kong (China), Netherlands, Singapore, US, South Korea, UK, France, Philippines	Yes	No
Africa Kenya	6 27,148[b]	US, UK, Hong Kong (China), India, Sri Lanka	No (numerous labor-law exemptions granted)	n.a.
Namibia	11 29,000	Japan, Hong Kong (China), South Korea, Taiwan, Malaysia, Singapore	No (strikes prohibited, inspection exemptions)	No
Zimbabwe	7 22,000	n.a.	No (strikes prohibited, special employment terms)	n.a.
Mauritius	Entire island 83,609	South Africa, Singapore, India, France, Malaysia, Hong Kong (China)	Yes	Yes

Sources: Boyenge (2003), ICFTU (2003b)

Notes:

a Each cell displays the number of EPZs that have been created and total employment therein.

b Includes employment from other types of trade zones.

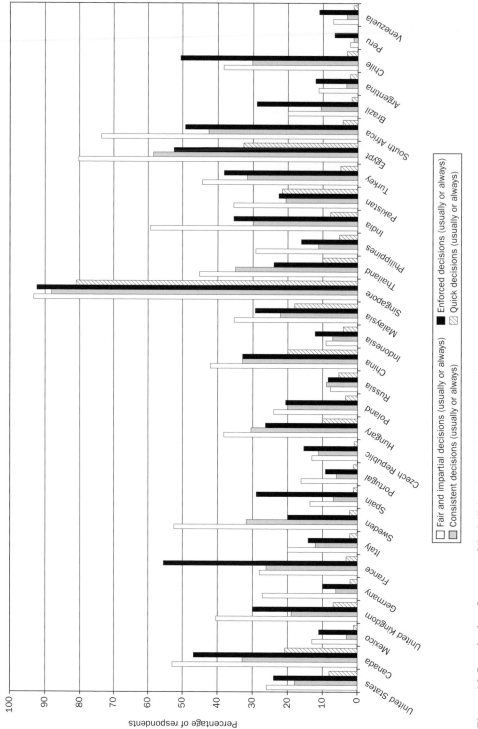

Figure 4.2 Perceived performance of the judiciary in resolving business disputes, select countries

disputes. In 28 of the 30 nations listed, less than one-quarter of respondents agreed that court cases were processed quickly. Discontent was less pervasive for decision consistency, as the number of countries recording like results dropped to 18. National court systems scored much better on fairness, impartiality, and enforcement of decisions, although it is the exception rather than the rule when a majority felt these attributes were usually or always present. Continental European and Latin American nations were least likely to hold favorable opinions of the judiciary on all of the dimensions mentioned.

The paths in Figure 4.1 going from the courts to the executive and legislative branches reflect potential judicial oversight of their actions. For example, the Czech Constitutional Court invalidated legislation that authorized the labor ministry to impose the terms of multi-employer collective bargaining agreements on nonsignatory firms (EIRO 2004a). It was the failure to limit extension to settings where the bargaining is representative and the case is exceptional that raised serious constitutional problems—not extension *per se*. A draft amendment responding to these concerns was prepared with consultation from the social partners and put before Parliament soon thereafter. Similarly, a U.S. federal appeals court unanimously overturned President Clinton's executive order restricting the use of replacement workers during strikes and the accompanying DOL regulations. The court essentially held that the President's discretionary powers over federal procurement did not provide a legal basis to override a well established right that employers had to use replacements under the federal labor laws. Judicial review could extend to administrative rule making in general to verify that the ministry or agency in question had not exceeded its statutory authority or ignored procedural requirements.

The rationale for linking the judiciary to law creation is obvious in common law systems. To illustrate, the obligation that U.S. labor unions have to impartially represent all members of the bargaining unit (i.e., duty of fair representation) has its genesis in American case law. Courts ultimately came to the conclusion that this implied duty was a necessary counterbalance to the power and control that unions acquired as exclusive bargaining agents under the National Labor Relations Act. But judicial law making occurs in civil law systems as well, albeit on a more limited scale. The opportunity for this to happen is greatest when labor law has undergone little codification, as in Germany (Schneider 2002). The phenomenon also can be witnessed in other settings. Japanese courts evolved the notion of "adjustment dismissals" to afford employers some flexibility in a regulatory environment that discourages employment terminations (Ouchi 2002). Pursuant to the doctrine, collective redundancies for economic reasons will not be considered illegal if a series of situational requirements are met.

Since enforcement is the fundamental purpose of judicial administration, we do not need to look for reasons why judges are involved in this aspect of law. A few comments are warranted about national case loads and court structure. As Figure 4.3 displays, there is considerable variation across countries in the propensity to litigate workplace conflicts. Brazil handles more than one million cases a year, and Germany is not far behind. At the other end of the spectrum are Japan and Thailand, which is not surprising given the longstanding characterization of Asian HR systems (outside of South Korea) as conciliatory and consensus oriented. Even there, EPL rates are increasing. The United States seems to have moderate activity in this area, despite having a reputation for being highly litigious. However, comprehensive time-series data were not available for instances where state courts made rulings on federal and state employment laws. Their

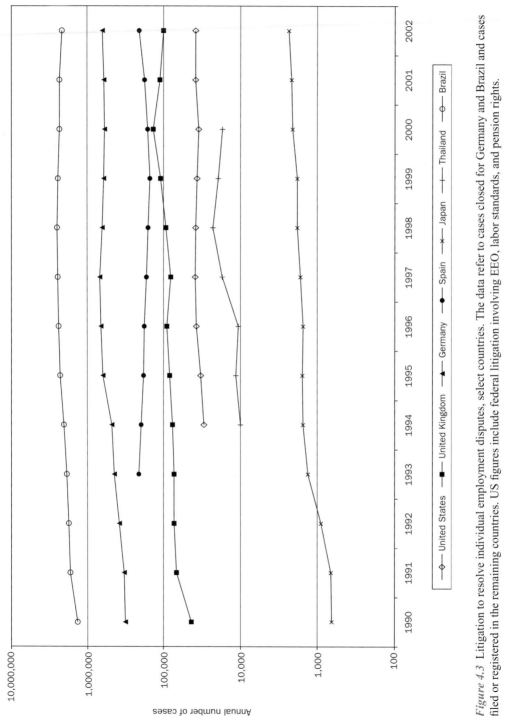

Figure 4.3 Litigation to resolve individual employment disputes, select countries. The data refer to cases closed for Germany and Brazil and cases filed or registered in the remaining countries. US figures include federal litigation involving EEO, labor standards, and pension rights.

Sources: Administrative Office of the United States Courts website (http://www.uscourts.gov/judbusucs/judbus.html); Brown *et al.* (2002); EIRO website (http://www.eiro.eurofound.ie/thematicfeature7.html); Filho (2001); Nakakubo (1996); Staff (2003b)

inclusion would place the United States on par with Brazil at a minimum in all likelihood. Litigation over industrial relations rights is not reported for any of the countries.

Different structures have been created to handle complaints about work illegalities. Most nations have specialized courts to handle such cases that go by many names (e.g., labor court, employment tribunal, industrial court, industrial relations court). They are the norm across Europe and Latin America, and common in the Middle East (e.g., Israel, Jordan), Africa (e.g., Kenya, Mauritania, Nigeria, Zambia), and Asia (e.g., Malaysia, Pakistan, Indonesia). In the United States and Canada, administrative agencies with adjudicatory powers can be viewed as pseudo-labor courts (e.g., National Labor Relations Board, provincial labor boards). More often than not, labor courts are staffed in a tripartite manner, comprising professionally qualified judges and appointees from the ranks of management and labor. India, Argentina, and Spain are examples of places where only professional judges sit. The labor "division" of the court system may have multiple levels that process appeals. Eventually, even these settings feed cases into the system of ordinary courts for high-level appeals. Some labor courts have jurisdiction over individual and collective disputes (e.g., Brazil, Mexico, Israel); others only over individual (e.g., Argentina, Mauritania) or collective ones (e.g., Sweden). Interested readers are directed to Aaron (1985) for a comprehensive review of labor courts worldwide. When labor courts are not the chosen model, ordinary courts adjudicate all or most employment-related disputes (e.g., the United States).

One of the more interesting legal phenomena in recent years has been the growing tendency of foreign workers to challenge MNEs in their home-country legal systems over actions that occurred overseas. Brief illustrations of this were contained in some of the short case profiles that appeared in Chapter 1. Legal Systems in Action 4.3 supplies an expanded context to see how these lawsuits play out.

Legal Systems in Action 4.3

The working conditions of foreign guest workers in Saipan are challenged in American courts

By the thousand they came from every corner of Asia, lured by the promise of "high-paying, quality jobs" on American soil. Young workers, mostly female, were paying recruiters hefty placement fees for the opportunity to travel to Saipan to work in its bustling garment industry. Special export privileges had been extended to this and other parts of the Northern Mariana Islands—a U.S. Commonwealth—attracting substantial investment from China and South Korea. Clothing made here could be shipped to the American mainland duty-free in quantities that were largely unrestricted. The lucrative nature of this arrangement was not lost on major retailers. What had grown into a $1 billion industry was feeding millions of dollars in merchandise to such high-profile firms as Target, Gap, Nordstrom, Tommy Hilfiger USA, and Abercrombie and Fitch.

Unfortunately, foreign guest workers were in for a rude awakening at their intended destination. Meager living quarters, hazardous working conditions, and low pay were the rule rather than the exception. More than a thousand citations had been issued over the years for safety infractions and the failure to pay overtime premiums. Moreover, the

continued

prevailing wage was roughly half of what it was anywhere else that the U.S. flag flew, the commonwealth government having been given the authority to set its own minimum rate in 1984. There even was talk of mandatory "shadow contracts" that prohibited employees from joining unions, practicing their religion, quitting, marrying, or becoming pregnant.

Disgruntled workers took the offensive in January 1999 by initiating two highly publicized federal lawsuits with the assistance of a law firm that had successfully represented Holocaust victims. The first suit was filed in Saipan against 22 locally based contractors claiming systematic violations of federal overtime and commonwealth labor laws. Defendants moved quickly to alter how the case would proceed through a series of motions. The first sought to strip away the anonymity that had been obscuring the parties behind the complaint. Fearing retaliation by their employers and government officials, hundreds of individuals had consented to join the lawsuit as "Doe" plaintiffs, and, as such, were not identifiable for cross-examination at trial, among other things. A second motion argued that the single, overarching suit should be broken up into separate proceedings against each contractor because the alleged abuses varied from firm to firm. The presiding judge had a sympathetic ear for both requests, ordering the heretofore nameless plaintiffs to disclose their identities (or drop out of the litigation) as well as case severance. Plaintiffs countered by taking the first part of the decision to the Ninth Circuit Court of Appeals, and won. They also filed an amended complaint with new causes of action, hoping to lock defendants into a single action.

A contemporaneous lawsuit in Los Angeles was undergoing its own procedural odyssey. More than two dozen U.S. retailers and Saipan-based businesses were accused of conspiring to use forced labor and abridge internationally accepted human rights in violation of federal law (e.g., Alien Tort Claims Act). Defendants' first point of attack was to seek a change of venue. The district judge denied the motion to transfer the action to the place of employment, citing major concerns about the ability to conduct a fair trial there. A determination was made to send the case to federal court in Hawaii instead, which precipitated an appeal to the Ninth Circuit Court. While the appeal was pending, defendants concentrated on the proceedings in Honolulu. A motion was filed seeking summary judgment against plaintiffs on all of their claims, and the continued use of the "Doe" pseudonyms was opposed.

The case was relocated yet again before these and other issues were formally resolved; this time to Saipan. The number of retailers and garment makers being pursued also had increased due to an amended complaint. With the pool of present and former victims now encompassing approximately 30,000 individuals, plaintiffs submitted a motion for class certification. What possible basis was there for granting this request? Plaintiffs argued that all of the harm inflicted was the result of a single, overarching conspiracy to manipulate and oppress the industry's work force, necessitating a common action against the perpetrators.

As these cases continued their trek in the federal system, a third was unfolding in state court. The final suit of this litigation trilogy had been brought by human rights and labor NGOs over alleged infractions of California's business code. In essence, the retailers were accused of engaging in unfair business practices by falsely advertising their garments as "sweatshop-free", facilitating the interstate shipment of "hot goods" (i.e., items produced in the presence of federal labor law violations), and aiding and abetting the practice of involuntary servitude on Saipan. Defendants' attempts to get the case dismissed as a matter of law and severed into company-specific proceedings were unsuccessful. Discovery was ordered under the supervision of a referee to allow plaintiffs to access data in the retailers' possession that were germane. Before discovery had run its course, defendants sought summary adjudication on the alleged misrepresentations because (1) there was no proof anyone had been harmed by them, and (2) they were statements protected by the First Amendment. Plaintiffs opposed both contentions, setting the stage for a hearing.

The evolving web of litigation was accompanied by concerted efforts—almost from the outset—to negotiate a settlement with interested defendants. Nordstrom and J. Crew Group were part of the first wave of companies to strike a deal, followed by Donna Karan International, May Department Stores, Polo Ralph Lauren, Sears Roebuck, and many others. In total, 19 firms agreed to a set of measures designed to compensate class members that had been wronged and to discourage future violations. A mandatory code of conduct for supplier contracts was at the heart of this framework, along with provisions for rigorous on-site monitoring by an independent human rights organization. Recruitment fees in excess of reasonable travel costs, shadow contracts, and sweatshop conditions would not be tolerated any longer.

Before the parties were able to gain court approval, a coalition of nonparticipants led by Target, Gap, and J. C. Penney tried to block the arrangement. Their inability to do so, coupled with a second ruling permitting things to progress as a class action, dramatically raised the stakes for holdout firms. Not surprisingly, the number of firms coming to terms with plaintiffs rose to 27 retailers and 27 contractors in the months that followed. The settlement, which was the largest international human rights award to date at $20 million, was accepted by a federal judge in April 2003.

One retailer, Levi Strauss, continued to litigate the matter and steadfastly deny any wrongdoing. To justify its position, the company asserted that all of the suppliers it did business with until 2000 had complied with a code of conduct that was a benchmark for the industry. The case was dismissed by agreement in January 2004, plaintiffs deciding that further legal expenses would not materially enhance the overall gains that had been achieved. With this development, a five-year battle came to an end.

Sources: Bas *et al.* (2004), Shenon (1993), Strasburg (2004), Sweatshop Watch (2000, 2002a, b, c)

Countries normally develop choice-of-law principles to identify which nation's law will govern when the disputants in a case are from multiple countries. This is one of the elements underpinning the path in Figure 4.1 between court systems. In the Saipan workers' case, U.S. courts applied a domestic law that gave foreign individuals standing to sue for human rights abuses committed by home-country entities. Parent-country nationals working abroad as expatriates may still be covered by domestic law if there are extraterritoriality provisions. The matter is less straightforward when third-country nationals are expatriated. Most countries allow the parties to designate which law will control the employment contract. The judiciary often refers to the place of performance or seat of the enterprise if the issue is not addressed. This does not mean that other factors are irrelevant. The presence of common nationality, place of the contract, place from which pay or instructions originate, or the currency used as payment may affect the outcome of the case as well.[5]

Decisions regarding the recognition of foreign judgments in another legal system constitute a second component of the informal relationship between courts. Assume that Australian employees sue an Italian MNE in Italy to enforce a judgment that was rendered against it in Australia. Are the Italian courts obligated to give automatic effect to that ruling? Unless a bilateral treaty indicates otherwise, the answer would be no. The second judicial forum may voluntarily enforce that holding if it appears the judgment resulted from procedures which are compatible with domestic concepts of due process. Some nations still might withhold recognition if reciprocity does not exist in the country where the suit commenced.

Conclusion

National branches of government contribute in varied and synergistic ways to the evolution of labor and employment law. The executive branch facilitates law creation when the head of state issues decrees or orders that contain principles which are legally binding on private IR actors or the public sector. They also negotiate treaties that can have significant reform implications for local law. More influence is exerted through administrative rule making by subordinate units—a critical activity that fleshes out the full set of regulatory expectations that enacted legislation seeks to advance. Legislatures are likely to be the primary driver of new law, though, especially in civil law systems. The codes and statutes that they pass embody the general principles that government policy makers are trying to foster. The extent to which labor and employment laws have extraterritorial application and apply unmodified to export-oriented development zones are two controversial issues of the day. Legislative oversight is an important support activity in law creation because it not only makes sure that regulations remain true to the original legislative intent, but also produces information that can be used to develop new legislative initiatives. The judiciary's role in law creation will be heavily influenced by the type of legal system in place. Whether their presence is considerable (common law systems) or modest (civil law systems), case law and judicial review are the two modes judges can utilize to impact law creation.

Law enforcement is primarily in the hands of the executive and judicial branches. The former mobilizes and prioritizes the resources that will be dedicated to compliance monitoring, statistical reporting, and perhaps initial adjudication. Whether enforcement shortfalls are the product of willful misconduct or lack of institutional capacity will vary across countries and issues. Court systems administer the main forum for societal members to vindicate their endowed rights. At times, they will be asked to decide whether justice is best served by the application of domestic or foreign law. Choice-of-law principles guide this determination in cases that are being decided on the merits. Other principles will be consulted to determine whether rulings from abroad are entitled to deference and enforcement in this setting. The legislature indirectly impacts enforcement through legislative oversight and control over the appointment of nominees to the bench and key administrative positions.

The next chapter examines the role of the state in industrial relations, taking into account the rich body of substantive and procedural regulation that is superimposed on IR systems worldwide.

The state and industrial
5 relations in global perspective

One of the clearest indicators of a government's socioeconomic priorities is the regulatory stance that it takes toward industrial relations. For example, industrialization concerns have prompted several emerging markets to constrain labor rights in deliberate, methodical ways. Kuruvilla (1996) found evidence of this in the IR policies of Asian nations pursuing export-oriented development, particularly when labor-intensive manufactured goods were the perceived engine of national competitiveness. Suspending labor law protections in EPZs to attract foreign investment is another illustration of this mindset. The quest for macroeconomic stability instead may lead to formalized, corporatist structures that recognize trade unions as a critical policy-making stakeholder, if not co-equal partner in governance. Sweden, Mexico, Italy, and, to a lesser extent, Singapore have traveled this route, at least in the area of wages. There are other themes that the state may seek to advance, such as social justice or human rights. How these causes are and should be linked to freedom of association and collective bargaining rights has been a recurring topic of debate in legislative halls (e.g., GSP eligibility) and international bodies (e.g., social clauses in multilateral trade agreements, transnational social charters) alike.

But how does one gauge the practical significance and relative positioning of labor interests in a cross-border context? Such information would greatly enhance judgments about labor law efficacy. Table 5.1 highlights three core aspects of national IR systems that facilitate meaningful comparisons: labor-union presence; centralization of collective bargaining activity; and propensity for industrial conflict. Organized labor's potential grip on a given economy can be quantified in one of two ways. *Density* refers to the proportion of employed persons who are directly affiliated as members—a longstanding barometer of union strength in the industrial relations literature. As the table reveals, there was tremendous variability within and across regions on this measure in the mid to late 1990s. For example, Canadian and Mexican workers were approximately twice as likely as those in the United States to be formally aligned with the labor movement. Neither country's figures are impressive from a global perspective, though, constituting less than one-third of the national work force. A similar differential was evident in the handful of Middle Eastern and African countries profiled, albeit at uniformly higher levels. Disparities in organizing were even more dramatic in Europe, where density was more than eight times greater in Sweden (81.1 percent) than in France (9.7 percent). The rest of Europe lies somewhere in between, with most falling below 30 percent. Asia and Latin America also exhibited significant differences in membership rates. China's density

| Region | Country | Union presence | | Bargaining structure | | Work stoppages[d] | | |
		Density[a] (%)	Coverage[b] (%)	Dominant level[c] (trend)	Secondary level[c] (trend)	2000	2001	2002
North America	United States	12.8	14.0	Company/plant *Increasing*	National/sector *Decreasing*	39[e] (393,700) 20,419,400	29[e] (99,100) 1,151,300	19[e] (45,900) 659,600
	Canada	28.1	32.0	Company/plant *Increasing*	National/sector *Decreasing*	377 (143,570) 1,661,620	381 (220,499) 2,198,870	294 (167,945) 3,028,423
	Mexico	20.8	n.a.	Company/plant *Stable*	National/sector *Stable*	173[f] (69,635) 438,299	254[f] (37,001) 488,019	n.a.
Europe	United Kingdom	31.2	32.5	Company/plant *Increasing*	National/sector *Decreasing*	212 (183,200) 498,800	194 (179,900) 525,100	146 (942,900) 1,323,300
	Ireland	48.9	90.0	Company/plant *Stable*	National/sector *Increasing*	39[g] (28,192) 97,046	26[g] (32,168) 114,613	27[g] (3,553) 21,257
	Germany	25.0	68.0	National/sector *Stable*	Company/plant *Increasing*	n.a. (7,428) 10,776	n.a. (60,948) 26,833	n.a. (428,283) 310,149
	France	9.7	92.5	National/sector *Stable*	Company/plant *Increasing*	2,775 (21,094) 809,860	2131 (11,884) 691,914	n.a.
	Italy	34.9	82.5	National/sector *Stable*	Company/plant *Increasing*	966 (687,000) 884,100	746 (1,125,000) 1,026,000	616 (5,442,000) 4,861,000
	Sweden	81.1	92.5	National/sector *Stable*	Company/plant *Increasing*	2 (163) 272	20 (9,831) 11,098	10 (711) 838
	Spain	14.9	82.5	National/sector *Increasing*	Company/plant *Increasing*	750 (2,067,287) 3,616,907	737 (1,244,634) 1,923,758	688 (4,534,274) 4,945,091
	Portugal	24.3	82.5	National/sector *Increasing*	Company/plant *Increasing*	250[f] (38,830) 40,454	208[f] (26,058) 41,570	250[f] (80,168) 108,062
	Czech Republic	27.0	27.5	Company/plant *Stable*	National/sector *Increasing*	n.a.	n.a.	n.a.
	Hungary	19.9	32.5	Company/plant *Increasing*	National/sector *Decreasing*	10[h] (40,111) 636,267	7[h] (23,135) 11,676	4[h] (4,573) 1,377

continued

Table 5.1 continued

Region	Country	Union presence		Bargaining structure		Work stoppages[d]		
		Density[a] (%)	Coverage[b] (%)	Dominant level[c] (trend)	Secondary level[c] (trend)	2000	2001	2002
Europe continued	Poland	14.7	42.5	Company/plant Increasing	National/sector Decreasing	44[h] (7,900) 74,300	11[h] (1,400) 33,400	1[h] (13) 118
	Russia	n.a.	n.a.	Company/plant Increasing	National/sector Decreasing	817 (31,000) 236,400	291 (13,000) 47,100	n.a.
Asia and Oceania	Japan	21.5	17.5	Company/plant Increasing	National/sector Stable	118 (15,322) 35,050	90 (12,172) 29,101	n.a.
	Australia	24.5	82.5	Company/plant Increasing	National/sector Decreasing	698[g] (325,400) 469,100	675[g] (225,700) 393,100	766[g] (159,700) 259,000
	New Zealand	22.7	27.5	Company/plant Increasing	National/sector Decreasing	21[g] (2,632) 11,495	42[g] (22,022) 54,440	46[g] (23,309) 34,398
	South Korea	11.4	12.5	Company/plant n.a.	National/sector n.a.	250 (177,969) 1,893,563	235 (88,548) 1,083,079	n.a.
	China	63.4	15.1	Company/plant Increasing	–	n.a.	n.a.	n.a.
	Indonesia	3.4	n.a.	Company/plant n.a	–	n.a.	n.a.	n.a.
	Malaysia	13.4	2.6	Company/plant	–	11[f] (2,969) 6,068	13[f] (2,209) 5,599	4[f] (506) 1,638
	Singapore	15.9	18.8	Company/plant Stable	National/sector Stable	0 0	0 0	0 0
	Thailand	4.2	26.7	Company/plant Increasing	–	13 (5,969) 225,788	5 (526) 6067	n.a.
	Philippines	38.2	3.7	Company/plant Increasing	–	60 (21,442) 319,233	43 (7,919) 206,493	36 (18,240) 358,152
	Taiwan	33.1	3.4	Company/plant n.a.	–	n.a.	n.a.	n.a.
	India	18.8	<2.0	National/sector Stable	Company/plant Increasing	771 (1,418,299) 28,763,121	674 (687,778) 23,766,809	554 (1,061,025) 26,457,437

Region	Country	Density (%)	Coverage (%)	Bargaining structure	Bargaining trend	Work stoppages		
	Pakistan	n.a.	n.a.	Company/plant	–	4 (225) / n.a.	4 (711) / n.a.	4 (516) / n.a.
Middle East and Africa	Turkey	33.7	n.a.	National/sector	–	52[f] (18,705) / 368,475	35[f] (9,911) / 286,015	n.a.
	Israel	23.0	n.a.	National/sector / n.a.	National/sector / n.a.	54[g] (297,882) / 2,011,263	62[g] (426,560) / 2,039,973	47[g] (1,647,810) / 1,488,120
	Egypt	38.8	n.a.	National/sector / Increasing	National/sector / Increasing	6 (1,482) / 1377	1 (n.a.) / n.a.	3 (1,760) / 2654
	South Africa	40.9	n.a.	Company/plant / Increasing	National/sector / Increasing	n.a.	n.a.	n.a.
South America	Brazil	43.5	n.a.	Company / Increasing	National/sector / Increasing	n.a.	n.a.	n.a.
	Argentina	38.7	72.9	Company/plant / Increasing	National/sector / Stable	613 (6,760,850) / 12,392,241	n.a.	n.a.
	Chile	13.1	12.7	Company/plant / Increasing	–	125[f] (13,227) / 114,306	86[f] (11,591) / 127,157	117[f] (14,662) / 207,224
	Peru	7.8	n.a.	Company/plant / Increasing	National/sector / Decreasing	37[f] (5,280) / 22,711	40[f] (11,050) / 61,116	64[f] (22,925) / 111,815
	Venezuela	17.1	n.a.	Company/plant / Increasing	National/sector / Decreasing	n.a.	n.a.	n.a.

Sources: Ayadurai (1994), Bronstein (2000), Fairris and Levine (2004), Galin (1994), Hwang (1994), Jimenez (1994), Kuruvilla *et al.* (2002), Manusphaibool (1994), national government websites, OECD (2004c), Ozkan (2003), Quim (2003), Watson Wyatt Worldwide (2004). The most recent figures for density and coverage are reported when data were provided by multiple sources. Work stoppage data were obtained from the ILO's Laborsta website (http://laborsta.ilo.org) unless noted otherwise.

Notes:

a Union members as a percentage of wage and salary earners in the economy.

b Percentage of employees in the economy covered by collective bargaining agreements.

c Over the period 1985–95.

d The number of strikes and lockouts is presented in the first row of each cell, with the number of workers involved shown in parentheses. Row two lists the total number of work days lost.

e Work stoppages that did not involve at least 1000 employees are not included in DOL statistics.

f Lockouts are not included in national work stoppage data.

g Work stoppages must last for a minimum number of days irrespective of the number of participants to be included in national work stoppage data. For Ireland, Australia, and Israel, the dispute must persist for at least 10 days; for New Zealand, five days.

h EIRO (2003e).

level (63.4 percent)[1] was nearly 20 times that of Indonesia; Brazil's (43.5 percent) more than five times that of Peru. With a few notable exceptions, little headway had been made on either continent during this period in bringing workers into organized labor's fold.

While interesting in their own right, density statistics can be a very misleading bellwether of labor's ability to significantly impact the terms and conditions of employment in a particular setting. Membership *per se* is no guarantee that a collective agreement will be in place to fix work policies and practices for the organization's rank and file. Newly formed bargaining agents must tackle the challenges of negotiating their first contract, a process that could take months to run its course—if a settlement is produced at all. Existing labor–management relationships must absorb the transactions costs of new bargaining rounds to replace agreements that expire, without any assurances that a mutually acceptable framework will surface to fill the void. Opposite forces could be at work extending the provisions of negotiated settlements to other parts of the labor market by custom or the operation of law. These contingencies call for a second means of assessing strength, *coverage*, which will be defined as the percentage of workers whose employment entitlements and obligations are set by bargaining and its outcomes. This would include persons employed or represented by the original signatories to collective agreements, as well as all others who benefit from a spillover of their underlying terms by virtue of voluntary action or government edict.

In this light, one has a very different impression of the extent to which unions are a force to be reckoned with in many economies. The most startling reappraisal occurs in France, a country that appears on the basis of density alone to harbor a very impotent labor movement. Despite low membership levels and a highly fragmented political orientation, unions arguably exert as much influence in the aggregate as their Swedish counterparts, which seemingly operate in a vastly superior environment laden with bargaining power. As we will see, however, French labor's sphere of influence is rooted much more in decisions the state has made about its role in the labor market than in the competencies or behaviors of management and unions. Spain, Portugal, Italy, Germany, Poland, and Hungary are other places in the region where coverage far or moderately exceeds density. Illustrations of this phenomenon are harder to find elsewhere, but no less compelling (e.g., Australia, Argentina, Thailand).

Alternatively, coverage data may suggest that density levels overstate labor's influence on workplace decision making. This is particularly true for China, the Philippines, India, and Malaysia, where collective agreements extend only to a small fraction of those who are formally organized. What accounts for this shortfall? One possibility is that indigenous "labor" functions more as a social or political movement than as an economic one, prompting its leaders to emphasize social protest and other forms of political behavior over collective bargaining. This may partially explain what has been going on in the last three of these nations but not China, where unions and their peak federation are extensions of the state rather than independent external stakeholders in its policies. A competing explanation casts the divergence as an artifact of asymmetric labor laws, which place few barriers in the way of organizing activity but make it very difficult to secure enforceable agreements at the bargaining table. The merits of this argument will be easier to assess once we catalog key aspects of IR regulation later in the chapter.

Of course, these two variables are not always at odds. Coverage and density figures are quite similar for the United States, Canada, the United Kingdom, Japan, South Korea,

Singapore, New Zealand, and Chile. All of these locations share one thing in common—a decentralized IR system that concentrates negotiating activity at the company/plant level.[2] Custom and practice may cause certain industries to depart from this norm for historical reasons, but they represent a small proportion of the agreements that are formed (i.e., secondary-level bargaining). One sees this historically in the U.S. steel, auto, and rubber industries, where the dominant unions sought to informally standardize work practices across firms through the pursuit of pattern bargaining.[3]

Nations that rely instead upon more centralized structures for bargaining undergo a homogenization of employment terms on industry, sector, or regional levels. Some pressures may exist to make bargaining more responsive to the competitive challenges that individual employers face, but contractual accommodations are very much the exception, not the rule. These markets are much more likely to foster corporatist traditions in industrial relations and high coverage rates. At the same time, centralized structures demand a different set of competencies from firms interested in exerting some control over their IR fate. While collective bargaining skills are at a premium in decentralized (i.e., pluralist) systems, internal lobbying and persuasion capabilities are needed in centralized systems to impact the strategic direction and negotiating positions of the team negotiating on behalf of the larger federation.

Even well established bargaining structures may change over time. To illustrate, Ochel (2005) reported that area-wide wage agreements, which have been a core feature of German industrial relations, are becoming less prevalent, while company and plant wage agreements are gaining in popularity. And Germany is not an isolated case. It thus becomes critical to identify impending shifts in negotiating activity and factor them into the calculus of site selection and retention decisions.

The middle two columns in Table 5.1 document how bargaining structures around the world have been evolving of late. Few nations registered dual growth in their dominant and secondary levels (i.e., Spain, Portugal, Egypt, South Africa, Brazil). The complete absence of change was even more of a rarity, found only in Mexico and Singapore. Countries with historical leanings toward decentralized structures tended to see an expansion of firm-level activity at the expense of already limited sectoral bargaining (e.g., the United States, Canada, the United Kingdom, Australia, New Zealand, Hungary, Poland, Russia, Peru, Venezuela).[4] Nations with a historical affinity for more centralized structures did not see fundamental change in this practice, but were likely to witness a growing undercurrent of decentralized negotiations (e.g., Continental Europe, Sweden, India, Argentina). It was a decade where enterprise bargaining took on greater importance worldwide on balance, and there have been no signs of a systematic reversal since then.

Industrial conflict is the final IR-system attribute we will consider. Work stoppage data for the years 2000–02 can be found in the far-right columns of Table 5.1. Short time series admittedly do not allow us to delve deep into the tactical and cultural nuances of these events. Important observations nevertheless can be made. To begin with, credible data are not always available, particularly in emerging markets. When such information has been compiled, its comparability must be carefully weighed. Although most countries fold lockouts into their overall statistics, exceptions do exist (e.g., Portugal, Turkey, Chile). Size thresholds may need to be satisfied before disputes are recorded, potentially underreporting the propensity for conflict (e.g., the United States). The same concern arises when a minimum number of days must elapse before stoppages are counted (e.g., Ireland, Australia, Israel). Assuming the underlying variable definitions are fundamentally sound, one must avoid placing too much stock in single-year statistics. The table is filled with examples of nations that display huge variations in performance from one annual period to the next.

Our ultimate objective here is to devise comparative measures for decision-making purposes. Poole (1986: 123–148) advanced the argument that there are consistent tendencies in the way that individual countries manifest industrial conflict. A typology of strike activity was proffered based on the interplay of four core dimensions: frequency, breadth, duration, and impact.[5] Updated values for these indicators were generated, combining data from Table 5.1 with ILO Laborsta estimates of the economically active population in each country. Starting with impact, we see the following average number of work days lost annually to work stoppages (per 1,000 wage and salary earners):

- *Less than 30:* Mexico, Germany, Sweden, Portugal, Hungary, Poland, Russia, Japan, New Zealand, Singapore, Philippines, Egypt.
- *30–39:* United Kingdom, France, Turkey, Peru.
- *40–49:* Australia, South Korea.
- *50–59:* United States, Ireland.
- *140–149:* Italy.
- *170–179:* Canada.
- *270–279:* Spain.
- *950–959:* Israel, India.
- *Greater than 2,000:* Argentina.

Nations in the first tier up for discussion (i.e., fewer than 30 days lost) are best described as low-conflict environments. At the extreme is Singapore, which lost no work time during this period—a phenomenon that, incredibly, extends back into the late 1980s uninterrupted. Egypt, Japan, Poland, Russia, and Germany were not far behind, with less than 10 days idled by stoppages for every thousand workers. No single characteristics defined the occasional disruptions in these locations. That was not the case for other countries. Work disputes tended to be longer in duration in Mexico and Poland than elsewhere in this cluster. For Hungary, New Zealand, and South Korea, breadth was the distinctive feature.

Our next tier includes countries that lost 30–59 work days. The mounting losses in scheduled hours are not insignificant; however, they still are indicative of relatively peaceful IR systems. Nations in this second group have more distinctive conflict signatures. Duration is the dominant trait in the Philippines, Turkey, and United States, while breadth stands out for the United Kingdom and Ireland. A more complex situation arises in France, Australia, and Portugal, where dual features coexist. France and Australia both ranked high on the incidence of stoppages, but saw them manifest in different ways. French disputes also tended to last for a long time, while those Down Under were inclined to involve large groups of employees. The profile for Portugal resembles that for Australia with medium levels of frequency and breadth.

The remaining countries were conflict-prone, some extremely so. Italy, Canada, and Spain can be grouped in a third tier, forfeiting between 100 and 300 work days per annum for every thousand economically active persons in the labor market. Stoppages in Canada were relatively infrequent, but typically kept substantial numbers of workers idle for considerable periods. Italian and Spanish stoppages tended to be short-lived, but occurred often and normally elicited broad participation. Tier-four nations were in a league of their own, hemorrhaging no fewer than 950 workdays as a consequence of labor–management clashes. Extensive breadth was the primary feature of Israeli stoppages, second only to Argentina in scope. Indian disputes were a distant third in terms of breadth, but tended to last fairly long when they were triggered. Argentina was impacted most negatively, by far, having to contend with the greatest number of stoppages and most participants drawn in.

What, if anything, appears to have changed twenty years after Poole's work? All of the countries jointly investigated had markedly lower breadth and impact values except Israel. Frequency was universally lower. The lone attribute that remained somewhat stable in most places was duration. Exceptions to this were Israel, France, and the United States (longer), as well as Ireland, the United Kingdom, Sweden, and Spain (shorter).

Exactly how does the law factor into all of this? As depicted in Figure 5.1, four facets of the labor–management relationship can be regulated: union formation, union administration, agreement facilitation, and dispute resolution.[6] Union formation, our starting point, focuses attention on two primary activities: securing membership commitments from employees who lack formal representation, and establishing the labor organization's legal personality. What mode(s) of union recognition will be sanctioned by the state? How much oversight will it exert over the events and exchanges that are associated with union organizing? Assuming adequate numbers of workers are prepared to officially become rank-and-file members of organized labor, will multiple unions be allowed to represent similarly situated workers in a given firm, industry, or region? If not, then what legal obligations do unions inherit when they become certified as the exclusive representative bargaining agent for a particular group? What must unions do in the aftermath of being recognized to acquire the capacity to perform legal acts on their own behalf (e.g., enter into contracts, own property)? To secure certain kinds of preferential treatment under the law (e.g., limited liability, special tax benefits, access to state-sponsored dispute resolution procedures)?

Once these institutions become legally viable, there are potential concerns about their ongoing administration. What, if anything, will the government insist on to increase the probability that organizational decision making and resource consumption remain true to members' needs? Financial dealings could be regulated in various ways. Certain transactions might be prohibited constraining the revenue sources that can be tapped, expenditures made, or both. Transparency and accountability requirements are other means of bringing this about, relying on disclosure, independent verification, and public scrutiny to keep leaders on the straight and narrow. At the extreme, the state could provide direct or indirect subsidies conditioned on union leaders engaging in behaviors deemed beneficial to workers.

The subject of internal governance continues in this vein. What safeguards will be installed to ensure that the rank and file have a meaningful voice in union affairs? How will leadership positions be staffed? What requirements must potential officeholders meet, and how long will they be permitted to serve once chosen? Are there delineated fiduciary duties that officials must adhere to? Under what circumstances will officials be subject to removal from office, and by what process?

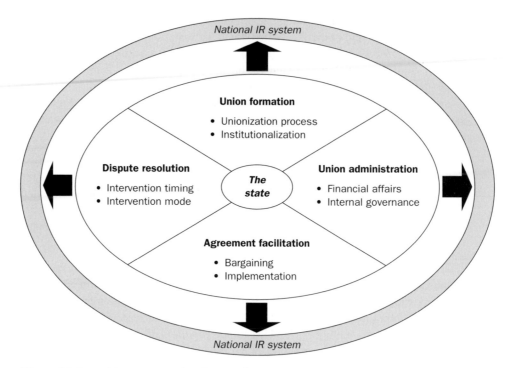

Figure 5.1 Potential government involvement in IR systems

With economically palatable agreements and industrial peace as superordinate goals, the state has decisions to make about the parameters of collective bargaining and what to do if the process gets bogged down. Will certain terms and conditions of employment be placed beyond the reach of negotiations because they are extensively codified into law or categorically barred from discussion? What will be expected from the parties behaviorally to create an environment conducive to productive interactions and jointly supported settlements? Do the provisions agreed to have to be approved by the executive or judicial branch before they can take legal effect? If so, what criteria will public officials apply when passing judgment? If not, would it be desirable to require that agreements be registered with the labor ministry to help monitor the status of bargaining relationships? Can part or all of the work practices supported by the signatory parties be imposed on other firms that did not participate in the underlying negotiations?

What if collective bargaining instead winds up at impasse? Have management and labor satisfied all that is expected of them by the state in reaching this point, or are there additional measures they are obligated to take to overcome the deadlock (i.e., conciliation, mediation, and/or interest arbitration)? Will the state be a direct supplier of dispute-resolution services or leave it to the parties to find competent private providers? Should recourse to economic weapons like strikes and lockouts be tolerated? What must be done to legitimately deploy them if they are available? What has to happen before the government will intervene to suspend or terminate work stoppages?

The sections that follow compare and contrast how different sovereignties have opted to fill these policy voids.

Union formation and administration

The impetus for unionization can come from myriad sources. Political ideology can be a driving force, as individuals seek to create an institutional springboard to advance their worldview (e.g., Communism, Socialism). For others, the political-economy paradigm is not the focal point of concern. Rather than trying to alter the system, the goal is to accumulate sufficient bargaining power within it to share equitably in the fruits of their labor. This pragmatic mindset leads workers to join and remain members if it is perceived to be an effective way of enhancing employment and income security. The North American IR literature in particular is steeped in the notion of instrumentally oriented unionization decisions.[7] Cultural attitudes may influence the perceived desirability of union membership as well. Two works have linked union density levels to Hofstede's national-culture framework (Black 2002; Singh 2001). As predicted, density was negatively related to high scores on masculinity, power-distance, and uncertainty avoidance.

Assuming one or more of these factors prompts individuals to engage in organizing activity, how will the state inject itself into the process and toward what end? Table 5.2 summarizes how union recognition is regulated among the group of nations we have been considering. One could make the argument that Germany, Sweden, and Poland offer organizers the most inviting haven, having no direct hand in recognition *per se*. Ancillary criteria (e.g., governance features or successfully negotiating a collective agreement) will need to be demonstrated at some future point in time, though, if there is interest in accessing the legal system to vindicate certain rights.

The dominant pattern is to institute some kind of certification mechanism. Twenty-six of the countries reviewed allow for unilateral registration by labor organizations subject to minimum size requirements regarding the number of workers that will be represented (Japan and South Korea are exceptions). For example, the threshold number is set at three in the Czech Republic, 15 in New Zealand, 20 in Mexico, 30 in Taiwan, and 50 in Egypt. Uganda sets the bar at 1,000 employees (ICFTU 2004: 61). Brazil predicates recognition on demonstrating that at least one-third of the regional workers in a given labor class have been organized. In some nations, the critical mass needed depends on the type of union workers are seeking to form. Venezuelan law embraces a sliding scale of sorts as follows: company unions (20 or more); trade, industrial and regional unions (40 or more); and general unions (100 or more). The critical realization is that employers have no institutionalized role to play until recognition occurs and bargaining responsibilities attach. Of course, government officials may not automatically accept recognition requests that meet the statutory criteria which have been laid out. To illustrate, Malaysia has been criticized for the practice of refusing registration without any official explanation (ICFTU 2004: 192). The same source alleges that Equatorial Guinea consistently refuses to register independent trade unions despite constitutional affirmation of the right to organize.

Other sovereignties afford labor unions parallel or alternative modes of validation. To illustrate, a subset of Canadian provinces continue to use card-check systems, which automatically convey recognition once unions entice more than 50 percent of the group targeted to sign membership cards.[8] Secret-ballot elections are fully available to the parties in the United States, Mexico, the United Kingdom, Singapore, the Philippines,

Table 5.2 Regulating union formation and internal union affairs, select countries

Region	Country	Avenues of government intervention — Modes of union recognition for collective bargaining purposes	Union security arrangements are legally enforceable		
			Closed shop	Union shop	Agency shop
North America	United States	Government certification (secret-ballot election, bargaining order)			✓[a]
		Voluntary employer recognition (card-check agreements legal but not mandatory)			
	Canada	Government certification (secret-ballot election mandated by seven provinces, card-check system elsewhere)			✓
		Voluntary employer recognition (except Quebec)			
	Mexico	Government certification (unilateral registration by union, secret-ballot election[b])	✓	✓	
Europe	United Kingdom[c]	Government certification (declaration request by union, secret-ballot election)			
		Voluntary employer recognition			
	Ireland	Voluntary employer recognition			
	Germany	Formal recognition not required (ability to engage in bargaining predicated on having at least one member employed in the firm and satisfying criteria regarding resources, independence, and governance)		✓[d]	
	France	Government certification (ability to engage in company or sector bargaining as a 'representative' trade union predicated on meeting criteria regarding size, resources, influence, and independence, or formally aligning with one of the major confederations)			
	Italy	Government certification (ability to engage in sector bargaining as 'most representative' trade union predicated on formally aligning with one of the major confederations)			
	Sweden[e]	Formal recognition not required (securing a sector agreement (i.e., an 'established union') perfects the right to participate in certain aspects of employer decision making)			
	Spain	Government certification (ability to engage in sector bargaining as 'most representative' trade union predicated on getting a sufficient proportion of one's members elected employees' delegates or works council members[f])	✓		
	Portugal	Government certification (unilateral registration by union)			
	Czech Republic	Government certification (unilateral registration by union)	✓	✓	✓

Region	Country	Basis of recognition			
	Hungary	Government certification (unilateral registration by union)			
	Poland	Government certification (unilateral registration by union)			
	Russia	Government certification (unilateral registration by union)			
Asia and Oceania	Japan	Government certification (unilateral registration by union)		✓	
	Australia[c]	Voluntary employer recognition			
	New Zealand	Government certification (unilateral registration by union)	✓[g]		
	South Korea	Government certification (unilateral registration by union)		✓[h]	
	China[i]	Government certification (request for ACFTU approval)			
	Indonesia	Government certification (unilateral registration by union)			
	Malaysia	Government certification (unilateral registration by union)			
		Voluntary employer recognition			
	Singapore	Government certification (secret-ballot election)	✓		
		Voluntary employer recognition			
	Thailand	Government certification (secret-ballot election)	✓		
	Philippines	Government certification (secret-ballot election)			
		Voluntary employer recognition			
	Taiwan	Government certification (unilateral registration by union)	✓	✓[j]	
	India	Government certification (unilateral registration by union, secret-ballot election mandated by three states)	✓		
	Pakistan	Government certification (secret-ballot election)			
Middle East and Africa	Turkey	Government certification (ability to engage in sector bargaining as "most representative" trade union predicated on organizing ≥ 10% of an industry's employees and the majority of workers in a firm)	✓[k]		
	Israel	Voluntary employer recognition	✓		
	Egypt	Government certification (unilateral registration by union)	✓		
	South Africa	Voluntary employer recognition	✓	✓[l]	
South America	Brazil	Government certification (recognition predicated on organizing ≥ 33.3% of the region's workers in a particular labor category)		[m]	
	Argentina	Government certification (ability to engage in sector bargaining as a "trade union with personality" predicated on organizing ≥ 20% of an industry's employees and proving one is most representative)			
	Chile	Government certification (secret-ballot election)			✓
	Peru	Government certification (unilateral registration by union)			
	Venezuela	Government certification (unilateral registration by union)	✓[n]		

continued

Table 5.2 Notes

Sources: Bronstein (2000), Brown (2003), Córdova and Ozaki (1980), Egorov (2002), International Labor Law Committee, ABA Labor and Employment Law Section (2000a, b, 2002a, b), Jung (2002a), Kubínková (2002), O'Connell (1999), Sharma (1985)

Notes:

a Twenty-two states have outlawed union security agreements that otherwise would be legal under federal law, taking advantage of authority that was extended to them by the Taft–Hartley amendments to the National Labor Relations Act (i.e., Section 14(b)). Interested readers can consult the National Right to Work Legal Defense Foundation website (http://www. nrtw.org/rtws.htm) for more details about pertinent state legislation and case law.

b Limited to situations where one union asserts it has majority support with the accompanying right to take title to a collective agreement administered by a rival. In these circumstances, the relevant CAB will conduct a vote (i.e., *recuento*) to establish which labor organization has majority support.

c A longstanding tradition of accommodating closed shops and lesser forms of union security was outlawed in the 1990s.

d While union security arrangements are not regulated by specific legislation, Irish case law suggests that union shops would not be an unconstitutional infringement on the freedom of association so long as they are not imposed on existing workers.

e In 2001, the Swedish Labor Court held that "examination fee" obligations—which resemble agency shops—do not violate the European Convention for the Protection of Human Rights, and therefore are enforceable. Undeterred, the country's largest employer federation filed a complaint with the Council of Europe's Committee of Ministers reiterating its contention that this practice violated major EU instruments. Although the committee did not categorically reject the imposition of examination fees, Swedish officials received instructions to allow only charges that were incurred inspecting wages. Thus, this form of union security remains at least partially viable. In an interesting sidebar, the complaint also sought to ban closed-shop provisions. Concluding that these clauses were at odds with the European Social Charter, the committee convinced the state to engage its social partners in negotiations to abolish their use. A decision nevertheless was made to list closed shops as legal in the table since no agreement had been reached at the time of this writing. In-depth coverage of these events can be found in EIRO (2001b, 2003b).

f Labor organizations become "most representative" at a national level if at least 10% of the persons elected to serve as employee delegates or on works councils are members. A higher threshold must be met to achieve "most representative" status within Autonomous Communities (i.e., 15%). Unions with either designation have the ability to negotiate sector agreements.

g A "bargaining fee" clause cannot take effect unless it receives majority support in a secret ballot of nonunion and union workers who would be impacted. If this requirement is met, the firm must notify nonunion employees of the outcome and indicate the time period for opting out if there is a desire to do so.

h Union-shop clauses are enforceable where the union represents more than two-thirds of the workers in the same business.

i Security arrangements have little relevance since unions have no independent legal existence and are required to be established in firms that have 25 or more workers. Moreover, all employers are required to contribute 2% of their monthly payroll to trade union funds (China Internet Information Center 2002).

j While one article of the Collective Agreement Law authorizes parties to negotiate union-shop clauses, another indicates that they can be voided if their effect is to limit the firm's usual business requirements (Hwang 1994: 283). This apparent inconsistency appears to have limited practical significance, though, since the government provides direct subsidies to trade unions, accounting for a substantial portion of their operating funds.

k Unions have the right to collect an amount equal to two-thirds of regular membership dues from nonmembers who want to be covered by the collective bargaining agreement.

l This column is marked rather than the first one even though Section 26 of the Labor Relations Act refers explicitly to "closed shop" agreements. The main reason for the reclassification here flows from subsection (3), which reads, "A closed shop agreement is binding only if . . . (c) there is no provision in the agreement requiring membership of the representative trade union before employment commences. . . ." That language is more consistent with a union shop than a closed shop as they are defined here and in most IR sources.

m A *de facto* agency shop appears to exist, given the way that trade unions are funded. The Labor Ministry regularly levies a trade union tax on all workers and allocates the monies to national labor federations on the basis of membership size.

n Nonmembers who choose to work under the terms of a collective agreement must be charged an amount equivalent to 75% of dues to be forwarded to the union.

Pakistan, and Chile. A majority of Canadian provinces now mandate this practice, as do three states in India. The intent here is to provide a government-supervised forum where both sides can compete for the hearts and minds of employees in orderly, balanced campaigns. Spain piggybacks on the voting process used to select employee delegates and works-council members to determine which labor entities are "most representative" for the purpose of negotiating sectoral agreements. A similar situation prevails in France, where electoral support in these two venues can be a basis for establishing that unions are "representative." In contrast, Ireland, Israel, South Africa, and Australia[9] rely exclusively on voluntary employer recognition, while the United Kingdom, Malaysia, Singapore, the Philippines, Canada, and the United States permit it as one of the legally sanctioned routes.

Labor organizations face wide-ranging demands after they come into being. Registration is a common requirement, necessitating the filing of contact information, constitutions, bylaws, and, at times, the minutes of meetings where the latter two instruments were approved. Periodic disclosure and reporting obligations may be imposed, especially when it comes to financial matters. To illustrate, Mexican unions must provide the rank and file with a detailed accounting of the administration of union assets on no less than a semi-annual basis. Their Canadian peers need to supply copies of audited financial statements to members and the government (e.g., labor ministry, IRB) at yearly intervals. South Africa and the United Kingdom also call for the submission of independently audited annual financial reports to union members and a designated agency. In the case of the United Kingdom, the document would be filed with the Independent Certification Officer. The United States revised its reporting scheme for organized labor, but failed to incorporate an auditing requirement for the annual LM-2 forms. Overcoming past criticism that these forms contained insufficient information for members to evaluate the performance of the union and its leadership (e.g., Masters *et al.* 1989), unions now must provide the Labor Department with something closer to a functional accounting statement. Furthermore, unless a hardship exemption is obtained, the reports must be filed electronically, utilizing government-issued software.

The legal status of union security agreements has serious financial and strategic ramifications for labor, particularly where density and coverage are limited. Closed shop, union shop, and agency shop clauses are common variations on this theme, each seeking to strengthen the union's institutional position by committing all persons in the bargaining unit to formally affiliate on some level. Closed shops are the most attractive arrangement from organized labor's vantage point, making union membership a condition of employment. Union shops would be viewed as a fallback position. Here, firms are permitted to hire nonmembers with the stipulation that such persons must join the rank and file within a short period to remain employed. Agency shop provisions are the least restrictive of the three, allowing nonmembers to remain unaffiliated in a technical sense so long as they periodically reimburse the bargaining agent for IR services that are received from it (e.g., collective bargaining, grievance processing). The antithesis of these provisions would be open shops, which allow workers to contemplate affiliation as a personal, voluntary decision.

Returning to Table 5.2, we find an overwhelming regulatory predisposition against coerced union membership. Twenty-one of the countries reviewed do not consider *any* kind of security agreement to be legally enforceable. This position has been characterized as "negative freedom of association" in the European context and the "right to work" in many US states. Diametrically opposed are Canada and Sweden, which treat all three as binding if they appear in otherwise valid collective agreements. Closed shops are rarely tolerated, being available in a total of four nations. More countries (eight) make allowances for union shops, but tend to circumscribe their application. Under Irish law, it is unlikely that existing workers who opposed unionization can be forced to join—just new hires. This is not the case in South Africa, where labor can insist that individuals in both categories become members or lose their jobs when such a clause is in place. South Korea restricts the operation of union shops to businesses where unions already represent a two-thirds supermajority of workers. Taiwan also recognizes the legal validity of union shops, but has expressly reserved the right to void them if they limit the firm's usual business requirements.

Agency shops, which are formally accepted in 12 countries, have their own enforcement nuances. In New Zealand, bargaining-fee clauses cannot take effect unless they receive majority support in a secret-ballot election involving the union and nonunion members who would be impacted. American "outsiders" are not afforded the same procedural safeguard—voting on contract ratification is vested solely in the hands of union members. Brazil simply imposes a universal tax (*contribuição sindical*) on all workers that will be allocated proportionately to labor federations based on size.

The fee amount that can be extracted from nonmembers itself is regulated in different ways. Turkish law gives unions the right to collect an amount equal to two-thirds of regular dues from nonmembers who want to be covered by a collective agreement. In Chile, employers are required to charge nonmembers the equivalent of 75 percent of dues in such circumstances and forward these monies to the bargaining agent. Other countries permit unions to define what would be reasonable to defray the costs of providing representational services (e.g., the Philippines, South Africa, the United States). However, what is considered to be an appropriate representational service, and what is deemed a reasonable charge, can be very controversial issues. American case law prohibits unions from extracting funds from nonmembers to subsidize political behavior, organizing activity, members-only benefits, and other "nonchargeable" expenditures. In addition, they are required to provide employees with an independently verified financial breakdown of forced dues before such fees are collected, and to process complaints about the calculations in an expeditious, objective manner.

Another important activity impacting union democracy is the staffing of leadership positions. Most nations loosely regulate this area through the registration process, requiring labor to specify an orderly process for the identification and selection of officeholders, as well as terms of office, in their constitution or bylaws (e.g., South Africa, Mexico). Where this is not done, the state may formulate guidelines on how the succession process should be managed. The Philippines illustrates this approach, recommending the formation of an election committee with well defined duties and powers that are to be executed on a specified timeline.[10] A handful of nations get more extensively involved. For example, Australia and the United Kingdom have prescribed that new elections must occur at least once every four and five years, respectively. The United States sets the maximum period between elections at three years for local unions and five years for national and international labor entities. All three countries further micromanage select aspects of the election life cycle as well.[11]

Agreement facilitation

Bargaining power, rooted in the capacity to make it more expensive for the other party to reject than to give in to one's demands, is not determined solely by market forces. What the parties are able and willing to accomplish in collective bargaining is greatly influenced by the accompanying regulatory environment. The state may categorically bar the parties from negotiating on certain topics, or insist on certain behaviors at the bargaining table that go beyond what power inequalities would yield (e.g., bargaining in good faith). Similarly, maximum or minimum duration periods may be specified for agreements. Brazil and Chile illustrate these competing approaches, both drawing the line at two years. Labor and management instead may be denied or granted only limited access to tactics that would drive up the opponent's cost of disagreeing (e.g., strikes, lockouts). In some instances, the power to set specific terms may be usurped by government through general employment legislation or edicts that extend the provisions of collective agreements negotiated elsewhere. Each of these themes will be expanded on below.

The range of subjects that can be considered is our first major issue. Kuruvilla (2003: 16) identified a continuum of public policies on this matter, with no significant encumbrances anchoring one end. Sweden and much of Continental Europe exemplify this practice, having been unwilling to place any business issues impacting work beyond the reach of bargaining. The antithetical policy position has the state categorically excluding certain topics from discussion. One sees this in Taiwan and China, where negotiations on the introduction of new technology have been foreclosed, as well as in Malaysia and Singapore, which prohibit bargaining over critical talent-management practices (e.g., hiring, job assignments, transfers, RIFs). The United States is portrayed as embracing an intermediate approach, bifurcating issues into two distinct categories with differing behavioral standards. Mandatory subjects of bargaining encompass all items that directly affect the wages, hours, or conditions of employment of active workers. Subsequent case law and administrative rulings have clarified that this language extends beyond salaries and work schedules to include incentive compensation, fringe benefits, discipline policies, safety practices, staffing adjustments, and union security arrangements. Refusing to meaningfully discuss one or more of these themes once raised by the other side would create legal liability for the offending party. In contrast, permissive subjects deal with aspects of the firm that are viewed as management prerogatives (e.g., product portfolio, form of operations, advertising practices, investment strategy). Nothing in the law precludes the parties from jointly deciding how these matters should be handled—if there is mutual interest in doing so. Bargaining requests can be rejected out of hand without committing an illegal act whether it is prudent to do so or not.

Table 5.3 documents other ways that government can leave its imprint on the process and outcomes of collective bargaining. Beginning with the far-right column, one discovers that the mere presence of legally certified labor unions does not necessarily foreshadow an obligation to enter into negotiations. Thirteen countries lack national legislation that elevates bargaining to a legal duty, let alone regulate how it is conducted. As we have seen before, they are not confined to a single region or level of industrial development. Although the remaining nations require the parties to meet, no consensus position is evident regarding the behaviors that must be demonstrated. Half of the group

Table 5.3 Regulating collective bargaining, select countries

Region	Country	Content		Process
		Negotiated agreements must be reviewed and approved by the state	Agreements can be extended to nonsignatory firms in the industry/region by government decree	Legal duty to bargain exists
North America	United States	No	No	Yes ("good faith")
	Canada	No—agreement still must be registered in most provinces	No (except Quebec)	Yes ("good faith")
	Mexico	Yes—review limited to legal compliance	Yes—STPS can make a "law contract" declaration if petitioned to do so by unions representing at least two-thirds of the industry/region's workers	No
Europe	United Kingdom	No	No	No
	Ireland	No	Yes—agreements voluntarily registered with the Labor Court will be extended if the signatory parties are substantially representative of the industry	No
	Germany	No—agreement still must be registered	Yes—Labor Ministry can do so if an *ad hoc* joint committee supports the action and ≥ 50% of the sector's employees are covered beforehand	No
	France	No	Yes—Labor Ministry can act unilaterally or by request of a signatory party utilizing input from National Collective Bargaining Commission[a]	Yes ("good faith")
	Italy	No	No	No
	Sweden	No	No	Yes
	Spain	No	Yes—Labor Ministry can do so if a commission of "most representative" unions and employers' organizations supports the action	Yes ("good faith")

	Portugal	No	Yes—Labor Ministry can act unilaterally or by request of a signatory party after considering input from concerned parties[b]	Yes ("good faith")
	Czech Republic	No—agreement still must be registered	Yes[c]	Yes
	Hungary	No—agreement still must be registered in ≤ 30 days[d]	Yes—Labor Ministry can do so if presented with a joint request from signatory parties representative of the sector[b]	Yes
	Poland	No—agreement still must be registered	Yes—Labor Ministry can extend part or all of a "supra-enterprise" agreement if requested to do so by a national union/employer organization	Yes
	Russia	No—agreement still must be registered	Yes—Labor Ministry can invite nonsignatory firms to join industry agreements and bind those failing to reject the offer within 30 days	Yes
Asia and Oceania	Japan	No	Yes—Labor Ministry can do so by request of a signatory party if the LRC issues a supportive resolution	Yes ("good faith")
	Australia	Yes—certified agreements and industrial awards are given effect by the state	No	No[e]
	New Zealand	No—agreement still must be registered	No	Yes ("good faith")
	South Korea	No—agreement still must be registered in ≤ 15 days	No	Yes ("good faith")
	China	Yes—agreements lacking required terms will be returned for revision and resubmission—all agreements must be registered in ≤ 30 days	No	Yes
	Indonesia	No—agreement still must be registered	No	Yes ("good faith")
	Malaysia	Yes—review limited to legal compliance	No	No

continued

Table 5.3 continued

Region	Country	Content		Process
		Negotiated agreements must be reviewed and approved by the state	Agreements can be extended to nonsignatory firms in the industry/region by government decree	Legal duty to bargain exist
Asia and Oceania continued	Singapore	Yes—must be submitted in ≤ seven days (won't be certified if considered against public interest)	Yes—Minister of Manpower can do so after considering input from the IAC as to whether this action would be in the public interest	No[f]
	Thailand	No—agreement still must be registered in ≤ 15 days	No	Yes
	Philippines	No—agreement still must be registered in ≤ 30 days	No	Yes ("good faith")
	Taiwan	Yes[g]	No	No
	India	No—agreement still must be registered	No	No
	Pakistan	No	No	Yes
Middle East and Africa	Turkey	No	Yes—Council of Ministers can act if requested to do so by a signatory party, a concerned firm or the Labor Minister after considering input from the High Court of Arbitration	Yes
	Israel	No—agreement still must be registered in ≤ 60 days	Yes—Labor Ministry can act unilaterally or by request of a signatory party after considering input from concerned parties[b]	Yes ("good faith")
	Egypt	Yes[h]	No	No
	South Africa	No	No	No
South America	Brazil	No—agreement still must be registered	No	No
	Argentina	Yes[i]	Yes—Labor Ministry can act unilaterally	Yes ("good faith")
	Chile	No	No	Yes
	Peru	No	No	Yes
	Venezuela	No—agreement still must be registered	Yes	Yes

Sources: Adler and Avgar (2002), Bacik (2002), Briggs (1995), Bronstein (2000), Bureau of International Labor Affairs, USDOL (2002b), Casale (2002), Cristovam (2002), EMIRE database (http://www.eurofound.eu.int/emire/emire.html), Galin (1994), Hwang (1994), International Labor Law Committee, ABA Labor and Employment Law Section (2000a, b, 2002a, b), Jimenez (1994), Jung (2002b), Madhuku (1997), Manusphaibool (1994), Mathew (2003), O'Connell (1999), Quinn (2003), Wexels-Riser (2004).

Notes:

a A meeting may be scheduled with interested unions and affected employers before a decision is made. Though rarely used, an "enlargement" process also is available whereby the state imposes the terms of a collective agreement on all firms within its material scope that have a history of failed collective bargaining efforts.

b Notice of the proposed directive/order is first published in an official government source. Concerned parties in Portugal (15 days) and Israel (30 days) have a set period to submit reasoned objections. In Hungary, objecting parties have the option of directly appealing the minister's decision to a competent labor court.

c The Czech government was in the process of finalizing major revisions to the country's extension procedures at the time of this writing.

d While the underlying legislation makes it mandatory to register collective agreements, the Labor Ministry has not articulated procedures for doing so or specified an enforcement mechanism in the event of noncompliance.

e In 2002, Western Australia adopted the Labor Relations Reform Act, which authorized its IRC to issue good-faith bargaining orders where there is territorial jurisdiction. Similar reforms had been sought at the national level two years earlier, when the opposition party proposed amendments to the Workplace Relations Act that would have expanded the AIRC's powers in the same manner. That Bill never passed (McCallum 2002a).

f The Commissioner of Labor nevertheless will intervene whenever it is learned that a bargaining invitation has been refused, to persuade the objecting party to soften its position. The parties can request that the commissioner mandate conciliation if an agreement is not reached with 14 days of the original notice of invitation.

g Terms thought to be incompatible with progress of the employer's business or not suited to maintain workers' normal standard of living can be amended or cancelled. Existing collective agreements can be annulled as well where severe economic changes have occurred since their inception.

h As late as 1991, Egyptian labor law invalidated any clause in a collective agreement that jeopardized the nation's economic interest (Drits and Lebowitz 1994). Updated information could not be located.

i Labor Ministry approval is required to make collective agreements enforceable. The Labor Ministry also schedules and attends the underlying negotiations between the parties.

appear to demand little more than attendance, while the other half require "good faith bargaining." Exactly what the latter expectation entails will be a function of national culture and local labor history. By way of example, decades of litigation over the meaning of this term can be distilled into the following summary statement for the United States: the parties must come to the bargaining table with an open mind and make reasonable efforts to negotiate a mutually acceptable agreement covering mandatory subjects that have been raised.

Two overarching issues about content deserve mention. How much control do private IR actors have over the final set of terms and conditions incorporated in their agreements? Negotiated settlements are not always accepted passively by the state, as the table reveals. In eight nations, agreements do not become effective until the government takes some kind of official action. Some merely review documents for statutory compliance, declaring nonconforming instruments to be unenforceable until the defects are corrected (e.g., Mexico, China, Malaysia). Australia similarly requires that collective agreements must pass a "no disadvantage test" (i.e., no net reduction in the overall terms and conditions set out in industrial awards and employment laws) before they can be certified by the AIRC. Others intervene more aggressively, invalidating provisions or entire agreements that are not considered to be in the public interest (e.g., Taiwan, Singapore, Egypt). Argentina only follows this policy for regional and industry agreements. Even when pre-approval is not mandated, there may be a need to register final contracts with the labor ministry. To illustrate, the parties must register new agreements within 15 days in South Korea and Thailand, 30 days in Hungary and the Philippines, and 60 days in Israel.

Whether government has a penchant for imposing the terms of collective agreements on nonsignatory parties says even more about the freedom to contract. Returning to Table 5.3, we see that 15 countries and Quebec have a specific apparatus in place to extend settlements to establishments that were not represented in the negotiations giving rise to them. How are such procedures triggered? Will the deliberations involve one or multiple institutions? Six countries empower their labor ministries to initiate the process unilaterally: France, Israel, Portugal, Russia, Turkey, and Singapore. More often, the signatory parties must step forward and ask the state to intervene. Only organized labor has the right to do so in Mexico, provided it already represents at least two-thirds of the group that would be affected. The remaining countries permit any signatory party to petition for the extension (e.g., Poland, Japan, Spain, Germany), or mandate joint action (e.g., Hungary, Ireland).[12] Some jurisdictions accept requests from multiple sources. Approximately one-half of the nations surveyed confine the process to a single government entity, which affords concerned parties an opportunity to present their objections. The rest insist on some kind of institutional collaboration between the labor ministry and social partners (Germany, Spain, France), labor courts (Singapore, Turkey), or lead IR agency (Japan) to establish the appropriateness of issuing a decree. One's ability to navigate these waters puts a premium on extensive indigenous knowledge.

The last section examines how various IR systems respond to bargaining impasse.

Dispute resolution

As bargaining runs its course, it is to be hoped that the parties will be able to arrive at settlement terms which pave the way for a finite period of industrial peace. The reality of the situation is that they may not be able to bridge fundamental economic and ideological differences, or may fall victim to irrational behaviors which obscure the fact that their bargaining positions actually overlap. Accordingly, government has to decide how much latitude will be extended to labor and management to overcome deadlocked negotiations. Will self-help measures be permitted, and in what forms (i.e., economic versus noneconomic)? What procedural safeguards will be imposed to properly balance freedom-of-association rights with other legal entitlements (e.g., contract and property rights)? Will the state formally intercede to forestall conflict and broker an agreement, or merely prescribe that a dispute-resolution process be followed, leaving it to the combatants to find a way to competently implement it?

Table 5.4 showcases abundant regulatory variation despite its limited scope.[13] Three activities are profiled, each instigated by a different actor in the system: strikes, the deployment of replacement employees, and involuntary terminations of work stoppages. Strike decisions can be constrained in several ways. Insisting that conflict-resolution services be utilized beforehand is one avenue. Some countries mandate conciliation whenever bargaining breaks down (e.g., Hungary, Thailand, Pakistan, Argentina). Others insist on mediation in these circumstances (e.g., Poland, Turkey).[14] A few nations add binding arbitration to the mix on an automatic (e.g., Russia, Indonesia) or selective (e.g., Malaysia, South Korea, South Africa, Taiwan, the United States) basis. More laid-back governments vest discretionary authority with a particular unit to refer disputes to conciliation or mediation as seen fit. One finds this in France (labor ministry), Sweden (National Mediation Office) and Japan (labor relations commissions). Only six of the countries listed allow work stoppages to take place without first pursuing one of these alternatives: the United Kingdom, Ireland, Germany, Spain, Australia, and Israel. Even there, conflict-resolution expertise is made available through official sources upon request.

Another option is for the state to take the decision out of the hands of union leaders by requiring rank-and-file authorization. Sixteen nations in the table compel labor organizations to conduct strike votes, normally insisting that all affected union members be eligible to cast ballots, and that there be majority support. Interesting variations nevertheless can be found. Chile and Peru extend voting participation to all workers who would be impacted, not just those represented by the union. Malaysia has established a two-thirds supermajority as the minimum level of support needed to legitimize strikes. In Canada, employees in federally regulated industries and six provinces also may be asked to vote on the firm's last contract offer. Taiwanese labor must secure permission from the state to call a meeting where such polling will be conducted, and may find government officials on site during the event. For example, representatives from the Council of Labor Affairs and three regional labor departments were in attendance when the Chunghwa Telecom Workers Union voted to authorize a strike over concerns about job and economic security after the state-owned firm became fully privatized (Shih 2004). The government apparently stationed a public servant at each transmitting location in the landmark, video-conference voting process to certify its legality.

Table 5.4 Regulating industrial conflict, select countries

Region	Country	Strike vote mandatory[a]	Strike notice required (to Firm/State)	Use of replacement workers during work stoppages (source can be drawn from)	Regulatory mechanism to delay, suspend or terminate legal work stoppages
North America	United States	No	No	Permitted (hires and transfers)—locked-out employees have reinstatement rights, strikers do not	Pre-strike mediation required in railroad and airline industries; President can direct Attorney General to seek 80 day injunction against ongoing/impending strikes that threaten national health/safety
	Canada	Yes[b]	No	Permitted[c] (hires and transfers)—strikers have reinstatement rights	Pre-strike mediation required in "federal" industries and six provinces; ad hoc back-to-work legislation may be enacted if economically important enterprises are involved
	Mexico	No[d]	≥ 6 days (F, S)	Prohibited	President can issue executive order suspending strikes in transportation and telecom industries if there is a prominent danger to national economy
Europe	United Kingdom	Yes	≥ 7 days (F)	Permitted (hires and transfers)—strikers lack reinstatement rights[e]	No
	Ireland	Yes	≥ 7 days (F)	Permitted (hires and transfers)—strikers lack reinstatement rights[e]	No[f]
	Germany	No	No	Permitted (transfers only)—strikers have reinstatement rights	No
	France	No	No	Prohibited	Labor minister can refer disputes to tripartite commission for conciliation (mediator appointed if parties do not do so when conciliation fails[g])
	Italy	No	No	Prohibited	Pre-strike conciliation required in essential service industries
	Sweden	No	≥ 7 days (F, S)	Permitted (hires[h] and transfers)—strikers have reinstatement rights	National Mediation Office can postpone disputes for a two-week period; Parliament can enjoin disputes threatening important societal interests
	Spain	No	≥ 5 days (F, S)	Permitted (transfers only)—strikers have reinstatement rights	No

	Portugal	No	≥ 5 days (F, S)	Prohibited	Labor Ministry can refer disputes to binding arbitration if Economic and Social Council recommends it (arbitrator appointed if parties fail to do so)
	Czech Republic	Yes	≥ 3 days (F)	Prohibited	Pre-strike mediation required (mediator appointed if parties fail to do so)—arbitrator appointed if mediator fails to resolve dispute in ≤ 30 days
	Hungary	*	No	Prohibited	Pre-strike conciliation required for a minimum of seven days
	Poland	Yes	≥ 14 days (F)	*	Pre-strike mediation required (mediator appointed if parties fail to do so)—proceeding must be concluded in ≤ 14 days, producing an agreement or documentation of the parties' divergent positions
	Russia	Yes	≥ 10 days (F)	*	Pre-strike conciliation mandatory (a mediator must be appointed by the parties if their joint conciliation committee cannot resolve the dispute)—labor arbitration panel formed with state participation if mediation fails; state can postpone or temporarily suspend strikes for 30 days if there is an immediate threat to public health and safety
Asia and Oceania	Japan	Yes	No	Permitted (hires and transfers)—strikers have reinstatement rights	LRC can refer disputes in essential service industries to a mediation committee; Prime Minister can suspend strikes that gravely imperil national economy or daily lives of the populace (requires LRC input)
	Australia	No[j]	≥ 3 days (F)	Permitted (hires and transfers)—strikers have reinstatement rights	No[j]
	New Zealand	No	≥ 3–28 days[k] in essential service industries (F, S)	Permitted (transfers only)—limited to work necessary for health and safety reasons—strikers have reinstatement rights	Pre-strike mediation required in most industries[j]
	South Korea	Yes	≥ 10 days[l] (F, S)	Permitted (transfers only)—strikers have reinstatement rights	Pre-strike mediation required; Labor Ministry can refer disputes in essential service industries to binding arbitration if an LRC ad hoc special mediation committee recommends it
	China	No[m]	No	No	Conciliation, arbitration, and litigation are the only legally sanctioned means of resolving labor disputes
	Indonesia	No[n]	≥ 7 days (F, S)	Permitted (transfers only)—strikers have reinstatement rights	Negotiations failing to produce an agreement in ≤ 30 days must be submitted to Manpower Ministry for mediation (mediator has 30 days to facilitate a settlement)—arbitrator appointed if mediation is unable to settle dispute in ≤ 30 days

continued

Table 5.4 continued

Region	Country	Strike vote mandatory[a]	Strike notice required (to Firm/State)	Use of replacement workers during work stoppages (source can be drawn from)	Regulatory mechanism to delay, suspend or terminate legal work stoppages
Asia and Oceania continued	Malaysia	Yes[o]	≥ 7 days[p] (F, S)	*	Pre-strike conciliation required (Human Resource Ministry will try to foster a settlement during the strike-notice period); Human Resource Ministry can refer any dispute to the Industrial Court for binding arbitration
	Singapore	Yes	≥ 14 days in essential service industries (F, S)	Permitted (hires and transfers)—strikers have reinstatement rights	Pre-strike conciliation required (Labor Commissioner engages in conciliation for a minimum of seven days with possible extensions); President or Manpower Minister can refer certain disputes to the IAC for binding arbitration
	Thailand	Yes	≥ 1 day (F, S)	Permitted (hires and transfers)	Pre-strike conciliation required (conciliation officer appointed by Labor Department has five days to facilitate a settlement); Interior Minister can suspend disputes endangering the national economy or public order, or authorize the LRC to review the case and issue an order
	Philippines	Yes	≥ 30 days (F, S)	Permitted (hires and transfers)—strikers have reinstatement rights	Pre-strike conciliation required (Secretary of Labor obligated to promote a settlement through conciliation and mediation); Secretary of Labor can issue a "return to work" order when disputes affect the national interest
	Taiwan	Yes[q]	No	Permitted (hires[r] and transfers)	Pre-strike conciliation required; Council of Labor Affairs can refer any dispute to binding arbitration
	India	No[s]	No	*	State can refer labor disputes to Industrial Tribunal or Labor Court for compulsory adjudication (mandatory for public utility services)
	Pakistan	No	≥ 7 days (F)	Permitted (transfers only)	Pre-strike conciliation required; state can invoke binding arbitration before dispute begins, or within 15–30 days of its onset, if stoppage is prejudicial to national interest or creates serious hardship for society
Middle East and Africa	Turkey	No[t]	≥ 6 days (F)	Prohibited	Pre-strike mediation required (mediator has 15 days to foster settlement); Council of Ministers can postpone dispute for 60 days if national security or general health and safety is endangered (those remaining unresolved must be referred to High Arbitration Board for binding arbitration); Labor Court can suspend disputes if harmful to society/national wealth
	Israel	No	≥ 15 days (F, S)	*	No[u]

Egypt	No	≥10 days (F, S)	Permitted (hires and transfers)	*
South Africa	No	≥2 days (F)	Permitted[v] (transfers only)—strikers have reinstatement rights	Pre-strike conciliation required (bargaining council or CCMA has 30 days to facilitate an agreement or issue a certificate of non-resolution); all disputes in essential service industries must go to binding arbitration
South America Brazil	Yes	≥2 days[w] (F, S)	Prohibited	State can petition labor court for expedited arbitration of labor disputes
Argentina	No	No	Prohibited	Pre-strike conciliation required (conciliator appointed by Labor Ministry has 15–20 days to facilitate an agreement)
Chile	Yes[x]	No	Permitted[d] (hires and transfers)—strikers have reinstatement rights once strike is ≥30 days in length	State can refer labor disputes in essential service industries to binding arbitration
Peru	Yes	No	Prohibited	President can issue resumption-of-work order for disputes persisting an "excessive period of time" if a firm/sector is being seriously jeopardized
Venezuela	*	≥2 days (F)	Permitted (hires and transfers)	Pre-strike conciliation mandatory (Labor Inspectorate has five days from the time it receives notice of an impasse to facilitate an agreement). President can issue a "return to work" order when disputes pose an immediate threat to the population and refer them to binding arbitration

Source: Adler and Avgar (2002), Bacik (2002), Bhoola (2002), Briggs (1995), Bronstein (2000), Bureau of International Labor Affairs, USDOL (2002a), Casale (2002), Ciudad (2002), Cristovam (2002), Das (2003), Davenport (2001), EMIRE database (http://www.eurofound.eu.int/emire/emire.html), Fernandes (2002), Fernández (2002), Galin (1994), Grandi (2002), Gross (2001), Hwang (1994), International Labor Law Committee, ABA Labor and Employment Law Section (2000a, b, 2002a, b), Jimenez (1994), Jung (2002b), Labib (2003), Madhuku (1997), Manusphaibool (1994), Mathew (2003), O'Connell (1999), Park (1994), Quinn (2003), Rebhahn (2004), Watson Wyatt Worldwide (2004), Wexels-Riser (2004).

Notes:

* Extensive web-based searches failed to locate information on how this subject is regulated.

a A simple majority is the required threshold of support wherever voting is required unless specified otherwise. As a general rule, all affected members must be eligible to participate in the vote. In Japan, the latter standard is met if all of the delegates elected by members are eligible to vote. Chile and Peru deviate from this pattern by extending eligibility to all affected workers.

b Provincial legislation may precipitate voting on the employer's last contract offer as well. Some provinces authorize the labor relations board or labor minister to impose this requirement unilaterally, while others (i.e., Alberta, British Columbia, New Brunswick, Manitoba, Ontario) permit employers to request this action be taken.

c Quebec and British Columbia are exceptions, with total bans on replacements

d Employers, strikers and interested third parties have 72 hours to request certification of the strike's legal existence (i.e., whether it has majority support among affected employees). In addition to conducting a hearing, CAB officials can initiate a strike vote to ascertain the level of backing for the work stoppage. The strike will be declared legally nonexistent if majority support is lacking, obligating workers to return to their jobs within 24 hours to avoid dismissal.

continued

e   Under British and Irish law, firms must treat all strikers equally regarding reinstatement (i.e., allowing all or none to return). Acting otherwise can give rise to an unjust dismissal cause of action for the subset of individuals who were not given an opportunity to reclaim their jobs.

f   The Labor Minister can refer disputes that affect the public interest, or are of special importance, to the LRC for conciliation. If conciliation efforts are unsuccessful (i.e., LRC waives its conciliation function or reports that settlement cannot be facilitated), the Labor Court may conduct an independent investigation and recommend terms for settlement.

g   While the state has a longstanding obligation to maintain mediator lists pursuant to the French Labor Code, its ongoing commitment to this practice has been called into question. In 1998, the Economic and Social Council, a major advisory body, issued a report that bemoaned the increasingly common reliance on *ad hoc* appointments to handle mediation requests (EIRO 1998a).

h   Finding such persons is no easy task. Pursuant to the Unemployment Insurance Act (1997), individuals can decline work in struck firms without jeopardizing their unemployment benefits. Similarly, organized, nonstriking workers ordinarily are excused from performing struck work by "neutrality arrangements" in their collective agreements. This leaves unorganized supervisors and managerial employees as viable internal replacements.

i   The AIRC has discretionary authority to administer a strike vote pursuant to section 135 of the Workplace Relations Act (simple majority required).

j   A well developed system of compulsory conciliation and/or arbitration was largely dismantled in the 1990s.

k   No strike will be deemed legal unless the parties have been engaged in otherwise timely bargaining for at least 40 days.

l   More than 15 days for public interest industries.

m   The right to strike is not formally recognized in the present constitution or labor laws. In fact, the Trade Union Law indicates that the union's main goal in a labor dispute is to assist the firm to resume work and restore order as quickly as possible *irrespective* of the extent to which employee demands have been met (Fair Labor Association 2004: 239–40).

n   The original Manpower Bill (Article 136 explanatory note) specified that strike votes had to be taken and reported in strike notices (Zimmerman 2002: 28). However, none of that language made its way into the statutory text that was passed (Article 140).

o   A two-thirds supermajority is required to authorize strikes.

p   More than 42 days for essential service industries.

q   Permission must be secured from the state to call a meeting where a strike vote will be taken.

r   In 2002, the Employment Service Act was amended to ban public employment agencies from referring job seekers to companies idled by a labor dispute.

s   The National Commission on Labor (2002: 46) recommended a series of IR reforms in 2002, including a requirement that strikes be conditioned on secret-ballot elections with majority support. Formal legislative action on the proposal has not been reported to date.

t   A strike vote will be conducted if ≥ 25% of the workers affected request it. The union preserves its ability to continue the strike if a simple majority votes to support it.

u   The Knesset has rejected several compulsory arbitration Bills over the years.

v   Locked-out employees cannot be replaced unless the employer was responding to an existing strike.

w   More than three days for essential service industries.

x   The negotiating committee representing employees can call for a vote to send the dispute to mediation or arbitration at any time during a strike.

y   Firms seeking to preserve their ability to hire replacements at the onset of strikes must put forward a final offer that includes a cost-of-living adjustment of existing wages and benefits before the statutory period for collective bargaining (i.e., 45 days) expires. Firms that do not submit a timely final offer are barred from hiring replacements during the first 15 days of the strike. In addition, participants in the work stoppage must be paid a bonus equal to four times the wages of replacement workers (divided equally) once the latter begin to work. In 1995, a legislative proposal that would have banned the use of replacement workers was debated but never enacted.

Interestingly, three countries that have not systematically democratized strike decisions make allowances for voting in certain instances. Mexican employers, strikers, and interested third parties have 72 hours to petition the appropriate CAB to certify that an industrial action is legal (i.e., that it has majority backing). A strike vote may be administered by the board to confirm this is true. Turkey similarly conditions the continuation of a work stoppage on polling results if at least 25 percent of the affected workers request that their voices be heard. Down Under, the AIRC has the discretion to order a strike vote whenever the commission feels that this procedure might help the settlement process.

An obligation to provide advance notice is the final hurdle trade unions may encounter in this area. Approximately one-third of the nations under review have not incorporated any notice requirements in their labor laws (e.g., the United States, Italy, Hungary, Japan, India). The rest harbor different expectations regarding the entities that should be informed as well as how far ahead of time a warning about industrial action must be received. Compliance is achieved in ten countries by communicating the impending strike to management alone (e.g., Ireland, the Czech Republic, Russia, Pakistan, Venezuela), as opposed to the firm and the state, which is demanded in 14 other locations (e.g., Mexico, Sweden, New Zealand, Egypt, Brazil). Properly timing the message is equally important. Most jurisdictions hold all planned strikes to a single standard, which rarely exceeds ten days in length—the exceptions being Poland (14 days), Singapore (14 days), and the Philippines (30 days). Other governments extend the notice period for "essential service" or "public interest" industries. Malaysia offers the most striking illustration of this, increasing the lead time from seven to 42 days. In New Zealand, the message must be transmitted anywhere from three to 28 days in advance, depending on the economic sector.

Replacement workers are a potent countermeasure against strikes because they preserve the firm's ability to engage in revenue-generating activities. However, governments are not necessarily willing to allow employers to resort to this tactic. Eight countries in the table have outlawed their introduction entirely, and two others limit deployment to a very narrow set of positions. Another way of discouraging this practice is to restrict the sources that can be tapped to secure their services. Nations that permit replacements frequently ban firms from hiring new employees specifically for this role, forcing the enterprise to rely on internal transfers (e.g., Spain, South Korea, Pakistan, South Africa). Moreover, virtually every state that accepts the use of replacements expects their presence to be temporary (i.e., strikers have automatic reinstatement rights once the dispute ends). The primary rationale for this is to avoid unduly punishing economic strikers for becoming involved in otherwise legal work stoppages. The United States, United Kingdom, and Ireland are outliers in this regard, legally sanctioning the permanent replacement of those joining industrial action.

Many states have evolved mechanisms to delay or abort work stoppages that may engender grave societal consequences. The legislature may be given the lead role in triggering an intervention (e.g., Sweden, Canada), although this is rare. From 1950 to 1999, 30 strikes falling under Canadian federal jurisdiction were ended with back-to-work legislation (Commission for Labor Cooperation 2002: 68). More likely it will be the executive branch that functions as gatekeeper, whether it is the head of state (e.g., the United States, Japan, Peru), labor ministry (e.g., the Philippines) or a cabinet-level body (e.g., Turkey). Directing the conflict to the labor courts for binding arbitration is one solution, as noted above. Court injunctions and executive orders are the preferred response in several countries. The requirement in all cases is that the underlying circumstances be extraordinary, such as when there is a threat to "national health and safety," "important societal interests," or the "national economy." Adherence to this standard can be in the eye of the beholder, though, as exemplified by events in Turkey. Under Turkish law, the Council of Ministers has the power to order a 60 day suspension of industrial action that imperils national security or public health. This power was exercised twice within a ten week period to interrupt broad industrial actions in the glass industry (Kristal-Is Online 2004). Shortly after the first decree took effect, the Turkish Supreme Court ruled that there were insufficient grounds to support its enforcement. Delighted with the ruling, the union went out on strike. The council issued a new suspension decree one week later in apparent defiance of the high court's ruling. Its legality became a moot point in March 2004, when management and labor entered into a collective agreement.

Disputes also can arise between unions and management beyond the realm of bargaining. For example, there may be disagreements over contract administration or general compliance with labor and employment laws (e.g., consultation rights). In response, aggrieved parties may seek to defend their interests by (1) commencing adversarial proceedings before domestic tribunals, labor courts, or the judiciary, (2) lobbying the legislative or executive branches for legal reforms, or (3) mobilizing public opinion against the "offending" party. Multinational firms bring increased complexity to these situations, since their actions can play out simultaneously in multiple markets.

Marks and Spencer's decision to close all of its stores outside of the United Kingdom and Ireland is a prime illustration. Seven Continental European nations and Hong Kong were among the locations that would be negatively impacted by the decision. Organized labor responded at the country level in numerous ways. French unions challenged the action in court and filed a "specific instance" request with the OECD national contact point in France. The Belgian labor movement submitted an identical review request to that country's NCP. Spanish labor federations threatened to initiate demonstrations at the United Kingdom's embassy in Madrid if the company failed to negotiate an acceptable termination package for affected employees. The only unified response was a mass protest in London, where domestic and foreign workers met to demand that the stores be kept open and bargaining commence with unions on a European level. Hoping to foster a means of peacefully resolving such transnational conflicts, the European Commission has expressed interest in erecting a mechanism to supply voluntary EU-level conciliation and mediation services (EIRO 2002e). A consultation paper on the subject was prepared, based on a Commission-sponsored study of national dispute-resolution practices in the region. Little headway appears to have been made, though, since the idea was first broached with the social partners' peak organizations. Other blocs have not even attempted to follow suit, which is not surprising, given the materials presented in Chapter 3.

So far, we have taken an issue-based approach to labor law comparisons, concentrating on the similarities and differences in specific facets of organizing, bargaining, and conflict resolution. Ending our analysis at this point would not give a holistic sense of the way individual nations regulate the labor–management relationship, or how that ranks among the community of nations. Devising an appropriate methodology for this purpose is a complex undertaking. One possible strategy, an indexation system based on ratified ILO conventions (e.g., Cooke and Noble 1998; Flanagan 2003; Hasnat 2002; Mah 1997; OECD 1996), is rejected up front. The inherent flaws of this type of design were discussed at length in Chapter 2. Verité's (2003) study of ILS compliance in emerging markets is spared most of these criticisms, since the scores factored in content analyses of national constitutions, codes, and regulations to assess actual adherence to convention terms.

Even more ambitious is the 85 nation labor and employment law database developed by Botero *et al.* (2004a). Every major category of work regulation is copiously documented and quantified in a set of dichotomous, ordinal, and interval scales. Their composite "collective relations law" (CRL) index conveys the extent to which local law favors unions and employees in the areas of organizing, negotiation, industrial action, and corporate governance (i.e., board appointments, works councils).[15] CRL values were extracted for the subset of countries we have been discussing and converted into z scores. The results are displayed in Figure 5.2. This assessment tool better conveys intra- and interregional differences than reading down the individual columns of Tables 5.2–5.4. Still, the figure is meant to illustrate an approach to, rather than generate an end product for, country evaluations. Several important refinements are essential—a topic we will revisit in Chapter 7.

Conclusion

The desire to compare IR systems brings with it the challenge of identifying meaningful criteria to guide the process. The three features that anchored our discussion can be thought of as IR vital signs to evaluate on a cross-sectional and longitudinal basis. Density and coverage levels offer complementary perspectives on the labor movement's presence and influence in a given economy. Formal membership data certainly provide insight into organized labor's larger cultural appeal, but size alone does not guarantee that it will have much bargaining power *vis-à-vis* employers. Numerous settings were identified where large segments of the labor force were impacted by negotiated settlements despite the fact that a relatively small fraction was unionized—and vice versa. Thus, density figures can lead one to grossly under- or overestimate national union strength without factoring in coverage.

Bargaining structure was the second system attribute profiled. Some nations have a longstanding tradition of negotiating at the enterprise level. Others have aggregated bargaining activity to produce agreements that apply generally within an industry or a set geographic area. Unions face higher transaction costs in decentralized structures because they must go from firm to firm trying to negotiate settlements that have common terms and conditions. Management may be harder pressed to engineer desirable bargaining outcomes in centralized structures because idiosyncratic competitive pressures may be ignored in the negotiating stance adopted by the larger federation. Recent trends indicate that company bargaining is becoming even more entrenched where it has been predominant, and surfacing increasingly where it has been relegated to a secondary level. The spin put on this development depends on the side of the bargaining table one favors.

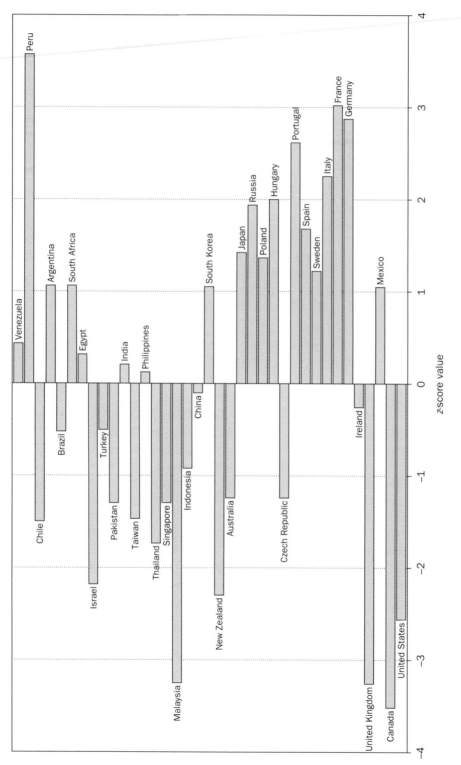

Figure 5.2 Quantifying labor law protections for unions and employees, select countries

The propensity for industrial conflict was the final characteristic examined. Here, we uncovered substantial variation not only in the absolute number of work stoppages, but also in their qualitative nature. Utilizing classification schemes articulated by previous researchers, we reaffirmed that patterned differences exist in strike frequency, duration, breadth, and impact across nations. The practical significance of these findings is somewhat self-evident. For example, the continuity of operations in host business units and foreign suppliers is less predictable in countries that are prone to broad-based industrial action. Individual firm efforts to promote a constructive labor-relations climate may be overwhelmed by the cultural or ideological draw of advancing organized labor's general position. High frequency also signals increased risk that sourcing arrangements will be disrupted, since there is a greater likelihood that labor unrest will escalate into economically damaging behaviors. Duration holds the key to whether the strikes that do occur tend to create short- or long-term scheduling problems for enterprises. These dimensions collectively form a baseline indicator warranting serious consideration in host entry and retention decisions—standardized number of work days lost (i.e., impact). Limited time-series data suggested that duration is the only strike feature to remain stable over the last couple of decades. Breadth, frequency, and impact all tracked at lower levels.

The state influences these patterns through policy choices made in four major IR domains: union formation, union administration, agreement facilitation, and dispute resolution. Unions should have an easier time securing recognition through *ex parte* requests than card-check systems, formal elections, and employer recognition, assuming local law is consistent with the dictates of ILO Convention No. 87.[16] Consequently, unilateral registration mechanisms should bolster density rates, especially when there are low numerical thresholds to qualify.

Government often is intent on ensuring that employees are represented by economically viable, democratic organizations, prompting the regulation of internal union affairs to varying degrees. The aspects of union administration most likely to draw attention are financial and governance practices. Labor leaders frequently have an obligation to report income and expenditure activity, although the required level of detail, audience, timing, and need for external validation change from one country to the next. The state's expectations for internal union democracy also fluctuate, with some sovereignties shunning oversight while others aggressively regulate the decision-making forums.

Union-security arrangements are a controversial means of nurturing institutional revenue streams because they deny interested persons negative freedom-of-association rights. Labor's justification for such measures is the need to fend off "free riders" (i.e., bargaining-unit employees who consume representational services without bearing an equitable share of the underlying cost). Very few nations accommodate union concerns to the point where closed shops are allowed. Union shops and agency shops are much more likely to be tolerated, but still fall short of being majority practice.

Government can extend its presence into collective bargaining in many ways. Specific issues may be deemed nonnegotiable as a matter of law, preempting discussion regardless of the interest one of the parties has in the topic. Certain behaviors may be mandated, such as a duty to bargain in good faith. Tentative settlements may need to survive government scrutiny or be formally registered before they can be implemented. Slightly more than half of the countries we analyzed have extension procedures available to bind nonsignatory firms to industry or national agreements. This option, in particular, should promote higher coverage levels and more centralized bargaining activity. The latter phenomenon should occur because firm-specific bargaining power is no guarantee that employment terms can be tailored to favor the enterprise's interests.

Governmental responses to failed negotiations can take on many forms. Most nations prohibit the parties from engaging in economic warfare until peaceful approaches to conflict resolution are exhausted. The required mix of conciliation, mediation, and arbitration services varies from country to country. Satisfying this obligation does not necessarily open the floodgates to overt conflict. Unions may not be able to launch or maintain industrial action unless they are formally authorized by a strike vote. The timing of the walkout needs to comply with notice requirements. Management's access to replacement workers may be heavily restricted or entirely foreclosed. The same may hold true for preemptive lockouts. When the economic or social stakes are high enough, the state may intervene to suspend or terminate work stoppages. All of these policy initiatives should improve the prospects for industrial peace.

Having become immersed in the rich diversity of national labor laws, one must not lose sight of the fact that vast stretches of labor-market regulation were not surveyed in this chapter. Workplace discrimination, nontraditional employment relationships, job discontinuity, variable pay practices, and retirement needs are critical social issues eliciting public-policy responses in their own right, generically grouped under the heading of "employment law." Appendix B provides interested readers with an overview of government efforts to facilitate equal opportunity, job security, and income security for the same set of countries. Considered in tandem, these materials indicate that nations are amply distributed across the cells of a 2×2 matrix which captures weak and strong regulation of labor versus employment matters.

Mindful that compliance is a necessary and desirable posture for firms to maintain, the next chapter examines how firms also attempt to reconfigure the legal environment to better suit their needs.

Managing domestic and transnational political behavior

6

A core premise in our discussion to this point has been that organizations need to proactively manage the regulatory environment if they want to be thorough in pursuing competitive advantage. This entails more than just becoming aware of the international and domestic forces that influence law creation and enforcement at the country level. Capabilities must be developed to proactively influence these processes in furtherance of overarching strategic goals. Consistent with this point, Masters (1987) recommended the inclusion of human-resource political analyses in strategic planning, and closer links between the corporate units responsible for HRM and public affairs. Such analyses would include the costs of compliance, the costs of projected regulatory changes, and the financial benefits of more favorable laws. While couched in a single-country context, this innovation would hold even greater value for MNEs, since the information would not only make host-site selection and retention decisions more economically sound, but also promote ongoing assessments of the firm's ability to build and diffuse political-process competencies.

Some might argue that corporate political behaviors (e.g., lobbying, public education initiatives, *amicus curiae* briefs) that attempt to align employment regulation with the competitive pressures that businesses face are an abdication of corporate social responsibility—not to mention a fundamentally unethical course of action for HR executives and professionals to participate in. A distinctly European view of HRM ethics tends to assess the morality of employment-related activities from the vantage point of the work force and wider society (e.g., Cornelius and Gagnon 1999; Drumm 1994; Greenwood 2002; Winstanley *et al.* 1996). Advocates of this line of thinking typically place emphasis on social justice and the extent to which employees are treated as an end in themselves, even if that calls for economic tradeoffs unfavorable to shareholders. In this light, firms that actively try to qualify for legal exemptions and waivers—or opportunistically locate in jurisdictions with weaker labor standards—would be vulnerable to charges of unethical behavior[1] (Schwartz and Carroll 2003: 521). Attempts to modify laws outright to deal with business exigencies would be even more suspect from this perspective. Acknowledging the need to respect core labor rights that have garnered widespread international support, passive submission to all forms of labor-market regulation seems counterintuitive if it threatens the economic viability of the operations and jobs in question. Maximizing employee welfare becomes a moot point in the absence of gainful employment.

In contrast, the "American" model of HRM has been described as management-focused, with a fundamental objective of promoting organizational efficiency (e.g., Greenwood 2002; Payne and Wayland 1999). At the extreme, criticisms are leveled that (1) employees are treated as little more than objects to be deployed in pursuit of the firm's strategic ends, and (2) the employee-champion role (see Ulrich 1997) only superficially defends employee interests by injecting an awareness of compliance-management responsibilities into efforts to mobilize people and organizational processes in furtherance of economic and market goals. A more balanced description of the profession and its priorities can be found in the codes of ethics and organizational activities of the Society for Human Resource Management (SHRM), the leading professional association for U.S. practitioners. The organization's code unmistakably rejects professional behavior that represents a minimalist approach to compliance management (i.e., doing nothing more than mechanically administering existing laws, whatever their limitations). To the contrary, HRM professionals are expected to add value with an eye toward enhancing their employer's ethical success and social responsibility. Accordingly, SHRM's governmental affairs program not only reports on legislative and regulatory proposals affecting the work of practitioners, but also works to increase their ability to engage in an ongoing, meaningful dialogue with law makers (see http://www.shrm.org/government/). For example, SHRM developed legislative fact sheets, advocacy materials, and sample letters encouraging government officials to update archaic definitions of white-collar work that were making it difficult to accurately judge whether legitimate overtime-pay obligations were present in many work settings, let alone steadfastly observe them. This behavior is not confined to the United States. To illustrate, Hong Kong's peak HRM association prepared a consultation paper offering suggestions to the Equal Opportunities Commission on ways to effectively implement impending race discrimination legislation (Hong Kong Institute of Human Resource Management 2005).

What is the litmus test for ethical behavior in IHRM where the work force may straddle numerous cultures and industrial development stages? The OECD Guidelines for MNEs are an obvious source to consider (see Box 2.2). Chapters IV and II clearly instruct firms to observe and promote internationally recognized labor standards. There also is an expectation of adherence to ILS-compatible host standards which are widely practiced by local employers. Nothing in the pertinent text suggests that multinationals are duty-bound to maximize workforce entitlements wherever they operate. Appropriate conduct in the area of government relations is less certain, given the vague language of Chapter II. Two core actions seem to be discouraged: attempts to secure *firm-specific* exemptions from existing employment regulation, and improper involvement in local politics. This section of the guidelines explicitly acknowledges the propriety of securing regulatory exemptions that are generally available to the business community, provided it does not conflict with the labor-standard thresholds mentioned above. There also appears to be acquiescence to some forms of political action, so long as the activity is not deemed "improper" in the host country and the views of "other stakeholders" are taken into account. These qualifiers suggest that the drafters did not intend to bar MNEs from trying to facilitate regulatory reforms that would benefit all firms in a given sector or the economy, especially when they are participating in a broader coalition of host employers (e.g., trade association or employer federation). A means-and-ends test of sorts still should be met to promote compliance. The modality of political behavior must be locally sanctioned, and the envisioned amendment or legislation must not conflict with the core labor rights articulated in Chapter IV.

The diverse approaches to political-party financing and their regulation exemplify the variance MNEs must contend with in the development and implementation of political-action strategies. In some regions, elections and party operations are funded primarily with public monies (e.g., Continental Europe, Latin America). Direct cash subsidies, often meted out in proportion to the party's representation among elected officeholders, may be complemented by in-kind benefits (e.g., free media use) and special tax concessions. Other nations rely heavily on private sources to fund the domestic political infrastructure (e.g., the United States, the United Kingdom, Australia, Japan, Central and Eastern Europe, Africa). The potential impact of corporate campaign contributions depends on which sourcing approach is emphasized. It also is a function of the way(s) that private donations are regulated. For example, many countries categorically ban political contributions from foreign sources (e.g., Argentina, Brazil, Chile, Mexico, France). U.S. election law also prohibits foreigners from making contributions directly or indirectly to any federal or state election. However, foreign companies are allowed to set up American-based political action committees, so long as they are not run by, and do not receive monies from, foreign nationals. Some nations ban all or a subset of firms from financially contributing to the political process. Poland and France do not allow any corporate entities to donate to political parties or individual candidates. Italy precludes only firms that are 20 percent or more publicly owned from doing so. Japan allows businesses to provide funds to political parties but not to individual candidates. Germany does not categorically restrict which companies can donate, but denies corporate donors any tax benefits. Wherever corporate donations are permitted, ceilings are likely to be imposed on the amounts disbursed during a given year or election cycle. Not only will the level of donation be capped at different levels, but there may be significant variation in disclosure obligations and state oversight. And this is only the tip of the regulatory iceberg.[2]

Significant opportunities nevertheless exist to shape business regulation in most nations if the appropriate political-action tools are selected. As discussed in the last chapter, various arms of the state can create law through individual and collective behaviors. The executive and legislative branches tend to be the primary drivers of regulatory activity, though—even in common law systems—making them popular targets for influence tactics. Figure 6.1 offers comparative data on the perceived influence that firms have over these governmental bodies for the set of countries we have been examining. While the legislative branch is treated as a monolithic bloc, its executive counterpart is dissected into three parts: executive branch (i.e., central government), ministries, and regulatory agencies. Several interesting patterns emerge. First, there are only five countries where less than 40 percent of the respondents felt that the business community was not "frequently influential" or "very influential" in shaping new laws that could substantially affect its interests—the United States, Portugal, Indonesia, Malaysia, the Philippines, and Pakistan. Second, with rare exceptions (e.g., the United States, the Czech Republic), influence levels are fairly uniform across governmental units in a given country. This suggests that firms not only recognize that law making originates in multiple sources, but also try to broadly participate in the process rather than concentrate government-relations resources on a single state entity. Third, economic development stage does not seem to be a good predictor of "influence potential."

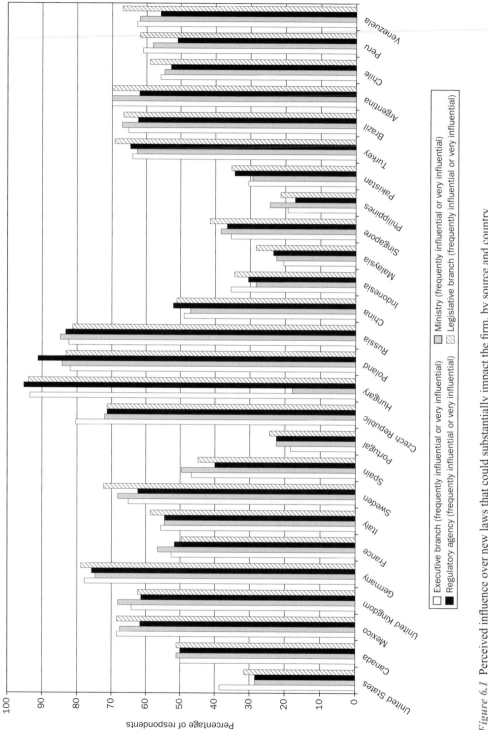

Percentage of respondents

Figure 6.1 Perceived influence over new laws that could substantially impact the firm, by source and country

□ Executive branch (frequently influential or very influential)
□ Ministry (frequently influential or very influential)
■ Regulatory agency (frequently influential or very influential)
▨ Legislative branch (frequently influential or very influential)

Emerging markets are not automatically more susceptible or receptive to corporate overtures than are AIEs. To illustrate, while influence levels are perceived to be moderately high in Mexico, Central and Eastern Europe, Turkey, and Latin America, the same does not apply for Asia in general. Fourth, considerable variability is present within and across regions. Intraregional differences are most notable in North America and Europe. For example, the levels reported for Mexico are more than twice as high as those for the United States. Germany, the United Kingdom, and Sweden exhibit substantially higher ratings than the rest of the European Union's "old guard" members, with Portugal and Spain faring the worst on this dimension. Corporate influence in the Czech Republic, Hungary, and Poland matches or exceeds that of Germany. We even see a significant gap in Asia, with China registering much higher levels of influence than its regional neighbors, especially the Philippines.

We now delve further into the nature of government–firm relations, with special emphasis on the complexities that multinational firms bring to the mix.

Dynamics of government–firm relations

There is a rich literature exploring the multifaceted nature of firm–government dyads in one-country settings (e.g., Mitnick 1980; Mahon 1993; Oberman 1993). These works deal with such issues as the theoretical impetus for regulation (public versus private interest-driven), appropriate means of regulation (directive versus incentive mechanisms), life cycle of regulatory agencies, determinants of corporate political strategy, and political action choice (direct versus indirect). The situation obviously becomes much more complicated for MNEs which are likely to encounter legal systems, governance infrastructures, and cultural norms regarding political involvement that vary greatly from one nation to the next. We have already seen a poignant example of this in the regulation of political financing.

Several models have been advanced to explain the underlying dynamics of MNE–government relations.[3] Three of the more established paradigms—sovereignty at bay, dependency, and bargaining—differ on such key dimensions as the nature of the political process (open–public or closed–elitist), firm–government relationship (conflictual–adversarial or cooperative–partnership), and firm power (Brewer 1992). The sovereignty-at-bay model vests MNEs with substantial power *vis-à-vis* home and host governments and assumes inherent conflict in the parties' objectives. This asymmetry, in turn, leads to adversarial relations everywhere. The dependency model also embraces the notion that powerful MNEs inherently infringe on host sovereignty, especially in emerging markets. However, the firm's relationship with its home government is depicted as cooperative. Bargaining-based models return to the notion that interactions between multinationals and governments are fundamentally distributive (i.e., win–lose) with the formers' power being a function of the unilateral control exerted over key value-chain resources. Brewer goes on to question the appropriateness of sweeping "macro" models for MNE–government interfaces, arguing instead that a "micro"-level, issues-based treatment of the subject offers a more useful framework for understanding the behaviors of each side. We will return to this prospect later in the chapter.

Continuing with a bargaining-based orientation, the ability to secure favorable treatment[4] in a given market will be dependent on more than the amount of corporate control over key resources. The extent to which the needs of political decision makers are supported must be considered as well. This is especially true for multinational enterprises. Kim (1987) found that MNEs' political responsiveness deterred "undesirable" host intervention in emerging economies—more so as the degree of industry competition escalated. Among the factors used to measure political responsiveness were the proportion of host employees in managerial positions and the overall work force, as well as expenditures on education and job-training activities for host nationals. Legal Systems in Action 1.2 similarly furnished illustrations of the benefits that can accrue from assisting host governments to upgrade the housing and transportation infrastructure for local workers.

These materials ground the dominant theme of this chapter—that indigenous firms and MNEs alike must treat government as another factor of production or set of agents that needs to be managed in the pursuit of competitive advantage (see Boddewyn and Brewer 1994). A market-oriented model of this interface depicts the business sector as a demander of public policies that are conducive to successful operations and government entities as potential suppliers. To maximize the probability of facilitating desired policy outcomes, multinationals need to adopt a contingency-based approach to political action where the techniques utilized are modified to accommodate differences in the constitutional form of government, the structure of the policy-making process, the organization of political interests, and public-sector staffing patterns in a given country (Hillman and Keim 1995). This is not meant to suggest that there will not be any intersubsidiary coordination of political activities. Such coordination is especially likely to occur if the firm relies on integrated sourcing in its operations, and the host economy has close economic ties (e.g., trade agreements) with other national economies (Blumentritt and Nigh 2002).

What specific political-action mechanisms can be leveraged? Florkowski and Nath (1993) noted that host environments could be proactively modified through negotiations or lobbying, but this certainly is not an exhaustive listing. Masters (1987) identified a broader set of political-action tactics that have been utilized for IR/HRM purposes, including political action committee (PAC) contributions, voter education programs, lobbying (independent or associational), and constituency building among employees, shareholders, suppliers, and community residents. To this we add coalition building with government officials (see Legal Systems in Action 6.2, p. 178) and judicial lobbying in the form of *amicus curiae* briefs on matters of law before the courts.[5]

How often are these measures utilized for IR/HRM issues within and across host countries? What factors influence the form, intensity, and coordination of such political activity by the IHRM function of multinational firms? Regrettably, there are no comprehensive studies of the political-action portfolios that private IR actors rely upon in domestic and international settings, or their relative efficacy. The closest thing the literature has to offer is a handful of U.S. investigations of the impact that PAC contributions have on the behaviors and election prospects of federal law makers. Saltzman (1987) reported that this source of political financing had a small but significant effect on the propensity of House members to register labor-supported positions during roll-call votes. Overall, PAC contributions increased the probability of Democrat officeholders voting as organized labor desired by 6–10 percent, and their Republican counterparts by 2–3 percent. The difference along party lines is not surprising, given that Democrats receive virtually all of the PAC monies allocated by trade unions, and Republicans were more likely to receive funding from corporate PACs. He also discovered that the political vulnerability of incumbents had a much greater impact on the disbursement of labor-linked PAC monies than did the incumbent's ability to do political favors because of tenure, committee membership, etc. Concentrating instead on corporate-sponsored organizations, Masters and Keim (1986) found that the likelihood of forming a PAC and the amount of money donated to it were positively related to the level of unionization in the firm's primary industry. They attributed this relationship to (1) an attempt to fend off labor's anticipated encouragement of government involvement in the workplace, and (2) an opportunistic response to select policy areas where joint political action may be sustainable (e.g., protective trade barriers). Unfortunately, no attempt was made to investigate the actual contribution patterns of PACs in the sample.

More recent studies have investigated how PAC contributions are impacted by congressional voting on specific policy matters. To illustrate, Phillips and Tower (2005) assessed the extent to which organized labor retaliated against House members who voted in favor of NAFTA's passage, in accordance with its pre-vote warnings. The most salient findings were that political funding decreased considerably for Democrats who voted "yes" and increased substantially for Republicans who voted "no". Francia (2001) also documented that labor PACs contributed less money to pro-NAFTA incumbents during the 1994 congressional elections—including Democrats who were at risk in contested races. Not surprisingly, corporate PACs tended to behave in an opposite manner. Incumbents who voted in favor of NAFTA received more than $8,000 more from this source on average than did House members failing to do so. Similar patterns have been uncovered with respect to congressional voting on Bills conveying fast-track negotiating authority to the President. Republicans supported by labor PACs and those Democrats receiving above-average levels of funding from this source were much more likely to oppose such legislation than were their party peers (Biglaiser et al. 2004). The reverse held true for incumbents from both parties receiving contributions from business PACs that were above the norm.[6]

In addition, empirical investigations of MNE political behavior in home- versus host-country contexts (and across multiple overseas locations) are unknown as it pertains to IR/HRM. Will multinationals superimpose their domestic priorities and tactics for this area on overseas locations or expect host units to adapt to the local political economy? Centralizing such activity bolsters headquarters' control but runs the risk of engaging in culturally ineffective or inappropriate tactics. Even worse is the prospect of a local backlash against what is perceived to be foreign meddling in the internal affairs of host nations. Being more polycentric increases the chances of deploying resources in ways that are locally responsive, but carries its own downside risks. Suboptimization in government relations at the country level is one concern if host units become overly preoccupied with appeasing local officials. Inefficient resource allocation for the MNE as a whole is another, to the extent that there is unnecessary duplication of government-relations infrastructure across units.

Some insights may be gleaned from a subset of studies examining the political activity of foreign-owned subsidiaries vis-à-vis indigenous firms. Mitchell et al. (1997) found that foreign-owned subsidiaries in the United States were less likely to form PACs in the first place, and contributed less money to candidates when such committees were erected. These results were interpreted as evidence that headquarters' concerns about the perceived legitimacy of political involvement depressed their participation in the process. Analogous observations have been made for British subsidiaries of multinational enterprises (Pinto-Duschinsky 1981: 232). However, no attempts were made to control for MNE home country in either work—a significant omission, given the variation in national political financing regimes and their potential impact on behavioral tendencies. One investigation did so, but was unable to link PAC funding or contribution patterns to country of origin (Mitchell 1995). A second political-action tool, agent lobbying, was investigated as well, with the same outcome. Again, the findings were heralded as support for foreign adaptation to the host setting. While corroborating the negative relationship between foreign ownership and PAC activity in general, Rehbein (1995) disclosed that culture distance was a salient factor. Parent companies in home countries that were culturally similar to the United States were more likely to fund committees ($p < 0.10$). Future investigations need to go beyond single-country analyses, study the entire portfolio of influence tactics across host units, and probe the specific coordination mechanisms that MNEs use to orchestrate government relations on a worldwide scale.

Given the dearth of studies on IR/HRM political behavior, we will rely on a preliminary 2×2 matrix to organize and discuss anecdotal accounts of such activity. The first column looks at domestic settings, where indigenous labor-market actors seek to influence the state, while the second column captures events occurring in foreign locations. Firms and pro-business NGOs are the focal point of row 1, with unions and pro-labor NGOs clustered together in row 2. The latter row is important to acknowledge, because corporate political behavior does not occur in a vacuum. Firm initiatives are likely to be at least partially determined by the political decisions implemented by those seeking to champion the labor movement's interests (Mitchell *et al.* 1997: 1100).

Starting in the upper left-hand cell, one can find ample evidence of IR/HRM-related political action by, or on behalf of, the business community. For example, the major employer federations in Germany waged an aggressive lobbying campaign in 1976 against what would become landmark legislation on codetermination (Callaghan 2003: 8). Their core contention was that representational parity for labor on supervisory boards would have a dramatic negative impact on economic performance. Unable to forestall its passage, the federations initiated legal action to have the law overturned by the nation's constitutional court, to no avail.[7] Legal Systems in Action 6.1 chronicles a more recent scenario, detailing the reactions of French employers to the mandatory 35 hour work week. In North America, we see the U.S. Council for International Business, which represents the country's corporate interests in several international bodies, testifying before congressional committees (e.g., supporting ILO convention ratification, disagreeing with government efforts to incorporate a social clause in the WTO/GATT framework), and writing letters to senators urging continued U.S. funding of the ILO and OECD. Since the beginning of 2000, the U.S. Chamber of Commerce has filed a multitude of *amicus* briefs with federal (46) and state (seven) courts as well as the National Labor Relations Board (seven) advocating that particular legal positions be adopted as a matter of law in labor and employment cases (see National Chamber Litigation Center, http://www.uschamber.com/nclc/default).

French employers, political action, and the legislated 35 hour work week

With a newly elected Socialist-led government in power, France set itself apart from other industrialized nations in 1998 by passing legislation that called for a 35 hour work week. Companies that agreed to reduce overall working hours by at least 10 percent—without lowering pay—while increasing the number of persons employed by 6 percent or more would qualify for up to seven years of financial incentives in the form of reduced social security contributions. No organization would be required to cut back the length of the work week. Firms that retained the traditional 39 hour schedule simply had to pay an overtime premium for all hours worked beyond the new threshold. They also forfeited the opportunity to lower their contributions for social programs. The envisioned benefits included a meaningful reduction in the country's double-digit unemployment rate and greater flexibility in employment contracting.

Reactions to the new policy were understandably varied. Labor leaders hailed the new mandate as the most significant development in the country's social contract in 60 years. The business community expressed bitter opposition not only to the policy's tenets, but also to the mode chosen to advance them. Rather than reducing unemployment, they argued, the ill-advised, ideologically driven initiative would cost jobs and place French firms at a significant competitive disadvantage. The European Commission even weighed in, conveying its view that the policy did not promote flexible labor markets and job creation as recommended in the macroeconomic guidelines for EU members.

There was little employers could do in 1997 when the state first communicated its resolve to enact a work-hours Bill during a tripartite national conference that was under way at the Prime Minister's residence. Employers had arrived expecting a spirited, but cooperative, dialogue on employment issues, not a *fait accompli*. Their public statements at conference end nevertheless made it clear they intended to fight back. The head of France's leading employer association, the CNPF, openly commented that the proceedings had been a "scandal." Other officers intimated that the organization might withdraw from all bodies jointly run with trade unions and stop national negotiations. Shortly thereafter, the association issued a press release foreshadowing the development of an alternative program to combat French unemployment in time for its general assembly in December— around the time when the government had projected submitting a "guidelines and incentives" Bill for reduced hours to Parliament.

It appeared that employers had been outmaneuvered on the political front a few months later when the National Assembly decided to make the statutory 35 hour work week effective in 2000. Their only apparent victory was an increase in the size threshold for companies given a two year reprieve from complying. Yet, this was not the end of the story. MEDEF, the newly renamed employers' federation, intensified its lobbying efforts to neutralize the legislation. In June 1999, the Labor Minister announced that overtime premiums would be lowered from 25 percent to 10 percent of normal pay during the law's first year of operation. A second peace offering found its way into the draft Bill being prepared that summer to better define how this area would be regulated—compliance would be assessed on the basis of annualized rather than weekly hours. The general work force could be scheduled for a maximum of 1,600 hours per year with overtime capped at 130 hours. How those hours were distributed would be left to collective bargaining. A different

continued

decision rule was fashioned for middle managers and white-collar employees, who could work up to 217 days in a 12 month period. If mollification was expected, the government was in for a surprise. MEDEF co-sponsored a protest rally in Paris the day before French law makers were set to debate the second reduced-hours measure. Thousands of business owners attended, focusing public attention on the issue even if they were unable to halt the legislative process.

Employers made life difficult for government officials in other ways. The financial incentives promised to qualifying firms did not come cheap, with an estimated price tag approaching 100 billion francs in the first year alone. Alcohol and tobacco taxes were supposed to be the primary revenue sources replacing waived social security contributions. A rash of negotiated agreements early on resulted in substantial cost overruns, though, prompting the state to turn its eye elsewhere for funding. Accordingly, the second draft work hours Bill included a provision seeking to tap into the surpluses in France's jointly administered unemployment insurance (UNEDIC) and social security (SECU) funds. This option was flatly rejected by employers (and unions for different reasons). MEDEF not only tried to publicly embarrass the government by questioning the appropriateness of using contributions collected for one purpose in a completely unrelated manner, but also threatened to permanently end its participation in any joint body that had monies siphoned off toward that end. The Labor Minister backed down and announced that alternative funding mechanisms would be sought. However, both follow-up proposals (i.e., 10 percent tax on overtime work in nonparticipating firms; diversion of alcohol duties currently being used to fund the Old Age Solidarity Fund) were opposed by business leaders.

Frustrated with the perceived lack of progress, MEDEF released a declaration in November 1999 outlining its expectations and future plans. Employers wanted the state to pledge that there would be a five-year moratorium on attempts to pay for the reduced-hours initiative with new corporate taxes or budget reallocations from social protection agencies. They also demanded that firms be granted a five year period to shorten work weeks in accordance with the law's provisions *or* through collective bargaining. Without these changes, the federation was intent on withdrawing from all jointly managed bodies dealing with employment matters. A very short window for action was specified to underscore its resolve. At most, the government had a few months to reverse its position.

The second part of the declaration was even more threatening to the nation's corporatist IR system. Big business invited organized labor to enter into bilateral discussions to establish a new social constitution that would eliminate "confusion as to the respective jurisdictions of the social partners and the government" and enable "autonomous, decentralized dialogue between the social partners." The state's role and influence in workplace decision making were under attack. Letters were sent to the major labor confederations extending an invitation to hold talks. All accepted, if for no other reason than to better ascertain what employers had in mind. The tactic elicited a conflicted response from government. President Chirac went on record stating he was willing to accept fundamental changes in the parties' interrelationships if that paved the way for successful outcomes in industrial relations. Prime Minister Jospin was more confrontational, asserting that he would "wage a political war against the idea" in defense of the Republic.

The government's subsequent decision to offset some of the costs associated with the reduced-hours policy with social program surpluses had the expected fallout. MEDEF suspended its involvement on the administrative boards of those funds and refused to appoint new representatives to them when it came time to do so in the summer of 2001. That fall, the association launched a nationwide campaign to rally support for a new series of initiatives. In January 2002, approximately 2,000 business representatives attended a special federation meeting that emphasized the need for greater political involvement and adopted a set of resolutions directed at politicians running for office in the upcoming presidential and general elections (the first demanding drastic reform or outright repeal of the statutory 35 hour work week). It was an unprecedented act by French employers.

The elections did produce a new center-right government, a development MEDEF believed had been influenced by its systematic efforts to publicize the previous coalition's shortcomings. Meetings were scheduled with the new Labor Minister to encourage a swift overhaul of the reduced-hours mandate. In September 2002, the state announced that the cabinet was reviewing a draft law relaxing several aspects of the underlying legislative framework. Things finally seemed to be moving in the right direction.

The feeling proved to be short-lived. No significant reforms occurred over the next two years, much to the chagrin of employers. Perhaps more disturbing from their perspective was Chirac's comment during a televised Bastille Day interview that the 35 hour working week was here to stay. He later added that the law was an untouchable fixture of the nation's social contract. What had changed? Management wasn't the only stakeholder group with a vested interest in the matter or the capacity to lobby. The high-stakes game of political action is not for those who are impatient, unorganized, or fainthearted.

Sources: Associated Press (1999), Barber (1998), EIRO (1997, 1999c, 2000b, 2001d, 2002d), Graham (1998, 1999a, b, 2000, 2002a, b), Johnson (2004a, b), Mallet (2002)

Moving to the upper right-hand cell, we see successful lobbying efforts by MNEs for restrictive labor legislation in Great Britain, Singapore, and Malaysia (e.g., Compa and Vogt 2001; Weinberg 1977). Japanese MNEs have obtained exemptions from the Thai minimum wage law for new employees during extended training periods. It has been reported that multinational firms pressured Ireland in the late 1990s not to alter the voluntary nature of union recognition by suggesting that existing FDI and future expansion plans would be placed in serious jeopardy if change occurred (EIRO 1998c). Several leading MNEs in the temporary services industry formed an association in India to petition the Labor Minister to usher in labor reforms that would facilitate more flexibility in employment relationships there (Jayashankar 2004). The United States is not immune to these forces, as Legal Systems in Action 6.2 reveals.

Turning to the lower left-hand cell, we confirm that organized labor and its supporters are no strangers to political action. According to one source, China's official labor federation (ACFTU) assisted with the development of more than 1,200 local laws and policies regulating workplace issues from 1997 to 2002 (China Internet Information Center 2002). Its South African counterpart, COSATU, aggressively tried to persuade the

India's government and IT sector lobby against potential outsourcing restrictions in the United States

As the twenty-first century dawned, there were many reasons to expect that India's IT sector would sustain the tremendous growth it had registered throughout the 1990s. A confluence of labor factor advantages and aggressive policy initiatives was transforming the country into a software engineering powerhouse, as well as an increasingly popular destination for business process outsourcing. Highly skilled English-speaking workers were in abundance, with more than 75,000 IT graduates being turned out annually by the country's educational institutions. In tandem, indigenous salary structures were 20–40 percent of what similarly trained individuals commanded in Western economies. Cultural training and accent neutralization programs were becoming the rage as established vendors sought to offer more customized services to foreign clients. Infrastructure upgrades and quality-oriented business practices made these human capital endowments even more formidable. Software technology parks had been or were being built in more than two dozen locations fueled by large-scale public-sector investment and export-oriented taxation policies. Locally based IT firms also seemed to have a passion for excellence, accounting for approximately two-thirds of the companies worldwide with SEI-CMM 5 process certification. In little more than a decade, industry worth had increased thirty-fivefold to nearly US$6 billion.

If one entity deserved credit for India's rise to prominence in the IT/BPO field, it was the National Association of Software and Service Companies (NASSCOM), a trade association sporting world-class operations. With a membership base that generated 95 percent of the industry's revenue, NASSCOM had amassed considerable political clout at home and respectability overseas. In many ways, it was the country's nerve center for IT policy and decision making, advising all levels of government on specific projects and participating directly in the central ministries of commerce, labor, and external affairs, among others. NASSCOM's dedication to, and savvy in, international marketing also was evident in the long list of Western firms—especially from the United States and United Kingdom—that were channeling significant volumes of work and relocating entire business units to India.

Yet, not all of the news associated with this storyline was good. A storm was brewing in the sector's primary market, the United States, as trade unions, politicians, and NGOs mobilized to fend off what was depicted as a mass exodus of skilled nonmanufacturing jobs. Mounting frustration and resentment in the American labor market was illustrated by the AFL-CIO's testimony before the US House Committee on Small Business in June 2003. Federation leaders railed against patterned misuse of temporary employment visas to facilitate seamless transfers of work abroad, and the substantial downward pressure that cheap foreign labor was exerting on the pay of domestic IT workers. Citing forecasts from Forrester Research, they also warned that over 3 million white-collar skilled jobs would be permanently lost over the next 15 years, depriving American workers of $136 billion in wages. From labor's vantage point, outsourcing work to places like India undermined the American middle class, deprived government treasuries of substantial tax revenues, and contributed substantially to the U.S. trade deficit.

While the merits of such points were debatable, elected officials grew wary of leaving the phenomenon unchecked and fostering perceptions among the electorate of "fiddling while

Rome burned". State governments were the first to act, sensing that the nation's capital would be loath to engage in protectionism at the same time it was trying to revive stalled multilateral negotiations to further liberalize trade. Ten governors issued executive orders on offshore outsourcing or took unilateral action to stop it (e.g., the cancellation of a $15.2 million contract with Tata Consulting Services to outsource agency work in Indiana[1]). State legislators eagerly followed suit as more than 100 anti-offshoring Bills were introduced in dozens of jurisdictions by the fall of 2004. Many sought to ban contractors from performing outsourced state work overseas. Others were designed to discourage the use of foreign call-center operations (e.g., requiring staff to identify their location and offer customers the option of rerouting their call stateside).

The movement received a major boost from federal lawmakers in the first quarter of 2004 as election-year pressures mounted. Twelve anti-outsourcing measures were championed by various members of Congress during that span. They ran the gamut of banning foreign contractors or subcontractors from performing government work that had been assigned to federal employees (or subsidized with federal monies) to denying companies that relied on such vendors federal financing and loan guarantees. One piece of legislation actually escaped detection until 24 hours after it had cleared the Senate, having been buried in an omnibus appropriations Bill.[2] Separate attempts were made to restrict the use of foreign guest workers, particularly those entering on L-1 (intracompany transfer) and H-1B (skilled worker) visas. Potential L-1 reforms included a two-year reduction in the authorized residence period, capping the number of visas issued annually, longer pre-entry employment with the employers, outlawing on-site assignments in client firms, and prohibiting visa holders from providing services to client firms that laid off any U.S. employees during the six months that preceded or followed their hiring. The two most controversial proposals for H-1B visas limited the in-residence period to a single, nonrenewable three-year term, and required hiring firms to show that they had increased the number of full-time U.S. employees, as well as their total and average wages, during the previous year.

With nearly half of its earnings deriving from the U.S. market, the Indian software services industry had too much at stake to passively accept such changes. Key stakeholders responded with a wide array of political behaviors on multiple fronts to turn the tide. The central government's main goal was to make the protectionist backlash against outsourcing a recurrent agenda item in bilateral and multilateral trade talks. In June 2003, the Commerce and Industry Minister pressed the Bush administration to do more than denounce state attempts to legislatively hinder outsourcing—India wanted its federal counterpart to formally intervene. While it was able to goad the USTR into labeling such initiatives "bad policy," federal intervention was dismissed for constitutional reasons. The topic was revisited the following spring as Indian politicians tried to come to grips with the unfavorable national legislation that was surfacing. Although the President had not come out in favor of any of these measures, Trade Representative Zoellick's comments did little to dispel the notion that the unsigned Bills were being used as bargaining chips to pressure India to accelerate trade reforms (e.g., reducing agricultural subsidies, liberalizing government procurement rules, strengthening intellectual property protections). Trying to bolster its bargaining position, New Delhi suggested that India might work against U.S. efforts to get global trade talks back on track after their derailment in Cancún unless the free flow of service jobs abroad was ensured. With strong backing from NASSCOM, India

continued

started to seek support within the WTO for the creation of a special professional services visa with no fixed expiration as well.

Leading law firms and lobbyists also were retained to improve India's understanding of, and ability to participate in, the local legal system. An advertising campaign of sorts was developed to highlight the net benefits arising from present economic ties. To illustrate, India's ambassador asserted that American companies had saved $26 billion by outsourcing work to his country, significantly enhancing the efficiency of the U.S. economy and its ability to invest in business innovation. Message in hand, the lobbyists began making their rounds on Capitol Hill as the Indian embassy maintained a low profile in the background.

The more hands-on approach to Washington politics dovetailed nicely with independent efforts by NASSCOM to "get in the ear" of law makers. A two-pronged strategy was implemented toward that end. Guided by an internationally renowned public relations firm, the association systematically lobbied Congress, the Bush administration, major U.S. states, and even the UK Parliament to let market forces, rather than regulation, determine the fate of offshore outsourcing. A grass-roots initiative also was launched, encouraging well-to-do Indian-Americans to become more politically involved. The primary objective was to shift their mode of participation from individual campaign contributors to supporters of formal advocacy groups or political action committees.

A different game plan was chosen to combat fundamental changes in the structure of temporary employment visas. Here, prudence dictated that the Information Technology Association of America (ITAA) should take the lead role in rallying host firms against additional restrictions. After years of informal dealings, the two organizations had signed a memorandum of understanding in 2001 pledging among other things to cooperate on public policy efforts with their respective governments. Teaming with nearly 200 domestic trade groups, the ITTA made the defeat of the aforementioned Bills a top priority. At times, the coalition also flexed its lobbying muscle to convince federal and state law makers to leave offshore outsourcing unregulated.

What did all of this political activity accomplish? Most of the restrictive state legislation proposed in 2003–04 never found its way out of committee or was voted down. Of the 11 laws that did pass, seven failed to survive gubernatorial vetoes. The remaining four were signed into law but are limited in scope.[3] At the federal level, even less materialized to constrain offshore outsourcing. None of the restrictions contemplated by the House or Senate in 2004 ever made it to the President for signing, and they were conspicuously absent from preliminary versions of the fiscal appropriation Bills for 2005. The budget measure ultimately approved by Congress in November 2004 simply earmarked $2 million to study offshoring's impacts on the U.S. economy and work force.

Modest success also would be achieved limiting immigration reform if the latest federal Bill becomes law as expected. While some setbacks are evident, the changes are not as onerous as the full set of amendments proposed early on. H-1B visa fees would rise to as much as $2,000–$1,500 for "worker retraining" (a 50 percent increase) and $500 for "fraud prevention and detection." Nondisplacement attestations would be reinstated, and employers would be obligated to match or exceed the prevailing wage for each job. The rule mandating one year of continuous employment with the petitioning firm prior to entry would be resurrected as well. (The period had been temporarily lowered to six months.) In addition, L-1 visa holders no longer could be stationed at third-party work sites unless they remained under the control and supervision of the petitioning employer and performed services demanding specialized knowledge specific to that firm. On the positive side, up to 20,000 persons completing U.S. graduate degree programs might be exempted each year from the annual cap on new H-1B visas (i.e., 65,000).

Lacking empirical evidence, it is difficult to establish the relative influence that each actor had on these outcomes. It may be more instructive to view this case as a compelling example of how the global economy challenges employers to be more committed to government relations and creative in its execution. Alliances often are necessary, whether they involve home government officials or foreign peer groups. Alliance management is becoming an increasingly salient organizational capability as a result. At the same time, there is no substitute for direct involvement in the host country. It is interesting to contemplate whether the visa situation would have played out differently had NASSCOM relied less on political action by proxy. Finally, one must be careful not to be lulled by lobbying victories. Like the mythical Phoenix, 112 anti-outsourcing Bills were introduced in all but a handful of American states during the first quarter of 2005. The battle was not over by a long shot.

Notes

1 Carved into smaller pieces, the project underwent a new round of bidding in hopes of enticing local companies to compete for the business.
2 The Bill only applied to a small number of entities (treasury, transportation, independent agencies) and would not be valid beyond September 2004. The Indian embassy and NASSCOM were quick to make these points, along with the fact that outsourced government work comprised approximately 2 percent of India's BPO business.
3 Readers interested in tracking state and federal legislation on global sourcing are directed to the NFAP website (http://www.nfap.net/researchactivities/globalsourcing/).

Sources: Agencies (2004), Bibby (2002), BS Corporate Bureau (2004), Businessdesk (2004), Frauenheim (2004), Gruber (2004), Haniffa (2003), Joseph (2004), Kumar and Bansal (2004), National Foundation for American Policy (2005), neoIT (2003), Parasuram (2004), PTI (2003, 2004a, b, c, d), Riedy (2003), Schroeder (2003, 2004), Ticoll (2004)

constitutional assembly to incorporate workers' rights in the new constitution as the nation politically reinvented itself during the 1990s. It also negotiated with the state to impact the provisions of diverse labor-market legislation that followed shortly thereafter. Sizable victories were achieved on both fronts (COSATU 2000). Of course, the outcomes are not always positive. The ACTU has mounted three unsuccessful campaigns over the last 12 years to convince Australia's Labor Party and labor-coalition governments to support core-labor-standard requirements in international trade agreements (Griffin *et al.* 2004). Several different tactics were utilized, with the emphasis shifting over time from internal party-politicking to external lobbying with other stakeholders. America's AFL-CIO has been very politically active for decades through a wide array of mechanisms. Besides publishing congressional voting records and funding PACs, the labor federation engages in voter registration drives (as does its British counterpart), testifies before Congress, provides a web-based infrastructure for rank-and-file members to individually lobby their representatives, and disseminates legislative fact sheets and model employment legislation (see http://www.aflcio.org/issuespolitics/). Since the mid-1990s, attempted or desired labor law reforms have sparked general strikes in Argentina, Greece, Israel, Italy, South Africa, and South Korea, with mixed results. In 2001, the Collective of Honduran Women, an NGO, lobbied government officials to back stronger labor protections in *maquiladoras* by co-signing a code of ethics along with producers (Quinteros 2001). U.S. human rights organizations like the ILRF and HRW frequently submit testimony to influence the decisions of federal law makers (e.g., DR-CAFTA passage) and file *amicus* briefs in labor and employment lawsuits.

Our final cell has unions and supporting transnational organizations entering the political arena to interact with international bodies and foreign states to advance labor's position. In previous chapters, we encountered the ICFTU systematically providing unsolicited ILS-compliance reports to the WTO Trade Policy Review Board for consideration, the ICFTU and European Trade Union Confederation trying to influence EU-GSP policies and their implementation, and the AFL-CIO securing representation on the U.S. delegation negotiating EPZ labor reforms with Bangladesh officials and Asian investors (see Legal Systems in Action 4.1). More recently, the ICFTU initiated what it hoped would become a firestorm of protest over draft legislation that weakened several aspects of Nigeria's Trade Union Act. It began with a letter sent directly to the Nigerian President, urging him to take whatever steps were legally necessary to withdraw the Bill from the National Assembly, and to better support the work of an ILO-sponsored tripartite committee trying to formulate recommendations to bring the country's labor and employment laws into conformity with international standards (ICFTU 2004). This was accompanied by an appeal to all global union federations and interested NGOs to send letters advocating the same position to the President and Nigerian embassy in their own countries.

The rest of the chapter develops research propositions for the corporate strategy–public policy interface as it relates to IHRM.

Wielding political-action mechanisms

We start with the assumption that MNEs establish and maintain international operations intending to advance a set of strategic objectives bearing on profitability, growth, diversification, or some combination thereof. These objectives, in turn, require that HRM policies and practices not only equip business units to compete effectively in their local environments, but also strengthen the MNE's interunit linkages (Schuler *et al.* 1993). In contrast, government leaders are expected to be pursuing more diverse, and potentially inconsistent, objectives containing economic, sociocultural, and political elements. At a minimum, host officials should harbor expectations that foreign-owned operations will preserve or improve living standards and the indigenous skill base. Guided by these criteria, each side attempts to advance its sphere of influence within the host HRM system through political and economic tactics—their ultimate aim being control over the flow of talent, work practices and standards, and general business information (e.g., trade secrets) into and out of the host unit. Targeted are such critical facets of HRM as labor-market emphasis (i.e., internal versus external); human resource development policies; reward, safety, and voice practices; and the role that industrial relations institutions play in workplace decision making.

The two sides are likely to be saddled with situational constraints that influence what kinds of initiatives will be undertaken to control the internal policies of local operations and corporate interactions with the larger society. An MNE's ability to identify, prioritize, and implement measures which are consistent with its strategic human-resource needs should be moderated by such factors as the HRM function's role in strategic planning, its structure, and the resource base from which it must operate. Similarly, host officials may find desired government action constrained by the state's historical role in industrial relations, administrative structure, political sensitivity to capital markets, and obligations to superordinate polities. Host officials should encounter difficulty maintaining significant departures from government's historical role absent major national crisis. Idiosyncratic economic incentives or regulatory exemptions for foreign investment are inconsistent with a strong societal-corporatist tradition, inviting focused opposition from well organized interest groups. State-corporatist settings should offer the presiding administration more latitude in decision making unless strong rival political factions are present. Plural states may lack the political consensus to vest authorities with sufficiently broad powers to create labor-market conditions that will induce large-scale foreign investment.

Even when government stays within the bounds of expected behavior, host officials may be unable to effectuate desired HRM changes if there is extensive fragmentation in the administrative systems that implement government policies toward MNEs (Lecraw and Morrison 1991). To illustrate, national labor ministries may lack sufficient control over quasi-independent federal agencies or state sovereignties to ensure that financial incentives for relocation in targeted development areas are supported by vocational training and manpower programs under the control of regional authorities. In the same vein, compliance agencies with overlapping jurisdiction may issue inconsistent employment regulations that doom MNEs to violate one set of standards in their attempts to satisfy the other. It will become increasingly difficult to advance economic development or social responsibility objectives as these structural deficiencies become more pronounced.

The net value that each side reaps from host-unit performance will determine the perceived adequacy of their current spheres of influence in HRM decision making, and suggest where change should be effectuated.

What specific factors will affect the management and resourcing of political behaviors across MNE operations? The firm's larger competitive environment is expected to be a major determinant. Environments can differ markedly based on the extent to which firm advantage must be derived from global integration, national responsiveness, or some combination of the two (Ghoshal and Nohria 1993). International environments call for little in terms of responsiveness or integration, inviting MNEs to establish autonomous host units that deliver standardized products to buyers. Global environments also demand low product differentiation, but necessitate widespread interunit collaboration to achieve the operational efficiencies essential to success in the industry. In contrast, multinational and transnational environments both contain strong pressures for national responsiveness. The former competitive arena again tolerates independent country operations, while the latter dictates that MNEs find ways of orchestrating high integration and high responsiveness simultaneously. As overall competitiveness becomes increasingly dependent on interunit linkages across countries, there is a growing need to oversee and control the political strategies pursued within each host. Therefore, it is anticipated that:

Proposition 1. Decision making for HRM political activity will be more centralized when the MNE is competing in market environments exhibiting strong pressures for global integration than when it is competing in those exhibiting weak pressures for integration.

The breadth and intensity of MNE efforts to manage the political dynamics of host legal systems also should be influenced by three critical aspects of the composite legal environment: complexity, relevancy, and heterogeneity (Florkowski and Nath 1993). Regulatory complexity is defined by the range of HRM issues that are controlled by law and the extensiveness of the requirements within each functional area. Regulatory relevance describes the extent to which host countries—and other stakeholders—assign a high enforcement priority to MNE compliance within their borders. Regulatory heterogeneity refers to the amount of differentiation in legal superstructures across countries (i.e. mix of pluralist, corporatist, and concertation-without-labor settings). Returning later to the likely forms political behavior will take in local political economies, it is projected that:

Proposition 2. HRM political-activity levels will be greater overall for MNEs when regulatory heterogeneity, complexity, and relevancy are high than when they are low.

Additional factors are expected to shape the political behavior of multinationals at the host-country level. Boddewyn and Brewer (1994) hypothesized that MNE political behavior intensifies as the stakes become higher, the opportunities for leverage and arbitrage of government policies become more abundant, and the firm's political competencies are more developed. The relatively small size of HRM budgets also suggests that firms will allocate resources parsimoniously to units where the probability of delivering successful interventions is high. As state systems become more fragmented, there are greater opportunities to capitalize on decentralized administrative decision making for firm-specific advantage. For example, Mercedes-Benz and BMW pitted local development authorities in numerous U.S. states against one another to secure economic and training incentives for greenfield sites that would not have been available from the federal government. Building on these concepts, it is expected that:

Proposition 3(a). HRM political activity will be greater within host countries that have high strategic salience to an MNE than in those that have low strategic salience.

Proposition 3(b). HRM political activity will be greater within host countries when there is high fragmentation in the government systems that implement labor-market policies than when there is low fragmentation.

Proposition 3(c). The level of boundary spanning for HRM political activity by other stakeholders will be greater within host countries that have high strategic salience to the MNE and high fragmentation of the government systems overseeing labor markets.

Political competencies are not automatically transferable across national borders (Boddewyn and Brewer 1994). MNE actions which generate political capital in one country may not garner tangible benefits in another because they do not advance the latter's macroeconomic goals or raise perceived legitimacy questions. Moreover, the procedural expertise needed to capitalize on processes in one political system can differ substantially from that required elsewhere. We saw several examples of national responsiveness pressures on political financing. There also are localization pressures in terms of the appropriate unit to influence. Executive-branch units tend to be the most promising targets for political behavior in parliamentary systems, while the legislative branch tends to occupy this position in the United States (Hillman and Keim 1995). Government actors in the two systems also are not equally predisposed to anchor decision making on cost–benefit justifications, nor do they gauge the merits of policy options using the same time horizon. Therefore, corporate political savvy is expected to be strongest in the home countries of MNEs, becoming less applicable abroad as regulatory heterogeneity increases. Consequently, it is predicted that:

Proposition 4(a). HRM political activity will be more effective when host labor-market policies are implemented by governmental processes which are similar to those of the MNE's home country than when they are dissimilar.

Host governments should be more receptive to MNEs that are able and willing to assist the state in promoting valued economic and social policies. Fewer government resources should be devoted to adversarial interactions in such instances, leading one to expect:

Proposition 4(b). HRM political activity will be more effective when MNEs seek to transfer HRM systems that have high public-policy salience to host countries than when they seek to transfer HRM systems with low policy salience.

What forces dictate which subset of political activities MNEs will apply within a given host nation? Various portions of our discussion suggest the following will be true:

Proposition 5(a). Direct contact will be MNEs' dominant form of HRM-related lobbying in countries with pluralist and state-corporatist IR systems, while participation in associational lobbying will be the dominant form in societal-corporatist IR systems.

Proposition 5(b). PAC contributions and voter education programs will consume more of the resources that host units allocate to HRM political activities in pluralist IR systems than will be the case in corporatist IR systems.

Proposition 5(c). Political financing will consume more of the resources that host units allocate to HRM political activities as the local political economy becomes more dependent on private sources for funding.

Within pluralist systems, MNE expenditures on PACs and voter education should be higher during periods when national unions are experiencing negative political munificence (i.e., the political party which labor has affiliated with is not in power or sympathetic to its concerns) (see Ofori-Dankwa 1993).

Conclusion

The decision to actively participate in the local political economy is not one taken lightly by companies, especially MNEs. Countries vary considerably in the way that law is evolved and the political behaviors that private actors are allowed to engage in to impact the process. Political competencies honed in one national setting may not adequately prepare multinationals to deal with other governments when it comes to labor-market regulation. Yet, the need to effectively manage the state's influence on operations is critical—more so as multinationals become dependent on integrated sourcing to establish a competitive advantage in their markets.

With so little known about political behavior as it relates to IHRM, we highlighted pertinent anecdotes from business and nonbusiness actors in a preliminary attempt to map the activity domain. This was followed by a discussion of the forces believed to influence the form and management of political action in cross-border situations. It is hoped that these materials will inspire more systematic investigations in the future.

The final chapter provides a more expansive discussion of the effects that global legal systems have on firm competitiveness and what might be done to achieve and sustain it.

Managing global legal systems for competitive advantage

7

We reach the end of our journey facing several simple truths. Though nation states utilize an assortment of legal superstructures to formulate and police the rights of societal members, labor markets the world over are governed by common law or civil law principles. Vast differences nevertheless exist in the form and level of government involvement in IR/HRM systems. It also can be said that employment regulation remains strongly rooted in national traditions and culture notwithstanding the efforts of regional and transnational political entities to foster greater convergence. This is not meant to suggest they are without influence, particularly in the hands of an increasingly sophisticated cadre of external stakeholders that are part of, or sympathetic to, organized labor. Labor standard disparities have become a thorny issue in trade policy and foreign affairs largely through their efforts. At the same time, the dramatic growth of employment-practice lawsuits around the globe has opened up a second front for business organizations to contend with. How firms choose to respond to these developments could significantly affect their economic future.

Accordingly, corporate decision makers, HR professionals, and academics need to redouble their efforts to find effective ways of navigating global legal systems. Some pieces of the puzzle are known, others await discovery in future studies. A few comments on both are in order.

Implications for management practice

Building on earlier chapters, Figure 7.1 summarizes the multitude of ways that employers can impact the legal superstructure regulating employment relationships. Firm-specific initiatives can take the form of NCP review requests concerning alleged noncompliance with the OECD guidelines, as well as direct interactions with bloc and national institutions during the course of lobbying or adjudication. More often, companies must work through larger federations to gain access to, or meaningfully influence the internal processes of, transnational institutions like the ILO and OECD (e.g., furnishing structured input during the initial proposal and formal adoption stages for ILO conventions, advising national contact points on specific instances or operating policies). The ability to influence regional blocs and individual governments likewise may be rooted largely in unique access opportunities enjoyed by trade groups and employer

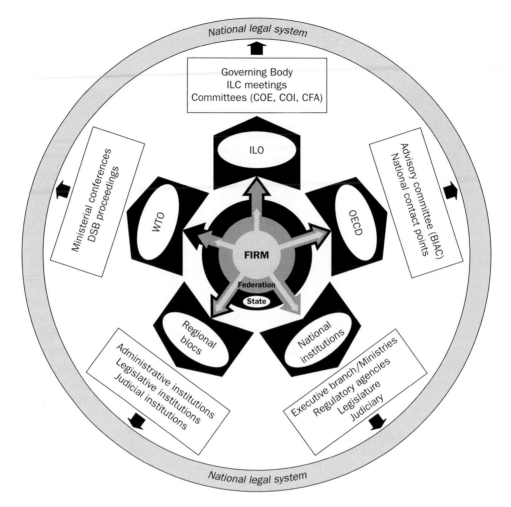

Figure 7.1 Opportunities to influence national legal systems

associations. At times, companies and federations may be dependent on the state to advance their interests in supranational political entities. This is categorically true for dealings with the WTO (e.g., invoking DSB procedures in trade disputes, building a consensus position on social clauses in multilateral trade agreements). Certain aspects of the ILO, OECD, and regional blocs are of the same mold (e.g., ILO Article 26 proceedings, OECD accession reviews, EU Council voting on proposed work directives).

In response, an issue-based triangulation strategy should be formulated to maximize one's chances of steering labor-market regulation at home and abroad. By way of analogy, research on corporate political behavior in Europe shows that firms not only lobby EU institutions on multiple levels, but also face different probabilities of securing access depending on the mode chosen (Bouwen 2002; McLaughlin *et al.* 1993). Bouwen's probe is highly instructive, documenting the different levels of success that European associations, national federations, and individual companies experience when trying to gain access to the Council of Ministers, European Commission, and European

Parliament. This lesson should not be lost on those willing to create the worldwide government relations "war room" envisioned in Figure 7.1.

What are the professional and organizational ramifications of this complicated legal picture? One study disclosed that knowledge-based guidelines for employment law—presumably domestic—had been devised by nearly 70 percent of the responding national affiliates of the World Federation of Personnel Management Associations (Brewster *et al.* 2000: 27). The report ultimately suggests that legislative and regulatory frameworks may be critical components of the external environment that human resource practitioners need to master (p. 41). This book ups the ante, arguing that HR executives and HR professionals lack core competencies if they are not broadly versed in regional, if not global, labor-market regulation. Indigenous firms that have no immediate interest in taking their operations overseas still may be competing against foreign firms that benefit from employment-regulation variance. If offshore relocations and foreign supplier alliances are contemplated, there is the specter of crisis management with key external stakeholders if they are not handled properly. The ability to offer strategic input on these matters depends on knowing how employment law potentially affects international value chains.

Legal compliance audits have been recommended in single-country settings for some time, although the types of items discussed tend to capture a small portion of the firm's potential exposure (e.g., Biles and Schuler 1986: 59–67; Jennings *et al.* 1990). Dowling (2001: 7) asserted that multinationals regularly engage in worldwide compliance audits for employment regulation but failed to supply any documentation associated with this practice. From a content standpoint, the tables in Chapter 5 and Appendix B should provide ample guidance for the construction of appropriate questions. The process side of this exercise should be co-chaired by a senior HR executive and corporate counsel, with the actual audit being performed by an outside law firm with a strong transnational presence. Some information technology vendors offer software products that can be useful support tools for compliance management reporting,[1] but they are no substitute for external, independent expertise that may be needed to defend the broader audit's integrity should regulators come calling in the future. Concerns have arisen in the United States that voluntary internal audits may increase liability if problems are detected and the results become known. To maximize one's ability to protect such information against forced disclosure, it has been recommended that:

- a written retainer agreement be developed, explicitly defining the parameters, methodology, and access procedures for the audit, as well as its purpose (i.e., being prepared because of a formal request for legal advice);
- primary responsibility for the analyses and final report be vested with the attorneys being retained;
- confidentiality agreements be signed by all members of the audit team;
- appropriate safeguards be maintained to preserve the secrecy of the findings and underlying materials (HR Focus 2004).

Whether these actions are necessary or desirable in other nations is itself a matter warranting legal advice.

Employment-practices liability insurance is another response to consider. Underwriters in North America, Europe, and select Asian markets (e.g., Australia) offered EPL products in numerous forms, as noted in Chapter 1. Though expensive, this risk-mitigating tactic could be a net positive benefit during the early stages of market entry if host legal systems and labor-market regulation are substantially different from what the foreign-based firm has experienced. It also should be weighed carefully whenever multinationals are committed to high levels of centralization in international HR decision making or satisfy a substantial part of their global staffing needs through expatriation.

More central to effective expatriate management is the structuring of international employment contracts. Properly drafted choice-of-law and choice-of-forum clauses should be cornerstones of such agreements. The radical divergence in national economic- and income-security regulation[2] affords plaintiffs a smorgasbord of potential remedies, inviting forum shopping whenever disagreements arise over the execution or modification of work responsibilities. Table 7.1 captures an even bigger concern when high-level managerial and technical talent is brought into host countries—preempting future threats to competitiveness should these individuals decide to leave the organization. The capacity to restrict the disclosure or use of trade secrets and strategic information post-employment differs substantially across countries, not to mention the accompanying cost. Recall from Chapter 4 that governments unilaterally decide which law courts will apply to international litigation within their borders if the parties failed to designate this beforehand. Choice-of-law provisions reduce the risk that judges will clothe expats with entitlements that never were intended, but they are not ironclad defenses. Supranational obligations may act as an override mechanism. Under the 1980 Rome Convention, EU member states are expected to subordinate the chosen law to stronger worker protections that are available from an EU nation whose law would have been invoked in the absence of choice. Elsewhere, courts simply might refuse to enforce it, on the basis of the argument that it is repugnant to local public policy. They nevertheless should be inserted because of the judicial tendency to uphold them if the law comes from a sovereignty that has a substantial interest in the employment matter.

Choice-of-forum provisions try to corral litigation risk by contractually establishing the place where alleged breaches will be challenged. The selection can be framed in terms of a particular nation or court therein. Waiting until the aggrieved expat decides where to sue confines the MNE's options to mounting a defense or seeking dismissal based on the principle of *forum non conveniens*. Like its companion, this legal strategy still must survive judicial scrutiny.

Implications for future research

While senior management and HR professionals have abundant opportunities to shape the regulatory environment, we are far removed from being able to comprehensively define what constitutes "best practice," let alone identify which firms should be labeled as engaging in such. The underdeveloped and highly fragmented nature of research in this topical domain should be viewed as an open invitation to the research community to dramatically upgrade the scope and quality of subsequent investigations. Three thematic improvements, in particular, would greatly enhance our understanding of how legal systems function and their ultimate relevance to corporate stakeholders. First, prevailing levels and trends in HR-related political action must be thoroughly documented in single- and multi-country settings. This encompasses not only the kinds of influence strategies adopted, but also how they are resourced, coordinated, and evaluated by individual organizations. Second, researchers must be more consistently sensitive to construct validity issues when they operationalize labor and employment regulation. Even those works that have recognized the need to incorporate content and process dimensions could be substantially improved. Third, impact studies must be broadened to include the reaction of capital markets to changing domestic and foreign workplace regulation. Little is known about the significance that investors attach to new legal requirements or the compliance posture of firms at home or abroad. Each point is discussed more fully below.

Having mapped the options that individual firms have to wield influence in global legal systems, we must progress beyond the Dark Ages in our understanding of what companies are doing in indigenous and overseas settings. At a minimum, comparative data are needed on the resourcing and execution of external boundary spanning bearing on employment regulation. To what extent is it a proactive, in-house activity as opposed to passive receipt of information from employer associations and HR professional societies? How much time is spent by HR executives and others in the organization interacting with regulators on employment matters? What percentages of these dealings are ministerial, adversarial, and participative? How common are formal government-relations strategies on labor-market regulation? Are such strategies and activities more likely to be observed in labor-intensive or in capital-intensive industries? In pluralist than in corporatist IR systems? In AIEs or emerging markets? How is performance in IR/HRM-related government relations evaluated at the firm level, and what is the track record to date based on survey or archival data? Where does ultimate accountability reside for efficacy (e.g., senior HR executive, corporate counsel, or public affairs executive)? To these questions we add items stemming from the research propositions on political action raised in the previous chapter.

To return to Figure 7.1, ethnographic studies and other forms of qualitative research would be highly desirable to shed more light on the inner workings of tripartite and other structures in the supranational bodies depicted. Regional blocs utilize diverse vehicles to engage the social partners in the development and implementation of labor standards that transcend national borders. Some have purely advisory roles; others have oversight responsibilities. There are settings where the state is officially represented, and others where it is not. How similar are the behavioral dynamics of these entities to those prevailing in national tripartite arrangements and firm-level labor–management cooperation programs? Are there common life-cycle stages that they pass through? Similarly, numerous blocs have dedicated forums where labor ministers collectively advise on labor-rights issues and, in some instances, promote dispute resolution. The intraorganizational bargaining process behind their concerted actions should be much better understood. A "grounded theory" approach should permeate these investigations with the specific aim of theoretical development.

Botero *et al.*'s (2004a) pioneering effort to empirically capture the intricate web of labor-market regulation is unprecedented in scope and detail, and should be applauded. That does not mean their approach is beyond refinement. The coding scheme used in several areas raises concerns about public-policy hairsplitting that has little practical significance. For example, ordinal variables capturing the right to unionize, collectively

Table 7.1 Trade secrets, restrictive agreements, and the employment relationship, select countries

Region	Country	Implied duty to protect former employer's trade secrets	Nondisclosure clauses enforceable?	Non-competition clauses			
				Enforceable?	Maximum duration allowed	Consideration required?	Mandated consideration during the restricted period
North America	United States	Yes	Yes	Yes[a]	Case-by-case determination	No[b]	None[b]
	Canada	Yes	Yes	Yes	6–12 months (24 months in Quebec)	No	None
	Mexico	Yes	Yes	No	–	–	–
Europe	United Kingdom	Yes	Yes	Yes[c]	18 months for senior employees 12 months for other employees	No	None
	Ireland	Yes	Yes	Yes	Case-by-case determination	No	None
	Germany	Yes (third-party use)	Yes	Yes	24 months	Yes	50% of former salary throughout
	France	Yes	Yes	Yes	24 months (48 months rarely)	Yes	33% of former salary for first 24 months and 100% thereafter
	Italy[d]	Yes	Yes	Yes	30 months for managers 36 months for other employees	Yes	50–100% of former salary throughout
	Sweden	No	Yes	Yes	24 months[e]	Yes[e]	60% of former salary throughout[e]
	Spain	Yes	Yes	Yes	24 months for senior managers 6 months for other employees	Yes	Case-by-case determination

Region	Country					
	Portugal	Yes	Yes	36 months	Yes	Case-by-case determination
	Poland	Yes (three years)	Yes	*	Yes	≥ 25% of former salary throughout
Asia and Oceania	Japan	Yes	Yes	24 months	Yes	Case-by-case determination
	Australia	Yes	Yes	12 months	No	–
	South Korea	Yes	Yes	12 months	Yes	Case-by-case determination
	China	Yes	Yes	Unclear		
	Singapore	Yes	Yes	18 months for senior managers 12 months for other employees	Yes	Case-by-case determination
	Philippines	Yes	Yes	60 months	No	–
Middle East and Africa	Israel	Yes	Yes	Case-by-case determination[g] *	*	*
	South Africa	Yes	Yes	Case-by-case determination	Yes	Case-by-case determination
South America	Brazil[d]	Yes	Yes	36 months	*	*
	Argentina	Yes	Yes	6 months	Yes	Case-by-case determination
	Chile	No	No[f]	–	–	–
	Peru	Yes	No	–	–	–

Sources: Jerusalem College of Technology (2001), Maatman (1997), MacLaren (1997), Ogawa (1999)

Notes:

* Extensive web-based searches failed to locate information on how this subject is regulated.

a The following states prohibit or severely weaken the enforcement of noncompete agreements: California, Colorado, Florida, Hawaii, Louisiana, Montana, Nevada, North Dakota, Oklahoma, Oregon, South Dakota, and Wisconsin.

b Unless this arrangement is sought post-hire. When that occurs, courts will determine whether adequate additional consideration has been provided on a case-by-case basis.

c As distinct from "gardening leave" clauses that call for employers to pay employees not to come to work from the time they are notified about termination until a specific date following their release. Existing rulings make it doubtful that courts will allow employers to extend the time one is precluded from working elsewhere by having noncompetition clauses become operative when gardening leave expires.

d To date, constitutionality concerns have not stopped courts from enforcing noncompete agreements.

e Collective bargaining agreements between the Swedish Employers' Confederation and several white-collar unions regulate these arrangements (Hall et al. 1996).

f The lone exception deals with the sale of a business.

g A nine-month standard has emerged in the high-tech sector.

bargain, and participate in industrial action are set to zero if there is no constitutional reference to these issues. One can acknowledge the symbolic value of characterizing something as a "constitutional right," but such language does not guarantee that the populace actually has well-defined entitlements that can be vindicated in the legal system. Implementing legislation or executive decrees provide much better insight in this respect. It also is true that elaborate rights can evolve over time in these areas solely through legislation, court rulings, and administrative regulations (e.g., the United States). By assigning the United States zeroes for all three variables, the researchers totally ignore over 70 years of federal intervention in labor-management affairs. Curiously, other aspects of labor law are codified without regard to their source.

Some dichotomous variables mask key national differences as well. Extension procedures arguably pose different levels of risk, depending on whether they are triggered by union petitions alone, joint requests from labor and management, or unilateral government action. Notice requirements for industrial action vary considerably in terms of the industries affected (general versus essential services) and minimum lead time (a few days to more than one month). These distinctions are not recognized in the present system. Analogous concerns arise for the regulatory areas outside of IR that have been included in the larger data set.

Most important of all, no adjustments are made to account for a given sovereignty's institutional capacity or propensity to enforce labor and employment laws. Chapter 4 made it clear that enforcement efforts in many emerging markets are openly thwarted by government officials or seriously compromised by resource deficiencies. AIEs are better able to fund, staff, and direct such activities, but that does not mean they are uniformly generous in this undertaking. There also is a danger they will evolve bureaucratic infrastructures which are so complex and cumbersome that they are afflicted with serious enforcement inefficiencies. To illustrate, by the late 1990s the U.S. Department of Labor was administering more than two dozen different types of adjudication procedures to give effect to the nearly 180 statutes under its charge—raising significant coordination problems for agency staff (Weil 1997: 431–432). These realities make it imperative that national measures of employment regulation go beyond content analyses of substantive rights. Two works start us down that path. Block and Roberts (2000) added an enforcement component to their labor-standards indices for Canadian provinces and U.S. states. The proxy chosen was quite limited, however, defined as the ability to secure judicial review of decisions rendered by the agency charged with compliance oversight.[3] Verité (2003) was more ambitious in its evaluation of key emerging markets, generating institutional capacity scores for labor law enforcement based on government and proprietary data. Countries were classified as having "strong institutional capacity," "effective institutional capacity but significant holes in effectiveness," "institutional capacity of limited effectiveness," and "seriously limited or ineffective institutional capacity." Researchers are urged to extend and enhance this element in future research designs.

It has become standard fare in the finance and economics literature to utilize event studies to ascertain the effects that business-related occurrences have on shareholder wealth. Pursuant to this methodology, actual stock-price movements during an event window (i.e., span during which investors are anticipated to be influenced by a news item) are compared to expected returns that are generated using one of several potential models.[4] Disparities between the two sets of values are classified as "abnormal" returns, which are tested to establish whether they are statistically different from zero. More likely to be invoked in studies of corporate restructuring, financial disclosures, or international trade (e.g., Epstein and Schnietz 2002; Oxley and Schnietz 2001), this technique occasionally finds its way into HR publications. For example, it has been used to assess stock-market reaction to major reductions in force, compensation and benefit changes, and positive HR reputation signals (Abowd *et al.* 1990; Hannon and Milkovich 1996). Rock (2003) added an international twist by examining the impact that NGO disclosure campaigns have on the stock price of U.S. firms doing business with foreign sweatshops. Unfavorable news stories generally resulted in statistically significant negative abnormal returns. The positive bump in share values that one multinational experienced for good-news events (e.g., resort to supplier monitoring systems, guarantees to phase out relationships involving sweatshop labor) was held out as corroboration of investors' general sensitivity to this topic.

Closer to home, there have been scattered instances where employment-law enforcement or passage was the event under investigation. Discrimination litigation was the central issue in two studies, being linked to modest declines in shareholder wealth (Selmi 2003; Wright *et al.* 1995).[5] More intriguing still is Billger's (2005) assessment of share-price movements during key stages of the U.S. Occupational Safety and Health Act's legislative evolution. Abnormal negative returns were identified around the time when (1) the initial Bill was released from committee to the floor of the House of Representatives, and (2) the House followed the Senate's lead in approving the conference committee report which contained the Bill's final language. Follow-up analyses indicated that the downturns were greatest in the industries most likely to experience safety and health problems, and that stock prices did not recover quickly. The latter finding was attributed to investor expectations that there would be a long-term negative effect on profitability.

Leveraging event-study methodology to study regulatory processes is not without potential pitfalls. Event windows can span months or years, especially when new legislation is the subject matter of interest. As Lamdin (2001) notes, news of the impending change may leak out gradually over time, making it extremely difficult to isolate a reevaluation effect from market noise. Alternatively, the change may have been fully anticipated and assimilated into share-price levels well before the legislative branch concludes its ritual of formal passage. Therefore, he advocates using a parameterized version of the market model which incorporates dichotomous variables for multiple event periods within the larger event window. Each period represents a distinct phase in the creation or enforcement of a particular regulatory scheme that one anticipates will influence investors. Billger (2005), and to a lesser extent Selmi (2003), adhere to this practice in their investigations. When doing so, the focus should be on firm-specific returns or a portfolio-return measure that is equally weighted or value-weighted to test for industry effects.[6] Where nonzero abnormal returns are uncovered, Lamdin further recommends that they be regressed on appropriate firm-level characteristics to confirm that significant relationships are present in the expected directions.

Skeptics may argue that this type of analysis has little relevance outside of AIEs, which have well developed stock markets that efficiently process promising or damaging information. While there is a dearth of event studies targeting emerging markets, some do exist. For example, adverse news about local environmental performance—typically warnings or penalties stemming from regulatory noncompliance—has triggered negative abnormal returns in several Latin American countries and the Philippines (Dasgupta *et al.* 2001). Tomz (1997) found that the stock prices of Mexican firms in labor-intensive industries rose on the heels of two critical events which preceded NAFTA's onset: passage of the House Bill that paved the way for U.S. implementation (Senate support was not in doubt), and an announcement from Canada's newly elected Prime Minister that his government would abide by the Canadian Congress's approval of NAFTA despite earlier campaign rhetoric to the contrary.

Where should we go from here? Beginning with developed economies, it would be valuable to engage in cross-country comparisons of the market's reaction to the enactment, amendment, and enforcement of employment regulation. Are there regional differences in the direction and magnitude of investors' reactions? Does the orientation of the national IR system (i.e., pluralist versus corporatist) have a moderating effect on share-price movements when laws do change? Investors might be less sensitive to labor-market interventions in the latter because tripartite structures afford management ample opportunities to alter the content of proposed regulation to minimize the disruptive impact on business activities. Failing to achieve that, employers may have secured a *quid pro quo* concession in a nonlabor area of regulation that potentially blunts greater transaction costs in the workplace. If there are no discernible differences in capital-market behavior, then it would appear that strong signals are being sent that tripartism is believed to be unduly redistributive in nature.

Other intriguing questions come to mind. How do stock markets react to regulatory shocks in employment regulation in other AIEs—especially those with which there are strong inward or outward investment links? In emerging markets that have attracted significant levels of FDI from the country being studied? Does the reverse hold true (i.e., positive abnormal returns for companies in developing nations when labor or employment protections intensify in AIEs that have a track record of making inward investments)? How interested are home-country capital markets in the successes or failures that international business units have in work-related compliance management and political action? In an increasingly global economy, these issues are too important to be left unanswered.

Conclusion

With their many layers and interrelationships, global legal systems place a premium on well orchestrated, multifaceted corporate initiatives that are steeped in a deep awareness of the substantive and procedural diversity of employment regulation. Borrowing from the strategy area, firms need to conduct ongoing SWOT (i.e., strengths, weaknesses, opportunities, and threats) analyses of the legal environment that is pertinent to their operations. Are organizational capabilities sufficiently developed and funded to advance the employer's interests across the range of ministerial, adversarial, and participative interactions they are likely to encounter at home and abroad? While it is not necessary to transform the international HRM function into a cadre of global employment lawyers, more professional emphasis should be placed on transnational legal education. Systematic legal audits of domestic and foreign units are a necessary complement. It would be wise to include potential investment targets in these reviews as well. The siren song of offshore outsourcing may draw unwary firms into alliance or market-entry decisions that prove to be a regulatory quagmire in the workplace. Researchers can be a positive force in the evolution of these processes by expanding our knowledge base in the ways that were suggested. Finally, great care needs to be exercised in structuring the contracts governing international assignments. No matter how substantively appealing a nation's employment laws may be to MNEs, choice-of-law clauses are only as valuable as the judiciary's interest in enforcing them in countries that believe they have a right to assert jurisdiction.

In closing, it is hoped that this contribution to the Global HRM series will serve the reader on multiple levels. Rather than treating the law and legal systems as exogenous variables, we examined the inner workings of the regulatory environment for IR/HRM and showed how it can be impacted by private actors on a domestic and international level. A concerted effort was made to provide detailed summaries of the labor and employment laws of several dozen nations as well. Although country and regional materials abound on specific aspects of workplace regulation, the ability to efficiently assess a given polity's *modus operandi* for labor-market interventions has been quite limited to date. The same can be said for the capacity to judge a particular sovereignty's regulatory behavior in employment matters *vis-à-vis* the larger international community. Finally, considerable documentation was amassed to support the argument that government relations must be treated as more than an exercise in compliance management when it comes to international human capital management. Legal systems are a value-chain component that must be actively managed, simultaneously impacting the "employee champion" and "strategic partner" roles laid before the HR profession. Perhaps raising more questions than it answered, this book should be viewed as a modest first step toward mastering that challenge.

Appendix A

Key ministries and agencies for industrial relations and equal employment opportunities, select countries

Country	Industrial relations	Equal employment opportunity

United States	National Labor Relations Board
	Federal Mediation and Conciliation Service
	National Mediation Board
	Federal Labor Relations Authority
	Federal Service Impasses Panel
		Equal Employment Opportunity
		  Commission
		State human rights agencies
		Office of Federal Contract Compliance
		  Programs

Canada	Industrial Relations Boards—federal, local Federal Mediation and Conciliation Service Ministry of Labor—Quebec • Office of the Labor Commissioner	Canadian Human Rights Commission Provincial human rights agencies

Mexico	Secretariat for Labor and Social Welfare
	• Federal Labor Delegations
	• Conciliators Corp.
	Conciliation and Arbitration
	  Boards—federal, local
		National Council for the Prevention of
		  Discrimination
		Conciliation and Arbitration Boards
		Commission for Racial Equality

United Kingdom	Advisory Conciliation and Arbitration Service Central Arbitration Committee Certification Officer	Equal Opportunity Commission (gender) Disability Rights Commission
Ireland	Labor Relations Commission	Office of the Director of Equality Investigations

Germany	Ministry of Economics and Labor—federal,
	  local
		Tripartite monitoring body
		  (private sector)

France	Ministry of Labor • Labor Inspectorate Conciliation Commissions—national, local	Ministry of Labor • Labor Inspectorate Three advisory bodies (race and ethnicity)

Country	Industrial relations	Equal employment opportunity
Italy	Ministry of Labor and Social Policy • Labor Inspectorate	Ministry of Labor and Social Policy • Labor Inspectorate National Equal Opportunities Committee Equal Opportunities Counselors

Sweden	Ministry of Industry, Employment and
	  Communication
	• National Mediation Office
		Equal Opportunities Commission
		Office of the Equal Opportunity
		  Ombudsman
		Office of the Disability Ombudsman
		Office of the Ombudsman against Ethnic
		  Discrimination
		Ombudsman against Discrimination
		  because of Sexual Orientation

Spain	Ministry for Labor and Social Affairs • Labor Inspectorate Interconfederal Mediation and Arbitration Service (SIMA)[a] Labor Authorities—local	Ministry for Labor and Social Affairs • Labor Inspectorate Advisory body (gender)

Portugal	Ministry of Employment and Social Security
	• Institute for the Improvement and
	  Inspection of Working Conditions
	  (IDICT)
		Commission for Equality in Labor and
		  Employment

Czech Republic	Ministry of Labor and Social Affairs • Department for Labor Law Legislation and Collective Bargaining	Labor Offices National advisory body
Hungary	Ministry of Employment and Labor • Department for Industrial Relations and Civil Dialogue • Labor Mediation and Arbitration Service	Ministry of Employment and Labor • Labor Inspectorate
Poland	Ministry of Economy, Labor and Social Affairs • Labor Law Department • Social Assistance Department • Mediation Service	National Labor Inspectorate Conciliation Committees

Russia	Ministry of Labor and Social Development
	• Collective Labor Disputes Settlement
	  Service
		Ministry of Labor and Social
		  Development

Japan	Ministry of Health, Labor and Welfare
	Labor Relations Commissions—central,
	  local
		Ministry of Health, Labor and Welfare
		Equal Opportunity and Mediation
		  Commissions

Australia	Industrial Relations Commissions—federal,
	  state
	Department of Employment and Workplace
	  Relations
	• Office of the Employment Advocate
		Australia Human Rights and Equal
		  Opportunity Commission
		Sex Discrimination Commissioner

New Zealand	Department of Labor • Employment Relations Authority	New Zealand Human Rights Commission Office of Human Rights Proceedings

continued

Country	Industrial relations	Equal employment opportunity
South Korea	Ministry of Labor • Labor Relations Policy Bureau Labor Relations Commissions—central, local	Ministry of Labor • Equal Employment Bureau Equal Employment Commission
China	Ministry of Labor and Social Security • Labor Administration Departments (i.e., labor bureaus and labor dispute arbitration committees)	Ministry of Labor and Social Security • Labor Administration Departments
Indonesia	Ministry of Manpower and Transmigration • Directorate of Terms of Employment (collective agreements) • Directorate of IR Dispute Settlement • Directorate of IR Institution Development	Ministry of Manpower and Transmigration
Malaysia	Ministry of Human Resources • Department of Trade Union Affairs • Industrial Relations Department Industrial Court	Ministry of Human Resources
Singapore	Ministry of Manpower • Labor Relations Department Industrial Arbitration Court	Labor Relations Department • Labor Relations and Welfare Division
Thailand	Ministry of Labor • Department of Labor Protection and Social Welfare • Labor Disputes Arbitration Office Labor Relations Committee	Ministry of Labor • Department of Labor Protection and Social Welfare
Philippines	Department of Labor and Employment • Bureau of Labor Relations National Labor Relations Commission National Conciliation and Mediation Board	Department of Labor and Employment
Taiwan	Council of Labor Affairs • Department of Labor Management Relations Conciliation Committees—local	Employment Discrimination Review Commissions—local
India	Ministry of Labor • Chief Labor Commissioner's Organization (CIRM) Boards of Arbitration—central, local	CIRM Disabilities Commissioner
Pakistan	Ministry of Labor, Manpower and Overseas Pakistanis • National Industrial Relations Commission	–
Turkey	Ministry of Labor and Social Security • Official Mediation Organization High Arbitration Board (YHK)	–

Country	Industrial relations	Equal employment opportunity
Israel	Ministry of Labor and Social Affairs • Division of Labor Relations • Mediation Officers Labor Courts (intermediation programs)	Ministry of Labor and Social Affairs
Egypt	Ministry of Manpower and Emigration • Conciliation Committees	Ministry of Manpower and Emigration
South Africa	Commission for Conciliation, Mediation and Arbitration	Commission for Conciliation, Mediation and Arbitration Labor Department, Director General Commission for Employment Equity
Brazil	Ministry of Labor and Employment • Labor Offices (DRTs)	Public Prosecutor for Employment (MPT) Departments of Labor and Employment—regional
Argentina	Ministry of Labor and Social Security Federal Service of Mediation and Arbitration	Ministry of Labor and Social Security
Chile	Ministry of Labor and Social Security • Labor Inspectorate	Ministry of Labor and Social Security • Labor Inspectorate
Peru	Ministry of Labor and Employment Promotion • Center for Conciliation, Arbitration and Investigation (CENCOAMITP)[b]	n.a.
Venezuela	Ministry of Labor • Labor Inspectorate	Ministry of Labor • Labor Inspectorate

Notes:

a While SIMA is administered by a private foundation created by the Reglamento de Aplicación del ASEC, RASEC, it is financed entirely by the national government.

b Formed in 2003 with technical assistance from the United States FMCS.

Appendix B

Supplemental tables: equal employment opportunity, economic security and income security laws, select countries

Table B.1 Regulating equal employment opportunity, select countries

Region	Country	Protected characteristics in employment settings[a]								
		Race/ color	Gender	Religion/ creed	Age	Disability	Sexual orientation	Political ideology	Nationality/ ethnic origin	Other
North America	United States	✓	✓	✓	✓	✓			✓	Marital status, family status
	Canada[b]	✓	✓	✓	✓	✓	✓		✓	Marital status, language, social status
	Mexico	✓	✓	✓	✓	✓	✓	✓	✓	
Europe	United Kingdom	✓	✓	✓		✓	✓		✓	Marital status
	Ireland	✓	✓	✓	✓	✓	✓			Marital status, family status
	Germany	✓	✓	✓	✓	✓	✓	✓	✓	Language
	France	✓	✓	✓	✓	✓	✓	✓	✓	Language
	Italy	✓	✓	✓		✓		✓	✓	Marital status, language, social status
	Sweden	✓	✓	✓	✓	✓	✓		✓	
	Spain	✓	✓	✓	✓	✓		✓	✓	Marital status, language, social status
	Portugal	✓	✓	✓	✓	✓		✓	✓	Language, social status
	Czech Republic	✓	✓	✓	✓	✓		✓	✓	
	Hungary	✓	✓	✓	✓	✓		✓	✓	Marital status
	Poland	✓	✓	✓	✓	✓		✓	✓	
	Russia	✓	✓	✓	✓			✓	✓	Language, propertied status
Asia and Oceania	Japan		✓	✓	✓				✓	Social status
	Australia	✓	✓	✓	✓	✓	✓		✓	Social origin
	New Zealand	✓	✓	✓	✓	✓	✓	✓	✓	Marital status, family status
	South Korea		✓	✓	✓	✓			✓	Social status
	China	✓	✓	✓						
	Indonesia[c]		✓	✓						
	Malaysia		✓	✓					✓	
	Singapore[d]		✓[e]		✓					
	Thailand	✓	✓	✓		✓		✓	✓	Language, social status, economic status

continued

Table B.1 continued

Region	Country	Protected characteristics in employment settings[a]								
		Race/color	Gender	Religion/creed	Age	Disability	Sexual orientation	Political ideology	Nationality/ethnic origin	Other
Asia and Oceania continued	Philippines	✓	✓	✓		✓				Marital status, language
	Taiwan[f]	✓	✓	✓		✓		✓	✓	
	India	✓	✓[g]	✓		✓				
	Pakistan									
Middle East and Africa	Turkey		✓			✓				
	Israel	✓	✓	✓	✓	✓	✓	✓	✓	Marital status, parental status
	Egypt		✓		✓					
	South Africa	✓	✓	✓	✓	✓	✓		✓	Marital status, language, social origin, conscience, belief, culture
South America	Brazil	✓	✓		✓					Family status
	Argentina	✓	✓	✓	✓			✓	✓	Social status
	Chile	✓	✓	✓				✓	✓	Social extraction
	Peru	✓	✓	✓	✓			✓	✓	Economic status
	Venezuela	✓	✓	✓	✓			✓	✓	Marital status, social status

Sources: Baker and McKenzie (2000), de la Vega (2004), EIRO (2004b), ILO website, International Labor Law Committee, ABA Labor and Employment Law Section (2000a, b, 2002a, b), Marin and Seife (2003)

Notes:

a National constitution, statutes, and/or regulations.

b Federal EEO legislation only covers chartered banks, airlines, television and radio stations, certain mining operations, and firms providing interprovincial communications and transportation services. Other private-sector firms are subject to provincial EEO regulation.

c While the Indonesian labor code (Chapter III, Article 5) requires that job opportunities be made available to individuals without discrimination, it does not identify specific characteristics that are protected.

d The Ministry of Manpower has issued guidelines recommending that race, gender, religion, age, and marital status should not be used in recruitment decisions, but this instrument does not have the force of law.

e Pregnancy only.

f Race, religion, language, and birthplace are prohibited factors in hiring decisions only.

g Extends to public- and private-sector employment based on statutory provisions in the Equal Remuneration Act (1976) and Maternity Benefit Act (1961).

Table B.2 Regulating collective dismissals/redundancies, select countries

Region	Country	Collective dismissals/redundancies[a]		
		Aggregation period for economic terminations (job losses triggering regulation)	Lead time for third-party notice/involvement that must elapse before RIF decisions can be implemented	Amount of severance pay mandated
North America	United States	Period-90 days: firms with 100+ workers (≥ 50 at one site)	**Union/employee representative and appropriate government ministry:** 60 days	None
	Canada	Period-4 weeks: (≥ 50 at one sited-federal jurisdiction), (≥ 10–25 at one site-BC, Manitoba, Newfoundland, Ontario) and (≥ 50 at one site in the remaining provinces)	**Union/employee representative and appropriate government ministry:** federal jurisdiction (16 weeks), provincial jurisdiction (4–18 weeks based on how many will be let go[b])	Federal jurisdiction: 2 days' pay for each year of service or 5 days' pay (larger) Provincial jurisdiction: 0–1 week's pay for each year of service
	Mexico	Time not relevant: sites with 20+ workers (≥ 1)	**Union/employee representative:** adequate time for negotiations **Appropriate government ministry:** must request and receive CAB approval to act	20 days' pay for each year of service (plus 3 months' pay irrespective of service)
Europe	United Kingdom	Period-90 days: all firms (≥20 at one site)	**Union/employee representative and appropriate government ministry:** 20–99 will be let go (30 days), 100+ will be let go (90 days)	0.5, 1.0 or 1.5 times weekly pay for each year of service based on age
	Ireland	Period-30 days: sites with 50–99 workers (≥ 10), 100–299 workers (10%), and 300+ workers (≥ 30)	**Union/employee representative and appropriate government ministry:** 30 days	2.0 times weekly pay for each year of service (plus one week's pay irrespective of service)
	Germany	Period-30 days: sites with 21–59 workers (≥ 5), 60–499 workers (≥ 10% or ≥ 25), and 500+ workers(≥ 30)	**Union/works council:** in "good time" for negotiations **Appropriate government ministry: 30–60 days**	12, 15 or 18 months' pay based on length of service and age (if parties don't agree on a social plan)
	France	Period-30 days: all firms (≥ 10)	**Union/works council and appropriate government ministry**[c]—firms with < 50 (> 50) workers: 21–35 (30–60) days based on how many will be let go	0.1 times monthly pay for each year of service plus 0.066 times monthly pay for each year accrued beyond 10 years

continued

Table B.2 continued

Region	Country	Collective dismissals/redundancies[a]		
		Aggregation period for economic terminations (job losses triggering regulation)	Lead time for third-party notice/involvement that must elapse before RIF decisions can be implemented	Amount of severance pay mandated
Europe continued	Italy	Period-120 days: firms with 15+ workers (≥ 5 at one site or multiple sites within the same province)	**Union/employee representative and appropriate government ministry:** up to 75 days if joint examination committee and conciliation are invoked	0.074 times yearly salary for each year of service[d]
	Sweden	Time not relevant: all firms (≥ 1)	**Union/employee representative:** in "good time" for negotiations. **Appropriate government ministry:** 5–25 will be let go (60 days), 26–100 will be let go (120 days), and over 100 will be let go (180 days)	None
	Spain	Period-90 days: firms with < 100 workers (≥ 10), 100–299 workers (≥ 10%), and 300+ workers (≥30)	**Union/works council**—firms with < 50 (> 50) workers: 15 (30) days. **Appropriate government ministry:** 15 days	20 days' pay for each year of service (capped at the equivalent of 12 months' pay)
	Portugal	Period-90 days: firms with 51 or more workers (≥ 5)	**Union/employee representative and appropriate government ministry:** 75–90 days	1 month's pay for each year of service or 3 months' pay (greater sum)
	Czech Republic	Period-30 days: firms with 20–100 workers (≥ 10), 101–300 workers (≥ 10%), and over 300 workers (≥ 30)	**Union/employee representative and appropriate government ministry:** 90 days	2 months' pay irrespective of service
	Hungary	Period 30 days: firms with 20–99 workers (≥ 10), 100–299 workers (≥ 10%), and 300+ workers (≥ 30)	**Union/works council and appropriate government ministry:** > 10 will be let go (30 days), and 25% or 50+ will be let go (90 days)	1–6 months' pay based on length of service with firm
	Poland	Period-90 days: firms with < 100 workers (≥ 10), 100–299 workers (≥ 10%) and 300+ workers (≥ 30)	**Union/employee representative and appropriate government ministry:** 45 days	1–3 months' pay based on length of service with firm
	Russia	Period-varies: 50–200 workers will be let go (30 days), 201–500 workers will be let go (60 days) and 500+ workers will be let go (90 days)	**Appropriate government ministry:**[e] 60 days	1 month's pay plus another 1–2 months' pay while unemployment persists if the person is registered with the state employment agency

Region	Country	Coverage	Notification	Severance pay
Asia and Oceania	Japan	Time not relevant: all firms (≥ 1)	*Union/employee representative and appropriate government ministry:* 30 days	None
	Australia	Period-not specified: all firms (≥ 15)	*Union/employee representative and appropriate government ministry:* as soon as practicable after the redundancy decision has been made	4–8[f] weeks' pay based on length of service with firm (typical TCR clause in federal industrial awards)
	New Zealand	Time not relevant: all firms (≥ 1)	*Union/employee representative:* adequate time for consultations (procedural fairness obligation)	None
	South Korea	Period-not specified: firms with < 100 workers (≥ 10), 100–999 workers (≥ 10%), 1000+ workers (≥ 100)	*Union/employee representative:* 60 days; *Appropriate government ministry:* 30 days	30 days' pay for each year of service
	China	Time not relevant: all firms (≥ 1)	*Union/employee representative and appropriate government ministry:* 30 days	1 month's pay for each year of service
	Indonesia	Period-30 days: all firms (≥ 10[g])	*Union/employee representative:* at least 30 days if mediation sought; *Appropriate government ministry:* firm must request and receive Manpower Ministry approval	2–10 months' pay based on length of service with firm
	Malaysia	Time not relevant: all firms (≥ 1)	*Union/employee representative:* adequate time for consultation[h]; *Appropriate government ministry:* 30 days	10, 15, or 20 days' pay for each year of service based on length of service with firm
	Singapore	Time not relevant: all firms (≥ 1)	*Appropriate government ministry:* as soon as individual notice is issued	None
	Thailand	Time not relevant: all firms (≥ 1)	*Appropriate government ministry:* 60 days	30–300 days' pay based on length of service with firm[j]
	Philippines	Time not relevant: all firms (≥ 1)	*Appropriate government ministry:* 30 days	15 or 30 days' pay for each year of service based on underlying cause
	Taiwan	Period-60 days:[i] firms with 31–499 workers (> 33.3%) and 500+ workers (≥ 20%)	*Union/employee representative and appropriate government ministry:* 60 days	30 days' pay for each year of service
	India	Time not relevant: sites with 50+ workers (≥ 1)	*Union/employee representative and appropriate government ministry:* 51–99 workers at site: 30 (60) days for retrenchments (plant closings) —100+ workers at site: 30 (90) days for retrenchments (plant closings); must request and receive state approval[k]	15 days' pay for each year of service

continued

		Collective dismissals/redundancies[a]		
Region	Country	Aggregation period for economic terminations (job losses triggering regulation)	Lead time for third-party notice/involvement that must elapse before RIF decisions can be implemented	Amount of severance pay mandated
Asia and Oceania *continued*	Pakistan	Period-not specified: sites with 20+ workers (> 50%)	***Appropriate government ministry:*** firm must formally request and receive Labor Court approval to act	20 days' pay for each year of service
Middle East and Africa	Turkey	Period-30 days: firms with 20–100 workers (≥ 10%), 101–300 workers (≥ 10%), and over 300 workers (≥ 30)	***Appropriate government ministry:*** 30 days	30 days' pay for each year of service
	Israel	None	***Union:*** adequate time for consultation[l]	30 days' pay for each year of service
	Egypt	n.a.	***Appropriate government ministry:*** firm must request and receive approval from a committee appointed by the Prime Minister to act	30 or 45 days' pay for each year of service based on length of service with firm
	South Africa	Period-12 months: firms with 50–200 workers (≥ 10), 201–300 workers (≥ 20), 301–400 workers (≥ 30), 401–500 workers (≥ 40) and > 500 workers (≥ 50)	***Union/employee representative:*** adequate time for consultation ***Appropriate government ministry:*** up to 60 days from consultation notice if facilitation is requested or the dispute is referred to a bargaining council or the CCMA	1 week's pay for each year of service
South America	Brazil	Time not relevant: all firms (≥ 1)	***Union/employee representative and appropriate government ministry:*** firm must secure union support prior to seeking approval to act	All FGTS deposits[m] made on behalf of the employee plus 0.40 times the person's accumulated FGTS balance
	Argentina	Time not relevant: firms with < 400 workers (15%), 400–1000 workers (10%) and > 1000 workers (5%)	***Union/employee representative and appropriate government ministry:*** up to 25 days for terminations triggering the Preventative Crisis Procedure[n] (PCP)	0.5 times monthly pay for each year of service
	Chile	Time not relevant: all firms (≥ 1)	***Appropriate government ministry:*** 30 days	30 days' pay for each year of service (capped at 330 days' pay)

Peru	Period–not specified: all firms: (≥ 10%)	Union/employee representative and appropriate government ministry: up to 33 days if full review process for approval runs its course	1.5 times monthly pay for each year of service (capped at the equivalent of 12 months' pay)
Venezuela	Period–90 days: sites with < 50 workers (10), 50–100 workers (20%) and > 100 workers (10%)	Union/employee representative and appropriate government ministry: firm must file notice of its intention, but authorization is not required[o]	30 days' pay for each year of service (capped at 150 days' pay)

Sources: Adler and Avgar (2002), American Chamber of Commerce in Egypt website (http://www.amcham.org.eg/dbe/Labor.asp#2), Asher and Mukhopadhaya (2004), Baker and McKenzie (2000, 2004), Cazes and Nesporova (2003), Ciudad (2002), Egorov (2002), EIRO (2003b), EIRO Redundancies and Redundancy Costs (http://www.eiro.eurofound.ie/thematicfeature6.html), ethailand.com (http://www.ethailand.com/index.php?id=1802), Gonzaga (2003), International Labor Law Committee, ABA Labor and Employment Law Section (2000a, b, 2002a, b), ILO (2000b), KPMG (2004), Marshall (2004), national labor ministry websites, OECD (2002c, 2004a), Ouchi (2002), PricewaterhouseCoopers (2004), Riad (2004), Watson Wyatt Worldwide (2004), World Bank Doing Business database (http://rru.worldbank.org/DoingBusiness/ExploreTopics/HiringFiringWorkers/), Zaman (2003)

Notes:

a Although they are not profiled, temporary layoffs and reductions in hours may be treated similarly if they reach a certain scale. To illustrate, the U.S. Worker Adjustment and Retraining Notification (WARN) Act considers "mass layoffs" to be a triggering event for its notice requirements. Mass layoffs are deemed to occur if 500 or more full-time workers at the same site will be laid off for at least six months; or 50–499 workers if they comprise 33% or more of the total active work force there. Notice also must be given if at least 50 employees will have their scheduled hours reduced by 50% or more for six consecutive months. Plant closings are subject to the same general requirements as collective redundancies as well.

b Only British Columbia, Manitoba, New Brunswick, and Saskatchewan require that unions receive notice of impending RIFs.

c The state's involvement has been decidedly different since the Conservative government took office after the spring 2002 elections. Two changes in particular highlight the shift in emphasis from decision overseer to problem solver. In October 2002, a ministerial position akin to "redundancy czar" was created to head a new interministerial body charged with improving the government's (1) awareness of technological and market forces pressuring firms to restructure, and (2) ability to formulate policies that effectively transition displaced individuals into better employment prospects. Several redundancy restrictions championed by the former Socialist-led government also were suspended for 18 months, such as mandatory mediation and the accompanying stipulation that rejected recommendations would be subject to judicial review. See EIRO (2001c, 2002c).

d This private termination indemnity (trattamento di fine rapporto) is unrelated to the mobility allowance (indennità di disoccupazione) individuals may receive from a government-administered program. Displaced workers qualify for the latter if they (1) lose their jobs outright in a collective dismissal (and are registered as such on a list maintained by the local labor office), or (2) remain in an economic layoff long enough to exhaust their eligibility for CIGs (cassa integrazione guadagni straordinaria) payments. The mobility allowance replaces 80% of lost earnings during the first 12 months of unemployment and 64% thereafter for a period that varies with age and company location (e.g., 36 additional months for persons over 50 years old in the south). Firms are required to pay the government an amount that equals nine (three) months of the full allowance for each eligible worker (if the union agreed to the RIF). Table B4 provides more details about the level and duration of GIGs distributions.

e While firms have no legal obligation to provide unions with advance notice under Russian law, labor still has the right to intervene by petitioning the appropriate unit of government to postpone or temporarily suspend announced mass redundancies (http://www.ilo.org/dyn/natlex/docs/WEBTEXT/42900/64988/E96RUS01.htm).

f The AIRC substantially increased employers' redundancy-pay obligations in a national test case put forward by the ACTU in 2004, raising the severance cap in federal awards to 12–16 weeks' pay for employees with at least nine years of service (Redundancy Case Decision [PR032004, 26 March 2004]; Redundancy Case Supplementary Decision [PR062004, 8 June 2004]). One of the most controversial elements of the award was a decision to impose the post-1984 "lesser" standard of up to eight weeks' pay on small business, a group heretofore

continued

Table B.2 notes

exempted from severance requirements. A Bill seeking to overturn this part of the decision was introduced in the House of Representatives in December 2004, only to be referred to a Senate committee for further inquiry. The committee's report was scheduled to be released on March 14, 2005 (http://www.workplace.gov.au/WP/Content/Files/WP/WR/Legislation/EWRBills41stParliament.pdf).

g There also must be an intent to initiate mass dismissals (Termination of Employment in Private Undertakings (TEPU) Act, § 3).

h This behavior would satisfy the Code of Conduct for Industrial Harmony, which is officially endorsed by the Malaysian Council of Employers, Malaysian Trades Union Congress, and Ministry of Manpower (http://www.mohr.gov.my/mygoveg/makluman/harmony.htm#25).

i Workers with more than six years of continuous service are entitled to "special severance pay" as well if they are retrenched because of new machinery or technology. This supplemental benefit amounts to 15 days' pay for each year of service from the beginning of the seventh year forward, capped at 360 days' pay (US–ASEAN Business Council 2003, http://64.233.167.104/search?q=cache:U-pCCQj9qzwJ:www.us-asean.org/Thailand/business_guide/regulations.asp+thailand+and+%22special+severance+pay%22&hl=en).

j Single-day terminations also can trigger notice and consultancy obligations under the Protective Law for Mass Redundancies of Employees (2003). PLMRE procedures must be followed if at least 20 (50) individuals are released on a given day in firms with 31–199 (> 200) workers.

k In its final report, the Second National Commission on Labor recommended repealing the provision which mandated government approval and increasing notice in retrenchment situations from 30 to 60 days (Labor File 2002a). A tripartite meeting convened by the Prime Minister in October 2002 failed to overcome stiff labor opposition to these and other proposed labor law reforms (Labor File 2002b).

l This obligation stems from a 2001 National Labor Court ruling that employers must consult with labor unions about the size and implementation of collective dismissals. Whether the firm's economic circumstances warrant collective dismissals continues to be viewed as a decision that is a managerial prerogative, much like the situation in the United States.

m Withholdings amounting to 8.5% of each person's monthly earnings are deposited into individual Fundo de Garantia por Tempo de Serviço (FGTS) accounts that were established at the time of hire. All funds are managed by the Caixa Econômica Federal, a state bank. Since 2001, firms also have been required to pay the government a fine equivalent to 10% of the FTGS balance for these "unjustified" dismissals.

n The PCP is a tripartite process intended to produce a negotiated, government-sanctioned agreement that minimizes the RIF's negative impact on employees.

o The Labor Minister has been vested with the authority to suspend decisions to implement mass dismissals and order arbitration for social reasons, though (Basic Labor Law, § 34).

Table B.3 Regulating contingent employment, select countries

Region	Country	Contingent employment — Fixed-contract employment — Availability	Maximum duration	Temporary work agencies — Availability	Maximum duration
North America	United States	Unrestricted	Not limited	Unrestricted	Not limited
	Canada	Unrestricted	Not limited	Unrestricted	Not limited
	Mexico	Objective[a] situations primarily	12 months	Prohibited	–
Europe	United Kingdom	Unrestricted	48 months	Unrestricted	Not limited
	Ireland	Renewals limited to objective[a] situations	48 months	Unrestricted	Not limited
	Germany	Unrestricted	24–48 months	Unrestricted	Not limited
	France	Objective[a] situations only	18–24 months	Objective situations only	18–24 months
	Italy	Unrestricted	Workers (36 months) Managers (60 months)	Unrestricted	Not limited —
	Sweden	Objective[a] situations primarily	6–36 months	Unrestricted	6–36 months
	Spain	Objective[a] situations only	6 months	Objective situations only	6 months
	Portugal	Objective[a] situations only	48 months	Objective situations only	6–12 months
	Czech Republic	Unrestricted	not limited	Unrestricted	Not limited
	Hungary	Unrestricted	60 months	Unrestricted	Not limited
	Poland	Unrestricted	Not limited	Objective situations only	12–36 months
	Russia	Objective[a] situations only	60 months	Unrestricted	Not limited
Asia and Oceania	Japan	Objective[a] situations only if lasts ≥ 3 years	36–60 months	Prohibited for certain occupations	36 months
	Australia	Unrestricted	Not limited	Unrestricted	Not limited
	New Zealand	Reasonable grounds	Not limited	Unrestricted	Not limited
	South Korea	Objective[a] situations only if lasts > 1 year	Not limited	Prohibited for certain occupations	24 months
	China	Unrestricted	Not limited[b]	Unrestricted	Not limited
	Indonesia	Objective[a] situations only	36 months	Objective situations only	36 months
	Malaysia	Unrestricted	Not limited	Unrestricted	Not limited
	Singapore	Unrestricted	Not limited	Unrestricted	Not limited
	Thailand	Objective[a] situations only	24 months	Unrestricted	24 months
	Philippines	Objective[a] situations only	12 months	Objective situations only	12 months
	Taiwan	Unrestricted	Government review if lasts > 12 months[c]	Unrestricted	6–9 months

continued

Table B.3 continued

Region	Country	Contingent employment		Temporary work agencies	
		Fixed-contract employment			
		Availability	*Maximum duration*	*Availability*	*Maximum duration*
Asia and Oceania *continued*	India	Prohibited[d]	–	Objective situations only[g]	Not limited
	Pakistan	Prohibited	–	Objective situations only	9 months
Middle East and Africa	Turkey	Objective[a] situations only	Not limited	Prohibited	–
	Israel	Unrestricted	Not limited	Unrestricted	9 months
	Egypt	Unrestricted	60 months	Unrestricted	Not limited
	South Africa	Unrestricted	Not limited	Unrestricted	Not limited
South America	Brazil	Usage capped[e]	24 months	Unrestricted	9 months
	Argentina	Rare situations only and use capped[f]	60 months	Rare situations	Not limited
	Chile	Unrestricted	12 months	Unrestricted	Not limited
	Peru	Objective[a] situations only	60 months	Usage capped[h]	Not limited
	Venezuela	Unrestricted	36 months	Unrestricted	Not limited

Sources: Adler and Avgar (2002), American Chamber of Commerce in Egypt website (http://www.amcham.org.eg/dbe/Labor.asp#2), Baker and McKenzie (2000, 2004), Cazes and Nesporova (2003), Ciudad (2002), Egorov (2002), International Labor Law Committee, ABA Labor and Employment Law Section (2000a, b, 2002a, b), ILO (2000b), KPMG (2004), Marshall (2004), national labor-ministry websites, OECD (2002c, 2004a), Ouchi (2002), PricewaterhouseCoopers (2004), Riad (2004), Watson Wyatt Worldwide (2004), Zaman (2003)

Notes:
a   Seasonal work, temporary replacements, temporary spikes in business demand, trainees, and other situations where the demand for labor is atypical.
b   Individuals who work continuously for the same firm for more than ten years have the right to request, and be awarded, nonfixed-term contracts if the firm wants to renew its employment agreement (PRC Labor Code, Article 20).
c   Persons with fixed-term contracts that extend longer than three years have the right to terminate them after the third year subject to 30 days' advance notice.
d   A policy reversal seems to be in the offing. The Amendment Contract Labor Act, which sought to legalize fixed-term agreements lasting up to ten years, was submitted to the national cabinet for approval late in 2003 (Indo-Asian News Service 2003). However, one news source reported that a formal decision still had not been made 12 months later (Indiainfo.com 2004). More concrete changes are evident at the local level. For example, state governments unanimously agreed to set up a standing committee chaired by a chief minister to provide guidance on labor law reforms needed to facilitate contractual employment in the public sector (Maiti 2003). Maharashtra has taken this one step further, creating a special economic zone for FDI that makes contractual employment a legal practice (India Infoline.com 2004).
e   Marshall (2004: 15) mentions the existence of numerical limits but fails to provide any details. It should be noted that Sorj *et al.* (2004: 42) asserted that the law sanctioning fixed-term contracts was repealed in January 2003, but the cited hypertext link was inoperative and no corroborating translation was found.

f   There is conflict in the literature about the continuing legal viability of fixed-term contracts here as well. While some sources list these arrangements as valid employment relationships (e.g., Baker and McKenzie 2004; Bronstein 2000), others have indicated that such temporary contracts were outlawed in 1998 (e.g., Marshall 2004: 18; Saavedra 2003: 241). Domeland and Gill (2002: 7) appear to reconcile this discrepancy, characterizing the 1998 reforms as merely stripping away severance-pay and payroll-tax exemptions that had been created earlier in the 1990s.

g   The use of temporary employees has been subject to governmental review since 1970 pursuant to the Contract Labor (Regulation and Abolition) Act. Section 10 of the law explicitly authorizes the prohibition of contract labor "in *any* process, operation or other work in any establishment" (emphasis added). This outcome is deemed especially appropriate where the work in question is (1) performed in a core area of the business, (2) perennial in nature, and (3) of sufficient volume to warrant hiring individuals on a full-time basis. One of the more interesting legal questions has been the responsibility that client firms have to temporary workers if their positions are abolished by the state. In 2001, the Supreme Court of India reversed itself on this issue, ruling that displaced individuals did not have a right to be absorbed into the work force as permanent employees (Mitta 2001). Instead, the vendor remains responsible for redeploying them elsewhere.

h   Temporary employees cannot comprise more than 50% of the client firm's overall work force (Ciudad 2002: 39).

Table B.4 Regulating income loss associated with work interruptions, select countries

Region	Country	Income loss associated with work interruptions		Workplace injury	
		Unemployment	Maximum duration of benefits[a]	Temporary disability	Permanent disability
		Earnings replacement rate[a]		Earnings replacement rate	
North America	United States	≈ 50% (varies by state)	26–30 weeks[b]	60–80% for ≥ 300 weeks or until recovery (varies by state)	Full: ≈ 66.6% (varies by state) Partial: prorated for degree of disability
	Canada	55%	45 weeks	75–90% until recovery (varies by province)	Full: 75–90% (varies by province) Partial: prorated for degree of disability
	Mexico	0	n.a.	100% until recovery	Full: 70% Partial: prorated for degree of disability
Europe	United Kingdom	Benefit level not fixed as a percentage of earnings base[c]	6 months	Universal amount until recovery (increased at 29 and 52 weeks)	Full: universal amount awarded Partial: prorated for degree of disability
	Ireland	Benefit level not fixed as a percentage of earnings base[c]	15 months	Universal amount for ≤ 26 weeks	Full: universal amount awarded Partial: prorated for degree of disability
	Germany	60% or 67% (varies with family status)	6–32 months (varies with age and span of employment)	70% until recovery	Full: 66.6% Partial: prorated for lost earning capacity
	France	57.4–75.0% (varies with age and employment span)	4–60 months (varies with age and span of employment)	80% until recovery (60% rate during first 28 days)	Full: 100% Partial: prorated for degree of disability
	Italy	40%[d]	6–9 months[d] (varies with age)	75% until recovery (60% rate applies during first 3 months)	Full: varies[j] (earnings-based component) Partial: prorated for degree of disability[j]

	Country				
	Sweden	0[e]	n.a.	80% until recovery	Full: 100% Partial: prorated for lost earning capacity
	Spain	60% or 70% (higher rate during first 180 days)	24 months	75% for ≤ 12 months (extension of up to 6 months possible)	Full: 100% Partial: prorated for degree of disability
	Portugal	65%	12–30 months (varies with age)	75% until recovery (70% rate applies during first 12 months)	Full: 80–100% (varies with family status) Partial: 70% of lost earning capacity
	Czech Republic	40% or 50% (higher rate during first 90 days)	6 months		Full: varies (earnings-based component) Partial: varies (50% of earnings-based component for full disability)
	Hungary	65%	9 months	100% for ≤ 12 months (extension of up to 12 months possible)	Full: 68% Partial: 51–63% (varies with span of employment)
	Poland	Benefit level not fixed as a percentage of earnings base[c]	6–18 months (varies with rate of regional unemployment)	100% for 26–39 weeks	Full: varies (earnings- and contribution-based components) Partial: 75% of total disability amount
	Russia	45–75% (varies with period that benefits are drawn)	12 months	100% until recovery	Full: 75% Partial: 30–75% (varies disability level)
Asia and Oceania	Japan	60–80%	3–12 months (varies with age and span of employment)	80% until recovery	Full: 85.7% Partial: prorated for degree of disability
	Australia	0	n.a.	80–100% for ≥ 26 weeks (varies by state/territory)	Full: same level as temporary disability Partial: prorated for earning capacity lost
	New Zealand	0	n.a.	80% until recovery	Full: same level as temporary disability Partial: prorated for degree of disability

continued

Table B.4 continued

Region	Country	Income loss associated with work interruptions			
		Unemployment		Workplace injury	
		Earnings replacement rate[a]	Maximum duration of benefits[a]	Earnings replacement rate: Temporary disability	Permanent disability
Asia and Oceania continued	South Korea	50%	3–8 months (varies with age and span of employment)	70% until recovery[k]	Full: 90% Partial: prorated for degree of disability
	China	Benefit level not fixed as a percentage of earnings base[c]	12–24 months (varies with contribution period)	100% until recovery	Full: 75–90% Partial: 10–30% (varies with earnings loss)
	Indonesia	0	n.a.	50–100% until recovery (varies with period benefits are drawn)	Full: 49 months' pay Partial: 2–40% of 70 months' pay based on degree of disability
	Malaysia	0	n.a.	80% until recovery	Full: 90% Partial: prorated for degree of disability
	Singapore	0	n.a.	66.6% for ≤ 12 months (100% rate applies during first 2 months)	Full: 72–144 months' pay (varies with age) Partial: prorated for degree of disability
	Thailand	50%[f] (only 30% if left work voluntarily)	6 months[f]	60% until recovery	Full: 60% for ≤ 180 months Partial: prorated for degree of disability for ≤ 120 months
	Philippines	0	n. a.	90% for ≤ 8 months	Full: varies (earnings- and contribution-based components) Partial: prorated for degree of disability
	Taiwan	60%	6 months	50–70% for ≤ 24 months (varies with period benefits are drawn)	Full: 60 months' pay Partial: 1.5–50 months' pay based on degree of disability

Region	Country				
	India[g]	0	n.a.	≈ 70% until recovery (varies with wage class)	Full: varies (flat amount for wage classes) Partial: prorated for degree of disability
	Pakistan	0	n.a.	60–100% for ≤ 6 months if SI law applies (50% for ≤ 12 months if WC law applies)	Full: 75% (100% in Punjab and Sindh) Partial: prorated for degree of disability
Middle East and Africa	Turkey	0	n.a.	50% until recovery	Full: 70% Partial: prorated for degree of disability
	Israel	40–80% (varies with earnings)	50–175 days (varies with age and family status)	75% for ≤ 13 weeks	Full: 75% Partial: prorated for degree of disability
	Egypt	60%	4–7 months (varies with contribution period)	100% until recovery	Full: 80% Partial: prorated for degree of disability
	South Africa	38–60% (varies with span of employment and earnings)	34 weeks	75% for ≤ 12 months (extension of up to 12 months possible)	Full: 75% Partial: prorated for degree of disability
South America	Brazil[h]	Benefit levels not fixed as a percentage of earnings base[i]	3–5 months (varies with span of employment)	91% until recovery	Full: 100% Partial: 50%
	Argentina	35–50% (varies with period benefits are drawn)	4–12 months (varies with contribution period)		Full: 70% Partial: prorated for degree of disability
	Chile	30–50% (varies with period benefits are drawn)	5 months	100% for ≤ 12 months (extension of up to 12 months possible)	Full: 70% Partial: prorated for degree of disability
	Peru	0	n.a.	100% for ≤ 11+ months	Full: 80% Partial: prorated for degree of disability
	Venezuela	60%	18–26 weeks	66.6% for ≤ 12 months (extension of up to 12 months possible)	Full: 66.6% Partial: prorated for degree of disability

continued

Table B.4 sources and notes

Sources: Adler and Avgar (2002), American Chamber of Commerce in Egypt website, Asian Labor News (2004a), Bhoola (2002), Bronstein (2000), Bureau of International Labor Affairs, USDOL (2002c, d, 2003), Deloitte Touche Tohmatsu (2004), Gordon and Toledano (1998), Gross (1999), Gross and Weintraub (2004), HWCA (2003), ILO (2004), International Labor Law Committee, ABA Labor and Employment Law Section (2000a, b, 2002a, b), Jung (2002a), Kochavi (2003), Kubinková (2002), Liu and Wu (1999), national government ministries, OECD (2004b: 23–4), Social Security Administration (2002, 2003a, b, 2004), US-ASEAN Business Council (2003), U.S. Department of State (2004a, b, c), World Bank Doing Business database, World of Labor Institute (2004).

Notes:

a   Unemployment insurance benefits are profiled as opposed to means-tested unemployment assistance.

b   Benefits can be extended for 13 additional weeks in one of two instances. Extensions are triggered automatically whenever the 13-week unemployment rate for insured workers in a given states reaches 5% and is 20% higher than the rate for the same period in either of the two preceding years. Alternatively, states have been given the authority to invoke an optional trigger if their prevailing insured (total) unemployment rate is 6.0% (6.5%) or higher.

c   Instead, flat-rate benefits are paid out that may or may not be adjusted based on select characteristics. In the UK, the contribution-based job seekers' allowance varies with age and family status. Ireland issues different awards depending on prior earnings and family status. Poland, in contrast, factors in previous labor-market attachment. Workers with less than five years of covered employment receive 80% of the base benefit, those with five to 20 years 100%, and those with greater than 20 years 120%. China appears to issue uniform benefits to all persons within the jurisdiction of the local government body that sets UI payments.

d   This "ordinary unemployment benefit" (*indennità di disoccupazione*) should not be confused with CIGo (*cassa integrazione guadagni ordinaria*) or CIGs (*cassa integrazione guadagni straordinaria*) income-support payments that laid-off employees may receive from the jointly funded, state-run Wages Guarantee Fund. CIGo benefits try to redress the economic hardship caused by temporary market forces beyond the employer's control, replacing as much as 80% of the earnings associated with lost work hours. However, individuals are limited to 12 months of benefits over a 24 month period. CIGs payouts are reserved for settings where the firm must undergo significant restructuring or reorganization, or faces the prospect of bankruptcy or liquidation. The replacement rate is identical, and can be disbursed for a longer interval (i.e., 24–36 months of benefits over a five-year period). In both instances, the employer submits an application to the state requesting the Fund's intervention and must meet certain prerequisites (e.g., prior union consultation in both cases, inclusion of a formal recovery plan for CIGs consideration). Franzini (2001) provides a more detailed overview of Italy's labor market policies.

e   The Swedish government subsidizes most of the administrative expenses for a membership-based, voluntary insurance program subscribed to by approximately 90% of all employees. Participants receive an earnings-linked payout during the first 100 days, with a lesser amount distributed thereafter for up to 200 additional days. A 300 day extension is available in some instances (see http://www.sweden.se/templates/cs/BasicFactsheet_3978.aspx).

f   Although the 1990 Social Security Act identified unemployment compensation as a benefit category, the legislation failed to specify an effective date and other critical details needed to make the program operational. A royal decree finally redressed these omissions in 2003, setting the stage for benefits to become a reality January 1, 2004. However, the government's alleged failure to adequately budget for them in fiscal 2004 pushed back implementation at least six months (Asian Labor News 2004b).

g   Concerted attempts were made at least twice during the 1990s to foster a national UI system. In 1992, the Social Security Association of India came out in favor of an unemployment compensation scheme and presented a series of operational recommendations to the Finance Minister. A committee appointed by the Labor Minister also studied the matter and endorsed program creation. However, neither initiative generated sufficient momentum for change (National Commission on Labor 2002: 6, http://labour.nic.in/lcomm2/2nlc-pdfs/Chap-8part2.pdf). While further details are unavailable, 11 states/territories have independently adopted temporary unemployment plans (Social Security Administration 2002: 68).

h   Financed from federal taxes, the unemployment insurance program provides benefits which are unrelated to the severance payments individuals receive from their FGTS accounts.

i   The benefit amount ranges from one to three times the minimum wage, depending on previous earnings.

j   Permanent disability pensions are supplemented with a flat-rate "unemployability pension" in cases where the degree of disability exceeds 34%.

k   Seriously disabled individuals may qualify for an "injury-and-disease pension" after 24 months, potentially increasing the replacement rate to 96% for 278–329 days per annum depending on the degree of disability.

Table B.5 Regulating work-related income, select countries

| Region | Country | Work-related income | | Variable pay |
| | | Direct pay | | |
		Minimum wage imposed	Overtime (OT) requirements	Profit sharing (PS)/equity plans (E) promoted
North	United States	Hourly rates fixed by federal and state legislation (uprating process: none)	50% pay premium for > 40 hrs/wk[d] (no cap on OT hours)	PS: tax incentives (deferred plans) E: tax incentives (ESOPs)
	Canada	Hourly rates fixed by legislation or provincial boards (uprating process: 3 provinces only)	50% pay premium for > 8 hrs/day or > 40–48 hrs/wk (no cap on OT hours)	PS: tax incentives (deferred plans) E: tax incentives (stock options)
	Mexico	Daily regional and occupation rates fixed by wage commission (uprating process: annual)	100% (200%) pay premium for > 48 (57) hrs/wk (no cap on OT hours)	PS: compulsory (10% pre-tax profit) E: tax incentives (stock options)
Europe	United Kingdom	Hourly national rate fixed by DTI with input from Low Pay Commission (uprating process: informal)	None	PS: tax incentives (cash plans: PRPs) E: tax incentives (CSOPs, SAYE plans)
	Ireland	Hourly national rate fixed by tripartite agreement or Labor Minister with Labor Court input (uprating process: none)	Premium not regulated (cap on OT hours: 2 hrs/day, 12 hrs/wk, 240 hr/yr, 36 hrs over 4 consecutive weeks)	E: tax incentives (ASOS, SAYE plans)
	Germany	No	None	No
	France	Hourly and monthly national rate[a] fixed by indexing system or Cabinet with NCBC input (uprating process: annual)	25% (50%) pay premium for > 35 (44) hrs/wk (cap on OT hours: 180 hrs/yr)	PS: dual approach (cash plans—tax incentives; deferred plans—compulsory) E: tax incentives (stock options)
	Italy	No	10% pay premium for > 40 hrs/wk (cap on OT hours: 250 hrs/yr)	E: tax incentives (share plans)
	Sweden	No	Premium not regulated (cap on OT hours: 12 hrs/wk, 200 hrs/yr)	No
	Spain	Monthly national rate fixed by legislation with tripartite consultation (uprating process: annual)	Premium not regulated (cap on OT hours: 80 hrs/yr)	E: tax incentives (share plans)
	Portugal	Monthly national rate fixed by legislation with tripartite consultation (uprating process: annual)	50% (75%) pay premium for > 8 (9) hrs/day or > 44 (45) hrs/wk (cap on OT hours: 200 hrs/yr)	No

continued

Table B.5 continued

Region	Country	Work-related income		Variable pay
		Direct pay		
		Minimum wage imposed	Overtime (OT) requirements	Profit sharing (PS)/equity plans (E) promoted
	Czech Republic	Monthly national rate fixed by Cabinet (uprating process: none)	25% pay premium for > 40 hrs/wk (cap on OT hours: 8 hrs/wk, 150 hrs/yr)	No
	Hungary	Hourly and monthly national rate fixed by tripartite agreement (uprating process: annual)	50% pay premium for > 8 hrs/day or > 40 hrs/wk (cap on OT hours: 200 hrs/yr)	E: tax incentives (stock options)
	Poland	Monthly national rate fixed by Cabinet if tripartite negotiations fail (uprating process: ≤ 1 yr)	50% (100%) pay premium for > 8 (10) hrs/day or > 40 (42) hrs/wk (cap on OT hours: 4 hrs/day, 150 hrs/yr)	No
	Russia	Monthly national and regional rates fixed by legislation with IR-actor input (uprating process: none)	50% (100%) pay premium for > 8 (10) hrs/day > 40 (42) hrs/wk (cap on OT hours: 4 hrs/2 days, 120 hrs/yr)	No
Asia and Oceania	Japan	Hourly and daily prefecture and industry rates fixed by wage councils or industrial committees (uprating process: annual)	25% pay premium for > 40 hrs/wk (cap on OT hours: 15 hrs/wk, 45 hrs/month, 120 hrs/3 months)	No
	Australia	Weekly national and state rates fixed by AIRC awards[b] (uprating process: claims-driven triggered by labor)	50% (100%) pay premium for > 40 (44) hrs/wk (no cap on OT hours)	E: tax incentives (share plans, stock options)
	New Zealand	Hourly, daily, and weekly national rate fixed by Labor Minister with IR-actor input (uprating process: annual)	None	No
	South Korea	Hourly, daily, and monthly national rate fixed by Labor Minister with wage-council input (uprating process: annual)	50% pay premium for > 40 hrs/wk (cap on OT hours: 12 hrs/wk)	No
	China	Hourly and monthly regional rates fixed by local labor bureaus with IR-actor input (uprating process: annual)	50% pay premium for > 40 hrs/wk (cap on OT hours: 3 hrs/day, 36 hrs/month)	E: tax incentives (ESOPs—varies by region)

Indonesia	Monthly regional and industry rates fixed by governors with input from wage commissions or tripartite negotiations (uprating process: annual)	50% (100%) pay premium for > 40 (41) hrs/wk (cap on OT hours: 3 hrs/day, 14 hrs/wk)	No
Malaysia	No	50% pay premium for > 48 hrs/wk (cap on OT hours: 104 hrs/month unless pre-approved)	No
Singapore	No	50% pay premium for > 44 hrs/wk (cap on OT hours: 72 hrs/month)	E: tax incentives (ESOPs, EEBRs)
Thailand	Daily regional rates fixed by Labor Minister with wage-committee input (uprating process: annual)	50% pay premium for > 48 hrs/wk (cap on OT hours: 36 hrs/wk)	No
Philippines	Daily regional rates fixed by regional wage-board orders (uprating process: petition-driven triggered by labor)	25% pay premium for > 8 hrs/day (no cap on OT hours)	PS: tax incentives (plans complying with 1990 Productivity Incentives Act)
Taiwan	Monthly national rate fixed by Executive Yuan with CLA input (uprating process: annual)	33% (66%) pay premium for > 8 (10) hrs/ day or 84 hrs/2 weeks (no cap on OT hours)	No
India	Daily industry and occupation rates fixed by state wage-board orders or index system (uprating process: periodic[c])	100% pay premium for > 48 hrs/wk (cap on OT hours: 12 hrs/wk)	E: tax incentives (share plans, stock options)
Pakistan	Daily and monthly national and province rates fixed by Labor Minister or governors with input from provincial wage boards (uprating process: ≤ 3 yrs)	100% pay premium for > 48 hrs/wk (no cap on OT hours)	PS: compulsory (5% net profits)
Middle East and Africa Turkey	Daily and monthly national rates fixed by Labor Minister with wage-board input (uprating process: ≤ 2 yrs)	50% pay premium for > 45 hrs/wk (cap on OT hours: 3 hrs/day, 270 hrs/yr)	No
Israel	Monthly national rate fixed by legislation or index system (uprating process: ≤ 1 yr)	25% (50%) pay premium for > 8 (10) hrs/day (cap on OT hours: 4 hrs/day, 12 hrs/wk)	E: tax incentives (stock options)
Egypt	Monthly national rate fixed by Prime Minister with wage-council input (uprating process: ≤ 3yrs)	35% (70%) pay premium for > 8 hrs/day or > 48 hrs/wk for day (night) work (cap on OT hours: 2 hrs/day)	PS: compulsory (10% of distributable profit)
South Africa	Hourly, weekly and monthly industry and occupation rates fixed by Labor Minister with ECC input (uprating process: none)	50% pay premium for > 9 hrs/day or > 45 hrs/wk (cap on OT hours: 3 hrs/day, 10 hrs/wk)	E: tax incentives (share plans, stock options)

continued

Table B.5 continued

| Region | Country | Work-related income | | Variable pay |
| | | Direct pay | | |
		Minimum wage imposed	Overtime (OT) requirements	Profit sharing (PS)/equity plans (E) promoted
South America	Brazil	Monthly national rate fixed by legislation (uprating process: annual)	50% pay premium for > 44 hrs/wk (cap on OT hours: 12 hrs/wk)	PS: compulsory (jointly negotiated plan features)
	Argentina	Monthly national rate fixed by tripartite board or presidential decree (uprating process: none)	50% pay premium for > 8 hrs/day or > 48 hrs/day, 3 hrs/day, 48 hrs/month, 320 hrs/yr)	PS: constitutional right (not enacted)
	Chile	Monthly national rate fixed by legislation with tripartite input (uprating process: annual)	50% pay premium for > 8 hrs/day or > 45 hrs/wk (cap on OT hours: 2 hrs/day)	PS: compulsory (30% of net profit after deducting a 10% return on equity (ROE)
	Peru	Monthly national rate fixed by tripartite council or presidential decree (uprating process: none)	25% (35%) pay premium for > 48 (50) hrs/wk (cap on OT hours: 10 hrs/wk)	PS: compulsory (5–10% of pre-tax profit)
	Venezuela	Monthly national rate fixed by Labor Minister with wage commission input or presidential decree (uprating process: < 1 yr)	50% pay premium for > 8 hrs/day or > 44 hrs/wk (cap on OT hours: 2 hrs/day, 10 hrs/wk, 100 hrs/yr)	PS: compulsory (≥ 15% net profit)

Sources: Abai China Law Net (2000), Adler and Avgar (2002), American Chamber of Commerce in Egypt website, Asian Labor News (2004a), Bhoola (2002), Bronstein (2000), Bureau of International Labor Affairs, USDOL (2002c, d, 2003), Deloitte Touche Tohmatsu (2004), EIRO (2002a, 2003d), European Commission (2002), Gordon and Toledano (1998), Gross (1999), Gross and Weintraub (2004), HWCA (2003), ILO Minimum Wages database (http://www.ilo.org/travaildatabase/servlet/minimumwages), ILO (1997a, b, c, 1998c, 2004), International Labor Law Committee, ABA Labor and Employment Law Section (2000a, b, 2002a, b), Jung (2002a, b), Kochavi (2003), Kubínková (2002), Liu and Wu (1999), national government ministries, OECD (2004b: 23–4), Russia Journal Daily (2003), US-ASEAN Business Council (2003), U.S. Department of State (2004a, b, c), Varga (2003), White and Case (2004), World Bank Doing Business database, World Law Group (2003), World of Labor Institute (2004), Yanuaritta (2002)

Notes:

a Separate rates continue to apply to those working 39- and 35-hour weeks, respectively, while the government promotes a convergence plan to both social partners (EIRO 2000a, 2002b, 2004c).

b The AIRC conducts *de facto* annual reviews of the wage rates found in federal industrial awards pursuant to adjustment requests from labor (e.g., ACTU). The commission's legal obligation to engage in this activity was formalized in §7 of the 1993 Industrial Relations Reform Act, which specified that industrial awards are intended to "act as a safety net of minimum wages and conditions of employment underpinning direct bargaining." Consequently, each safety net decision establishes whether there will be uniform or selective increases across wage groups, and articulates a "federal minimum wage" clause that must be incorporated in all existing awards. See O'Neill (2005) for a more detailed discussion of the evolution of safety net reviews since the 1990s (http://www.aph.gov.au/library/intguide/ECON/safety.htm).

c   The "variable dearness allowance" is used by 22 states/territories to adjust minimum-wage levels on a semi-annual basis to reflect changes in prices. In addition, the 1948 Minimum Wage Act specifies that all covered political subdivisions must revise their minimum-wage rates at least once every five years.

d   Four states (i.e., Alaska, California, Colorado, Nevada) mandate that overtime premiums be paid for each hour worked beyond eight in a given day, even if the overall work week does not exceed 40 hours.

Table B.6 Regulating the income security of retirees, select countries

Region	Country	Age cohort ≥ 65 years old (% of population)	Statutory pensionable age[a] Men	Statutory pensionable age[a] Women	Plan type(s) mandated — Government-administered plan — Funded solely by private actors (payroll tax contributions from employers, employees or both) — Provident fund pay-outs	Flat-rate pay-outs	Earnings-related pay-outs	Funded solely by government — Means-tested allowances	Occupational plan set up by employers (employer or jointly funded)	Personal plan with choice of public or private fund manager (employee funded)
North America	United States	12.3	65	65			✓	✓		
	Canada[b]	12.6	65	65			✓	✓		✓
	Mexico[c]	4.7	65	65			✓			✓
Europe	United Kingdom	15.7	65	60		✓	✓	✓		
	Ireland	11.3	66	66		✓		✓		
	Germany	16.1	65	65			✓			
	France	15.8	60	60			✓	✓	✓	
	Italy	17.8	65	60			✓	✓		
	Sweden	17.4	65	65			✓	✓		✓
	Spain	16.7	65	65			✓			
	Portugal	15.4	65	65			✓	✓		
	Czech Republic	13.7	61	59		✓	✓			
	Hungary[d]	14.6	62	62			✓			✓
	Poland[e]	11.9	65	60		✓	✓			✓
	Russia	12.3	60	55		✓	✓			
Asia and Oceania	Japan	17.2	65	65		✓	✓			
	Australia	12.3	65	62.5				✓	✓	
	New Zealand	11.7	65	65				✓		
	South Korea	7.1	60	60			✓			
	China	6.9	60	60		✓				✓

	Indonesia	4.8	55	55			✓
	Malaysia	4.1	55	55			✓
	Singapore	7.2	55	55			✓
	Thailand	5.2	55	55	✓		
	Philippines	3.5	60	60		✓	
	Taiwan	9.0	60	55		✓	
	India	5.0	55	55	✓	✓	
	Pakistan	3.7	60	55		✓	
Middle East and Africa	Turkey	5.8	55	50	✓	✓	
	Israel	9.9	65	60	✓	✓	
	Egypt	4.1	60	60	✓	✓	
	South Africa	3.6	65	60		✓	
South America	Brazil	5.1	65	65	✓	✓	
	Argentina	9.7	65	60	✓	✓	
	Chile[c]	7.2	65	60	✓	✓	✓
	Peru	4.8	65	65	✓	✓	✓
	Venezuela	4.4	60	55	✓		

Source: Social Security Administration (2002, 2003a, b, 2004)

Notes:

a The earliest age at which one becomes eligible for retirement income is listed if employees can participate in multiple plans.

b An income-tested supplement is added to retirement benefits as needed to achieve a universal pension.

c The government plan was closed to new entrants in 1997 for Mexico and 1982 for Chile, requiring participation in the personal insurance plan. Both governments provide a top-up as needed to orchestrate a guaranteed minimum pension.

d Individuals covered by the traditional insurance system before June 30, 1998, or who became eligible for coverage afterward before reaching the age of 42, do not have to participate in the private insurance plan.

e Persons between the ages of 30 and 50 can elect to participate in the traditional social insurance program and private insurance plan, while those younger than 30 must subscribe to both.

Notes

1 Global legal systems and the employment relationship

1 For purposes of this book, national HRM systems are the macro-level patterns in decision-making processes, substantive practices, and institutional relationships that firms develop and manage in nonunion settings. National IR systems, in turn, encompass the procedures for making decisions, actual employment policies, and interorganizational interfaces that are predominant where labor organizations and their members are present. The two systems coexist, although the administrative challenge of reconciling their outcomes varies considerably from country to country.

2 There are instances where systems with hybrid features are articulated. For example, Kochan (1980: 60) appears to straddle the unitary and pluralist camps in framing the major functions that public policy serves as (1) interpreter and transmitter of political and social norms, (2) regulator of the balance of economic power, and (3) arbitrator of conflicting policy objectives. Begin (1992) advocates more of a contingency-based framework where government exercises regulatory restraint during the early stages of economic development to allow firms flexibility in restructuring themselves to respond effectively to complex, dynamic competitive pressures, followed by significant oversight and regulation in later stages to protect society's interests.

3 For example, several labor federations met in Stockholm to develop a formal agenda to advance the cause of corporate social responsibility (ICFTU 2003c). The European Union also has been active in this area. The Directorate General of Employment and Social Affairs has issued a Green Paper on the subject (European Commission 2001), and the European Parliament voted in 2002 for new legislation that would create extraterritorial jurisdiction over illegalities that European companies perpetrate in developing countries. Not wanting to stand idly by, employers have developed a position paper on the desirability and tracking of corporate codes of conduct as well (IOE 1999).

4 There is a growing body of studies in the finance and IR/HRM literature indicating that capital markets do monitor and react to major HR policies and events, potentially influencing shareholder wealth and access to capital (e.g., Arthur 2003; Diller 1999; Hannon and Milkovich 1996; Watson Wyatt 1999, 2000; Wright *et al.* 1995).

5 To date, tribunal awards in the United Kingdom and Japan have topped off at slightly over US$1 million. Various factors may account for plaintiffs receiving much smaller sums, including the use of tribunals rather than juries to assess damages, the unavailability of punitive damages, and caps on compensation awards.

6 It is interesting to note that the plaintiffs' argument was grounded in gender discrimination rather than age discrimination because there were no formal laws at the time prohibiting the latter. They asserted that the law had an adverse impact on males since significantly more men than women continued working after the age of 65. The government's original rationale for precluding such actions by senior citizens was their general eligibility for state pensions.

7 Disputes brought before a panel of judges (e.g., appeals) can elicit multiple opinions that carry varying degrees of legal significance. Unanimous and majority opinions not only establish an outcome in favor of one of the parties, but also may provide the textual fodder for extending, refining, or altering the prevailing law for future litigants. Plurality opinions, cobbled with concurring ones, resolve the immediate dispute, but do little to impact the overarching law.

8 Legal systems in this region would go through extensive upheaval over the course of the twentieth century with the forced reception of Socialist law and its eventual rejection following the collapse of the former Soviet Union. Interested readers can consult David and Brierley (1978: 208–280) for a discussion of the structures and sources of Socialist law. Biryukov (2002) provides excellent insights

into the challenges that newly independent states like Ukraine face trying to return private law mechanisms to their legal systems.

9 Some caveats are in order. Since respondents may not have standardized expectations of the state, straight comparisons of percentage differences can be misleading. Furthermore, no attempt is made at this point to control for differences in regulatory life-cycle stages—a topic we will return to in Chapter 7.

2 Global institutions and the evolution of employment regulation

1 Dating back at least a millennium, this set of business-oriented principles and customs was developed largely by merchants. Legal scholars differ in how they characterize the nexus between *lex mercatoria* and national law. Some view it as an autonomous cluster of rules that transcends individual legal systems, while others see it operating only to the extext that there has been implementing legislation in a given country. Interested readers should consult Rodríguez (2002) for more details about the origins and application of this construct.

2 The Governing Body encompasses 56 regular and 66 deputy members with a fixed proportion in each category coming from the ranks of employers (25 percent), workers (25 percent), and governments (50 percent). Ten of the 28 regular seats allocated to the state are permanently held by countries of "chief industrial importance"—Brazil, China, France, Germany, India, Italy, Japan, the Russian Federation, the United Kingdom, and the United States. An electoral process is used to fill the remaining slots, with the winners serving three-year terms. The following nations were added as regular members after the round of balloting in 2002: Argentina, the Bahamas, Bulgaria, the Dominican Republic, Ecuador, Gabon, Indonesia, the Libyan Arab Jamahiriya, Lithuania, Mali, Mexico, Nigeria, Norway, Pakistan, the Republic of Korea, Saudi Arabia, South Africa, and Sudan (ILO website, http://www.ilo.org/public/english/ standards/relm/gb/refs/pdf/gbmember.pdf).

3 An official proclamation or publication still may be required afterwards, but it would be a purely ministerial act. Important country-level idiosyncrasies nevertheless exist. For example, the U.S. constitution confers sole power to negotiate and conclude treaties to the executive branch in all areas except trade. Efforts to secure international trade agreements must contend with the fact that Congress, not the President, has the constitutional power to regulate commerce with foreign states. Without formal legislative action by Congress, no trade agreement negotiated by the executive branch would take on the force of law. Since 1974, "fast-track" legislation has been enacted periodically to delegate congressional authority over trade treaties to the executive branch subject to a series of conditions. Common elements of these trade Bills include (1) delineated negotiating objectives and a specified form of agreement to be pursued, (2) a congressional oversight group to supervise negotiations and overall compliance with the statute, (3) an enforcement process for violations of its requirements, and (4) a commitment to vote on the results of negotiations and proposed implementing legislation within 90 days without amendments. There has been disagreement, acrimonious at times, between the branches regarding the appropriateness of including labor-standard objectives in such Bill—a development that will be examined more closely in later sections of the chapter. The Netherlands, Mexico, and Japan also limit direct application to certain kinds of treaties, although the underlying constitutional mechanisms producing this outcome differ (Jackson 1992). For ILO conventions, Japan customarily tends to amend nonconforming legislation and implement newly needed legislation before ratification takes place (Hanami 1981: 766). France tends to embody convention provisions in formal amendments to its internal law as well, seemingly at odds with a constitutional mandate for automatic incorporation. However, this is primarily done to communicate their existence to administrators and judges, thereby increasing the probability they will be applied—not to give them legal effect at the outset (Leary 1982: 30).

4 U.S. case law has evolved three criteria to determine whether treaty clauses are self-executing: the discernible intention of the contracting sovereignties, the level of precision and detail evident in the chosen language, and whether judicial application of the terms would infringe powers constitutionally allocated to other government branches. As Leary (1982: 65–70) noted, the self-executing nature of treaty provision has not been viewed as a significant legal issue in other nations historically.

5 See David (1984) for additional information on the hierarchical standing of legislation in various legal systems.

6 Recommendations are accepted rather than ratified because they are not put forward with the expectation of creating treaty-like obligations. The decision to endorse ratification can reflect the belief that all of the convention's substantive elements already exist in local law, or that the time has come to elevate national minimum standards in the area that it covers. One can anticipate the converse

as well. For example, the ILO received a communication from the Netherlands in 1974 stating that it would refrain from ratifying conventions that did not conform to existing national laws or that required new implementing legislation (Leary 1982: 40).

7 For the earliest adopter, a new convention doesn't enter into force as a binding international labor standard until 12 months after the date when the second country registers its ratification with ILO.

8 The length of these cycles differs over time and across conventions. It is standard practice to require countries to supply two detailed reports on all newly ratified conventions—the first one a year after they go into effect and the second two years thereafter. Recent evidence indicates that while about two-fifths of the states required to file first reports do not do so on time, all but a few have satisfied this requirement within 24 months (ILO 2003a). The subsequent timeline for reporting varies depending on the specific convention at hand. For ten "priority" conventions (i.e., those pertaining to freedom of association, abolition of forced labor, equal treatment and opportunities, employment policy, labor inspection, and tripartite consultation), detailed reports are automatically requested at two-year intervals. Other conventions generally call for five year simplified reports. Common substantive elements of the reports include (1) a characterization of how national laws comply with the convention, (2) a detailed summary of administrative and judicial decisions where it has been applied, and (3) a copy of communications with peak IR associations relating to the convention.

9 The former is composed of 20 external individuals appointed by the ILO Governing Body for renewable three year terms, while the latter is a tripartite body of appointed ILC delegates that may have 150 members or more at any given time.

10 The Governing Body assigned the case to the Committee on Freedom of Association (CFA) instead of an *ad hoc* committee, an option that will be discussed later in this section.

11 Complainants need not be formally affiliated with the ILO. Any national or international organization of workers or employers with a direct interest in the matter may file. The fact that the initiating party has not fully exhausted the avenues of appeal provided by local law will be considered, but is not viewed by the committee as determinative of its right to examine a given case. Finally, complaints may be submitted directly to the Governing Body or be referred to it by the United Nations. The latter situation is likely to involve governments that do not belong to ILO, and these sovereignties must consent to having the matter transferred to the ILO for disposition.

12 The commission was created in 1950 pursuant to an agreement with the UN Economic and Social Council. It is composed of nine independent persons appointed by the Governing Body, who normally work in three-person panels. Since 1964, a total of six cases have been brought to the commission, demonstrating the difficulty in securing consent. See von Potobsky (1998: 218–220) for a brief synopsis of the interactions that occurred and how the disputes were resolved.

13 The United States (1989), European Union (1997), and Canada (1997) already had imposed trade sanctions by terminating Generalized System of Preferences (GSP) trade benefits. U.S. efforts extended further, including the refusal to renew a bilateral textile agreement (1992), a ban on new or expanded American private investment (1997), and the prohibition of any imports produced, grown, or manufactured in Myanmar until human rights abuses cease (2003).

14 Alternatively, it may be that the countries with superior labor-market practices are more likely to ratify conventions because the transaction costs associated with ratification would be relatively low. Flanagan provides empirical evidence that is consistent with this explanation.

15 Two studies conducted during the 1950s and 1960s found that (1) local legislation diverged from conventions about 25 percent of the time at the moment of ratification, and (2) the COE was able to at least partially redress most of the discrepancies through the supervisory system (cited in de la Cruz *et al.* 1996: 30–31).

16 *Estate of Rodriguez v. Drummond Co.*, 256 F. Supp. 2d 1250 (N.D. Ala. 2003). Local managers allegedly retained paramilitaries as private security personnel and authorized them to engage in a systematic campaign of intimidation and execution directed at labor officials representing the work force.

17 Although seven additional conventions were ratified during the first year, the obligation to adhere to their principles predated ratification and ultimate incorporation into domestic law. Eager to seize the opportunity to gain greater access to U.S. markets, Cambodia qualified for sizable quota bonuses all three years (Sayres 2002). Moreover, the agreement was extended for another three years with even larger incentives.

18 New trade agreements normally are the outgrowth of multi-year negotiations. The Doha Round (2001–2004) was the ninth initiative to advance trade liberalization in the post-World War II period. In reverse chronological order, earlier efforts include the Uruguay Round (1986–1994), Tokyo Round (1973–1979), Kennedy Round (1962–1967), Dillon Round (1960–1962), Geneva Round

(1956), Torquay (England) Round (1951), Annecy (France) Round (1949), and Geneva Round (1948)—where GATT came into being.

19 These impediments can be the work of home and host governments alike. Home-country barriers take the form of export controls (e.g., U.S. restrictions on the export of dual-use technologies), conduct controls (e.g., the U.S. Foreign Corrupt Practices Act), and investment controls (e.g., Cuban trade provisions of the U.S. Helms–Burton Act). Host-country barriers can be embodied in sourcing/ownership controls, onerous customs/product requirements, and import quotas.

20 Charnovitz (1987) provides an excellent overview of this longstanding battle.

21 Finger pointing did occur as to the underlying cause of the "omission." Some parties asserted that certain emerging markets had worked behind the scenes to get the invitation withdrawn, others that informal promises to secure an invitation never were delivered on, and still others that the host nation chose not to issue an invitation out of concern that similarly situated entities would feel slighted if one was extended to the ILO (Staff 1996). Little appears to have changed since then. Several behind-the-scenes meetings with developing countries failed to garner support for a full invitation to the Seattle Conference (Raghavan 1999). The WTO Director General expressed his support for formal ILO involvement, but in a nonvoting capacity (Union Network International 2002).

22 The vast majority were affiliated with labor interests. Organized labor was well represented at the global (ICFTU, WCL, TUAC), regional (ETUC), and national levels (ACTU, New Zealand Council of Trade Unions, Indian National Trade Union Congress, JTUC-Rengo, Malaysian Trade Union Conference, Trade Union Congress of Tanzania, AFL-CIO, Canadian Labor Congress, CGT, CGIL, CISL, UIL, Danish Confederation of Trade Unions, Swedish Confederation of Professional Employees). Far fewer employer organizations attended, led by the IOE and a few national associations (e.g., Confederation of British Industry, Federation of German Industries, All India Association of Employers).

23 This labor-based NGO brings together the International Confederation of Free Trade Unions, ten international labor federations, and the OECD's Trade Union Advisory Committee. More details about its objectives and activities can be found at http://www.global-unions.org.

24 They also can be distinguished in other ways. For instance, defensive action is predicated on different levels of harm. Dumping and subsidy cases require a showing of *material* injury, documented by the presence of such things as a substantial increase (absolute or relative) in tainted imports, significant price undercutting or depression stemming from their presence, and general economic difficulties domestic producers are experiencing (e.g., declining sales, profits, employment, return on investment, growth). *Serious* injury, a higher threshold, must be established to qualify for safeguard protections. Here, one must demonstrate that the aforementioned conditions were a substantial cause of the domestic industry's plight. The period during which remedial action can be maintained also varies—up to five years to combat dumping or actionable subsidies and eight years when safeguards can be instituted.

25 Ex-factory (i.e., without shipping) unit costs are to be used as the basis of comparison wherever possible. Article II of the agreement further specifies that allowances have to be made for factors that affect price comparability, such as different terms and conditions of sale, taxation, quantities, physical characteristics, and anything else that can be shown to be relevant.

26 Developing countries that individually supply less than 3 percent of product imports generally are exempted from safeguard measures. Those meeting this criterion still might be reached if, in the aggregate, they account for more than 9 percent of imports.

27 The Canadian government also argued that the ban was not justifiable as a "protection of human life" initiative under the general exceptions clause. The DSB panel rejected this argument, concluding that the *prima facie* case for the nonexistence of a reasonably available alternative had not been made.

28 This number may significantly underestimate how often labor has leveraged the process because it does not count the times when filings were threatened to prod firms to take settlement negotiations more seriously. For example, Hurricane Hydrocarbons, a Canadian-based energy multinational, received a letter from the ICEM protesting workers' rights violations in the firm's Kazakhstan subsidiary. The main thrust of the letter was a request for the CEO's immediate, personal intervention to stop the alleged infringement of local labor law and international labor standards. In the event such assistance was not forthcoming, the letter made it clear that an OECD complaint would be given serious consideration (ICEM 2002). Follow-up information for the case was not available at the time of this writing. However, the tactic has been tried in other settings with some degree of success (Nilsson 2003: 5).

29 OECD members share three overarching values: open markets, democratic pluralism, and respect for human rights. The supporting body of legal instruments is made up of more than 160 declarations, recommendations, and decisions. *Declarations* (e.g., International Investment and Multinational

Enterprises, Policies for the Employment of Women) articulate concrete, nonbinding policy commitments that are monitored by designated OECD units. *Recommendations* (e.g., Core Principles of Occupational Pension Regulation) also lack legal force, but are considered moral imperatives that members should to do their utmost to implement. In contrast, *decisions* (e.g., OECD Guidelines for Multinational Enterprises, 2000 revision) are legally binding on members that do not abstain at the time of adoption. Committed nations must undertake whatever measures are required to effectuate their implementation (OECD website http://www.oecd.org/document/46/0,2340,en_2649_201185_1925230_1_1_1_1,00.html).

30 To illustrate, Poland began its trek toward full OECD membership by capitalizing on opportunities for involvement through the "Partners in Transition" program, which supported nations making the transition to market economies. Polish representatives took advantage of the ability to attend OECD committees as observers and serve internships in the organization's secretariat directorates. Positive feedback from the OECD Council led Poland to formally apply for membership in 1994 (Bielawski 2003).

31 Korea had altered its labor laws to legalize affiliates of the Korean Confederation of Trade Unions, extended the right to organize to teachers, abolished restrictions on the ability of union federations and employer associations to support bargaining and industrial actions, removed the ban on union political activities, and narrowed the definition of essential public services as it related to employees' right to strike (Jeong 2000).

3 Regional insitutions and the development of employment regulation

1 Those overseeing noneconomic treaties have less to work with in this regard, although their contributions are felt from time to time. To illustrate, the Organization of American States (OAS) maintains a complaint-driven process to redress violations of a hemispheric human rights convention. Individuals and legally recognized NGOs can trigger an examination of alleged misconduct by filing a petition with the Inter-American Commission on Human Rights (IACHR). Commissioners also have the power to unilaterally issue a complaint. The ensuing investigation may prompt the IACHR to request observations from government officials, make on-site inspections, conduct hearings, and engage in mediation. A private, final report with conclusions and recommendations will be issued once sufficient information has been assembled. If the state does not rectify the situation within the time allotted, the commission will decide whether to issue a second report or bring the matter before the judicial arm of the OAS, the Inter-American Court on Human Rights. Bol (1998) discusses how this institutional framework could be used to combat child labor. Member states, in contrast, can directly refer such cases to the court for advisory opinions. That happened in the Hoffman lawsuit profiled briefly in Chapter 1. Unhappy with the U.S. Supreme Court refusal to recognize a back pay remedy for undocumented migrants who were terminated for union-organizing efforts, Mexico asked the Inter-American Court to assess the ruling's compatibility with the OAS Charter, American Declaration of the Rights and Duties of Man, American Convention on Human Rights, and other international treaties. In September 2003, the court held that a person's migratory status does not provide a justifiable basis for depriving individuals of fundamental workplace rights, including the freedom of association (http://www.corteidh.or.cr/serieapdf_ing/seriea_18_ing.pdf). Eight months later, Democratic legislators in the U.S. Congress introduced two Bills (i.e., SOLVE Act, S. 2381/HR4264; FAIRNESS Act, HR 3809) that would override the Supreme Court's ruling in Hoffman and create a legalization program for illegal immigrants meeting certain conditions if enacted. The timing seems to be more than coincidental.

2 The WTO/GATT framework allows member states to participate in RTAs without violating their general transparency and nondiscrimination obligations (Articles XXIV and V). The number of agreements cited includes bloc accession agreements for one or more countries, bilateral free trade agreements, and bloc formation agreements.

3 Antigua and Barbuda, the Bahamas, Barbados, Belize, Dominica, Grenada, Guyana, Haiti, Jamaica, Montserrat, St. Kitts and Nevis, St. Lucia, St. Vincent and the Grenadines, Suriname, and Trinidad and Tobago are full members. Anguilla, Bermuda, the British Virgin Islands, the Cayman Islands, and the Turks and Caicos Islands have been accepted as associate members because they are nonindependent territories.

4 The updates were presented at the eighteenth meeting of the Council for Trade and Economic Development in January 2005 (http://www.jis.gov.jm/special_sections/CARICOMNew/CARICOMTrade.html).

5 Many of the standing committees that had been operating under the 1973 treaty were consolidated

by the first CMSE protocol. The standing committee of labor ministers, which facilitated all of the labor-rights instruments discussed below, was folded into COHSOD in this process. Consequently, labor ministers regularly attend and participate in its sessions.

6 The 1998 framework agreement to create a South American FTA precipitated several years of negotiations that culminated in the 2004 Cuzco Declaration. The declaration, which was issued at the conclusion of the third South American presidential summit, instructed the ministers of foreign affairs to prepare an action plan to make the CSN a reality. The year 2019 has been mentioned as the point when full integration may be feasible. It will be very interesting to see how the social dimension is handled by negotiators. As this chapter reveals, the two blocs differ markedly on the mechanism and level of regional involvement in workplace regulation.

7 Chile (1996), Bolivia (1997) and Peru (2003) were admitted later as associate members. This status allows them to participate in the FTA without having to raise tariffs against non-affiliated countries to MERCOSUR's CET levels.

8 Unlike its counterpart in CAN, the joint parliamentary commission is not empowered to enact regional instruments that are automatically incorporated into local law.

9 The Inter-American Conference of Ministers of Labor (IACML) has been the lead unit on labor matters, although its participation was quite limited at first. The group officially became involved in 1998 in the wake of the second summit of the Americas. Section IV of the summit's action plan directed member states to share information on labor laws, mechanisms for implementing core labor standards, and progress in industrial relations at that year's IACLM meeting in a token effort to promote workers' rights. Since then, the group has been trying to put its own stamp on the FTAA initiative. The IACML's 2001 Ottawa declaration created two working groups, one focusing exclusively on the social and labor dimensions of the Summit of the Americas process. Details of their meeting in April 2005 are reported on the OAS website (http://www.oas.org/udse/english/po_trab_2grupos1-1.asp). The group went even further in 2003, asserting that it should play an essential role whenever FTAA negotiations have social and labor elements (Santiago declaration, paragraph 22, http://www.oas.org/udse/informe_trabajo/informe/ingles/index.html). Readers interested in the larger history of inter-American labor cooperation should consult Charnovitz (2004).

10 Even so, the former is not necessarily a dead issue. Responding to a proposal from the Venezuelan ambassador, the OAS General Assembly resolved in 2003 to develop a draft "social charter of the Americas" and supporting action plan for consideration at its next session (Gindin 2004). Trying to sustain the momentum for passage, Venezuela has taken the draft charter to different locations around the country to obtain constructive feedback and evolve the document. Chapter IV delineates the entitlements that are encompassed in the right to work, going well beyond ILO core labor standards (http://www.venezuela-oas.org/SocialCharteroftheAmericas.htm).

11 Angola, Botswana, Lesotho, Malawi, Mozambique, Namibia, Swaziland, Tanzania, Zambia, Zimbabwe. By 1997, four new members would be added: South Africa (1994), Mauritius (1995), Congo (1997), and the Seychelles (1997).

12 The entire text can be found at http://www.queensu.ca/samp/sampresources/migrationdocuments/documents/1998/protocol.htm.

13 Angola, Burundi, Comoros, the Democratic Republic of Congo, Djibouti, Egypt, Eritrea, Ethiopia, Kenya, Madagascar, Malawi, Mauritius, Namibia, Rwanda, the Seychelles, Sudan, Swaziland, Uganda, Zambia, and Zimbabwe. Infighting was reported between COMESA and SADC during the 1990s as the two blocs competed not only to win the hearts of nations with dual membership, but also to determine the economic model that would lead Africa forward economically. Simon and Johnston (1999: 4) highlight some of the exchanges in that power struggle. As late as April 2004, Swaziland's participation into the COMESA free trade area was put on hold pending SADC consent for it to join (http://www.comesa.int/trade/Part%20III%20The%20FTA/view).

14 http://www.iss.co.za/AF/RegOrg/unity_to_union/pdfs/comesa/17comjun04.pdf.

15 Benin, Burkina Faso, Cape Verde, Côte d'Ivoire, Gambia, Ghana, Guinea, Guinea Bissau, Liberia, Mali, Niger, Nigeria, Senegal, Sierra Leone, and Togo.

16 Prepared with ILO technical assistance, the convention extends protections to migrant workers that are similar to the ones contained in the CARICOM and MERCOSUR agreements. The ECOWAS's other labor-rights instruments, three freedom-of-movement protocols, have been in effect for years but remain severely compromised because of widespread misconduct by local officials.

17 Brunei Darussalam, Cambodia, Indonesia, Laos, Malaysia, Myanmar, Philippines, Singapore, Thailand, and Vietnam. The move still had a defensive thrust, influenced heavily by concerns that export performance in their chief markets would suffer once NAFTA and the European Union were fully consummated.

18 ASEAN website (http://www.aseansec.org/8558.htm). For more details about the AADCP project, see http://www.aadcp.org/ps/projectdetails.html.

4 National institutions and the evolution of employment regulation

1 The DOL's Office of Foreign Relations (OFR) manages a robust international cooperation program. Since 2000, it has channeled nearly $200 million to EMs to assist them in furtherance of three basic goals: (1) better adherence to internationally recognized core labor standards and acceptable conditions of work; (2) more effective skills training and employment services to dislocated workers and unemployed youth; and (3) greater success in combating the spread of HIV/AIDS through workplace-based prevention education programs. Technical cooperation programs of OFR are designed with the full participation of foreign governments and key representatives of employer and worker organizations to ensure they respond effectively to the priority needs of the country and obtain the necessary buy-in from stakeholders. OFR also works closely with other U.S. government agencies such as the State Department, U.S. Agency for International Development, and U.S. Trade Representative, to ensure that its programs fully support the broader U.S. foreign policy objectives, and complement the efforts of other U.S. government assistance efforts (http://www.dol-union-reports.gov/ILAB/programs/ofr/).
2 This seemingly was the United Kingdom's countermove when it failed to get the concessions it wanted from the Directorate General for Employment and Social Affairs.
3 See Manzetti and Morgenstern (2000) for an insightful analysis of the underlying factors that give rise to effective oversight. Their discussion focuses on the successes and limitations of this process in several Latin American countries, with special emphasis on Argentina.
4 That does not mean the European Union has not experienced resistance from nations that are having difficulties meeting the qualifying criteria that have been laid out. Cole (2003) and Howse (2003) offer interesting accounts of the exchanges between India and EU officials in this regard.
5 For example, Article 7 of the Horei instructs Japanese courts to go to the law of the place where the juristic act (e.g., employment contract) was "performed" when the parties' intent is uncertain. This normally would be the country where the contract was entered into, although some lower courts have found an implied intent to designate the law of the place where performance will occur as the governing law (see Yamakawa 1996). Krebber (2000), Morgenstern (1984), and Sabirau-Pérez (2000) provide further information about the resolution of international conflicts of law in employment contracts.

5 The state and industrial relations in global perspective

1 Whether China's legally recognized unions and their federation, the ACFTU, should be considered functional equivalents of the independent labor movements in societal-corporatist and pluralist nations is certainly debatable. Quasi-mandatory membership, especially in the state-owned sector, and structural linkages with the ruling political party argue against crediting union officials with great organizing prowess or influence. Informative discussions of the Chinese labor movement's ongoing evolution can be found in Hong and Warner (1998) and To (1986).
2 These measures do not always correspond closely in decentralized systems, though. Although it is rare for coverage to significantly exceed density in these settings (e.g., Australia), coverage can be much lower, as we saw for several Asian EMs.
3 For a more detailed discussion of pattern bargaining and its erosion in the United States, see Kochan (1980: 113–121) and Erickson (1996). In contrast, the practice appears to be alive and well in Europe as one mode of reinforcing more centralized bargaining structures (e.g., EIRO 2000c).
4 Japan's net growth in enterprise bargaining appears to be confined to new IR relationships created over the period rather than a rejection of sectoral negotiations where they were entrenched. Ireland and the Czech Republic seem to be going in the opposite direction, with more multi-employer bargaining. However, the underlying drivers are different for these two countries. In Ireland, a series of national partnership accords dating back to 1987 have been signed by the government and peak IR actors. Parameters for wages, working conditions, as well as macroeconomic and social policies, are incorporated in each framework agreement. The Czech Republic instead has been trying to perfect the right to extend privately negotiated agreements to nonsignatory parties. Recall from Chapter 4 that the Czech Parliament was scheduled to consider an amended version of the law authorizing extensions in 2004.

5 Frequency was defined as the number of work stoppages per 100,000 wage and salary earners, breadth as the number of strike participants per 1,000 wage and salary earners, duration as the number of work days lost per striker, and impact as the number of work days lost per 1,000 wage and salary earners. Aligisakis (1997) used analogous measures to construct relative, structural, and general "propensity to strike" indices for select West European nations.

6 Union dissolution simply will be viewed as the revocation of institutional rights and obligations that were perfected during the formation stage.

7 E.g., Kochan (1980: 142–147), Brief and Rude (1981), LeLouran (1979), Youngblood *et al.* (1981), and Florkowski and Schuster (1987).

8 For an interesting assessment of the impact this approach has on election outcomes, see Johnson (2002). Neutrality/card-check agreements can be entered into legally in the United States, but are uncommon outside of the context of high-profile corporate campaigns (e.g., Cingular Wireless in 2002). Two Bills before the 109th Congress (S. 842 and H.R. 1696) would require NLRB certification whenever a majority in the intended bargaining unit sign authorization cards. Not surprisingly, employers have been very critical of these arrangements. For example, the U.S. Chamber of Commerce has raised legal concerns or objections to their present treatment under the law in testimony before the Senate Subcommittee on Labor, Health, and Human Services (http://www. appropriations.senate.gov/subcommittees/record.cfm?id=224896) and an *amicus* brief filed with the National Labor Relations Board (http://www.uschamber.com/NR/rdonlyres/erh7f5d2kfxn3d2gwig vkxguuve5witpa5ftythg5q26hetl7mlv5svv5exn3puxho2fz3eetgrta7j6myh5yclcluf/DanaCorporation andClariceKAtherholtandInternationalUnionUnitedAutomobileAerospaceandAgriculturalImpl.pdf).

9 An excellent case history of Australia's handling of union recognition is contained in McCallum (2002b).

10 "Amending the Implementing Rules of Book V of the Labor Code of the Philippines," Department Order 40–03, Series of 2003, Rule XII (http://www.blr.dole.gov.ph/DO40-03.htm).

11 Australia (http://www.workplace.gov.au/NR/rdonlyres/DCC78220-F096-426F-B309-66E6FF 6218CA/0/raor2003.pdf); United Kingdom (http://www.dti.gov.uk/er/union/elections-pl866.htm); United States (http://www.access.gpo.gov/nara/cfr/waisidx_04/29cfr452_04.html).

12 For the sake of accuracy, extensions can be induced in two ways in Spain. Collective agreements are extended as a matter of law whenever a majority of the parties in a given industry, region, or sector sign the document. All companies and workers within the scope of its application automatically are bound by the terms once this occurs. Table 5.3 highlights the alternative scenario, where petitioners seek to fill a contractual void that is left by failed bargaining relationships (i.e., enlargement).

13 A comprehensive review would assess how other tactics are regulated, including picketing, boycotts, corporate campaigns, partial strikes, work slowdowns, sympathy strikes, lockouts, and alternative dispute resolution (ADR) procedures.

14 The two processes should not be viewed as identical. Fact finding and the encouragement of joint problem solving are the main tools wielded by the conflict-resolution specialist in conciliation. More aggressive tactics may be used during mediation to strengthen the impetus for compromise, such as controlling the pace of the negotiations, suggesting specific provisions for a tentative agreement, or creating an artificial crisis to foster a sense of urgency in concluding the negotiations (e.g., announcing to parties that have come to accept the mediator's involvement as critical that he/she must leave shortly due to other commitments). Viewed in this light, one can make sense of requiring mediation in the aftermath of failed conciliation, as specified in Filipino and Russian labor law.

15 More detailed information about European laws on codetermination and works councils is available in EIRO (1998b, d). Japanese labor law neither prohibits nor explicitly regulates nonunion forms of employee involvement. Survey data on the prevalence and impact of these bodies appear in Tsuru and Morishima (1999). U.S. law, in contrast, is hostile to group activity outside of traditional labor unions. Employee participation programs technically qualify as "labor organizations" under the National Labor Relations Act, and Section 8(a)(2) bars employers from assisting labor organizations in any manner. Thus, labor leaders would have the ability to shut down participatory structures involving bargaining unit members and in nonunion enterprises if they were so inclined (e.g., filing an unfair labor practice charge). The Teamwork for Employees and Management Act would have amended the NLRA to permit such activity as long as it didn't infringe on collective bargaining matters. That Bill was vetoed by President Clinton in 1996.

16 The ILO's position on registration formalities has been that administrative authorities must not be given discretionary power to accept or reject applications unless (1) such decisions are governed by clear statutory criteria, (2) the criteria chosen are not unduly burdensome or impossible for labor to satisfy, and (3) unions have a right to appeal applications that are declined and receive an expeditious judicial review.

6 Managing domestic and transnational political behavior

1 This is particularly true for the moral-rights and universalistic ethics paradigms.
2 An excellent resource for this topic is the *Handbook on Funding of Political Parties and Election Campaigns* (2004) published by the International Institute for Democratic and Electoral Assistance.
3 Rugman and Verbeke (1998: 124–130) provide a useful classification scheme and synthesis of the literature in this area.
4 For MNEs, this means being allowed to access existing entitlements, waivers, and exemptions available to local firms, and to orchestrate regulatory changes that are extended to other businesses in the sector or country.
5 For labor, one also could include general strikes, voter mobilization drives, social pacts with the state, and formal links with political parties (Hamann and Kelly 2003). The authors provide a cursory, but useful, discussion of the reasons why there are national differences in the propensity to utilize particular forms of political action in the United States, United Kingdom, Italy, Spain, and Germany. Their observation that links between labor and certain political parties have become tenuous of late is corroborated by other works. For example, Piazza (2001) documented varying levels of decoupling between unions and social democratic parties in 16 AIEs over the last half-century, marked by constituency-broadening efforts and the pursuit of more conservative public policies. A significant driver of this phenomenon was the level of globalization, which was operationalized in terms of general economic openness and the extent to which individual nations engaged in international trade and FDI abroad.
6 See Roscoe and Jenkins (2005) for a meta-analysis of the impact that PAC campaign contributions have on roll-call voting in general, as well as the influence that model specification has on reported results.
7 The U.S. Chamber of Commerce in former West Germany sought assistance from the U.S. government in an unsuccessful attempt to exempt American subsidiaries from the legislation (Weinberg 1977).

7 Managing global legal systems for competitive advantage

1 To illustrate, SAP claims that its human capital management suite ensures compliance with the reporting requirements of more than 50 nations. Even if this is true, the application offers no insight into legal obligations which lack recurrent disclosure obligations.
2 Legal obligations associated with individual dismissals and benefits should be added to the rights summarized in Appendix B.
3 Broad rights of appeal were considered detrimental to a statute's implementation based on the presumption that judges are less interested or less qualified decision makers than are agency personnel (Block 2005: 7). Not only does the literature fail to supply empirical justification for this belief, but it completely ignores the prospect of agency capture by special interest groups—a frequently referenced concern in regulatory processes. Dominant business or labor coalitions could subvert agency objectives to their own agendas, making ordinary courts a forum of last resort for justice. Their general framework was extended to a comparative analysis of EU and US (federal) labor standards without any mention of enforcement (Block, *et al*. 2003; Block 2005). One possible reason for this departure is the European Union's reliance on member states to police transposed work directives. At best, regional institutions become indirectly involved in enforcement whenever infringement proceedings are instituted pursuant to the EC treaty.
4 Interested readers can find an excellent overview of this research design in MacKinlay (1997).
5 Wright *et al*. (1995) also reported share-price gains for organizations that were publicly recognized by the federal government for having exemplary affirmative action initiatives. However, the methodology underpinning that portion of their study has been widely criticized, and has not been successfully replicated in subsequent investigations (see Bierman 2001; McWilliams and Siegel 1997).
6 With an equal-weighted portfolio, one cannot determine whether "no effect" findings indicate that all firms were unaffected, or that negative and positive effects for individual companies were similar enough in magnitude to cancel each other out.

Bibliography

Aaron, B. (1985) "Labor Courts and Organs of Arbitration." In Hepple, B. A. (chief ed.) *Labor Law, International Encyclopedia of Comparative Law*, vol. 15, chapter 16. Boston, MA: Martinus Nijhoff Publishers.

Abai China Law Net (2000) "Overtime." Online. Available: http://www.abailaw.com/english/labor/ overtime.htm.

Abbot, M. (2002) "Labor Side-Agreements Involving Canada: Current Practices and Comparative Effectiveness." Paper presented at the Thirty-ninth Canadian Industrial Relations Association Annual Meeting. Online. Available: http://www.cira-acri.ca/IIRA%20CIRA%20docs/Abbott,%20Michael.pdf.

Abdal-Haqq, I. (2002) "Islamic Law: An Overview of its Origins and Elements," *Journal of Islamic Law and Culture*, 7: 27–81.

Abowd, J. M., Milkovich, G. T., and Hannon, J. M. (1990) "The Effects of Human Resource Management Decisions on Shareholder Value," *Industrial and Labor Relations Review*, 43: 203S–236S.

Adams, R., and Jack, A. (1997) "French Set to Invade 'Garden of England'," *Financial Times,* April 17, 9.

Adams, R. J. (1992) "The Role of the State in Industrial Relations." In Lewin, D., Mitchell, O. S., and Sherer, P. D. (eds) *Research Frontiers in Industrial Relations and Human Resources*. Madison, WI: Industrial Relations Research Association.

Adler, S. J., and Avgar, A. (2002) "National Labor Law Profile: The State of Israel," International Observatory of Labor Law. Online. Available: http://www.ilo.org/public/english/dialogue/ifpdial/ ll/observatory/profiles/is.htm

AFL-CIO (2002) "Unions Worldwide Charge PPR with Violating Internationally Recognized Corporate Responsibility Standards," Press Release July 22. Online. Available: http://www.cleanclothes.org/ urgent/02-07-22.htm.

—— (2005) "Reject Flawed CAFTA, Union Leaders Tell Congress," Global Economy News. Online. Available: http://www.aflcio.org/issuespolitics/globaleconomy/ns04142005.cfm.

Agencies (2004) "Bush May Use BPO Backlash to Pressure India," *rediff.com*, March 8. Online. Available: http://www.rediff.com/money/2004/mar/08bpo2.htm.

Aggarwal, M. (1995) "International Trade, Labor Standards, and Labor Market Conditions: An Evaluation of the Linkages," US International Trade Commission, Working Paper 95-06-C.

Albarracin, J. (2005) "Globalization and Immigration: The New Immigration Policies of MERCOSUR from the Perspective of Argentina." Online. Available: http://www.unomaha.edu/ollas/Cumbre% 20Abstracts%20and%20Papers/Albarracin%20Julia%20paper.pdf.

Alben, E. (2001) "GATT and the Fair Wage: A Historical Perspective on the Labor–Trade Link," *Columbia Law Review*, 101: 1410–1447.

Aldred, C. (1998) "Multinationals Face New Claims: U.K. Government May Seek Legislation to Reverse Ruling," *Business Insurance*, 32 (51): 40.

—— (2000) "EPL Claims Rise Sharply in U.K.," *Business Insurance*, 34 (19): 49–50.

—— (2001) "U.K. Employment Ruling Could Be Felt Internationally," *Business Insurance*, 35 (42): 15–16.

Aligisakis, M. (1997) "Labor Disputes in Western Europe: Typology and Tendencies," *International Labor Review*, 136: 73–94.

American Center for International Labor Solidarity/AFL-CIO (2003) *Justice for All: A Guide to Worker Rights in the Global Economy*. Washington, DC: American Center for Labor Solidarity.

American Lawyer (2003) "Bar Talk: Diversity International," *American Lawyer*, 25 (7): 26.

Arthur, M. M. (2003) "Share Price Reactions to Work–Family Initiatives: An Institutional Perspective," *Academy of Management Journal*, 46: 497–505.

Asian Labor News (2004a) "Thailand: Safety Net for the Unemployed," January 2. Online. Available: http://www.asianLabor.org/archives/000460.php.

—— (2004b) "Thailand: Unemployed Go Waiting for Benefits," June 19. Online. Available: http://www.asianlabour.org/archives/000460.php.

Asher, M. G., and Mukhopadhaya, P. (2004) *Severance Pay in Selected Asian Countries: A Survey*. Online. Available: http://www.spp.nus.edu.sg/docs/wp/wp55.pdf.

Associated Press (1999) "French Employers Protest Shortened Workweek," *New York Times*, October 5, 4.

Ayadurai, D. (1994) "Malaysia." In Deery, S., and Mitchell, R. (eds) *Labor Law and Industrial Relations in Asia: Eight Country Studies*. Melbourne, Vic: Longman Cheshire.

Baanante, M. J. (2004) "Minimum Wage Effects under Incomplete and Endogenous Compliance: Evidence from Peru." Online. Available: http://www.up.edu.pe/ciup/cel/papers/S4_MiguelJaramillo_SalarioMinimoCumplimientoIncompletoEndogeno.pdf.

Bacik, I. (2002) "Labor Law Profile: Ireland," ILO International Observatory of Labor Law. Online. Available: http://www.ilo.org/public/english/dialogue/ifpdial/ll/observatory/profiles/ire.htm

Bain, T., and Hester, K. (2003) "Carrot or Stick? How MNCs Have Reacted to the European Works Council Directive." In Cooke, W. N. (ed.) *Multinational Companies and Global Human Resource Strategies*. Westport, CT: Quorum Books.

Baker and McKenzie (2000) *Worldwide Guide to Termination, Employment Discrimination, and Workplace Harassment Laws*. Chicago: CCH.

—— (2004) *Doing Business in Argentina*. Online. Available: http://www.bakernet.com/NR/rdonlyres/en3uc4fqxfpzozmb4ir7or4j7ylekbn74q7frlxrkbl5u7vechecqinr3kkth2gegmuvfq4a5fehe4mb b6oowmgsgka/Doing+Business+in+Argentina.pdf.

Bannon, L. (2000) "Slave-Labor Suit Targets Japanese Firms," *Wall Street Journal*, August 23, A18.

Barber, L. (1998) "Brussels Hits at 35-Hour Week Plans," *Financial Times*, May 13, 2.

Barnard, C. (2000) *EC Employment Law* (2d ed.). New York: Oxford University Press.

Bas, N., Benjamin, M., and Chang, J. C. (2004) "Saipan Sweatshop Lawsuit Ends with Important Gains for Workers and Lessons for Activist." Online. Available: http://www.cleanclothes.org/legal/04-01-08.htm.

BBC Monitoring International Reports (2003) "South Korean Government, Employers Clash over New Labor Model," July 2. Academic (Lexis-Nexus) Database, University of Pittsburgh Databases A–Z.

Begin, J. (1992) "Comparative Human Resource Management (HRM): A Systems Perspective," *International Journal of Human Resource Management*, 3: 379–408.

Berkowitz, D., Pistor, K., and Richard, J. (2003) "The Transplant Effect," *American Journal of Comparative Law*, 51: 163–203.

Bertola, G., Boeri, T., and Cazes, S. (1999) "Employment Protection and Labor Market Adjustment in OECD Countries: Evolving Institutions and Variable Enforcement." Employment and Training Papers 48. Geneva: International Labor Office. Online. Available: www.ilo.org/public/english/employment/strat/download/etp48.pdf.

Bhoola, U. (2002) "National Labor Law Profile: South Africa," ILO International Observatory of Labor Law. Online. Available: http://www.ilo.org/public/english/dialogue/ifpdial/ll/observatory/profiles/index.htm.

BIAC (2000) "Education, Employment, Labor and Social Affairs Report," *In Committee*, January–June. Online. Available: http://www.biac.org/members/elsa/docs/eelsa_report/EELSANEWS00-06.pdf.

Bibby, A. (2002) "IT Professionals' Forums in India: UNI Delegation to India in January 2002." Online. Available: http://www.union-network.org/unisite/Sectors/IBITS/ICT/documents/India%20mission %20report%20Jan2002.pdf.

Bielawski, J. (2003) "Poland's Input into OECD Revolution." Online. Available: http://www.sprawymiedzynarodowe.pl/yearbook/2003/bielawski.html.

Bierman, L. (2001) "OFCCP Affirmative Action Awards and Stock Market Reaction," *Labor Law Journal*, 52 (3): 147–156.

Biglaiser, G., Jackson, D. J., and Peake, J. S. (2004) "Back on Track: Support for Presidential Trade Authority in the House of Representatives," *American Political Research*, 32: 679–697.

Biles, G. E., and Schuler, R. S. (1986) *Audit Handbook of Human Resource Practices: Auditing the Effectiveness of the Human Resource Functions*. Alexandria, VA: American Society for Personnel Administration.

Billger, S. M. (2005) "The Heterogeneous Effect of the Passage of the Occupational Safety and Health Act on Stock Returns," Working Paper. Online. Available: http://www.econ.ilstu.edu/smbillg/papers/billger_osha.pdf.

Biryukov, A. (2002) "The Doctrine of Dualism of Private Law in the Context of Recent Codifications of Civil Law: Ukrainian Perspective," *Annual Survey of International and Comparative Law*, 8: 53–78.

Bisom-Rapp, S. (2001) "An Ounce of Prevention is a Poor Substitute for a Pound of Cure: Confronting the Developing Jurisprudence of Education and Prevention in Employment Discrimination Law," *Berkeley Journal of Employment and Labor Law*, 22: 1–48.

Black, B. (2002) "National Culture and Comparative Industrial Relations Theory." Unpublished paper. Online. Available: http://www.qub-efrg.com/uploads/B.Black_Working_Paper.pdf.

Blackett, A. (2002a) "Toward Social Regionalism in the Americas," *Comparative Labor Law and Policy Journal*, 23: 901–965.

—— (2002b) "The International Law of Trade: Mapping the Equilibrium Line: Fundamental Principles and Rights at Work and the Interpretive Universe of the World Trade Organization," *Saskatchewan Law Review*, 65: 369–392.

Blanpain, R. (1980) "The OECD Guidelines and Labor Relations: Badge and Beyond." In Horn, N. (ed.) *Legal Problems of Codes of Conduct for Multinational Enterprises*. Boston, MA: Kluwer.

Blecher, L. (2004) "Above and Beyond the Law," *Business and Society Review*, 109: 479–492.

Block, R. N. (2005) "Indicators of Labor Standards: An Overview and Comparison." Working Paper 54, ILO Policy Integration Department. Online. Available: http://www.ilo.org/public/english/bureau/integration/download/publicat/4_3_312_wp-54.pdf.

Block, R. N., and Roberts, K. (2000) "A Comparison of Labor Standards in the United States and Canada," *Relations Industrielles/Industrial Relations*, 55: 273–306.

Block, R. N., Roberts, K., Ozeki, C., and Roomkin, M. (2001) "Models of International Labor Standards," *Industrial Relations*, 40: 258–286.

Block, R. N., Berg, P., and Roberts, K. (2003) "Comparing and Quantifying Labor Standards in the United States and European Union," Paper presented at the Thirteenth World Congress of the International Industrial Relations Association. Online. Available: http://www.fu-berlin.de/iira2003/papers/track_3/Plenary_track_3_Block.pdf.

Blumentritt, T. P., and Nigh, D. (2002) "The Integration of Subsidiary Political Activities in Multinational Corporations," *Journal of International Business Studies*, 33: 57–77.

Boddewyn, J. J., and Brewer, T. L. (1994) "International Business Political Behavior: New Theoretical Directions," *Academy of Management Review*, 19: 119–143.

Boivain, J. (1989) "Industrial Relations: A Field and a Discipline." In Barbash, J., and Barbash, K. (eds) *Theories and Concepts in Comparative Industrial Relations*. Columbia, SC: University of South Carolina Press.

Bol, J. (1998) "Using International Law to Fight Child Labor: A Case Study of Guatemala and the Inter-American System," *American University International Law Review*, 13: 1135–1223.

Botero, J., Djankov, S., La Porta, R., Lopez de Silanes, F., and Shleifer, A. (2004a) *Labor Regulations for 85 Countries Dataset*. Online. Available: http://iicg.som.yale.edu/data/ datasets.shtml.

—— (2004b) "The Regulation of Labor." Online. Available: http://rru.worldbank.org/Documents/Doing Business/Methodology/HiringFiringWorkers/Labor.pdf.

Bouwen, P. (2002) "Corporate Lobbying in the European Union: The Logic of Access," *Journal of European Public Policy*, 9: 365–390.

Boyenge, J. S. (2003) *ILO Database on Export Processing Zones*. Geneva: International Labor Office.

Bradford, W. D. (2004) "Discrimination, Legal Costs and Reputational Costs." Working Paper. Online. Available: http://www.fma.org/Chicago/Papers/Suit090904.pdf.

Brewer, T. L. (1992) "An Issue-Area Approach to the Analysis of MNE–Government Relations," *Journal of International Business Studies*, 23: 295–309.

Brewster, C. (1993) "Developing a 'European' Model of Human Resource Management," *International Journal of Human Resource Management*, 4: 765–784.

Brewster, C., Farndale, E., and van Ommeren, J. (2000) "HR Competencies and Professional Standards." Report to the World Federation of Personnel Management Associations. Online. Available: http://www. wfpma.com/comp.pdf.

Brief, A., and Rude, D. (1981) "Voting in Certification Elections: A Conceptual Analysis," *Academy of Management Review*, 6: 261–267.

Briggs, C. (1995) "Lockout Law in Australia: Into the Mainstream?" ACIRRT Working Paper 95, University of Sydney. Online. Available: http://www.acirrt.com/pubs/WP95.pdf.

Briscoe, D. R., and Schuler, R. S. (2004) *International Human Resource Management* (2d ed.). New York: Routledge.

Bronstein, A. (2000) "National Labor Law Profile: Republic of Argentina." ILO International Observatory of Labor Law. Online. Available: http://www.ilo.org/public/english/dialogue/ifpdial/ll/observatory/profiles/arg.htm.

Brown, A., Bundit, T., and Hewison, K. (2002) "Labor Relations and Regulation in Thailand: Theory and Practice." Working Paper Series 27, Southeast Asia Research Center, City University of Hong Kong. Online. Available: http://www.cityu.edu.hk/searc/WP27_02_ Thailand_Labor.pdf.

Brown, D. (2000) "International Labor Standards in the World Trade Organization and the International Labor Organization," *Federal Reserve Bank of St. Louis Review*, July, 105–112. Online. Available: http://research.stlouisfed.org/publications/review/00/07/0007db.pdf.

Brown, E. V. (2003) "Thailand: Labor and the Law," Asian Labor Update 46. Online. Available: http://www.amrc.org.hk/4601.htm.

Brown, G. D. (2004) "NAFTA's 10 Year Failure to Protect Mexican Workers' Health and Safety." Online. Available: http://mhssn.igc.org/NAFTA_2004.pdf.

BS Corporate Bureau (2004) "India to Discuss BPO with US after Polls," *rediff.com*, February 17. Online. Available: http://www.rediff.com/money/2004/feb/17bpo.htm.

Bulmer-Thomas, V. (1998) "The Central American Common Market: From Closed to Open Regionalism," *World Development*, 26: 313–322.

Bureau of International Labor Affairs, USDOL (2002a) "Mexico," *Foreign Labor Trends*, FLT 02–08. Washington, DC. Online. Available: http://www.ilr.cornell.edu/library/downloads/ keyWorkplace Documents/ForeignLaborTrends/mexico-2002.pdf.

—— (2002b) "Brazil," *Foreign Labor Trends*, FLT 02–04. Washington, DC. Online. Available: http://www.ilr.cornell.edu/library/downloads/keyWorkplaceDocuments/ForeignLaborTrends/brazil-2002.pdf.

—— (2002c) "Argentina," *Foreign Labor Trends*, FLT 02–04. Washington, DC. Online. Available: http://ww.ilr.cornell.edu/library/downloads/keyWorkplaceDocuments/ForeignLaborTrends/argentina-2002.pdf.

—— (2002d) "Malaysia," *Foreign Labor Trends*, FLT 02–10. Washington, DC. Online. Available: http:// www.ilr.cornell.edu/library/downloads/keyWorkplaceDocuments/ForeignLaborTrends/malaysia-2002.pdf.

—— (2003) *Labor Rights in Chile: Report*. Online. Available: http://www.dol.gov/ilab/media/reports/usfta/ HR2738ChileLaborRights.pdf.

Burrows, N. (1997) "Opting In to the Opt-out: The UK and European Social Policy," *Web Journal of Current Legal Issues*. Online. Available: http://webjcli.ncl.ac.uk/1997/issue4/burrows4.html.

Burton, J. (2002) "Furore as Malaysia Expels Illegal Workers," *Financial Times*, September 14, 4.

Business Coalition for U.S.–Central American Trade (2005) "News and Op-eds." Online. Available: http://www.uscafta.org/articles/.

Businessdesk (2004) "Mansingh Allays Fears about Outsourcing," *rediff.com*, February 18. Online. Available: http://www.rediff.com/money/2004/feb/18bpo3.htm.

Callaghan, H. J. (2003) "Battle of the Systems or Multi-level Game? Domestic Sources of Anglo-German Quarrels over EU Takeover Law and Worker Consultation." Presented at the Fifteenth Annual Meeting of the Society for the Advancement of Socio-economics. Online. Available: http://www.sase.org/conf2003/papers/callaghan_helen.pdf.

Camp, B. J. (1994) "Mercedes Location Puts Alabama in World Spotlight," *Economic Development Review*, 12 (4): 66–67.

Canadian HR Reporter (2003) "This Just in from B.C.," May 19, 5.

Carley, M., and Hall, M. (2000) "The Implementation of the European Works Councils Directive," *Industrial Law Journal*, 29 (2): 103–124.

Casale, G. (2002) "Collective Bargaining and the Law in Central and Eastern Europe: Some Comparative Issues." ILO International Observatory of Labor Law. Online._Available: http://www.ilo.org/public/english/dialogue/ifpdial/ll/observatory/as_1.htm.

Cazes, S., and Nesporova, A. (2003) "Employment Protection Legislation (EPL) and its Effects on Labor Market Performance." Paper presented at the ILO High-level Tripartite Conference on Social Dialogue, Malta. Online. Available: http://www.ilo.org/public/english/region/eurpro/geneva/conf/malta2003/emp_prot_leg.pdf.

Champion, M. (2002) "U.K. Business Fears Expansion of Workers' Rights," *Wall Street Journal*, June 21, A6–7.

Charnovitz, S. (1987) "The Influence of International Labor Standards on the World Trading Regime: A Historical Overview," *International Labor Review*, 126: 565–584.

—— (2004) "The Emerging Labor Dimension of the Free Trade Area of the Americas." Center for Human Rights and Social Justice Working Paper 2. Online. Available: http://www.nyuhr.org/docs/s04 charnovitz.pdf.

Charny, D. (2000) "Regulatory Competition and the Global Coordination of Labor Standards," *Journal of International Economic Law*, 3: 281–302.

China Internet Information Center (2002) "All-China Federation of Trade Unions and its Work." Online. Available: http://www.china.org.cn/english/2002/Nov/48588.htm.

—— (2004) "Rules Set Minimum Wages for Workers." Online. Available: http://www.china.org.cn/english/2004/Feb/86531.htm.

Ciudad, A. (2002) "Labor Reforms and Integration Processes in the Member States of the OAS: 1980–2000." Working Paper 147, AICLM-ILO Project. Lima: International Labor Office. Online. Available: http://www.ilo.org/dyn/declaris/DECLARATIONWEB.DOWNLOAD_BLOB?Var_DocumentID=3588.

Clay, L. (2001) "The Effectiveness of the Worker Rights Provision of the Generalized System of Preferences: The Bangladesh Case Study," *Transnational Law and Contemporary Problems*, 11: 175–201.

Clean Clothes Campaign (2002) "UNITE Files Complaint with the OECD, Charging Brylane Inc. and Pinault-Printemps-Redoute with Violations of the Guidelines," July 2. Online. Available: http://www.cleanclothes.org/legal/02-07-02.htm.

Cole, A. N. (2003) "Labor Standards and the Generalized System of Preferences: The European Labor Incentives," *Michigan Journal of International Law*, 25: 179–209.

Collier, R. (2002) "For Anti-sweatshop Activists, Recent Settlement is Only Tip of Iceberg," *San Francisco Chronicle*, September 29. Online. Available: http://www.sfgate.com/cgi-bin/article.cgi?file=/chronicle/archive/2002/09/29/MN218571.DTL.

Collingsworth, T. (1996) "International Worker Rights Enforcement: Proposals Following a Test Case." In Compa, L. A., and Diamond, S. F. (eds) *Human Rights, Labor Rights, and International Trade*. Philadelphia: University of Pennsylvania Press.

Commission for Labor Cooperation (2002) "Labor Relations Law in North America." Comparative Guides to Labor and Employment Laws in North America. Online. Available: http://www.naalc.org/english/pdf/study2_intro.pdf.

Compa, L., and Vogt, J. S. (2001) "Labor Regulation and Trade: Labor Rights in the Generalized System of Preferences: A 20-Year Review," *Comparative Labor Law and Policy Journal*, 22: 199–238.

Cooke, W. N. (1997) "The Influence of Industrial Relations Factors on U.S. Foreign Direct Investment Abroad," *Industrial and Labor Relations Review*, 50: 3–17.

—— (2001) "The Effects of Labor Costs and Workplace Constraints on Foreign Direct Investment among Highly Industrialized Countries," *International Journal of Human Resource Management*, 12: 697–716.

—— (2003) "Global Human Resource Strategies: A Framework and Overview." In Cooke, W. N. (ed.) *Multinational Companies and Global Human Resource Strategies*. Westport, CT: Quorum Books.

Cooke, W. N., and Noble, D. S. (1998) "Industrial Relations Systems and US Foreign Direct Investment Abroad," *British Journal of Industrial Relations*, 36: 581–609.

Copp, R. (1977) "Locus of Industrial Relations Decision Making in Multinationals." In Banks, R. F., and Stieber, J. (eds) *Multinationals, Unions, and Labor Relations in Industrialized Countries*. Ithaca, NY: Cornell University Press.

Córdova, E., and Ozaki, M. (1980) "Union Security Arrangements: An International Review," *International Labor Review*, 119: 19–38.

Cornelius, N., and Gagnon, S. (1999) "From 'Ethics by Proxy' to Ethics in Action: New Approaches to Understanding HRM and Ethics," *Business Ethics: A European Review*, 8: 225–235.

Cortés, J. C. C., Toyama, J. L. M., Balbin, E., Caro, E. P., and Pizarro, M. D. (2003) *Regional Integration and Free Trade in the Americas: The Labor Challenge in CAN*. Regional Office for the Americas, ILO. Online. Available: http://www.apps.oas.org/foraorgint/attachments/ ENGCANAIRPREL EDITED.DOC.

COSATU (2000) "COSATU's Engagement with Policy and Legislative Processes during South Africa's First Term of Democratic Governance: First Term Report of the COSATU Parliamentary Office." Online. Available: http://www.cosatu.org.za/congress/cong2000/ parlrep.htm.

Cristovam, M. L. (2002) "EIRO Comparative Study on Collective Bargaining Coverage and Extension Procedures: The Portuguese Case." Online. Available: http://www.eiro.eurofound.eu.int/2002/12/ word/pt0209105s.doc.

Crutchfield George, B., Lynch, P., and Marsnik, S. F. (2001) "U.S. Multinational Employers: Navigating through the 'Safe Harbor' Principles to Comply with the EU Data Privacy Directive," *American Business Law Journal*, 38: 735–783.

Daily Yomiuri (1999) "More Workers Sue Firms for Unfair Labor Practices," October 13. Academic (Lexis-Nexus) Database, University of Pittsburgh Databases A–Z.

Das, S. K. (2003) "Role of Conciliation Officers in the Resolution of Industrial Disputes." In Sivananthiran, A., and Ratnam, C. S. V. (eds) *Prevention and Settlement of Disputes in India*. New Delhi: International Labor Organization. Online. Available: http://www.ilo.org/public/ english/region/asro/newdelhi/download/prevnton.pdf.

Dasgupta, S., Laplante, B., and Mamingi, N. (2001) "Pollution and Capital Markets in Developing Countries," *Journal of Environmental Economics and Management*, 42: 310–335.

Däubler, W. (1996) "Instruments of EC Labor Law." In Davies, P., Lyon-Caen, A., Sciarra, S., and Simitis, S. (eds) *European Community Labor Law: Principles and Perspectives*. New York: Oxford University Press.

Davenport, G. (2001) "National Labor Law Profile: New Zealand." ILO International Observatory of Labor Law. Online. Available: http://www.ilo.org/public/english/dialogue/ifpdial/ll/observatory/ profiles/nz.htm.

David, R. (1984) "Sources of Law." In David, R. (ed.) *The Legal Systems of the World: Their Comparison and Unification, International Encyclopedia of Comparative Law*, vol. 2, chapter 3. Boston, MA: Martinus Nijhoff Publishers.

David, R., and Brierley, J. E. C. (1978) *Major Legal Systems in the World Today: An Introduction to the Comparative Study of Law*. New York: Free Press.

Davis, B. (1993) "Illusory Bargain: Some U.S. Companies Find Mexican Workers Not So Cheap after All," *Wall Street Journal*, September 15, A1.

Davis, M. (1997) "ACTU Issues RSA Lawsuit Threat," *Australian Financial Review*, July 1, 10.

de Cruz, P. (1999) *Comparative Law in a Changing World* (2d ed.). London: Cavendish Publishing.

Dekker, L. C. G. D. (1989) "The Concept of Corporatism from an Industrial Relations Perspective." In Barbash, J., and Barbash, K. (eds) *Theories and Concepts in Comparative Industrial Relations*. Columbia, SC: University of South Carolina Press.

de la Cruz, H. B., von Potobsky, G., and Swepston, L. (1996) *The International Labor Organization: The International Standards System and Basic Human Rights*. Boulder, CO: Westview Press.

de la Vega, O. (2004) *Employment Discrimination in Mexico*. Online. Available: www.bnabooks.com/ ababna/rnr/2004/err172.pdf.

Deloitte Touche Tohmatsu (2004) "Pensions, Social Security and Other Employee Benefits." Online. Available: http://www.deloitte.com/dtt/whitepaper/0,1017,sid%253D30008% 2526cid%253D69326, 00.html.

Diller, J. M. (1999) "A Social Conscience in the Global Marketplace? Labor Dimensions of Codes of Conduct, Social Labeling and Investor Initiatives," *International Labor Review*, 138: 99–129.

Diller, J. M., and Levy, D. A. (1997) "Child Labor, Trade and Investment: Toward the Harmonization of International Law," *American Journal of International Law*, 91: 663–696.

Dombois, R., Hornberger, E., and Winter, J. (2003) "Transnational Labor Regulation in the NAFTA— A Problem of Design? The Case of the North American Agreement on Labor Cooperation between the USA, Mexico and Canada," *International Journal of Comparative Labor Law and Industrial Relations*, 19: 421–440.

Domeland, D., and Gill, I. S. (2002) "Labor Reform in Latin America during the 1990s." In Gill, I. S., Montenegro, C. E., and Domeland, D. (eds) *Crafting Labor Policy: Techniques and Lessons from Latin America*. New York: Oxford University Press.

Dow, G. K. (1997) "The New Institutional Economics and Employment Regulation." In Kaufman, B. E. (ed.) *Government Regulation of the Employment Relationship*. Madison, WI: Industrial Relations Research Association.

Dowling, D. C. (2001) "The Practice of International Labor and Employment Law: Escort your Labor/ Employment Clients into the Global Millennium," *Labor Lawyer*, 17: 1–24.

Drits, D., and Lebowitz, A. (1994) *1994 Survey: Critique of Trade Union Rights in Countries Affiliated with the League of Arab States*. New York: Jewish Labor Committee.

Drumm, H. J. (1994) "Theoretical and Ethical Foundations of Human Resource Management: A German Point of View," *Employee Relations*, 16: 35–47.

Dunlop, J. T. (1993) *Industrial Relations Systems* (rev. ed.). Boston, MA: Harvard Business School Press.

Economist Intelligence Unit (2003) "Executive Briefing: Has Outsourcing Gone Too Far?" *ebusinessforum.com*, August 18. Online. Available: http://www.ebusinessforum.com/index.asp.

Egorov, V. (2002) "National Labor Law Profile: Russian Federation." ILO International Observatory of Labor Law. Online. Available: http://www.ilo.org/public/english/dialogue/ifpdial/ll/observatory/ profiles/rus.htm.

Ehrenberg, D. S. (1996) "From Intention to Action: An ILO–GATT/WTO Enforcement Regime for International Labor Rights." In Compa, L. A., and Diamond, S. F. (eds) *Human Rights, Labor Rights, and International Trade*. Philadelphia: University of Pennsylvania Press.

EIRO (1997) "The Consequences of the October National Conference." Online. Available: http://www. eiro.eurofound.ie/1997/11/feature/fr9711176f.html.

—— (1998a) "New Proposals on the Prevention and Resolution of Industrial Disputes." Online. Available: http://www.eiro.eurofound.ie/print/1998/04/feature/fr9804102f.html.

—— (1998b) "The Impact of European Works Councils." Online. Available: http://www.eiro. eurofound.ie/1998/07/study/tn9807201s.html.

—— (1998c) "The Problem of Trade Union Recognition: Endangering Social Consensus in Ireland?" Online. Available: http://www.eiro.eurofound.ie/1998/03/feature/ie9803114f.html.

—— (1998d) "Board-level Employee Representation in Europe." Online. Available: http://www.eiro. eurofound.ie/1998/09/study/tn9809201s.html.

—— (1999a) "UK Government Publishes Proposals for Implementing EWCs Directive." Online. Available: http://www.eiro.eurofound.ie/1999/07/feature/uk9907220f.html.

—— (1999b) "ECJ Rules against Luxembourg for Non-transposition of EWCs Directive." Online. Available: http://www.eiro.eurofound.ie/1999/11/inbrief/eu9911209n.html.

—— (1999c) "MEDEF Proposes New Social Constitution." Online. Available: http://www.eiro. eurofound.ie/1999/12/feature/fr9912122f.html.

—— (2000a) "The SMIC in the Age of the 35-Hour Week." Online. Available: http://www.eiro. eurofound.ie/2000/07/inbrief/fr0007177n.html.

—— (2000b) "Debate Continues over a New Social Constitution and the Future of the Parity Principle." Online. Available: http://www.eiro.eurofound.ie/2000/01/feature/fr0001134f.html.

—— (2000c) "Wage Policy and the EMU." Online. Available: http://64.233.161.104/search?q=cache: sMkXwvkdIC4J:www.eiro.eurofound.eu.int/2000/07/study/tn0007402s.html+%22pattern+bargaining %22+and+study&hl=en.

—— (2001a) "European Works Councils Directive Finally Implemented." Online. Available: http://www. eiro.eurofound.ie/2001/01/feature/lu0101157f.html.

—— (2001b) "Court Rules that Examination Fees do not Violate Negative Freedom of Association." Online. Available: http://www.eiro.eurofound.ie/2001/04/inbrief/se0104191n.html.

—— (2001c) "Redundancy Legislation to Be Toughened." Online. Available: http://www.eiro.eurofound. ie/2001/07/feature/fr0107172f.html.

—— (2001d) "MEDEF Pulls Out of Social Security Funds." Online. Available: http://www.eiro. eurofound.ie/2001/07/inbrief/fr0107167n.html.

—— (2002a) "New Minimum Wage Legislation Criticized by Unions." Online. Available: http://www. eiro.eurofound.eu.int/2002/11/feature/pl0211109f.html.

—— (2002b) "SMIC Debate Gathers Momentum." Online. Available: http://www.eiro.eurofound.ie/ 2002/08/feature/fr0208102f.html.

—— (2002c) "'Redundancy Supremo' Appointed." Online. Available: http://www.eiro.eurofound.ie/ 2002/11/inbrief/fr0211103n.html.

—— (2002d) "MEDEF Holds Extraordinary Congress." Online. Available: http://www.eiro.eurofound.ie/ 2002/02/inbrief/fr0202103n.html.

—— (2002e) "Commission to Consult on EU-level Dispute Resolution Machinery." Online. Available: http://www.eiro.eurofound.ie/2002/06/feature/eu0206203f.html.

—— (2003a) "Thematic Feature: Works Councils and Other Workplace Employee Representation and Participation Structures." Online. Available: http://www.eiro.eurofound.ie/2003/09/tfeature/ de0309201t.html.

—— (2003b) "Council of Europe Criticizes Sweden over Closed Shop and Union 'Examination Fees'." Online. Available: http://www.eiro.eurofound.ie/2003/11/inbrief/se0311101n.html.

—— (2003c) "New Rules on Redundancies and Protection of Union Activists." Online. Available: http:// www.eiro.eurofound.ie/2003/06/inbrief/pl0306101n.html.

—— (2003d) "Overtime in Europe." Online. Available: http://www.eiro.eurofound.ie/2003/02/study/ tn0302101s.html.

—— (2003e) "Labor Dispute Settlement in Four Central and Eastern European Countries." Online. Available: http://www.eiro.eurofound.ie/2003/01/study/tn0301101s.html.

—— (2004a) "Czech Republic: Extension of Collective Agreements under Debate." Online. Available: http://www.eiro.eurofound.eu.int/2002/12/word/pt0209105s.doc.

—— (2004b) *Overview of the Implementation of the Framework Equal Treatment Directive.* Online. Available: http://www.eiro.eurofound.ie/2004/02/study/tn0402102s.html.

—— (2004c) "SMIC Minimum Wage Increased." Online. Available: http://www.eiro.eurofound.ie/ 2004/08/inbrief/fr0408102n.html.

El Mundo (2001) "Spanish High Court Turns Down U.S. Extradition Request for Arriortua Accused of Industrial Espionage whilst at General Motors," June 20. Academic (Lexis-Nexus) Database, University of Pittsburgh Databases A–Z.

Epstein, E. J. (1998) "Codification of Civil Law in the People's Republic of China: Form and Substance in the Reception of Concepts and Elements of Western Private Law," *University of British Columbia Law Review*, 32: 153–198.

Epstein, M. J., and Schnietz, K. E. (2002) "Measuring the Cost of Environmental and Labor Protests to Globalization: An Event Study of the Failed 1999 Seattle WTO Talks," *International Trade Journal*, 16: 129–160.

Erickson, C. L. (1996) "A Reinterpretation of Pattern Bargaining," *Industrial and Labor Relations Review*, 49: 615–634.

Essien, V. (1994) "Customary Law and Western Legal Influence in Modern-day Africa: Case Studies from Ghana and Nigeria." In Danner, R. A., and Bernal, M. H. (eds) *Introduction to Foreign Legal Systems*. New York: Oceana Publications.

European Commission (2001) *Promoting a European Framework for Corporate Social Responsibility.* Green Paper, European Commission Directorate General for Employment and Social Affairs. Online. Available: http://www.europa.eu.int/comm/employment_social/soc-dial/csr/greenpaper_ en.pdf.

—— (2002) *Employee Stock Options in the EU and the USA: Overview.* Online. Available: http:// europa.eu.int/comm/enterprise/entrepreneurship/support_measures/stock_options/overview.pdf.

Executive Briefing (2003) "Has Outsourcing Gone Too Far?" *ebusinessforum.com*, 18 (August). Online. Available http://www.ebusinessforum.com/index.asp?layout=rich_story&doc_id=6641.

Facts on File World News Digest (1996) "Volkswagen Executive Faces Charges," December 19. Academic (Lexis-Nexus) Database, University of Pittsburgh Databases A–Z.

Fair Labor Association (2004) *Year Two Annual Public Report: Part 4 of Four*. Online. Available: http://www.fairlabor.org/2004report/print.html.

Fairris, D., and Levine, E. (2004) "Declining Union Density in Mexico, 1984–2000," *Monthly Labor Review*, 127 (9): 10–17.

Falkner, G., Hartlapp, M., Lieber, S., and Treib, O. (2004) "Non-compliance with EU Directives in the Member States: Opposition through the Backdoor?" *West European Politics*, 27: 452–473.

Fedderson, C. T. (1998) "Focusing on Substantive Law in International Economic Relations: The Public Morals of GATT's Article XX(a) and 'Conventional' Rules of Interpretation," *Minnesota Journal of Global Trade*, 7: 76–122.

Fernandes, A. M. (2002) "Conciliation, Mediation and Arbitration: National Report – Portugal." Online. Available: http://europa.eu.int/comm/employment_social/Labor_law/docs/disputeresolution_portugal_en.pdf.

Fernández, M. L. (2002) "Out-of-court Methods for Resolving Conflicts in the Spanish System of Employment Relationships." Online. Available: http://europa.eu.int/comm/employment_social/Labor_law/docs/disputeresolution_spain_en.pdf.

Filho, R. F. (2001) "Perspectives on 'the Litigation Explosion' in Employment: Employment Litigation on the Rise? A Brazilian Perspective," *Comparative Labor Law and Policy Journal*, 22: 281–296.

Financial Times (1999) "British Executive 'Fired to Make Way for Saudi'," November 3, 8.

Flanagan, R. J. (2003) "Labor Standards and International Competitive Advantage." In Flanagan, R. J., and Gould, W. B. IV (eds) *International Labor Standards: Globalization, Trade, and Public Policy*. Stanford, CA: Stanford University Press.

Florkowski, G. W. (1991) "Profit Sharing and Public Policy: Insights for the United States," *Industrial Relations*, 30: 96–115.

Florkowski, G. W., and Nath, R. (1993) "MNC Responses to the Legal Environment of International Human Resource Management," *International Journal of Human Resource Management*, 4: 305–324.

Florkowski, G., and Schuster, M. (1987) "Predicting the Decisions to Vote and Support Unions in Certification Elections: An Integrated Perspective," *Journal of Labor Research*, 8: 191–207

Ford, J. (1998) "Virgin Express Plans to Move to Ireland," *Financial Times*, July 8, 17.

Forney, M. (2000) "Chinese Suing Japanese Firms Hope to Find Justice in the U.S.," *Wall Street Journal*, August 24, A19.

Francia, P. L. (2001) "The Effects of the North American Free Trade Agreement on Corporate and Labor PAC Contributions," *American Political Research*, 29: 98–109.

Franzini, M. (2001) "Unemployment Benefits and Labor Market Policies in Italy." Online. Available: http://www.econ-pol.unisi.it/welfare/franzini.pdf.

Frauenheim, E. (2004) "Offshoring Study Funded by New Bill," *CNET News.com*, November 24. Online. Available: http://news.com.com/Offshoring+study+funded+by+new+bill/2100-1022_3-5466394.html.

Galenson, W. (1981) *The ILO: An American View*. Madison, WI: University of Wisconsin Press.

Galin, A. (1994) "Israel." In Deery, S., and Mitchell, R. (eds) *Labor Law and Industrial Relations in Asia: Eight Country Studies*. Melbourne, Vic: Longman Cheshire.

Galloni, A., and Boudette, N. E. (2002) "Fiat Seeks Italian Aid for Big Layoffs," *Wall Street Journal*, October 10, A6.

Galloni, A., and Di Leo, L. (2002) "Italy Approves Layoffs for Fiat, Risking Strikes," *Wall Street Journal*, December 6, A6.

Ghoshal, S., and Nohria, N. (1993) "Horses for Courses: Organizational Forms for Multinational Corporations," *Sloan Management Review*, 34 (2): 23–35.

Giles, A. (1989) "Industrial Relations Theory, the State, and Politics." In Barbash, J., and Barbash, K. (eds) *Theories and Concepts in Comparative Industrial Relations*. Columbia, SC: University of South Carolina Press.

Gindin, J. (2004) "Venezuela Prepares Social Charter for the Americas," *Agencia Latinoamericana de Información y Análisis-Dos*, October 8. Online. Available: http://www.alia2.net/article_print.php3?id_article=2374.

Global News Wire (2001) "India Considering Law Reforms EPZs." Online. Available: http://web.lexis-nexis.com/universe/ document?_m=2ac1a7e071c5f852e7c0867dcce22dfe&_docnum=14&wchp=dGLbVtb-zSkVb&_ md5=14c3ac6d5f07f9e4b104ed190bfe9eb1.

Glover, T. (2003) "British Communications Union Threatens Strike over Call-Centre Move to India," *Sunday Business*, March 16. Online. Available: http://www.sundaybusiness.co.uk.

Goldstein, S. (1996) "Israel: Creating a New Legal System from Different Sources by Jurists of Different Backgrounds." In Örücü, E., Attwooll, E., and Coyle, S. (eds) *Studies in Legal Systems: Mixed and Mixing*. Boston, MA: Kluwer Law International.

Gonzaga, G. (2003) "Labor Turnover and Labor Legislation in Brazil," *Economia*, 4: 165–222.

Gordon, D., and Toledano, E. (1998) "Recidivism in Receipt of Unemployment Benefits 1990–1995." Online. Available: http://www.issa.int/pdf/jeru98/theme2/2-8d.pdf.

Graham, R. (1998) "France Cuts Working Week to 35 Hours," *Financial Times*, May 20, 2.

—— (1999a) "Paris to Delay 35-Hour Week," *Financial Times*, June 22, 2.

—— (1999b) "Turning Back the Clock: France's Controversial Plan to Introduce a 35-Hour Working Week is Less Radical than was First Feared," *Financial Times*, July 29, 13.

—— (1999c) "Paris Compromise on 35-Hour Week," *Financial Times*, October 26, 2.

—— (2000) "French Bosses Insist Labor Reforms are not Working: Even Trades Unions Admit Rigid System Provides Little Incentive to Seek Jobs," *Financial Times*, April 12, 2.

—— (2002a) "French Employers Challenge Politicians: Medef Congress Wish List of Reforms after Elections," *Financial Times*, January 16, 6.

—— (2002b) "French Employers Push New Government on Hours," *Financial Times*, September 2, 2.

Grandi, M. (2002) "Extra-judicial Resolution of Collective Disputes in Italy." Online. Available: http://europa.eu.int/comm/employment_social/Labor_law/docs/disputeresolution_italy_en.pdf.

Greenwood, M. R. (2002) "Ethics and HRM: A Review and Conceptual Analysis," *Journal of Business Ethics*, 36: 261–278.

Griffin, G., Nyland, C., and O'Rourke, A. (2004) "Trade Unions, the Australian Labor Party and the Trade–Labour Rights Debate," *Australian Journal of Political Science*, 39: 89–107.

Groom, B. (1997) "Attractions of Relocation Lure French Groups," *Financial Times*, September 8, 9.

Gross, A. (1999) "Human Resource Issues in Singapore." Online. Available: http://www.pacificbridge.com/Publications/Singapore99.htm.

—— (2001) "Thailand Human Resources Update." Online. Available: http://www.pacificbridge.com/pdf/pub_thailand_2001_hr.pdf.

Gross, A., and Weintraub, R. (2004) "2004 Human Resources Trends in Japan." Online. Available: http://www. pacificbridge.com/Publications/JapanDec2004.htm.

Gruber, A. (2004) "Congress Drops Measure Limiting Offshore Outsourcing," *Govexec.com*, October 13. Online. Available: http://www.govexec.com/dailyfed/1004/101304a1.htm.

Gumbel, P. (1993) "Exporting Labor: Western Europe Finds that it's Pricing itself out of the Job Market—Work Flees to East Europe: EC Takes a Hard Look at Employer Mandates," *Wall Street Journal*, December 9, A1.

Hall, D., Elenbaas, D., Lesellier, N., and MacLenna, B. (1996) "Counter-attacking against Staff Poachers," *International Commercial Litigation*, 13: 14–20.

Hamann, K., and Kelly, J. (2003) "Union Revitalization through Political Action? Evidence from Five Countries," *Proceedings of the Fifty-fifth Annual Meeting*, 105–112. Madison, WI: Industrial Relations Research Association.

Hanami, T. (1981) "The Influence of ILO Standards on Law and Practice in Japan," *International Labor Review*, 120: 765–779.

Haniffa, A. (2003) "US Strongly Opposed to Ban on Outsourcing," *rediff.com*, June 13. Online. Available: http://www.rediff.com/cms/print.jsp?docpath=/money/2003/jun/13bpo.htm.

Hannon, J. M., and Milkovich, G. T. (1996) "The Effect of Human Resource Reputation Signals on Share Prices: An Event Study," *Human Resource Management*, 35: 405–424.

Hasnat, B. (2002) "The Impact of Core Labor Standards on Exports," *International Business Review*, 11: 563–575.

Hillman, A., and Keim, G. (1995) "International Variation in the Business–Government Interface: Institutional and Organizational Considerations," *Academy of Management Review*, 20: 193–214.

Hong, N. S., and Warner, M. (1998) *China's Trade Unions and Management*. New York: St Martin's Press.

Hong Kong Institute of Human Resource Management (2005) "Comment on the 'Legislating against

Racial Discrimination: A Consultation Paper'." Online. Available http://www.hkihrm.org/ihrm_ eng/ih_hrr_law_01.asp?id=32.

Horn, N. (1980) "Codes of Conduct for MNEs and Transnational *Lex Mercatoria*: An International Process of Learning and Law Making." In Horn, N. (ed.) *Legal Problems of Codes of Conduct for Multinational Enterprises*. Boston, MA: Kluwer Law and Taxation Publishers.

Howard, L. S. (1998) "Tougher Laws to Spur World EPLI Demand," *National Underwriter/Property and Casualty Risk and Benefits*, 102 (36): 17–19.

Howse, R. (2003) "Back to Court after Shrimp/Turtle? Almost but not Quite Yet: India's Short Lived Challenge to Labor and Environmental Exceptions in the European Union's Generalized System of Preferences," *American University International Law Review*, 18: 1333–1381.

HR Focus (2004) "Disclosure on HR Compliance Audits," April, 2.

HR Briefing (1999) "As Claims Rise, Employers Fight Back," January 10, 3.

Human Rights Watch (2001) *Trading away Rights: The Unfulfilled Promise of NAFTA's Labor Side Agreement*. Online. Available: http://www.hrw.org/reports/2001/nafta/nafta0401.pdf.

—— (2004) "CAFTA's Weak Labor Rights Protections: Why the Present Accord Should Be Opposed." Briefing paper. Online. Available: http://www.hrw.org/english/docs/2004/03/09/cafta 90days.pdf.

—— (2005) "The United States–Dominican Republic–Central American Free Trade Agreement Falls Short on Workers' Rights." Written testimony submitted to the U.S. House of Representatives Committee on Ways and Means, April 21. Online. Available: http://hrw.org/backgrounder/arms/hearing0405/ hearing0405.pdf.

Hwang, Y. C. (1994) "Taiwan (ROC)," in Deery, S., and Mitchell, R. (eds) *Labor Law and Industrial Relations in Asia: Eight Country Studies*. Melbourne, Vic: Longman Cheshire.

HWCA (2003) *Comparison of Workers' Compensation Arrangements: Australia and New Zealand*. Online. Available: http://www.hwca.org.au/documents/Comparison2003.pdf.

IBM/Towers Perrin (1992) *Priorities for Competitive Advantage: A Worldwide Human Resource Study*. Chicago: Towers Perrin.

ICEM (2002) "Hurricane Reaps Whirlwind over Kazakh Oil Workers' Rights: Anti-unionism at Refinery Brings Global Protest," *ICEM Update* 35, August 22. Online. Available: http://www.icem.org/update/ upd2002/upd02-35.html.

ICFTU (1999) "Trade Union Proposals on the Future of EU–ACP Relations," April 27. Online. Available: http://www.icftu.org/displaydocument.asp?Index=990916176&Language=EN.

—— (2000) "Final Congress Statement on International Labor Standards and Trade Workers' Rights in the World Trading Systems, 17GA/8.11," April 5. Online. Available: http://www1.umn.edu/humanrts/ links/congresslabour.html.

—— (2001a) "Core Labor Standards Tabled at Doha WTO Ministerial," *ICFTU Online*, November 11. Online. Available: http://icftu.org/displaydocument.asp?Language=EN&Index=991214214.

—— (2001b) "Statement on the Agenda for the Fourth Ministerial Conference of the World Trade Organization." Online. Available: http://www.wto.org/english/forums_e/ngo_e/posp20_e.htm.

—— (2003a) "Supporting Development at the WTO: A Trade Union Report." Online. Available: http://www.icftu.org/displaydocument.asp?Index=991218400&Language=EN.

—— (2003b) *Annual Survey of Violations of Trade Union Rights*. Brussels: International Confederation of Free Trade Unions. Online. Available: http://www.icftu.org/www/pdf/pub_survey2003en.pdf.

—— (2003c) "Unions on Corp Social Responsibility," *LaborNET*, 16 April. Online. Available: http://www. labor.net.au/news/3025.html.

—— (2004) *Annual Survey of Violations of Trade Union Rights*. Brussels: International Confederation of Free Trade Unions. Online. Available: http://www.icftu.org/www/pdf/ Survey04-EN.pdf.

ILO (1995) *Report in which the Committee Requests to be Kept Informed of Developments: Complaint against the Government of Venezuela*, Case No. 1612. Online. Available: http://www.oit.org.pe/sindi/ english/casos/ven/ven199503.html.

—— (1997a) "Minimum Wage Fixing in Japan," Briefing Note 3. Online. Available: http://www.ilo.org/ public/english/dialogue/govlab/legrel/papers/brfnotes/minwages/japan3.htm.

—— (1997b) "Minimum Wage Fixing in South Korea." Briefing Note 4 (rev.). Online. Available: http://www.ilo.org/public/english/dialogue/govlab/legrel/papers/brfnotes/minwages/korea3.htm.

—— (1997c) "Minimum Wage Fixing in Brazil." Briefing Note 9. Online. Available: http://www. ilo.org/public/english/dialogue/govlab/legrel/papers/brfnotes/minwages/brasil3.htm.

—— (1998a) *Report of the Committee of Inquiry Appointed under Article 26 of the Constitution of the International Labor Organization to Examine the Observance by Myanmar of the Forced Labor Convention, 1930 (No. 29)*. Online. Available: http://www.ilo.org/public/english/standards/relm/ilc/ilc91/pdf/pr-24p1.pdf.

—— (1998b) *World Labor Report 1997–98*. Geneva: International Labor Office.

—— (1998c) "Minimum Wage Fixing Mexico." Briefing Note 13. Online. Available: http://www.ilo.org/public/english/dialogue/govlab/legrel/papers/brfnotes/minwages/mexico3.htm.

—— (1998d) "Minimum Wage Fixing: A Summary of Selected Issues." Briefing Note 14. Online. Available: http://www.ilo.org/public/english/dialogue/govlab/legrel/papers/brfnotes/minwages/issues3.htm.

—— (2000a) "International Labor Conference Adopts Resolution Targeting Forced Labor in Myanmar (Burma)." Press Release, June 14. Online. Available: http://www.ilo.org/public/english/bureau/inf/pr/2000/27.htm.

—— (2000b) *Termination of Employment Digest*. Online. Available: http://www.ilo.org/public/english/dialogue/ifpdial/downloads/term/digest.pdf.

—— (2003a) *General Report of the Committee of Experts on the Application of Conventions and Recommendations*. Online. Available: http://www.ilo.org/ilolex/gbe/cearc2003.htm.

—— (2003b) *Report of the Committee on the Application of Standards, International Labor Conference Provisional Record*, Ninety-first Session. Online. Available: http://www.ilo.org/public/english/standards/relm/ilc/ilc91/pdf/pr-24p1.pdf.

—— (2003c) Committee on Freedom of Association Committee. Report 332, November 2003. Online. Available: www.ilo.org/ilolex/english/cfarepsq.htm.

—— (2003d) "'Last Chance' for Myanmar (Burma)," *ILO News*, April 3. Online. Available: http://www.us.ilo.org/archive/news/2003/ilowatch_0304.cfm.

—— (2003e) *Complaint against the Government of Guatemala Presented by the ITGLWF*, Case 2179, Report 330, Committee on Freedom of Association. Online. Available: http://www.ilo.org/ilolex/english/caseframeE.htm.

—— (2003f) *Complaint against the Government of Guatemala Presented by the ITGLWF*, Case 2179, Report 332, Committee on Freedom of Association. Online. Available: http://www.ilo.org/ilolex/english/caseframeE.htm.

—— (2004) "Overtime." Information Sheet WT-2. Online. Available: http://www.ilo.org/public/english/protection/condtrav/pdf/infosheets/wt-2.pdf.

Independent (Bangladesh) (2000a) "Foreign Diplomats Often Meddling in Internal Affairs, JS Body Told." Academic (Lexis-Nexus) Database, University of Pittsburgh Databases A–Z.

—— (2000b) "Trade Union Activities in Export Processing Zones: BGMEA Moots Referendum among Workers'. Academic (Lexis-Nexus) Database, University of Pittsburgh Databases A–Z.

—— (2000c) "Trade Unionism in EPZs: Investors Appeal to Government to Save $1B Investment." Academic (Lexis-Nexus) Database, University of Pittsburgh Databases A–Z.

—— (2000d) "More Time Needed to Work Out an Acceptable Model." Academic (Lexis-Nexus) Database, University of Pittsburgh Databases A–Z.

Indiainfo.com (2004) "2004: A Year of Full Activity for Labor Ministry," December 19. Online. Available: http://news.indiainfo.com/2004/12/19/1912Labor.html.

India Infoline.com (2004) "Navi Mambai SEZ to Attract Foreign Investment." Online. Available: http://www.indiainfoline.com/news/news.asp?dat=10117.

Indo-Asian News Service (2003) "Contract Labor Can Generate More Employment – Minister," November 5. Online. Available: http://64.233.161.104/search?q=cache:WoR_YIJRdu0J:in.news.yahoo.com/031105/43/293of.html+india+and+%22contractual+employment%22&hl=en.

International Labor Law Committee, ABA Labor and Employment Law Section (2000a) *International Labor and Employment Laws*, vol. 1. Washington, DC: Bureau of National Affairs.

—— (2000b) *International Labor and Employment Laws*, vol. 2. Washington, DC: Bureau of National Affairs.

—— (2002a) *International Labor and Employment Laws, Cumulative Supplement to Volume 1*. Washington, DC: Bureau of National Affairs.

—— (2002b) *International Labor and Employment Laws, Cumulative Supplement to Volume 2*. Washington, DC: Bureau of National Affairs.

IOE (1999) *IOE Statement on Trade and Labor Standards for the WTO Ministerial Meeting*. Online. Available: http://www.ioe-emp.org/ioe_emp/pdf/ioe_seattle_statement.pdf.

—— (2000) *ILO Standards*. Position paper of the International Organization of Employers. Online. Available: http://www.ioe-emp.org/ioe_emp/pdf/standards_in_one%20documee9b.pdf.

—— (2001) *ILO and the Social Dimensions of Globalization*. Position paper of the International Organization of Employers. Online. Available: http://www.ioe-emp.org/ioe_emp/pdf/The%20ILO%20and%20the%20SD%20of%20G%20(Position%20Paper).pdf.

Iskandar, S. (1997) "Valeo Chief Threatens to Move Production Abroad," *Financial Times*, July 17, 16.

ITGLWF (2001) "Letter to the ILO Director General Regarding the Choi & Shin's Factories." Online. Available: http://www.usleap.org/Maquilas/Choi/letter/ITGtoILO7-23-01.html.

—— (2002a) "International Textile, Garment and Leather Workers' Federation Presents Choi Shin Case to OECD Korean National Contact Point," February 25. Online. Available: http://www.cleanclothes.org/legal/02-02-25.htm.

—— (2002b) "WTO Urged to Hold Guatemalan Government to Account over Maquila Abuses." Press release, January 16. Online. Available: http://www.itglwf.org/displaydocument.asp?DocType=Press&Index=342&Language=EN.

Jackson, J. H. (1992) "Status of Treaties in Domestic Legal Systems: A Policy Analysis," *American Journal of International Law*, 86: 310–340.

Japan Economic Newswire (1995) "Restructuring Leads to Drastic Increase in Labor Suits," October 29. Academic (Lexis-Nexus) Database, University of Pittsburgh Databases A–Z.

Jay, S. (1997) *Most Humble Servants: The Advisory Role of Early Judges*. New Haven, CT: Yale University Press.

Jayashankar, M. (2004) "Job Market: Temporary Solution," *Business World*, 2 August. Online. Available: http://www.businessworldindia.com/aug0204/news06.asp.

Jennings, C., McCarthy, W. E. J., and Undy, R. (1990) *Employee Relations Audits*. New York: Routledge.

Jensen, C. B. (2004) "Inspecting the Inspectors: Overseeing Labor Inspectorates in Parliamentary Democracies," *Governance: An International Journal of Policy, Administration and Institutions*, 17: 335–359.

Jeong, I. (2000) "OECD Recommendations on Labor Issues and Korean Compliance with Evaluations: Labor Law, Relations, Markets, and Social Security." Online. Available: http://www.kli.re.kr/20_english/02_work/file/oecd.pdf.

Jerusalem College of Technology (2001) "Covenants not to Compete," *Values for Management*, 4. Online. Available: http://www.besr.org/journal/besr_newsletter_4.html.

Jiménez, P. E. A., and Morales, I. (2004) "Contribution in Response to the Open and Ongoing Invitation: Roundtable on Labor Law." FTAA Committee of Government Representatives on the Participation of Civil Society. Online. Available: http://www.ftaa-alca.org/spcomm/soc/Contributions/Brazil/cscv133_e.asp.

Jimenez, R. T. (1994) "The Philippines." In Deery, S., and Mitchell, R. (eds) *Labor Law and Industrial Relations in Asia: Eight Country Studies*. Melbourne, Vic: Longman Cheshire.

Johnson, J. (2004a) "Chirac 'Timid' on 35-Hour Week," *Financial Times*, July 16, 2.

—— (2004b) "French Still Split on Work Hours," *Financial Times*, September 8, 4.

Johnson, S. (2002) "Card Check or Mandatory Recognition Vote? How the Type of Union Recognition Procedure Affects Union Certification Success," *Economic Journal*, 112: 344–361.

Joseph, J. (2004) "India Slams US over BPO Ban," *rediff.com*, February 16. Online. Available: http://www.rediff.com//money/2004/feb/16bpo1.htm.

Josephs, H. K. (2001) "Upstairs, Trade Law; Downstairs, Labor Law," *George Washington International Law Review*, 33: 849–872.

Jung, L. (2002a) "National Labor Law Profile: Republic of Korea (South Korea)." ILO International Observatory of Labor Law. Online. Available: http://www.ilo.org/public/english/dialogue/ifpdial/ll/observatory/profiles/kor.htm.

—— (2002b) "National Labor Law Profile: Japan." ILO International Observatory of Labor Law. Online. Available: http://www.ilo.org/public/english/dialogue/ifpdial/ll/observatory/profiles/jp.htm.

Kahn, S. (2003) "Bangladesh Scrambles to Meet US Deadline on Trade Unions." *OneWorld.net*, November 25. Online. Available: http://oneworld.net/article/view/73558/1/.

Kaiser, F. M. (2001) "Congressional Oversight," *CRS Report for Congress*, 97-936 GOV. Washington, DC: Library of Congress, Congressional Research Service.

Kalula, E. (2004) "Beyond the Workplace: Labor and Labor Market Regulation in South Africa and the SADC Region." Paper presented at the Seventeenth Annual Labor Law Conference. Online. Available: http://www.lexisnexis.co.za/ServicesProducts/presentations/17th/EvanceKalula.doc.

Kang, S. (2003) "Nike Settles Case with an Activist for $1.5 Million," *Wall Street Journal*, September 15, A10.

Kapner, F., and Barber, T. (2002) "Anger at Fiat Move to Axe 8,000 Jobs," *Financial Times*, October 10, 17.

Kaufman, B. E. (1997) "Labor Markets and Employment Regulation: The View of the 'Old' Institutionalists." In Kaufman, B. E. (ed.) *Government Regulation of the Employment Relationship*. Madison, WI: Industrial Relations Research Association.

Kerwin, K. (1996) "GM Wins One in the Lopez Case," *Business Week Online News Flash!* October 17. Online. Available: http://www.businessweek.com/bwdaily/dnflash/october/new1017b.htm.

Kim, W. C. (1987) "Competition and the Management of Host Government Intervention," *Sloan Management Review*, 28 (3): 33–39.

Kochan, T. A. (1980) *Collective Bargaining and Industrial Relations: From Theory to Policy and Practice*. Homewood, IL: Richard D. Irwin.

Kochavi, D. (2003) "Employees Stock Options: Israeli Tax Reform Overview." Online. Available: http://www.acca.com/chapters/program/israel/taxreform.pdf.

KPMG (2004) *Investment in Turkey*. Online. Available: http://www.kpmg.com.tr/dbfetch/52616e 646f6d4956b6e637c1c6ee340be9e40a053b92d678/investment_in_turkey.pdf.

Krebber, S. (2000) "Conflicts of Law in Employment in Europe," *Comparative Labor Law and Policy Journal*, 21: 501–541.

Kristal-Is Online (2004) "Lawlessness: Turkish Glass Strike Banned!" February 17. Online. Available: http://www.kristalis.org.tr/news.htm.

Kubínková, M. (2002) "National Labor Law Profile: The Czech Republic." ILO International Observatory of Labor Law. Online. Available: http://www.ilo.org/public/english/dialogue/ifpdial/ll/observatory/profiles/cz.htm#1.

Kucera, D. (2002) "Core Labor Standards and Foreign Direct Investment," *International Labor Review*, 141: 31–69.

Kumar, A., and Bansal, R. (2004) "Outsourcing Ban Caught Indian Mission Napping," *Financial Express*, January 28. Online. Available: http://www.financialexpress.com/fe_full_story.php? content_id=51307.

Kuruvilla, S. (1996) "Linkages between Industrialization Strategies and Industrial Relations/Human Resource Policies: Singapore, Malaysia, the Philippines, and India," *Industrial and Labor Relations Review*, 49: 635–657.

—— (2003) "Social Dialogue for Decent Work." International Institute for Labor Studies Discussion Paper Series DP/149/2003. Online. Available: http://www.ilo.org/public/english/bureau/inst/download/dp14903.pdf.

Kuruvilla, S., Das, S., Kwon, H., and Kwon, S. (2002) "Trade Union Growth and Decline in Asia," *British Journal of Industrial Relations*, 40: 431–461.

Labib, J. (2003) "Egypt's New Labor Law," *International Market Insight*, December 29. Online. Available: http://strategis.ic.gc.ca/epic/internet/inimr-ri.nsf/en/gr122518e.html.

Labor Advisory Committee for Trade Negotiations and Trade Policy (2004) *Report to the President, the Congress and the United States Trade Representative on the U.S.–Central American Free Trade Agreement*. Online. Available: http://www.ustr.gov/assets/Trade_ Agreements/Bilateral/CAFTA/CAFTA_Reports/asset_upload_file63_5935.pdf.

Labor File (2002a) "Labor News: Second NCL Report Submitted: PM to Meet TU Leaders." Online. Available: http://www.Laborfile.org/cec1/Laborfile/News%20Update2/News3.htm.

—— (2002b) "Labor News: Disagreement over Labor Reforms Continues: PM Agrees to Hold a Tripartite Meeting." Online. Available: http://www.Laborfile.org/cec1/Laborfile/News%20 Update2/News4.htm.

Lamdin, D. J. (2001) "Implementing and Interpreting Event Studies of Regulatory Changes," *Journal of Economics and Business*, 53: 171–183.

Lawyers' Committee for Human Rights (2002) "Before Central American Free Trade Agreement Can

Move Forward Country by Country Assessment of Workers' Rights Needed." Online. Available: http://www.lchr.org/media/2002_alerts/1119.htm.

Leahy, J. (2003) "UK Hears Claims," *Financial Times*, March 12, 21.

Leary, V. A. (1982) *International Labor Conventions and National Law: The Effectiveness of the Automatic Incorporation of Treaties in National Legal Systems*. Boston, MA: Martinus Nijhoff Publishers.

—— (1997) "The WTO and the Social Clause: Post-Singapore," *European Journal of International Law*, 8 (1): 118–122.

Lecraw, D. J., and Morrison, A. J. (1991) "Transnational Corporation–Host Country Relations: A Framework for Analysis," *Essays in International Business* No. 9. Columbia, SC: University of South Carolina.

LeLouran, J. (1979) "Predicting Union Vote from Worker Attitudes and Preferences," *Thirty-second Industrial Relations Research Association Proceedings*, 72–82.

Lenckus, D. (1998) "Employers not Doing Enough on Growing ELP Risks: Survey," *Business Insurance*, 32 (16): 2–3.

LeRoy, M. H. (1996) "Presidential Regulation of Private Employment: Constitutionality of Executive Order 12,954, Debarment of Contractors who Hire Permanent Striker Replacement," *Boston College Law Review*, 37: 229–302.

Levine, M. J. (1997) *Worker Rights and Labor Standards in Asia's Four New Tigers: A Comparative Perspective*. New York: Plenum Press.

Linos, K. (2004) "How Can International Organizations Shape National Welfare States? Evidence from Compliance with EU Directives." Paper presented at the 2004 Plenary Conference of the European Political Science Network. Online. Available: http://www.ces.fas.harvard.edu/publications/Linos Compliance.pdf.

Liu, E., and Wu, J. (1999) *Minimum Wage Systems*, RPO08/98–99. Online. Available: http://www.legco.gov.hk/yr98-99/english/sec/library/989rp08.pd.

Lyutov, N. (2003) "The Role of the ILO in the Adoption of the New Russian Labor Code," *International Journal of Comparative Labor Law and Industrial Relations*, 19: 163–177.

Maatman, G. L. (1997) "Structuring the Multinational Employment Agreement: Considerations for Reducing Liability Exposure and Preventing Disloyalty after the Termination," *Corporate Counsel's International Advisor*, 148: 2–9.

MacKinlay, A. C. (1997) "Event Studies in Economics and Finance," *Journal of Economic Literature*, 35: 13–39.

MacLaren, T. F. (ed.) (1997) *Worldwide Trade Secrets Law*. Deerfield, IL: Clark Boardman Callaghan.

Madhuku, L. (1997) "The Right to Strike in Southern Africa," *International Labor Review*, 136: 509–530.

Mah, J. H. (1997) "Core Labor Standard and Export Performance in Developing Countries," *World Economy*, 20: 773–785.

Mah, J. S. (1998) "ASEAN, Labor Standards and International Trade," *ASEAN Economic Bulletin*, 14 (3): 292–302.

Mahon, J. F. (1993) "Shaping Issues/Manufacturing Agents: Corporate Political Sculpting." In Mitnick, B. M. (ed.) *Corporate Political Agency: The Construction of Competition in Public Affairs*. Newbury Park, CA: Sage Publications.

Maiti, P. (2003) "New Federal Roadmaps," *Indiatogether.org*, December. Online. Available: http://www.indiatogether.org/2003/dec/opi-roadmap.htm.

Malkani, G. (1999) "US Groups Come under Spotlight over Human Rights Abroad," *Financial Times*, July 5, 5.

Mallet, V. (2002) "French Face Increase in their Working Week," *Financial Times*, September 19, 4.

Mankidy, J. (1995) "Changing Perspectives of Workers' Participation in India, with Particular Reference to the Banking Industry," *British Journal of Industrial Relations*, 33: 443–58.

Manyin, M., Lum, T., McHugh, L., Nguyen, P., and Zeldin, W. (2001) "Vietnam's Labor Rights Regime: An Assessment." CRS Report for Congress. Washington, DC: Library of Congress, Congressional Research Service.

Manusphaibool, S. (1994) "Thailand." In Deery, S., and Mitchell, R. (eds) *Labor Law and Industrial Relations in Asia: Eight Country Studies*. Melbourne, Vic: Longman Cheshire.

Manzetti, L., and Morgenstern, S. (2000) "Legislative Oversight: Interests and Institutions in the United

States and Latin America." Paper presented at the Notre Dame Conference on Horizontal Accountability in New Democracies. Online. Available: http://www.nd.edu/~kellogg/pdfs/ Manzetti.pdf.

Marcus, D. R. (1996) "GM v. Volkswagen," *American Lawyer*, May. Academic (Lexis-Nexus) Database, University of Pittsburgh Databases A–Z.

Marginson, P., Armstrong, P. K., Edwards, P. K., and Purcell, J. (1995) "Extending beyond Borders: Multinational Companies and the International Management of Labor," *International Journal of Human Resource Management*, 6: 702–719.

Marin, H., and Seife, F. (2003) "Law and Status of Peruvian Women." Online. Available: http://www. ishr.org/sections-groups/pac/peruvianwomen2003.htm#6b.

Mark, W., and Oxman, V. (2002) "The Social and Labor Dimensions of Globalization and Integration Process: Experience of CARICOM." Working Paper 152, IACLM–ILO Project. Lima: International Labor Office. Online. Available: http://www.oit.org.pe/spanish/260ameri/oitreg/activid/proyectos/ cimt/documetospdf/152eng.pdf.

Marshall, A. (2004) "Labor Market Policies and Regulations in Argentina, Brazil, and Mexico: Programs and Impact." ILO Employment Strategy Papers 13. Online. Available: http:// www.ilo.org/public/ english/employment/strat/download/esp13.pdf.

Martinson, J. (1999) "Doubts over EU Pension Test Case," *Financial Times*, March 22, 16.

Masters, M. F. (1987) "Corporations, Human Resources Management, and Political Action." In Ferris, G. R., and Rowlands, K. M. (eds) *Research in Personnel and Human Resources Management*, 5: 357–393. Greenwich, CT: JAI Press.

Masters, M. F., and Kevin, G. D. (1986) "Variation in Corporate PAC and Lobbying Activity: An Organizational and Environmental Annalysis," *Research in Corporate Social Performance and Policy*, 5: 249–271. Greenwich, CT: JAI Press.

Masters, M. F., Atkin, R. S., and Florkowski, G. W. (1989) "An Analysis of Union Reporting Requirements under Title II of the Landrum–Griffin Act," *Labor Law Journal*, 40 (11): 713–722.

Mathew, B. (2003) "A Brief Note on Labor Legislation in India," *Asian Labor Update* 46. Online. Available: http://www.amrc.org.hk/4605.htm.

Mazey, E. (2001) "Grieving through the NAALC and the Social Charter: A Comparative Analysis of their Procedural Effectiveness," *Michigan State University–DCL Journal of International Law*, 10: 239–257.

McCallum, R. (2002a) "Good Faith Bargaining, Protected Action and the Need for a Statutory Trade Union Recognition Procedure." Paper presented at the Tenth Annual Labor Law Conference. Online. Available: http://www.nt.gov.au/ocpe/swd/edp/alumni/200203_ mccallum_precis.pdf.

—— (2002b) "Trade Union Recognition and Australia's Neo-liberal Voluntary Bargaining Laws," *Relations Industrielles/Industrial Relations*, 57: 225–251.

McLaughlin, A. M., Jordan, G., and Maloney, W. A. (1993) "Corporate Lobbying in the European Community," *Journal of Common Market Studies*, 31: 191–212.

McWilliams, A., and Siegel, D. (1997) "Event Studies in Management Research: Theoretical and Empirical Issues," *Academy of Management Journal*, 40: 626–657.

Mercer Human Resource Consulting (2004) *International Social Security Agreements: August 2004*. Online. Available: http://www.mercerhr.com/knowledgecenter/reportsummary.jhtml?idContent= 1009605.

Millman, J. (1998) "High-tech Jobs Transfer to Mexico with Surprising Speed: How One Electronics Firm Boosts Productivity by Addressing Workers' Needs," *Wall Street Journal*. April 9, A18.

Mishra, B. (2003) "Labor Commission for South Asia Region to be Set Up," *Times of India*, September 15. Online. Available: http://timesofindia.indiatimes.com/articleshow/183158.cms.

Mitchell, N. J. (1995) "The Global Polity: Foreign Firms' Political Activity in the United States," *Polity*, 27: 447–463.

Mitchell, N. J., Hansen, W. L., and Jepsen, E. M. (1997) "The Determinants of Domestic and Foreign Corporate Political Activity," *Journal of Politics*, 59: 1096–1113.

Mitnick, B. M. (1980) *The Political Economy of Regulation: Creating, Designing, and Removing Regulatory Forms*. New York: Columbia University Press.

Mitro, M. T. (2002) "Outlawing the Trade in Child Labor Products: Why the GATT Article XX Health Exception Authorizes Unilateral Sanctions,' *American University Law Review*, 51: 1223–1273.

Mitsuhashi, H., Park, H. J., Wright, P. M., and Chua, R. S. (2000) "Line and HR Executives' Perceptions of HR Effectiveness in Firms in the People's Republic of China," *International Journal of Human Resource Management*, 11: 197–216.

Mitta, M. (2001) "A Flip-flop for the Better," *Indian Express*, September 6. Online. Available: http://www.indianexpress.com/columnists/mitta/20010906.html.

Moad, J. (2003) "Sun Hit with Discrimination Suit," *eWeek*, March 19. Online. Available: http://www.eweek.com/.

Morgenstern, F. (1984) *International Conflicts of Labor Law: A Survey of the Law Applicable to the International Employment Relation*. Geneva: International Labor Organization.

Morrison, S. (2003) "Sun Fights Allegations of 'Indian Bias'," *Financial Times*, March 19, 22.

Moye, W. T. (1980) "Presidential Labor–Management Committees: Productive Failures," *Industrial and Labor Relations Review*, 34: 51–66.

Müller, T., and Hoffmann, A. (2001) "EWC Research: A Review of the Literature." Warwick Papers in Industrial Relations 65. Online. Available: http://users.wbs.warwick.ac.uk/irru/publications/paper_65.pdf.

Münchau, W., and Althaus, S. (1997) "VW 'Lucky' to Escape with $100m Pay-out to GM," *Wall Street Journal*, January 11–12, 2.

Munro, R. (2003) "CIS Laborers, a Niche and a New Law," *Moscow Times.com*, March 25. Online. Available: http://www.moscowtimes.ru/stories/2003/03/25/011.html.

Murillo, M. L. (2001) "The Evolution of Codification in the Civil Law Legal Systems: Towards Decodification and Recodification," *Journal of Transnational Law and Policy*, 11: 1–20.

Murray, J. (2001) "A New Phase in the Regulation of Multinational Enterprises: The Role of the OECD," *Industrial Law Journal*, 30: 255–270.

Nakakubo, H. (1996) "Procedures for Resolving Individual Employment Disputes," *Japan Labor Bulletin*, 35 (6). Online. Available: http://www.jil.go.jp/bulletin/year/1996/vol35-06/05.htm.

National Commission on Labor (2002) "Conclusions and Recommendations," *Second National Commission on Labor Report*. Online. Available: http://Labor.nic.in/lcomm2/nlc_report.html.

National Employment Law Project (2002a) "Supreme Court to Hear Arguments on Back Pay for Undocumented Workers in National Labor Relations Act Case," January 14. Online. Available: http://www.nelp.org.

—— (2002b) "Supreme Court Rules on Back Pay for Undocumented Workers in National Labor Relations Act (NLRA) Cases," March 27. Online. Available: http://www.nelp.org.

—— (2003) *Inter-American Court of Human Rights: In the Matter of Request for Advisory Opinion Submitted by the Government of the United Mexican States OC-18-Brief of Amicus Curiae*. Online. Available: http://www.nelp.org.

National Foundation for American Policy (2005) "Proposed Restrictions on Global Outsourcing Continue at High Level in 2005." NFAP Policy Brief, April. Online. Available: http://www.nfap.net/research activities/studies/Global_Sourcing_2005B.pdf.

neoIT (2003) "Research Summary: Mapping Offshore Markets." Offshore Insights White Paper. Online. Available: http://www.neoit.com/gen/knowledgecenter/knowledgewhite.html#.

Nicaragua Solidarity Campaign (2005) "DR–CAFTA Ratification in Nicaragua Doubtful." Online. Available: http://www.nicaraguasc.org.uk/news/.

Nilsson, V. (2003) "Achieving Transparency for Investment: How?" OECD Global Forum on International Investment. Online. Available: http://www.oecd.org/dataoecd/34/27/19499083.pdf.

Oberman, W. D. (1993) "Strategy and Tactic Choice in an Institutional Resource Context." In Mitnick, B. M. (ed.), *Corporate Political Agency: The Construction of Competition in Public Affairs*. Newbury Park, CA: Sage Publications.

Ochel, W. (2005) "Decentralizing Wage Bargaining in Germany: A Way to Increase Employment?" *Labour*, 19: 91–121.

O'Connell, L. D. (1999) "Collective Bargaining Systems in Six Latin American Countries: Degrees of Autonomy and Decentralization." Working Paper 399, Inter-American Development Bank. Online. Available: http://www.iadb.org/res/publications/pubfiles/pubWP-399.pdf.

OECD (1996) *Trade, Employment, and Labor Standards: A Study of Core Workers' Rights and International Trade*. Paris: Organization for Economic Cooperation and Development.

—— (1998a) "Making the Most of the Minimum: Statutory Minimum Wages, Employment and Poverty." In *Employment Outlook 1998*. Paris: Organization for Economic Cooperation and Development.

—— (1998b) "Working Hours: Latest Trends and Policy Initiatives." In *Employment Outlook 1998*. Paris: Organization for Economic Cooperation and Development.

—— (2000) *OECD Guidelines for Multinational Enterprises: Revision 2000*. Paris: Organization for Economic Cooperation and Development.

—— (2001) *Annual Report of the OECD Guidelines for Multinational Enterprises: Global Instruments for Corporate Responsibility*. Paris: Organization for Economic Cooperation and Development.

—— (2002a) *The Activity of the French National Contact Point (NCP)*. Online. Available: http://www.minefi.gouv.fr/TRESOR/pcn/pcn2002_ang.pdf.

—— (2002b) *Background Document on the ICN/Adidas Case*. Online. Available: http://www.oecd.org/dataoecd/33/43/2489243.pdf.

—— (2002c) "Taking the Measure of Temporary Employment." In *Employment Outlook 2002*. Paris: Organization for Economic Cooperation and Development.

—— (2002d) Annual Report of the OECD *Guidelines for Multinational Enterprises: Focus on Responsible Supply Chain Management*. Paris: Organization for Economic Cooperation and Development.

—— (2003) *Annual Report of the OECD Guidelines for Multinational Enterprises: Enhancing the Role of Business in the Fight against Corruption*. Paris: Organization for Economic Cooperation and Development.

—— (2004a) "A Detailed Description of Employment Protection Regulation in Force in 2003: Background Material for the 2004 Edition of the OECD *Employment Outlook*." Online. Available: http://www. oecd.org/dataoecd/4/30/31933811.pdf.

—— (2004b) *Benefits and Wages: OECD Indicators*. Online. Available: http://www1.oecd.org/publications/e-book/8104071E.PDF.

—— (2004c) *Employment Outlook 2004*. Paris: Organization for Economic Cooperation and Development.

OECD Watch (2003) *Review of National Contact Points, June 2002 – June 2003*. Online. Available: http://www.ausncp.gov.au/content/docs/20030620_OECDwatch.rtf.

Official Journal of the European Communities (2001) *Legislation,* L 346, vol. 44, December 31.

Ofori-Dankwa. J. (1993) "Murray and Resef Revisited: Toward a Typology/Theory of Paradigms of National Trade Union Movements," *Academy of Management Review*, 18: 269–292.

Ogawa, M. (1999) "Noncompete Covenants in Japanese Employment Contracts: Recent Developments," *Hamline Journal of Public Policy and Policy*, 22: 341–377.

Olivier, M., Kalula, E., and Smit, N. (2002) "Equitable Trade and the Social Dimension in SADC: Recent Experiences and Proposals for Enhanced Protection." Paper presented at the Thirty-ninth Annual Meeting of the Canadian Industrial Relations Association. Online. Available: http://www.cira-acri.ca/IIRA%20CIRA%20docs/Olivier,%20Kalula%20and%20Smit.pdf.

O'Neill, S. (2005) "National Wage and Safety Net Claims and Outcomes 1991–2005," *E-Brief*, 21 June. Online. Available: http://www.aph.gov.au/Library/INTGUIDE/ECON/safety.htm.

O'Rourke, D. (2003) "Outsourcing Regulation: Analyzing Nongovernmental Systems of Labor Standards and Monitoring," *Policy Studies Journal*, 31: 1–29.

Ortwein, B. M. II (2003) "The Swedish Legal System: An Introduction," *Indiana International and Comparative Law Review*, 13: 405–445.

Ouchi, S. (2002) "Change in Japanese Employment Security: Reflecting on the Legal Points," *Japan Labor Bulletin*, 41 (1). Online. Available: http://www.jil.go.jp/bulletin/year/2002/vol41-01/05.htm.

Oxley, J. E., and Schnietz, K. E. (2001) "Globalization Derailed? Multinational Investors' Response to the 1997 Denial of Fast-track Trade Negotiating Authority," *Journal of International Business Studies*, 32: 479–496.

Ozkan, S. (2003) "More Global than Ever, as Local as Always: Internationalization and Shop-floor Transformation at Oyak-Renault and Tofas-Fiat in Turkey." Online. Available: http://socsci2.ucsd.edu/~aronatas/scrretreat/Ozkan.Sebnem.doc.

Panford, K. (1994) *African Labor Relations and Workers' Rights: Assessing the Role of the International Labor Organization*. Westport, CT: Greenwood Press.

Parasuram, T. V. (2004) "US Senate Passes Law against Outsourcing," *rediff.com*, January 24. Online. Available: http://www.rediff.com///money/2004/jan/24bpo.html.

Park, Y. (1994) "South Korea." In Derry, S., and Mitchell, R. (eds) *Labor Law and Industrial Relations in Asia: Eight Country Studies*. Melbourne, Vic: Longman Cheshire.

Parker, G. (2002a) "Ireland and UK Offered Deal to Spur Labor Law," *Financial Times*, October 10, 8.

—— (2002b) "Germany Backs Britain on 48-Hour Working Week," *Financial Times*, March 29, 2.

Payne, S. L., and Wayland, R. F. (1999) "Ethical Obligations and Diverse Values Assumptions in HRM," *International Journal of Manpower*, 20: 297–308.

Pelizzo, R., and Stapenhurst, R. (2004) "Tools for Legislative Oversight: An Empirical Investigation." World Bank Policy Research Working Paper 3388. Online. Available: https://mercury.smu.edu.sg/rsrchpubupload/4837/worldbank_wps3388.pdf.

Perez del Castillo, S. (1993) "MERCOSUR: History and Aims," *International Labor Review*, 132: 639–653.

Phillips, G. A., and Tower, E. (2005) "Organized Labor's Campaign Contributions after the NAFTA Vote: Rhetoric or Retribution?" In Plummer, M. G. (ed.) *Empirical Methods in International Trade: Essays in Honor of Mordechai E. Kreinin*. Northampton, MA: Edward Elgar.

Piazza, J. (2001) "De-linking Labor: Labor Unions and Social Democratic Parties under Globalization," *Party Politics*, 7: 413–434.

Pinto-Duschinsky, M. (1981) *British Political Finance, 1830–1980*. Washington, DC: American Enterprise Institute.

Ponessa, J. (1995) "Panel OKs Bill to Nullify Clinton's Strike Order," *Congressional Quarterly Weekly Report*, June 17, 1752.

Poole, M. (1986) *Industrial Relations: Origins and Patterns of National Diversity*. London: Routledge.

Porcano, T. M. (1993) "Factors Affecting the Foreign Direct Investment Decision of Firms from and into Major Industrialized Countries," *Multinational Business Review*, 2: 26–36.

PricewaterhouseCoopers (2004) *Doing Business in the Russian Federation*. Online. Available: http://www.pwcglobal.com/ru/eng/ins-sol/publ/PwC_Doing_Business_Guide_RF.pdf.

PTI (2003) "Nasscom to Seek US IT Association's Help," *Economic Times*, November 16. Online. Available: http://economictimes.indiatimes.com/articleshow/msid-286436,curpg-1.cms.

—— (2004a) "Yet Another Anti-BPO Bill in US," *rediff.com*, March 3. Online. Available: http://www.rediff.com/money/2004/mar/03bpo2.htm.

—— (2004b) "50 House Members Support BPO Ban," *rediff.com*, March 4. Online. Available: http://www. rediff.com/money/2004/mar/04bpo2.htm.

—— (2004c) "US Senate Votes to Bar Outsourcing Govt Jobs," *rediff.com*, March 5. Online. Available: http://www.rediff.com/money/2004/mar/05bpo.htm.

—— (2004d) "US States Fire Up Anti-BPO Moves," *rediff.com*, September 1. Online. Available: http://www.rediff.com/money/2004/sep/01bpo.htm.

Quinn, P. (2003) "Freedom of Association and Collective Bargaining: A Study of Indonesian Experience 1998–2003." ILO Working Paper (15). Online. Available: http://www.ilo.org/dyn/declaris/DECLARATIONWEB.DOWNLOAD_BLOB?Var_DocumentID=1963.

Quinteros, C. (2001) "Union Sundown?" *Foreign Policy*, 125: 63.

Radford, M. F. (2000) "The Inheritance Rights of Women under Jewish and Islamic Law," *Boston College International and Comparative Law Review*, 23: 135–184.

Raghavan, C. (1999) "ILO Head to Go to Seattle, and 'Make Known' ILO Views," *Third World Network*. Online. Available: http://www.twnside.org.sg/title/known-cn.htm.

Ratnam, V. C. S. (1995) "Economic Liberalization and the Transformation of Industrial Relations Policies in India." In Verma, A., Kochan, T. A., and Lansbury, R. D. (eds) *Employment Relations in Growing Asian Economies*. London: Routledge.

Rebhahn, R. (2004) "Collective Labor Law in Europe in a Comparative Perspective II," *International Journal of Comparative Law and Industrial Relations*, 20 (1): 107–132.

Rehbein, K. A. (1995) "Foreign-owned Firms' Campaign Contributions in the United States: An Exploratory Study," *Policy Studies Journal*, 23: 41–61.

Reith, P. (1998) "Pre-industrial Action Secret Ballots." Ministerial Discussion Paper. Online. Available: http://www.dewrsb.gov.au/ministersAndMediaCentre/reith/discussionpapers/ secret_ballots.pdf.

Reuters (2005) "Bush Steps Up Efforts to Pass CAFTA in Congress." Online. Available: http://www.independent-bangladesh.com/news/may/14/14052005bs.htm#A16.

Riad, T. R. (2004) "The New Egyptian Labor Law." Online. Available: http://www.legal500.com/devs/egypt/hr/eghr_001.htm.

Rice, R. (1997) "Zulus in Mercury Poisoning Settlement," *Financial Times*, April 12–13, 6.

Riedy, M. J. (2003) "Adverse Government Actions Facing the Outsourcing Industries." Online. Available: http://www.globalequations.com/MJRNasscomOct2003.pdf.

Roberts, R. (2005) "The Social Dimension of Regional Integration in ECOWAS." Policy Integration Department Working Paper 49. Online. Available: http://www.ilo.org/public/english/bureau/integration/download/publicat/4_3_310_wp-49.pdf.

Rock, M. (2003) "Public Disclosure of the Sweatshop Practices of American Multinational Garment/Shoemakers/Retailers: Impacts on their Stock Prices," *Competition and Change*, 7: 23–38.

Rodríguez, A. M. L. (2002) "Lex Mercatoria." Online. Available: http://www.rettid.dk/artikler/20020046.pdf.

Rodrik, D. (1996) "Labor Standards in International Trade: Do they Matter and What Do we Do about Them?" In Lawrence, R., Rodrik, D., and Whalley, J (eds) *Emerging Agenda for Global Trade: High Stakes for Developing Countries*. Washington, DC: Overseas Development Council.

Rohter, L. (2002) "South American Trading Bloc Frees Movement of its People," *New York Times*, November 24, 6.

Roscoe, D. D., and Jenkins, S. (2005) "A Meta-analysis of Campaign Contributions' Impact on Roll Call Voting," *Social Science Quarterly*, 86: 52–68.

Rosenzweig, P. M., and Nohria, N. (1994) "Influences on Human Resource Management Practices in Multinational Corporations," *Journal of International Business Studies*, 25: 229–251.

Rugman, A. M., and Verbeke, A. (1998) "Multinational Enterprises and Public Policy," *Journal of International Business Studies*, 29: 115–136.

Russia Journal Daily (2003) "Minimum Wage Raised to $20," September 24. Online. Available: http://www.russiajournal.com/news/cnews-article.shtml?nd=40580.

Ryuichi, Y. (1992) "The Applicability of Japanese Labor and Employment Laws to Americans Working in Japan," *San Diego Law Review*, 29 (2): 175–201.

Saa, R. (2001) "Argentina to Repeal Labor Reform Law," *AFX-Asia*, December 26. Academic (Lexis-Nexus) Database, University of Pittsburgh Databases A–Z.

Saavedra, J. (2003) "Labor Markets during the 1990s." In Kuczynski, P. P., and Williamson, J. (eds) *After the Washington Consensus: Restarting Growth and Reform in Latin America*. Online. Available: http://www.iie.com/publications/chapters_preview/350/9iie3470.pdf.

Sabirau-Pérez, M. (2000) "Changes of the Law Applicable to an International Contract of Employment," *International Labor Review*, 139: 335–357.

Saltzman, G. M. (1987) "Congressional Voting on Labor Issues: The Role of PACs," *Industrial and Labor Relations Review*, 40: 163–179.

SAP International (2004) "Declaration of Fourth South Asian People's Summit," January 21. Online. Available: http://action.web.ca/home/sap/news.shtml?sh_itm=fe72be88e88846883f8588d914a2b2f9&AA_EX_Session=1c2d0bdfea925b85c6bfa9b20a5f0f24.

Sayres, N. J. (2002) "The Vietnam–U.S. Textile Agreement Debate: Trade Patterns, Interests, and Labor Rights." Washington, DC: Congressional Research Service. Online. Available: http://www.us-asean.org/Vietnam/CRS_Textile.pdf.

Schmid, J. (1998) "German Court Drops Spying Charges against Lopez," *International Herald Tribune*, July 28. Online. Available: http://www.iht.com/IHT/JS/98/js072898.html.

Schneider, M. (2002) "Judicial Lawmaking in a Civil Law System: Evidence from German Labor Courts of Appeal." Discussion Paper 2002/02, Institute of Labor Law and Industrial Relations in the European Community. Online. Available: http://www.iaaeg.de/documents/Discussion_Paper_0202.pdf.

Schregle, J. (1985) "Labor Law and Industrial Relations in the Third World." In Blanpain, R. (ed.) *Comparative Labor Law and Industrial Relations* (2d ed.). New York: Kluwer Law and Taxation Publishers.

Schroeder, M. (2003) "India Aims to Calm U.S. Outsourcing Fears," *Wall Street Journal*, November 13, A4.

—— (2004) "Business Coalition Battles Outsourcing Backlash," *Wall Street Journal*, March 1, A1.

Schuler, R. S., Dowling, P., and De Cieri (1993) "An Integrative Framework for International

Human Resource Management," *International Journal of Human Resource Management*, 4: 717–764.

Schwartz, M. S., and Carroll, A. B. (2003) "Corporate Social Responsibility: A Three-domain Approach," *Business Ethics Quarterly*, 13: 503–530.

Selmi, M. L. (2003) "The Price of Discrimination: The Nature of Class Action Employment Litigation and its Effects," *Texas Law Review*, 81: 1249–1335.

Serrano, M. R., Marasigan, M. L. C., and Palafox, J. A. F. (2004) "Is a Social Charter Possible in the ASEAN? Exploring the Chances of an ASEAN Social Charter in Six ASEAN Member States." Online. Available: www.fesspore.org/pdf/Others/social%20study.pdf.

Sethi, S.P. (2003) *Setting Global Standards: Guidelines for Creating Codes of Conduct in Multinational Corporations*. Hoboken, NJ: John Wiley.

Sharma, B. (1985) *Aspects of Industrial Relations in ASEAN*. Occasional Paper 78. Singapore: Institute of Southeast Asian Studies.

Shenon, P. (1993) "Saipan Sweatshops are No American Dream," *New York Times International*, July 18, 1 and 6.

Shih, H. (2004) "Chunghwa Telecom Union Votes to Allow Strike," *Taiwan News Online*, December 6. Online. Available: http://www.etaiwannews.com/Taiwan/Society/2004/12/06/1102298929.htm.

Siddiqui, A. (2001) "Bangladesh: Human Rights in Export Processing Zones," *Asian Labor Update* 38, January–February. Online. Available: http://www.amrc.org.hk/Arch/3803.html.

Sijabat, R. M. (2004a) "Ministry Plans Suspension of Autonomy in Labor Field," *Jakarta Post*, August 13. Online. Available: http://www.bkpm.go.id/bkpm/news.php?mode= baca&info_id =496.

—— (2004b) "Indonesia: New Labor Law Causes Workers More Distress," *Jakarta Post*. August 26. Online. Available: http://www.asianLabor.org/arcdhives/002605.php.

Simon, D., and Johnston, A. (1999) "The Southern African Development Community: Regional Integration in Ferment." Briefing Paper, New Series, 8. Southern Africa Study Group, Royal Institute of International Affairs, December. Online. Available: http://www.riia.org/pdf/briefing_papers/the_southern_african_development.pdf.

Sinai, R. (2003) "PM: No Entry of Foreign Workers till End of 2003," *Haaretzdaily.com*. Online. Available: http://www.haaretzdaily.com/hasen/objects/pages/PrintArticleEn.jhtml?itemNo=215605.

Singh, G. (2001) "National Culture and Union Density," *Journal of Industrial Relations*, 43: 330–339.

Singh, S. (2000) "ILO Sets Up Working Party on Globalization," *Third World Network*. Online. Available: http://www.twnside.ord.sg/title/party.htm.

Skapinker, M. (1998) "Sabena May Move Pilots' Contracts to Switzerland," *Financial Times*, April 3, 7.

Smith, D. C. (1997) "Why Did Lopez Betray GM? VW Settlement Provides No Answer," *Ward's Auto World*, February. Academic (Lexis-Nexus) Database, University of Pittsburgh Databases A–Z.

Social Security Administration (2002) *Social Security Programs throughout the World: Europe, 2002*. Online. Available: http://www.ssa.gov/policy/docs/progdesc/ssptw/2002-2003/europe/index.html.

—— (2003a) *Social Security Programs throughout the World: Asia and the Pacific, 2002*. Online. Available: http://www.ssa.gov/policy/docs/progdesc/ssptw/2002-2003/asia/index.html.

—— (2003b) *Social Security Programs throughout the World: Africa, 2003*. Online. Available: http://www.ssa.gov/policy/docs/progdesc/ssptw/2002-2003/africa/index.html.

—— (2004) *Social Security Programs throughout the World: The Americas, 2003*. Online. Available: http://www.ssa.gov/policy/docs/progdesc/ssptw/2002-2003/americas/index.html.

Sorj, B., Fontes, A., Carusi, D., and Quintaes, G. (2004) "Reconciling Work and Family: Issues and Policies in Brazil." ILO Conditions of Work and Employment Series 8. Online. Available: http://www.ilo.org/public/english/protection/condtrav/pdf/8cws.pdf.

South Asia Citizens' Web (2005a) "Draft South Asian Labor Rights Charter and UN Labor Rights Convention for Discussion and Approval." Online. Available: http://www.sacw.net/Labour/SALRC.html.

—— (2005b) "Resolution on South Asian Labor Rights Charter." Online. Available: http://www.sacw.net/Labour/Resolution.html.

Staff (1996) "SMC Opens, amidst Doubts and Controversies," *Third World Network*. Online. Available: http://www.twnside.org.sg/title/smc-cn.htm.

—— (2003a) "Andean Community," *Intal*, Monthly Newsletter 84. Online. Available: http://www.iadb. org/intal/ingles/publicaciones/CARTAS/CartaINTAL84ing.pdf.

—— (2003b) "Number of Labor-related Lawsuits Hits Record High 2,321," *Japan Labor Bulletin*, 42 (5): 5. Online. Available: http://www.jil.go.jp/bulletin/year/2003/vol42-05.pdf.

—— (2005) "Ratification of U.S. Trade Agreement Polarizes Opinions in Costa Rica," *Tico Times Online Daily Page*. Online. Available: http://www.ticotimes.net/dailyarchive/2005_02/daily_02_22_05.htm.

Strasburg, J. (2004) "Levi's Lawsuit Dropped/Saipan Workers' Case Dismissed in Victory for Clothier," *San Francisco Chronicle*, January 8. Online. Available: http://swatch.igc.org/headlines/2004/levis_suit_jan04.html.

Sweatshop Watch (2000) "Summary of the Saipan Sweatshop Litigation." Online. Available: http://swatch.igc.org/marianas/summary5_00.html.

—— (2002a) "Saipan Sweatshop Litigation: An Update." Online. Available: http://swatch.igc.org/marianas/update_mar02.html.

—— (2002b) "Major Breakthrough in Saipan Sweatshop Lawsuits!" Online. Available: http://swatch.igc.org/swatch/headlines/2002/saipansuits_may02.html.

—— (2002c) "U.S. Clothing Retailers on Saipan Settle Landmark Workers' Rights Lawsuit." Online. Available: http://swatch.igc.org/marianas/settlement/html.

Szladits, C. (1975) "The Civil Law System." In David, R. (ed.) *The Legal Systems of the World: Their Comparison and Unification. International Encyclopedia of Comparative Law*, vol. 2. Boston, MA: Martinus Nijhoff Publishers.

Tait, N. (2003) "Government Appeals against Age Discrimination Ruling," *Financial Times*, May 23, 6.

Tallberg, J., and Jönsson, C. (2001) "Compliance Bargaining in the European Union." Online. Available: http://www.svet.lu.se/Staff/Personal_pages/Jonas_tallberg/TallbergJonsson %20ECSA.pdf.

Tett, G. (2000) "Kajima Settles with Wartime Chinese Slave Laborers," *Financial Times*, November 30, 1.

Ticoll, D. (2004) "IT Industry Trade Associations and the Globalization of Knowledge Work: A Review of NASSCOM and the Irish Software Association." Report prepared for the Information Technology Association of Canada. Online. Available: http://www.itac.ca/Library/PolicyandAdvocacy/Outsourcing/04OctITIndustryTrade-AReviewofNASSCOM.pdf.

To, L. L. (1986) *Trade Unions in China, 1949 to the Present*. Singapore: Singapore University Press.

Tomz, M. (1997) "Do International Agreements Make Reforms More Credible? The Impact of NAFTA on Mexican Stock Prices." Paper presented at the Annual Meeting of the American Political Science Association. Online. Available: http://www.stanford.edu/~tomz/working/credible.pdf.

Torres, C. (2000) "Argentine Unions Threaten Strike on Labor Bill," *Wall Street Journal*, February 23, A27.

Traxler, F., Balschke, S., and Kittel, B. (2001) *National Labor Relations in Internationalized Markets: A Comparative Study of Institutions, Change, and Performance*. New York: Oxford University Press.

Trebilcock, M. J., and Howse, R. (1999) *The Regulation of International Trade* (2d ed.). London: Routledge.

Tsogas, G. (2001) *Labor Regulation in a Global Economy*. Armonk, NY: M. E. Sharpe.

Tsui, A. S., and Milkovich, G. T. (1987) "Personnel Department Activities: Constituency Perspectives and Preferences," *Personnel Psychology*, 40: 519–537.

Tsuru, T., and Morishima, M. (1999) "Nonunion Employee Representation in Japan," *Journal of Labor Research*, 20: 93–110.

TUAC (2000) "Monitoring of Industrial Relations and Labor Law Reform in Korea." Online. Available: http://www.tuac.org/statemen/communiq/elsarok200004.htm.

Turnell, S. (2002) "Core Labor Standards and the WTO." Working Paper. Online. Available: http://www.econ.mq.edu.au/research/2001/Number%203%202001.PDF.

Ulgado, F. M. (1996) "Location characteristics of manufacturing investments in the US: A Comparison of American and Foreign-based Firms," *Management International Review*, 36: 7–26.

Ulrich, D. (1997) *Human Resource Champions: The Next Agenda for Adding Value and Delivering Results*. Boston, MA: Harvard Business Press.

Union Network International (2002) "WTO Moore Backs Closer Links," *UNI News Flash*, February 3.

Online. Available: http://www.union-network.org/uniflashes.nsf/0/31d9d0f9be48056ec1256b55003fbce9?OpenDocument.

—— (2004) "Unions for EPZs in Bangladesh," *UNI News Flash*, July 14. Online. Available: http://www.union-network.org/uniflashes.nsf/58f61ccf5875fe90c12567bb005642f9/83f3c709137a934ac1256ed1003757c8?OpenDocument.

United States Council for International Business (2002) *International Labor Affairs Report*, August: 4.

United States Trade Representative (1999) *U.S. Generalized System of Preferences Guidebook*. Washington, DC: Office of the United States Trade Representative.

—— (2005) *2005 Trade Policy Agenda and 2004 Annual Report of the President of the United States on the Trade Agreements Program*. Online. Available: http://www.ustr.gov/assets/Document_Library/Reports_Publications/2005/2005_Trade_Policy_Agenda/asset_upload_file454_7319.pdf?ht.

US–ASEAN Business Council (2003) "Doing Business in Indonesia." Online. Available: http://www.us-asean.org/Indonesia/business_guide/business_regulations.asp.

U.S. Department of State (2004a) *Country Reports on Human Rights Practices: Indonesia*. Online. Available: http://www.state.gov/g/drl/rls/hrrpt/2004/41643.htm.

—— (2004b) *Country Reports on Human Rights Practices: Argentina*. Online. Available: http://www.state.gov/g/drl/rls/hrrpt/2004/41746.htm.

—— (2004c) *Country Reports on Human Rights Practices: Venezuela*. Online. Available: http://www.state.gov/g/drl/rls/hrrpt/2004/41778.htm.

U.S. General Accounting Office (1993) *North American Free Trade Agreement: Assessment of Major Issues*, vol. II, GAO/GGD-93-137. Online. Available: http://archive.gao.gov/d48t13/149866.pdf.

U.S. Justice Department (2000) "Former GM Executive Charged with Defrauding Company by Taking Confidential Documents." Press Release, May 22. Online. Available: http://www.usdoj.gov/opa/pr/2000/May/291cr.htm.

US/LEAP (2003) "The Guatemala Surprise," *Maquilas Newsletter*, July. Online. Available: http://www.usleap.org/Recent%20Headlines/Guate%20Surprise%207-03.html.

U.S. National Administrative Office (1998a) *Public Report of Review of NAO Submission No. 9702*. Online. Available: http://www.dol.gov/ilab/media/reports/nao/pubrep9702.htm.

—— (1998b) *Public Report of Review of NAO Submission No. 9702, Part II: Safety and Health Addendum*. Online. Available: http://www.dol.gov/ILAB/media/reports/nao/9702partII.htm.

—— (2005) "Status of Submissions under the North American Agreement on Labor Cooperation (NAALC)." Online. Available: http://www.dol.gov/ILAB/programs/nao/status.htm#iia7.

Van Beers, C. (1998) "Labor Standards and Trade Flows of OECD Countries," *World Economy*, 21: 57–73.

Varga, K. (2003) "Hungary Passes Significant Changes to Income Tax Rules; Includes Changes to Taxation of Capital Gains and Stock Options," *Flash International Executive Alert*, 2003–002: 3–4.

Verité (2003) "Emerging Markets Research Project: Year End Report." Prepared for the California Public Employees' Retirement System. Online. Available: http://www.calpers.ca.gov/eip-docs/about/press/news/invest-corp/verite-report-2003.pdf.

Villamor, "Philippines Concern Stricter Enforcement Laws in EPZs." Online. Available: http://web.lexis-nexis.com/universe/document?_m=f8494aebfeb3c0d423b6cc98e65e8f55&_docnum=7&wchp=dGLbVlb-zSkVb&_md5=69d22e9b6d46376ec706a0bd0c4f1f8c.

von Potobsky, G. (1998) "Freedom of Association: The Impact of Convention No. 87 and ILO Action," *International Labor Review*, 137: 195–221.

Waldman, P. (2002) "Unocal to Face Trial over Link to Forced Labor," *Wall Street Journal*, June 13, A1 and B3.

Warn, K. (2000) "Argentina's Labor Reform Laws Passed," *Financial Times*, April 28, 5.

Watson Wyatt (1999) "Watson Wyatt Human Capital Index:® Human Capital as a Lead Indicator of Shareholder Value." Online. Available: http://www.watsonwyatt.com/research/resrender.asp?id=W-488&page=1.

—— (2000) "Human Capital Index: European Survey Report 2000." Online. Available: http://www.watsonwyatt.com/research/resrender.asp?id=EU21&page=1.

Watson Wyatt Worldwide (2004) "Taiwan." In *Benefits Report: Asia Pacific 2004*. Online. Available:

http://www.winklerpartners.com/htmlffiles-english/Publications/articles/WatsonWyatt%20ETC%20 Taiwan2004.pdf.

Weber, T., Foster, P., and Egriboz, K. L. (2000) "Costs and Benefits of the European Works Councils Directive." DTI Employment Relations Research Series 9. Online. Available: http://www.dti.gov. uk/er/emar/camp.pdf.

Weil, D. (1997) "Implementing Employment Regulation: Insights on the Determinants of Regulatory Performance." In Kaufman, B. E. (ed.) *Government Regulation of the Employment Relationship*. Madison, WI: Industrial Relations Research Association.

Weinberg, N. (1977) "Multinationals and Unions as Innovators and Change Agents." In Banks, R. F., and Stieber, J. (eds) *Multinationals, Unions and Labor Relations in Industrialized Countries*. Ithaca, NY: Cornell University Press.

Wexels-Riser, N. (2004) "National Labor Law Profile: Islamic Republic of Pakistan." Online. Available: http://www.ilo.org/public/english/dialogue/ifpdial/ll/observatory/profiles/pak.htm.

White and Case (2004) *Countries at a Glance: Employee Stock Purchase Plans*. Online. Available: http://www.wcuniverse.com/pub/resources/espps.pdf.

Williams, H. L. (2000) "Of Labor Tragedy and Legal Farce: The Han Young Factory Struggle in Tijuana, Mexico." Paper prepared for the University of California—Santa Cruz Conference on Human Rights and Globalization "When Transnational Civil Society Networks Hit the Ground." Online. Available http://www2.ucsc.edu/globalinterns/cpapers/williams.pdf.

Wilson, R. (2000) "The Decade of Non-compliance: The New Zealand Government Record of Non-compliance with International Labor Standards, 1990–98," *New Zealand Journal of Industrial Relations*, 25: 79–94.

Winstanley, D., Woodall, J., and Heery, E. (1996) "Business Ethics and Human Resource Management: Themes and Issues," *Personnel Review*, 25 (6): 5–12.

Wolffe, R. (1998) "Alabama Buzzes with the Sounds of Global Business," *Financial Times*, September 10, 4.

Wonacott, P. (2003) "Poisoned at Plant, Mr. Wu Became a Labor Crusader: Legal Reforms in China Have Created an Army of Self-taught Attorneys," *Wall Street Journal*, July 21, A1 and A6.

Working Group of the Vice Ministers Responsible for Trade and Labor (2005) "The Labor Dimension in Central America and the Dominican Republic. Building on Progress: Strengthening Compliance and Enhancing Capacity." Report Submitted to the Ministers Responsible for Trade and Labor in the Countries of Central America and the Dominican Republic. Online. Available: www.iadb.org/trade/ 1-english/pub/labor-CADR.pdf.

World Bank Group (2001) *World Business Environment Survey 2000*. Online. Available: http://info. worldbank.org/governance/wbes/index1.html.

World of Labor Institute (2004) "The Argentinian Labor Market in 2004 (First Half)." Online. Available: http://www.gpn.org/data/argentina/argentina-analysis-eng.doc.

World Law Group (2003) "The Changing Face of Global Stock Plans." Online. Available: http://www. gcd.com/db30/cgi-bin/pubs/WorldLawGroup.pdf.

Wright, P., Ferris, S. P., Hiller, J. S., and Kroll, M. (1995) "Competitiveness through Management Diversity: Effects on Stock Price Valuation," *Academy of Management Journal*, 38: 272–287.

Wright, P. M., McMahan, G. C., Snell, S. A., and Gerhart, B. (2001) "Comparing Line and HR Executives' Perceptions of HR Effectiveness: Services, Roles, and Contributions," *Human Resource Management*, 40: 111–123.

WTO (2000) *European Communities: Measures Affecting Asbestos and Asbestos-containing Products, Report of the Panel*. WT/DS135/R. Online. Available: http://www.wto.org/english/ tratop_e_dispu_e/dispu_subjects_index_e.htm#bkmk6.

—— (2002) *Trade Policy Review Body: Guatemala – Minutes of Meeting*. Online. Available: http://www.wto.org/english/tratop_e/tpr_e/tp_rep_e.htm.

Xinhua News Agency (2000a) "Bangladesh to Allow TU Rights in EPZs in Phases," March 3. Academic (Lexis-Nexus) Database, University of Pittsburgh Databases A–Z.

—— (2000b) "United States to Withdraw GSP Facilities to Bangladesh," November 1. Academic (Lexis-Nexus) Database, University of Pittsburgh Databases A–Z.

—— (2003) "China–US Agreement on Labor Law Cooperation Signed," November 18. Online. Available: www.chinadaily.com.cn/en/doc/2003–11/18/content_282624.htm.

—— (2004) "Bangladesh Allows Trade Unions in EPZ," May 11. Online. Available: http://64.233. 161.104/search?q=cache:zmXKbW68SqAJ:www.countrywatch.com/%40school/as_wire.asp%3Fv COUNTRY%3D014%26UID%3D1096780+Bangladesh+allows+trade+unions+in+EPZ%22+and+ %22Xinhua+News+Agency+%22&hl=en.

Yamakawa, R. (1996) "The Road Becoming More Traveled: The International Dimension of Japanese Labor Law," *Japan Labor Bulletin*, 35 (9). Online. Available: http://www.jil.go.jp/bulletin/year/1996/ vol35-09/05.htm.

Yanuarita, H. (2002) "Good Governance in Minimum Wage Setting in the Era of Regional Autonomy." USAID Report PEG 102. Online. Available: http://www.pegasus.or.id/Reports/102)%20Good%20 Gov%20in%20Min%20Wage.pdf.

Youngblood, S. A., Mobley, W. H., and DeNisi, A. S. (1981) "Attitudes, Perceptions, and Intentions to Vote in a Union Certification Election: An Empirical Investigation," *Thirty-fourth Industrial Relations Research Association Proceedings*, 244–253.

Zaheer, D. A. (2003) "Breaking the Deadlock: Why and How Developing Countries Should Accept Labor Standards in the WTO," *Stanford Journal of Law, Business and Finance*, 9: 69–104.

Zaman, H. (2003) "Changing Labor Laws to Suit Globalization," *Dawn*, July 14. Online. Available: http://www.dawn.com/2003/07/14/erb9.htm.

Zimmerman, D. A. (2002) *Legal Challenges to Industrial Relations Reform in Indonesia: An International Perspective*. Technical report submitted to USAID/ECG, Jakarta, Indonesia. Online. Available: http://www.pegasus.or.id/Reports/85)%20Industrial%20Relations2.pdf.

Zweigert, K., and Kötz, H. (1987) *An Introduction to Comparative Law*, vol. 1 (2d ed.). Oxford: Clarendon Press.

Internet resources

Global institutions

Governmental/tripartite

http://www.ilo.org/public/english/support/lib/dblist.htm
http://webfusion.ilo.org/public/db/dialogue/gllad/atlas/at-frame.cfm
http://www.ilo.org/public/english/dialogue/ifpdial/index.htm
http://www.ilo.org/public/english/employment/gems/eeo/
http://www.ilo.org/public/english/dialogue/sector/themes/epz.htm
http://www.oecd.org/document/10/0,2340,en_2649_34889_2663562_1_1_1_1,00.html

Nongovernmental organizations

http://www.ioe-emp.org/ioe_emp/sitemaps/sitemaps.htm
http://www.icftu.org/contents.asp?Language=EN
http://www.icftu.org/focus.asp?Issue=trade&Language=EN
http://www.icftu.org/focus.asp?Issue=multinationals&Language=EN
http://www.hrw.org/doc/?t=labor
http://www.hrw.org/doc/?t=corporations_trade
http://www.cleanclothes.org/legal.htm

Regional institutions

Trade blocs

http://www.aseansec.org/home.htm
http://www.caricom.org/
http://www.comunidadandina.org/ingles/agenda/social.htm
http://www.ecowas.int/
http://europa.eu.int/comm/employment_social/index_en.html
http://europa.eu.int/comm/employment_social/labour_law/directives_en.htm
http://www.sice.oas.org/Ftaa_e.asp

http://www.naalc.org/english/sitemap.shtml
http://www.sadc.int/index.php?action=a1001andpage_id=shdsp_labourSAARC
http://www.saarc-sec.org/main.php

Other

http://www.oas.org/udse/informe%5Ftrabajo/informe/ingles/index.html
http://www.cidh.oas.org/DefaultE.htm
http://www.corteidh.or.cr/index_ing.html

National institutions

http://edirc.repec.org/minlabor.html
http://www.hg.org/1table.html

Sources of country law/legal systems

http://www.ilo.org/dyn/natlex/natlex_browse.byCountry?p_lang=en
http://www.worldlii.org/catalog/51111.html
http://www.findlaw.com/12international/countries/
http://www.state.gov/g/drl/rls/hrrpt/2004/
http://www.ssa.gov/policy/docs/progdesc/ssptw/index.html
http://www.eiro.eurofound.ie/site_map.html
http://www.observatorio.net/
http://rru.worldbank.org/DoingBusiness/ExploreTopics/HiringFiringWorkers/
http://www.worldbank.org/wbi/governance/govdata/

Index